Ancient Puebloan Southwest

Ancient Puebloan Southwest traces the evolution of Puebloan society in the American Southwest from the emergence of the Chaco and Mimbres traditions in the AD 1000s through the early decades of contact with the Spanish in the sixteenth century. The book focuses on the social and political changes that shaped Puebloan people over the centuries, emphasizing how factors internal to society impacted cultural evolution, even in the face of the challenging environment that characterizes the American Southwest. The underlying argument is that while the physical environment both provides opportunities and sets limitations to social and political change, even more important evolutionary forces are the tensions between cooperation and competition for status and leadership. Although relying primarily on archaeological data, the book also includes oral histories, historical accounts, and ethnographic records as it introduces readers to the deep history of the Puebloan Southwest.

Case Studies in Early Societies

Series Editor
Rita P. Wright, New York University

This series aims to introduce students to early societies that have been the subject of sustained archaeological research. Each study is also designed to demonstrate a contemporary method of archaeological analysis in action, and the authors are all specialists currently engaged in field research. The books have been planned to cover many of the same fundamental issues. Tracing long-term developments, and describing and analyzing a discrete segment in the prehistory or history of a region, they represent an invaluable tool for comparative analysis. Clear, well organized, authoritative, and succinct, the case studies are an important resource for students, and for scholars in related fields, such as anthropology, ethnohistory, history, and political science. They also offer the general reader accessible introductions to important archaeological sites.

Books in the series

1. *Ancient Mesopotamia*
   Susan Pollock

2. *Ancient Oaxaca*
   Richard E. Blanton, Gary M. Feinman, Stephen A. Kowalewski, Linda M. Nicholas

3. *Ancient Maya*
   Arthur Demarest

4. *Ancient Jomon of Japan*
   Junko Habu

Ancient Puebloan Southwest

John Kantner

Georgia State University

PUBLISHED BY THE PRESS SYNDICATE OF THE UNIVERSITY OF CAMBRIDGE
The Pitt Building, Trumpington Street, Cambridge, United Kingdom

CAMBRIDGE UNIVERSITY PRESS
The Edinburgh Building, Cambridge, CB2 2RU, UK
40 West 20th Street, New York, NY 10011–4211, USA
477 Williamstown Road, Port Melbourne, VIC 3207, Australia
Ruiz de Alarcón 13, 28014 Madrid, Spain
Dock House, The Waterfront, Cape Town 8001, South Africa

http://www.cambridge.org

First published 2004

Printed in the United Kingdom at the University Press, Cambridge

Typeface Plantin 10/12 pt.   *System* LATEX 2ε   [TB]

A catalogue record for this book is available from the British Library

Library of Congress Cataloguing in Publication data
Kantner, John, 1967–
Ancient Puebloan Southwest / John Kantner.
   p.   cm. – (Case studies in early societies)
Includes bibliographical references and index.
ISBN 0–521–78310–0 (hb) – ISBN 0–521–78880–3 (pb)
1. Pueblo Indians – Antiquities.   2. Southwest, New – Antiquities.   I. Title.
II. Series.
E78.S7K35   2004
978.9′01 – dc22   2004047300

ISBN 0 521 78310 0 hardback
ISBN 0 521 78880 3 paperback

Contents

Figures

Boxes

Acknowledgments

This book includes contributions from many friends and colleagues. Michelle Hegmon, Cathy Cameron, Gwinn Vivian, Keith Kintigh, Mark Varien, Paul Minnis, Kathy Roler Durand, Ron Towner, Russ Bodner, Steve Lekson, Tim Kohler, Tom Windes, Sarah Herr, Todd VanPool, Christine VanPool, and Rita Wright provided invaluable comments on sections and chapters of the book. Barbara Mills, Bill Walker, Catherine Baudoin, Catherine Cocks, Chuck Adams, Doug Gann, Dave Phillips, David Noble, David Wilcox, Dennis Gilpin, Dennis Holloway, George Huey, Harry Shafer, Jeff Dean, Jerry McElroy, Jim Potter, Joan Mathien, John Neikirk, Keith Kintigh, Kelley Hays-Gilpin, Kim Spurr, Lynn Teague, Peggy Nelson, Mark Varien, Mary Eztkorn, Mick Robins, Paul Minnis, Mitch Allen, Chuck Riggs, Ruth Van Dyke, Steven LeBlanc, Tim Kohler, Mary Wachs, and Wes Bernardini helped to identify and/or provide permission to use figures that appear on these pages. I am especially indebted to Lynne Sebastian, whose vision is responsible for this book and who assisted and encouraged me throughout its production. Thanks also to Rita Wright and Simon Whitmore, who provided support, encouragement, and flexibility while this book was being assembled. A special thanks to Chris Kantner, who not only assisted in creating the figures, but who also has stood by me through the years.

1 The ancient Puebloan Southwest: an introduction

In the late 1800s, as Anglo-American settlers moved into the Four Corners area of the United States where New Mexico, Arizona, Utah, and Colorado meet, they encountered a large number of ancient ruins, some of which were exceptionally imposing. Racist views about the indigenous inhabitants of the region, combined with a comparatively widespread knowledge of the Aztec empire encountered by the Spanish *conquistadors*, led many newcomers to assume that the local ruins with their impressive artifacts represented outposts of Mexican civilization. A substantial minority believed that they derived from the "lost tribes" of Israel or even more fanciful sources.

Although the evolution of the Four Corners region was influenced by developments in the great civilizations of Mesoamerica, and while many groups in the Southwest did interact with their neighbors to the south, the Aztecs did not build these structures. Archaeologists have instead determined that ancestors of current Native American groups living in this part of the United States built and lived in the villages now lying in ruins throughout the Four Corners. However, many of the questions raised by the nineteenth-century pioneers – Who were these people? Where did they come from? When did they live here? Why did they leave? – still structure the archaeology of this region, and they will be essential themes in this book.

One of the interesting problems in writing a general-interest book on archaeology is deciding how to bound your topic, both in time and in space. Human societies tend to form a web of connections with their neighbors. Often these relationships are not the formal "government to government" kinds that we are used to observing and studying in more recent history, but instead are personal ties between individuals and families. These relationships can exist over long distances and persist for generations, and they involve both the movement of material goods and ideas and the actual relocation of people. The net effect of these webs of relationship is to make the "boundaries" of early societies fuzzy and difficult to define, especially when observed through the filter of long time

1

depth and the methods of archaeology, both of which tend to capture patterns rather than particular events.

This book discusses early societies in what is often called the "American Southwest." To establish appropriate and manageable boundaries for this topic, a good place to start is by addressing the basic newspaper reporters' questions that are drilled into journalism students everywhere: What, Where, Who, When, and Why? This first chapter will address the "big W" questions to explain how and why the temporal and spatial boundaries used in this study of early societies in the Southwest were chosen.

What?

At first glance, the American Southwest might seem out of place in a book series that includes such archaeological "heavy hitters" as *Ancient Mesopotamia* and *Ancient Oaxaca*. In each of these regions, the evolution of human societies culminated in one or more of the great urban civilizations of the ancient world. Although societies of the American Southwest prior to European Contact were among the most complex cultural developments in North America, they did not approach the scale or complexity of these ancient civilizations. And yet, despite the relatively modest achievements of societies of the ancient Southwest, this region has one of the most intensively studied and best-known archaeological records in the world.

This widespread interest among both the public and professional archaeologists is the result of several factors. Thanks to the work of artists, filmmakers, photographers, and writers, the landscape of the American Southwest and its indigenous people have achieved an almost mythic quality. John Ford did not invent Monument Valley, but because of his work, people in every corner of the earth can identify it as the home of John Wayne, Maureen O'Hara, and a cast of larger than life characters. Zane Grey imagined the Four Corners states so vividly that millions of people who have never been there can experience an intimate relationship with its inaccessible canyons and mesas, its rivers and vast deserts and stark mountains (Figure 1.1). Tony Hillerman and Louis Lamour, Charles Russell, Georgia O'Keefe, and David Muench, each through his or her own medium has made the Southwest familiar throughout much of the world.

The landscape of this mythic American Southwest includes the ancient and modern homes of American Indians. There are few places in the world where indigenous people have been able to maintain their own culture and lifeway in their ancestral land as successfully as the native people of the Southwest. The cultural richness of these people and the

1.1 Monument Valley is the stereotypical landscape of the American Southwest.

clear and tangible link between the modern and archaeological societies of this region have made the archaeology of the Southwest especially accessible and interpretable for the layperson.

At the same time, this clear link between the ethnographic present and the archaeological past has proved endlessly seductive for archaeologists. One of the great burdens of archaeology is our ultimate inability to *know*, to be certain that our interpretations of the past are correct. This is especially true for those of us working with societies that never developed writing. We can draw on multiple lines of evidence and test hypotheses with rigorous methodology, but we can never know for sure. And during late-night worrying sessions, we might be tempted into all kinds of Faustian bargains if we could just have the opportunity to ask those people in the past what on earth pattern X or phenomenon Y was all about.

So here we have the American Southwest, with living and relatively intact cultures descended from the pre-Contact people of the region, people with oral histories and cultural practices whom we could "interview" about the meaning of the past. Is it any wonder that archaeologists have been practically tripping over each other here for the past hundred years? The presence of descendent populations and the opportunity to use the ethnographic present to elucidate the pre-Contact past have been a bane of Southwestern archaeology as well as a boon to it, but certainly this opportunity has contributed heavily to both its popularity and its success (Figure 1.2).

Although the importance of the Southwest to developments elsewhere in the ancient world might appear limited, the contributions of Southwestern archaeology to the theory and method of the entire discipline have been substantial. The hundred years of intensive study, the historical links to Native people, the superb preservation, and the relative lack of disturbance have made this an excellent laboratory for several categories of archaeological investigations. In terms of the focus of this book, the most important of these are investigations of the origins and development of social and political complexity in human societies.

At several points in time and in several different locations, societies in the pre-Contact Southwest began moving along a developmental trajectory toward greater differentiation in social, political, and economic roles. The organization and material culture of these societies became increasingly complex and elaborate. Then, in each case, those developments were truncated – in the final instance, by the arrival of the Spanish, but in all others, by factors internal to the society and its relationship to its environment and its neighbors. Because the archaeological record left by these initial forays into increasing sociopolitical complexity were not obliterated by any subsequent development of more complex societies, the Southwest offers a unique opportunity to understand the origins and nature of the human impulse toward social and political elaboration.

Where?

Establishing boundaries around a culture area is always an exercise in artificiality. No matter how carefully the boundaries are based on physiographic or linguistic or ethnic data, there are always caveats and exceptions. For the purposes of this book, the American Southwest is defined as encompassing most of the US states of New Mexico and Arizona and the Mexican state of Chihuahua, along with neighboring areas of Utah, Colorado, and Sonora (Figure 1.3).

This huge region encompasses a wide range of environments, from high mountain peaks that retain portions of their snow cover throughout the year to torrid desert basins where summer temperatures are in the triple digits for weeks at a stretch. It is bisected by the Continental Divide – the western two-thirds is drained by a mighty web of tributaries to the Colorado River, while the eastern one-third drains into the Rio Grande. Biogeographers recognize five major environmental zones: the Colorado Plateau, the southernmost extension of the Rocky Mountain chain,

1.2 Similarities between the architecture of the ancient Puebloans, such as Chaco Canyon's Pueblo Bonito at the top, with the architecture of modern Pueblo people, exemplified by Taos Pueblo at the bottom, has erroneously led both casual observers and professional scholars to regard Puebloan culture as unchanging.

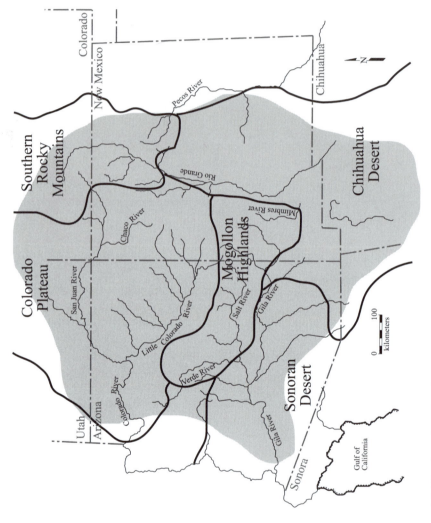

1.3 The American Southwest is often defined as encompassing most of New Mexico and Arizona and neighboring areas of Utah, Colorado, and the Mexican states of Sonora and Chihuahua. This enormous region includes portions of several major physiographic provinces.

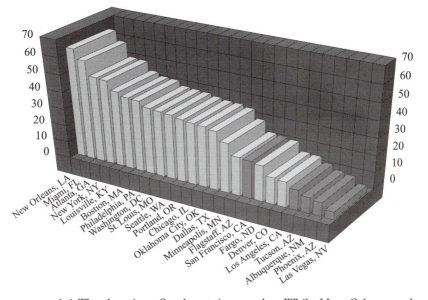

1.4 The American Southwest is very dry. While New Orleans and Miami receive around 60 inches (1524 mm) of rain each year, Albuquerque and Tucson are lucky to see 9 inches (230 mm) of precipitation. Flagstaff, located at a higher elevation than most Southwest towns, gets almost 23 inches (584 mm) of rain and snow each year (based on averages from 1971 to 2000).

the Mogollon Highlands, and the Chihuahuan and Sonoran Deserts. Chapter 2 provides a more detailed description of these varied environments, but it is worth mentioning a few aspects of the physical and social environment that have contributed heavily to both public popularity and successful scholarship in the American Southwest.

It is dry here. Really dry. In much of the Southwest, the average annual precipitation figures are in the single digits (Figure 1.4). Even in the better-watered areas, average precipitation amounts rarely exceed 500 mm, except in the highest – and thus most frigid – mountain ranges. For archaeological preservation, this arid climate means not only less damage from standing and running water, but less damage from vegetative growth and better surface visibility.

As for population density, the states of Arizona and New Mexico alone comprise a larger land area than the combined states of Maine, New Hampshire, Vermont, Connecticut, Massachusetts, New York, New Jersey, Delaware, Pennsylvania, Maryland, Rhode Island, and Virginia. The entire population of New Mexico is slightly greater than that of

Portland, Oregon; the population of Arizona is slightly less than that of Philadelphia. This extremely low population density has meant that a great deal of the archaeological record has not been destroyed by subsequent occupation and its associated development.

This is not true everywhere, of course. The growth of the region's larger cities, especially Phoenix, and to a lesser extent Albuquerque and Tucson, has eradicated the remains of earlier settlements. Additionally, the large water impoundment projects needed for modern settlement in this arid region and extractive industries like mining and oil and gas development have impacted the archaeological record. In recent years, however, historic preservation laws have ensured that much of the archaeological information is recovered prior to development, and overall the vastness of the region and the limited impact of modern land uses have left us with an extremely rich and relatively undisturbed archaeological record.

In many areas of the Southwest, the greatest threat to preservation has been not development but the curiosity and, sometimes, the greed of the modern inhabitants. Vandalism, looting, and unscientific excavation of archaeological sites have been a serious problem. On the positive side, the earliest preservation efforts in the USA directed toward archaeological sites originated in the Southwest and resulted in the passage by Congress of the Antiquities Act of 1906. Preservation is still an important value among the people of this region, where avocational archaeology societies and site stewardship programs have an excellent record of education, outreach, and public service.

Who?

Over the past 12,000 years, this landscape has been the home of a wide variety of human societies. For the past hundred years, the remains left behind by those societies have been the focus of thousands of investigations. Given this embarrassment of archaeological riches, the first challenge for planning this book was to select a manageable yet logical and coherent portion of this archaeological world on which to focus.

Because of my interests in the origins of sociopolitical and economic complexity, the field was narrowed considerably (the first 10,000 years could be distilled into a relatively brief synopsis!), but still a large proportion of the archaeological information from the American Southwest concerns just such societies. For the past 2,000 years, this region has been occupied by people of several distinct archaeological traditions exhibiting considerable dependence on agriculture and a largely sedentary way of life (Box 1.1). The three major archaeological traditions, the "Hohokam" and the two ancestral Puebloan groups that have been termed "Anasazi"

Box 1.1   Naming archaeological cultures of the Southwest

Early in the development of Southwest archaeology, scholars recognized that different geographical areas exhibited distinct archaeological remains. To distinguish these from one another, archaeologists working in the 1920s and 1930s assigned names to geographically discrete patterns of material culture. One of the first, "Anasazi," was used to label pre-Contact inhabitants of the northern Southwest who appeared to have shared a number of cultural traits and a common history. Borrowed from the Navajo, non-Puebloan people still living in the Four Corners area, the term "Anasazi" has been variously translated as "old people," "enemy ancestors," or "ancient non-Navajos" (Walters and Rogers 2001).

Patterns in pre-Contact remains common to the Gila and Salt Rivers led to another label, "Hohokam," which also entered the archaeological lexicon in the early 1930s. Literally meaning "all used up," this word was adopted from indigenous Piman inhabitants living in southern Arizona. At the same time, the pre-Contact patterns of the rugged highland areas of southwestern New Mexico and central Arizona were considered distinctive enough to warrant yet a third addition to the nomenclature: "Mogollon," from the Mogollon Mountains, which themselves were named after the eighteenth-century Spanish governor of New Spain, Don Juan Ignacio Flores Mogollón (see Cordell 1997:153–88 for a summary of Southwest archaeological nomenclature).

Since the early 1930s, more labels have been assigned to various pre-Contact cultural patterns that are constrained both across space and through time. From the "Patayan" of the far western Southwest, to the "Sinagua" of central Arizona, to the "Salado" found along the Hohokam–Mogollon boundary, these names are used to describe distinctive suites of cultural characteristics. These terms represent "archaeological cultures," meaning that they identify patterns only in the *material* culture; they do not necessarily reflect social groups, political affiliations, or ethnic identities. In fact, most of the nomenclature disguises almost as much variability as it describes – the Anasazi, for example, probably had very little shared identity but instead consisted of many different groups, some of whom were friends, some of whom were enemies, and some of whom never even knew the others existed. The challenge for archaeologists, then, is to take the patterns represented by the gross nomenclature and tease apart what life was like for different Anasazi and what meaningful identities they formed and maintained.

In addition to obscuring important variability, the terms adopted by early archaeologists inspire controversy. Many contemporary Pueblo Indian people, for example, take offense at use of the term "Anasazi." They consider these people to have been their ancestors, and they therefore see it as inappropriate to apply a term taken from another indigenous group, especially since they have comparable words in their own languages. For example, to refer to pre-Contact Puebloan remains, the Hopi use "Hisatsinom" while the Tewa Pueblos use "Se'da," with both words meaning "ancient ones." Since archaeologists cannot reasonably use *all* of these terms, most now employ "Ancient Puebloans" to refer to the ancestors of modern Pueblo people, which technically includes the Anasazi, Mogollon, and arguably even some Hohokam. Although I have never been happy with any of the alternatives, this book will largely follow the current convention and refer to the ancestors of contemporary Pueblo people as "Puebloans."

and "Mogollon" by archaeologists, developed elaborate ceremonial systems, monumental architecture and engineering features, sophisticated and labor-intensive craft items, and relatively complex social and political structures.

The Hohokam were desert dwellers. For most of their history, they settled along the river valleys of southern Arizona, especially the Gila and the Salt. Compared with their neighbors, the defining characteristics of the Hohokam were their extensive use of canal irrigation, the construction of platform mounds and ballcourts, cremation of their dead, and a ceramic technology using the paddle-and-anvil technique. Not only was the manufacturing technology used by Hohokam potters distinct from that used by Mogollon and Anasazi potters, vessel forms and shapes were also distinctive (Figure 1.5).

Other differences include substantial numbers of non-utilitarian artifacts that are unique to the Hohokam cultural tradition, including stone pallets and carved and etched shell jewelry. The basic house form during the entire Hohokam sequence (AD 300–1350) was a freestanding structure built of poles that were woven together and covered with mud, all set into shallow depressions. The architectural details of these houses varied, as did the settlement organization and the associated public architecture, but the Hohokam people never adopted the large, multistory "apartment

1.5 Vessel forms produced by Hohokam people are illustrated at the top, while forms common to Mogollon vessels are shown at the bottom. Anasazi people made pottery similar in form to their Mogollon neighbors.

buildings," or pueblos, favored by the other major pre-Contact traditions of the Southwest.

Marked differences in material culture, settlement patterns, organization, belief systems, and history exist between the Anasazi and Mogollon traditions – and for that matter, there is remarkable variability within each tradition. When one compares them with the Hohokam, however, their essential similarity is clear. Both the Anasazi and the Mogollon began as pithouse dwellers (Figure 1.6) but eventually shifted to residence in large, multistory, multifamily pueblos (Figure 1.2). They made their pottery by coiling long thin ribbons of clay into the desired shape and then scraping and smoothing the vessel. Although the colors and decorations of Anasazi and Mogollon pottery were distinctive, the vessel forms were largely the same, and through time the styles grew more similar.

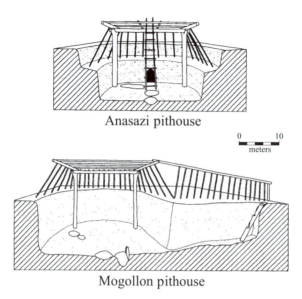

Anasazi pithouse

0   10
meters

Mogollon pithouse

1.6 Many people of the Anasazi and Mogollon traditions constructed
and lived in distinctively styled pithouses for over one millennium. These
two pithouses were built in Bear Village, a community in which Anasazi
and Mogollon residents lived side by side.

This book focuses on the Anasazi and Mogollon traditions and largely
excludes the Hohokam. This decision was based in part on the very different antecedents, adaptations, and organization evinced by the Hohokam
and in part on a desire to examine the specific historical trajectory of
Puebloan people who occupied what is now Arizona and New Mexico at
European Contact. Certainly there would have been connections among
all three cultural traditions – recall those fuzzy boundaries noted earlier –
and several modern Pueblo groups do trace links to the Hohokam in their
oral traditions. But the core of Pueblo society at Contact derived from
the Anasazi and Mogollon traditions and reflected the history of change
and amalgamation of those two cultural patterns.

When?

A broad reading of the archaeological literature of Southwestern USA
and northern Mexico reveals interesting temporal patterns. In particular,
a few dates keep appearing as pivotal in one cultural sequence after
another. George Gumerman and his colleagues (Cordell and Gumerman
1989; Gumerman and Gell-Mann 1994) call these "hinge points" and

describe them as marking widespread periods of rapid cultural change. For example, most scholars recognize AD 1275–1300 as one of these seminal points, because vast areas of the Southwest were depopulated while others experienced substantial population gains (Figure 1.7).

One of the most interesting of these "hinge points" occurred between AD 1130 and 1150. Beginning about AD 900 or 950, and accelerating in the period from AD 1000 to 1130, there had been a florescence across the entire Southwest. Settlement expanded into areas never occupied by sedentary populations before or since, population increased, and investments in construction and sociopolitical complexity reached what may have been their highest levels in the pre-Contact Puebloan world. In the Anasazi tradition, the culmination of this florescence was the "Chaco phenomenon." Huge masonry buildings were constructed in Chaco Canyon in northwestern New Mexico, and communities throughout the Four Corners region were incorporated into some form of social or political network. Chaco did not encompass the entire Anasazi world, but it came close. Within the Mogollon tradition, people living in the rugged highlands of east-central Arizona continued to reside in pithouse villages throughout the AD 900–1100 period. But in the Mimbres country of southwest New Mexico, settlement shifted quite rapidly to large villages composed of multiple cobble-masonry roomblocks. Mimbres villages were among the largest sites in the Southwest at this time, and there is evidence – including the famous Mimbres pottery – for a stylized ritual system.

Then came the AD 1130–1150 "hinge point." Chaco and Mimbres experienced a massive loss of complexity and cohesion, followed by a major (though short-lived) reorganization and relocation of population.

Interestingly, the same "hinge points" are seen beyond the boundaries of the Puebloan Southwest. In the Hohokam area, the period from AD 900 to 1100 saw expansion of settlement beyond the river valleys and into more diverse environments, and many of the largest Hohokam settlements reached what was to be their maximum size. This period also saw construction of large numbers of ballcourts and mounds and considerable expansion of the canal systems. Then, during the early twelfth century, Hohokam populations withdrew from the wide variety of environmental zones to which they had expanded, concentrating again in the river valleys, and the spatial structure of large Hohokam sites underwent major reorganization. Far beyond the boundaries of the Southwest, groups as diverse as sea-faring societies in coastal California and the mound-building cultures of the Eastern Woodlands also exhibit substantial cultural change in the mid-1100s. The AD 900s and 1000s also saw the rapid growth and elaboration of the Toltec polity in Mesoamerica

Date (AD)	Pecos Classification	Chaco Canyon Puebloan	Rio Grande Puebloan	Phoenix Basin Hohokam	Mimbres Mogollon	Casas Grandes
1400–1300	Pueblo IV		Classic		Cliff	
1300						Medio
1300–1200	Late Pueblo III	Mesa Verde	Coalition	Classic	Black Mountain	
1200–1100	Early Pueblo III	Late Bonito	Developmental		Reorganization/ Postclassic	
1100–1000	Late Pueblo II	Classic Bonito		Sedentary	Classic	
1000–900	Early Pueblo II	Early Bonito				Viejo
900–800	Pueblo I	Pueblo I	Archaic	Colonial	Late Pithouse	
800–700						
700				Pioneer		
700–600	Basketmaker III	Basketmaker III				
600–400					Early Pithouse	Plainware
400–100	Basketmaker II					

1.7 Each of the cultural traditions in the pre-Contact American Southwest followed its own path through time, as illustrated in these timelines for different Anasazi, Hohokam, and Mogollon groups. Scholars do recognize, however, various "hinge points," here indicated in gray, when most traditions underwent rapid cultural change.

and the northern Mayan florescence in the Yucatan. And both of these societies also effectively collapsed at about AD 1150.

In the late AD 1100s and early 1200s, Puebloan settlements were again flourishing in the Southwest. The distribution of these settlements was much more narrow than it had been in the AD 1000s, however, and the structure of these settlements and presumably the organization of the societies that created them appear to have been very different from those of the early twelfth century.

Because the focus of this book is on the sociopolitical and economic evolution of Puebloan society, it begins at the time of greatest pre-Contact complexity in each of the two Puebloan traditions – the Chaco phenomenon within the Anasazi tradition and the Mimbres developments within the greater Mogollon tradition. To examine and account for a specific historical trajectory, the book traces Puebloan development from the halcyon days of maximum expansion and complexity at the turn of the twelfth century through a series of major changes in settlement, demography, organization, and ideology, ending with the cultural configuration of Pueblo society as it was recorded in the early decades after European Contact in AD 1540. This reconstruction of Puebloan pre-Contact history will be largely based on archaeology but will refer to historical accounts, Pueblo oral history, and ethnographic records.

Why?

All interpretations of the past based on archaeology are inferences – conclusions derived from facts through some process of reasoning. And all of our inferences, particularly those about *why* things happened, are shaped by the theoretical framework within which the archaeologist observes and interprets the archaeological record.

Some of our inferences are so heavily based on detailed observation, physical analysis, and experiments that they virtually achieve the status of demonstrated facts. Many technologies – for example, the manufacture of stone tools and ceramics or the construction of houses, buildings, and public works – are understood in great detail, and the degree of inference involved is very small. However, as we move beyond technology and into more complex aspects of past societies – subsistence strategies, factors determining where sites will be located, relationships of exchange through which non-local goods were acquired, for example – the level of inference goes up and the degree of certainty goes down. We are able to observe the material remains of these strategies, decisions, and relationships, and we can identify some of the factors that constrained or influenced them. But the ultimate explanation, the argument that links the constraints and influences on human action with the objects and patterns observable in the archaeological record, is based on inferences that are further removed from demonstrable fact.

If we shift our questions about the past away from the material world and toward the realms of organization and ideology, the inferential leaps needed to interpret the past become even greater. Often, multiple layers of inference are required, and the degree of certainty with which we can know about organizational principles or belief systems is always much lower than the degree of certainty with which we can interpret technology or subsistence practices.

Inferences are not made in a vacuum. Our experiences in the modern world and our beliefs about how human societies function heavily influence the inferences that we draw about past human societies from the patterns observed in the archaeological record. For this reason, it is important for archaeologists to make clear the frame of reference or "theoretical orientation" that structures their inferences and interpretations that they offer about the past.

When archaeology first began in the American Southwest, the goals were twofold: first, to acquire museum-quality specimens of the material culture; and second, to understand who had built the impressive structures, how they had lived, and what had become of them. The theoretical orientation that structured and guided the interpretation of the Southwest at that time has been called the "direct historical approach," because Pueblo ethnography was employed to interpret pre-Contact patterns, based on the assumption that the observable behaviors of modern Pueblos were nearly identical to those of their ancestors (Cushing 1890; Fewkes 1893, 1896).

Subsequent research discredited some major claims of the direct historical approach, and Southwestern archaeologists turned sharply away from Pueblo ethnography and from any inferences not firmly founded on observable facts. Beginning in the early years of the twentieth century and continuing through the 1950s, Southwestern archaeology focused on empirical observation, description, and classification. Meticulous excavation and detailed analysis established the baseline for Southwestern archaeology during this time. Even today, our understanding of how the archaeological record of this region is organized temporally and across space was largely established during this period.

It is difficult for those of us working in the Southwest today to imagine what it was like to do archaeology here only a generation or two ago. In the days before radiocarbon dating and dendrochronology, the relative age of archaeological sites and even whole cultures could only be established through painstaking analysis and correlation of ceramic styles or through excavation of stratified sites in which stone tools and other artifacts from lower strata could be conclusively demonstrated to be earlier than those from upper strata. And even when these demonstrations of relative age could be made (and in those pre-computer days, this required recording and manipulating tens of thousands of pieces of data by hand, on paper), the whole relative chronology was left floating in time, with no way to assign an "X years ago" age to the phenomena in question.

Ultimately, fifty years of hard work in excavation, observation, description, and classification, along with technological innovations in dating techniques and other areas of the field, brought us to the point where we had a good understanding of the basic nature of the Southwestern archaeological record (e.g., Gladwin 1957; McGregor 1965). But because archaeologists had tended to eschew inference at any but the most basic level, we did not have a systematic approach to understanding *why* that record exhibited the patterns that it did. Often classification was treated as if it were explanation, especially when categories defined by cultural anthropologists, such as "bands," "tribes," and "chiefdoms," were used. Assignment of societies to these categories was seen as both descriptive and explanatory.

Beginning in the 1960s, Southwestern archaeology emphasized explanation and the use of consciously scientific methods to reconstruct the past. The major theoretical approach during this era was cultural ecology, in which the evolutionary trajectory of Southwestern societies was seen as driven by cultural responses to environmental and demographic changes (e.g., Lightfoot 1983; Plog 1974; Zubrow 1975). This theoretical approach was originally referred to as the "new" archaeology but ultimately came to be referred to as "processual" archaeology. The underlying premise of processual archaeology is that the behavior of human societies is connected in a direct, systemic way to their physical environment. The guiding principle for research based on this theoretical approach is that through application of scientific methods, one can discover regularities in the connections between culture and environment. Processual archaeology contends that through the glasses of science, not only can we explain a particular case under study, but ultimately we can identify the basic rules that govern cultural change.

The cultural ecological perspective continues to inform many archaeologists working in the American Southwest (e.g., Dean 1996a; Rautman 1996; Schelberg 1992). This research has been very successful at correlating cultural patterns with changing environmental conditions. In many cases, archaeologists have showed that new behaviors were clear responses to sudden climatic changes that challenged peoples' abilities to survive.

Scholars espousing the cultural ecological viewpoint also have developed explanations for cultural change that may be applicable to a wide variety of pre-Contact societies, including explanations of subsistence behavior by hunter-gatherer groups and scenarios for the development of dependence on domesticated plants.

Despite these successes, in recent years cultural ecology has been challenged from a number of different theoretical camps. Many of the detractors charge that traditional cultural ecology is too "adaptationist"; it proposes a relatively straightforward relationship between the environment and culture such that the latter is always a successful reaction to the former. To some archaeologists – and the debate is echoed in anthropology in general – this perspective denies any special qualities to the human species, such as intentional behavior that may be selfish or altruistic or in other ways shaped by human agency. Detractors point to cultural ecology's tendency to depict humans as responding to environmental situations *en masse* and acting primarily for the preservation of society as a whole, assumptions that do not ring true given many of the human behaviors we see in the world today.

Beginning in the 1980s, archaeology, like many other disciplines, came under the influence of postmodernism. In archaeology, the major theoretical approach influenced by postmodernism is referred to as "postprocessualism" and, like postmodern schools in other disciplines, it "is largely based on the beliefs that science is not objective, not based on absolute and true laws, and in practice has not improved humanity" (VanPool and VanPool 1999:35). The practitioners of postprocessualism in its more extreme forms reject all claims of truth and question the possibility that humans can perceive an objective reality. These individuals concentrate on "deconstruction," a form of critical analysis designed to reveal the contradictions, assumptions, and biases of the researcher. In this extreme form, deconstruction is not intended to yield an improved interpretation but simply to indicate the logical weaknesses and cultural or personal biases within the work. Less extreme postprocessualists acknowledge that there is such a thing as objective reality and do not reject all knowledge, but they, too, concentrate on deconstructionist techniques designed to identify assumptions and biases that have been unconsciously accepted by archaeologists. These more moderate postprocessualists provide interpretations of the archaeological past, but make no claim of objectivity.

Although very few practitioners of archaeology in the Southwest have embarked on the path of extreme postprocessualism, many are moving away from the strict adaptationist/culture ecological approaches that dominated research during the 1970s and 1980s. Some important influences of the postprocessual critique can be seen in recent Southwestern archaeology however, particularly in research that considers the different social identities that exist in any human context and the interesting tensions and negotiations that guide much of our social behavior. Work by Patricia Crown (2000a) and Kelley Hays-Gilpin (2000) on different gender roles in the archaeological record, for example, reflects a growing awareness of influential aspects of life in the pre-Contact Southwest that have not been addressed in previous archaeological research.

Many of the new theoretical approaches emerging in Southwestern archaeology emphasize political economy and practice theory. Although manifested in a variety of explicit approaches, these new perspectives stress the importance of individual agency in the quest for status, authority, and power, while exploring the many pathways to achieving higher-status and leadership roles (e.g., Kantner 1999a; Kohler and Van West 1996; Saitta 1997; Sebastian 1992; Whiteley 1988). An important aspect of these viewpoints is the cooperative and competitive interplay between different kinds of individuals, such as between leaders and followers, as they each try to realize their goals within a social world. These interactions, together with the physical environment, shape how authority, status, and power are manifested at varying levels and how, in turn, economic activities and material culture are shaped by these political and social relationships.

Discussions in this book reflect these newer theoretical perspectives. A guiding belief is that an understanding of sociocultural change can be enhanced by taking the strengths of the cultural ecological approach and combining them with some of the more valid criticisms emerging from the postprocessual traditions. The result is a viewpoint that acknowledges the importance of the social and physical environment and the efficacy of the scientific approach but that recognizes the importance of human agency and the effect of human actions and choices on culture change. Humans, like other species, have evolved behavioral mechanisms that contribute to individual preservation and enhance our ability to reproduce successfully. Because we are a self-aware species with heightened cognitive abilities, many of these evolved behaviors are self-interested or serve the interests of our relatives. This does not mean that humans are condemned by evolution to steal, bully, or fight for any little advantage; we are a social species whose very survival depends on the cooperation of others, and so self-interest often leads to cooperation. But we also do not often pass up opportunities to gain a little more than our neighbors, especially if we can do it without incurring the ire of others in our social group!

This process of negotiating individual advantage in a social context is critical to the development of increasingly complex social and political organizations. The evolution of leadership is especially important because leadership provides a socially sanctioned arena in which certain individuals and their kin can gain an advantage over others through their influence on group decisions. In the simplest societies, leaders are so heavily constrained by their social group and their authority is so restricted to particular situations that they barely have any advantage at all; in more complex contexts, leaders can receive substantial benefits. The relationship between leaders and the social groups they lead is therefore always a tenuous negotiation in which the gains provided by leadership are constantly evaluated against the costs. To complicate matters, gains and costs are measured through the filter of the society's cultural and ideological heritage, and as cultural ecology has shown us, the physical environment provides important constraints and opportunities that influence how people make decisions.

This perspective on human behavior and its potential effects on culture change provides the theoretical foundation for discussions in this book. Like all societies, ancient Puebloan groups in the American Southwest ultimately consisted of individuals who evaluated their sociopolitical situation according to the opportunities provided by the environment and through the filter of their own cultural history. For example, the tension between leaders who emerged during Chaco and Mimbres times and the other members of the societies in which they lived had an important influence on later cultural patterns in the region. This book explores the historical development of these tensions as manifested at various points in Puebloan history and the ways in which cooperative and competitive sociopolitical behaviors contributed to the evolution of the historic Pueblo people living in the Southwest when the Spanish arrived in the sixteenth century.

The Puebloan Southwest

This, then, is a book that assesses the history of pre-Contact Puebloan people of the American Southwest. It examines the Anasazi and Mogollon archaeological traditions and the culture of their most direct descendants, the Pueblo Indians of Arizona and New Mexico, as it was when these groups were first encountered by the Spanish. Beginning with the period of greatest expansion of settlement and greatest sociopolitical elaboration around AD 1100, the book traces the historical trajectory by which the Anasazi of the Chaco era and the Mogollon of the Mimbres period became the Contact-era Pueblo people.

Chapters 2 and 3 set the stage for this story. Chapter 2 briefly describes the landscape and the changing climatic conditions within which pre-Contact Puebloans lived, while considering their effects in constraining and enabling culture change. The Southwest is a precarious setting in which to make a living as a farmer, and the impact of even minor climatic changes can be far-reaching. This chapter contains a brief overview of existing paleoclimatic reconstructions for this large and topographically varied area and addresses critical issues of drought, growing season, and agricultural potential. This chapter will make explicit the view that environmental change set limits on or provided opportunities for cultural change but was not the primary cause of the long-term cultural trajectory being examined.

Chapter 3 features an overview of Puebloan history from the region's first human occupants through the early development of the Chaco and Mimbres cultures in the AD 1000s. This chapter is intended to provide a broad understanding of the extent and variability of Puebloan cultural development in the Southwest as a baseline for examination of sociopolitical development from the period of Chaco and Mimbres florescence through European Contact.

In Chapter 4, the Mogollon and Anasazi world at the starting point of the analysis – the apotheosis of Chaco and Mimbres cultures – is discussed in detail. In this and each succeeding chapter, the cultural domains of settlement and subsistence, trade and economics, and social, political, and religious structure are considered. I examine not only the cultural domains and the issues of power, authority, and leadership, but also the changing patterns of interaction among different groups. This examination includes not only the areas directly impacted or influenced by the Chaco and Mimbres developments, but the rest of the Puebloan and even non-Puebloan Southwest as well.

Chapters 5 through 8 present a historical examination of how the societies of the Puebloan Southwest got from Point A – the cultural patterns manifested at AD 1100 – to Point B – the cultural patterns at European Contact in AD 1540. In Chapter 5, the period from AD 1100 through the early AD 1200s is explored. The early part of this period was the time of maximum expansion and elaboration of the Chaco and Mimbres cultures. The mid-1100s, however, saw rapid loss of organizational complexity and material culture elaboration. Major population dislocation and regional abandonments can be attributed to a combination of both sociopolitical and environmental factors. The late AD 1100s and early 1200s saw the emergence of new cultural patterns in a post-Chacoan, post-Mimbres Puebloan Southwest.

Chapter 6 considers the widespread thirteenth-century pattern of multifamily pueblos and cliff dwellings with their numerous kivas and associated refuse mounds. As this period progressed, the residents of many sites intensified their agricultural production and took advantage of defensive locations, a pattern that corresponds with increasing evidence of conflict. Also during this era, the northern Mexican culture of Casas Grandes, or Paquimé, began exerting considerable influence on the Puebloan world, an influence that would continue well into the fourteenth century.

The last years of the thirteenth century were marked by a phenomenon that has fascinated archaeologists and the general public alike since it was first recognized. Within a fairly brief period, large areas of the Southwest were abandoned and populations aggregated in uplands and other better-watered portions of the region. Chapter 7 discusses this "Great Abandonment," noting which areas lost population and which gained, identifying the cultural and environmental patterns associated with these losses and gains, and suggesting ways in which these major dislocations and relocations impacted the organization of subsequent Puebloan societies. By the early AD 1300s, major changes in the social and political structure of Puebloan societies were occurring, as populations with widely differing histories were thrown together into large, aggregated communities. Among other topics, this chapter discusses the origin and nature of the Kachina Cult in the Puebloan Southwest.

Finally, chapter 8 examines the large communities of the fifteenth and early sixteenth centuries, the precursors of the Contact-era Pueblo traditions that are the book's ending point. Archaeological, written historical, ethnographic, and oral historical evidence is used to offer a reconstruction, grounded in the theoretical perspective described above, of the historical process by which the Anasazi and Mogollon world of AD 1100 was transformed into the Puebloan world as it was encountered and perceived by both the European and Pueblo participants in that encounter.

2 "The Daylight World": the paleoenvironmental context for Puebloan history

In September 1906, half of the 892 residents of the Hopi Pueblo village of Oraibi moved away as the result of a long-simmering factional dispute (Figure 2.1). Two months later, federal troops forced a large number of the former residents to return, but eventually new villages of Bacavi and Kykotsmovi were established by disenfranchised Oraibi inhabitants. Anthropologists and Hopi alike agree that the "Oraibi split" was one of the more significant events on the Hopi reservation during the twentieth century, and for this reason the Oraibi split has been the subject of anthropological inquiry for many decades. While the facts surrounding the event are fairly well understood, few scholars agree as to the most important causes that culminated in the disintegration of Oraibi. What is clear, however, is that while climate change roughly corresponds with the events of 1906, poor environmental conditions only provided a context for factionalism to reach disruptive levels – the environment did not so much *cause* the events as it did provide *opportunities* for them to occur, a perspective that guides interpretations throughout this book.

Oraibi is one of several Hopi villages located on Black Mesa in northwestern Arizona (Figure 2.2). Because of the ostensibly desolate and dry environment, historical and cultural change during both pre-Contact and modern periods often have been considered as the result of changing weather patterns. Richard Bradfield is one of several scholars who argue that the Oraibi split was caused by climatic shifts in the late 1800s, including an extensive drought beginning around 1865. According to Bradfield (1971), the dry conditions so severely impacted Oraibi's agricultural fields that tensions built between those village members with access to productive fields and those whose crops were most heavily stressed. Eventually, the Oraibi Wash became so deeply incised that irrigation farming was impossible and some of the best croplands were lost. The split of 1906, therefore, is seen by Bradfield and others as a necessary economic accommodation to the loss of the village's productive capacity.

These anthropological interpretations of the events in the Hopi villages during the 1900s reflect an awareness of how challenging it is to

2.1 This Frederíc Harner Maude photograph of the Hopi town of Oraibi dates from the turn of the twentieth century and shows a man preparing to descend into a plaza kiva. In 1906, half of Oraibi's residents left the town as a result of factionalism.

be a farmer in the American Southwest. The region's environment is famous for being dry, and anthropologists have tended to regard this aridity as a major – if not *the* major – factor shaping the cultural evolution of the region's indigenous inhabitants. Scholars also recognize, however, that the Southwestern landscape is highly diverse, defined as much by its irregular and prominent geologic features and remarkable geographic variability as it is by its dryness. And, as the example of Oraibi illustrates, conditions in the Southwest are notoriously unstable from season to season and from year to year, unpredictably ranging from devastatingly violent rainstorms to lengthy droughts. A complete understanding of cultural change in the Southwest is therefore necessarily predicated on a detailed knowledge of the region's physical environment. The following discussion is summarized from a variety of excellent sources, including Brown (1994), Elias (1997), and Williams (1986).

Dry, wet, hot, and cold: the varied climate of the Puebloan Southwest

The climate of the southwestern United States is largely shaped by the region's geological features. Perhaps most important is the relatively high elevation of the Southwest, marked by precipitous mountain ranges, or *cordilleras*, that are oriented along north–south axes. Because of these

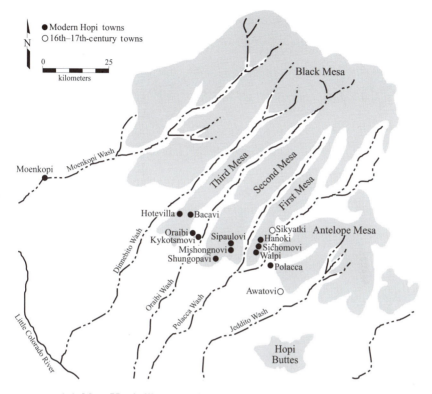

2.2 Most Hopi villages are found where ephemeral washes fed by occasional precipitation and small springs drain Black Mesa. Horticultural activity around these washes is vulnerable to droughts and erosion, and, as seen in the history of Oraibi, such crises can play important roles in village social, economic, and political life.

cordilleras, the major atmospheric systems that bring moisture from the west toward the east are broken up so thoroughly that the region's climatic zones are best characterized as longitudinal. A classic example of this pattern is provided by the Sierra Nevada cordillera, whose high elevations capture moist air moving east from the Pacific Ocean, resulting in a severely arid "rain shadow" on the lowlands of the eastern side. With the uneven geology of the Southwest, the result is an environment composed of many localized zones of cool and moist highlands alternating with hot and dry lowlands.

During the summer, rapid heating of high-elevation lands produces updrafts and a clockwise circulation pattern that captures moist air from the Gulfs of Mexico and California and brings it north. This moisture

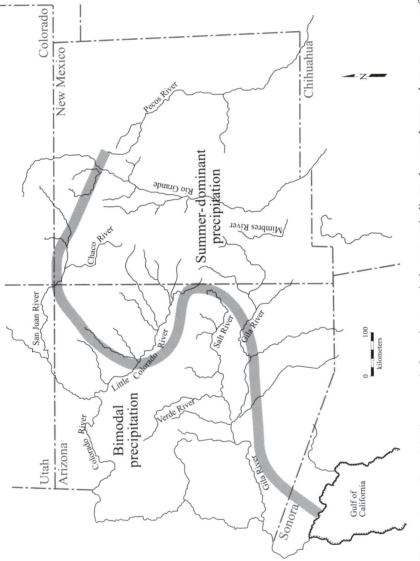

2.3 Analyses of precipitation records from the twentieth century indicate that northern and western areas of the American Southwest receive equal amounts of moisture during the winter and summer, while southern and eastern areas receive most of their moisture during summer storms.

creates monsoonal rains as the hot humid air from the south hits cooler, higher elevations. This precipitation falls either during orographic storms, which form as moisture-laden winds hit the cooler elevations of mountain ranges, or during brief convection storms, when the summer sun heats the ground, producing hot, moist air that rapidly rises into the cooler atmosphere and results in unpredictable and violent precipitation. All this atmospheric activity provides the Southwest with more summer thunderstorms than any other part of the United States. During these violent storms, enormous amounts of water often fall faster than can be absorbed by the sun-baked desert soils, resulting in fast-moving runoff that cuts deep channels, or *arroyos*, across the landscape. Many an unsuspecting tourist has been caught off guard as water dumped from a distant thundercloud rushes down the arroyo in which they are walking – in deep canyons with no escape, the results can be fatal.

The cooler temperatures of the winter months cause the flow of air to reverse to a counter-clockwise circulation, bringing in cold, dry air from the north and creating a high-pressure ridge that prevents weather systems from entering the region. Both schoolchildren praying for snow days and farmers hoping for deep snows that feed spring runoff know the frustration of watching the Weather Channel as a promising winter storm hits the dome of high pressure over the Southwest and turns north. Fortunately, anomalous conditions occasionally drive the high-pressure ridge to the west, allowing Pacific storms to enter the Southwest. When these conditions persist, a flow of winter storms can cross the region, bringing precipitation in the form of steadily falling rain or snow, pleasing schoolchildren, skiers, and farmers alike.

Because the high-pressure ridge tends to sit most frequently over the eastern portion of the Southwest, this area suffers most from low winter precipitation. This results in a unimodal pattern of annual precipitation, with the majority of the year's moisture falling during summer rainstorms (Figure 2.3). Areas to the west, however, benefit more directly from Pacific storms before the moisture is pushed north, and as a result, they enjoy a bimodal pattern, with precipitation occurring both in the winter and in the summer in roughly equal proportions. This pattern, when combined with the generally lower elevations and warmer temperatures of this part of the Southwest, creates environmental zones that differ substantially from areas to the east.

Diversity across space: the physiographic provinces of the Puebloan Southwest

Local differences in geology and elevation affect the general climatic patterns of the American Southwest in varied ways, which in turn contribute

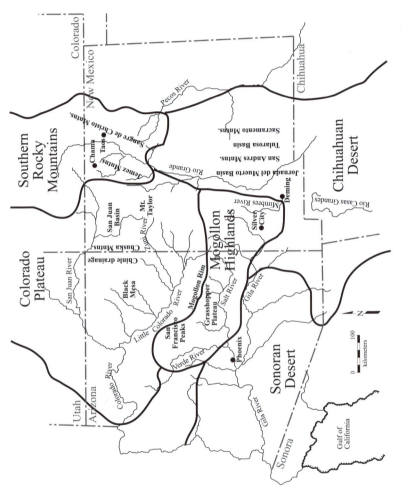

2.4 The American Southwest can be divided into five physiographic zones based on prevailing topography, climate, and plant and animal life. The Sonoran and Chihuahuan Deserts are often included together in a single Basin and Range zone, but here they are separated owing to their distinct flora and fauna. Place names from the chapter are also shown.

to unique distributions of plants and animals. Geographers find it useful to divide the region into a number of distinct physiographic provinces, each with its own geologic history and unique topographic and hydrographic features that distinguish it from neighboring provinces (Figure 2.4). Like any classification system, the division of the American Southwest into discrete provinces obscures significant local variability, but the classification is still useful for characterizing major differences seen in the Southwestern landscape.

Colorado Plateau

For all of Puebloan history, the 337,000 km^2 Colorado Plateau figures prominently. This high-elevation mass of soft sedimentary rock has been eroded to form magnificent features ranging from the sandstone pinnacles of Monument Valley to the vast depths of the Grand Canyon (Figure 2.5). Mountain uplifts pushing through the sedimentary surface are rare. Instead, most prominent points are tablelands whose elevations are enhanced because they border immense basins, such as in the case of the Chuska Mountains on the Arizona–New Mexico border, whose elevations are emphasized by the surrounding San Juan Basin and the Chinle drainage. A handful of features produced by volcanic activity can be found in the San Francisco Peaks to the west, which experienced an extensive period of volcanism beginning in the AD 1060s, and in the area surrounding Mount Taylor, where basalt flows were active as recently as 700 years ago. Despite these prominent features, however, most of the Colorado Plateau consists of broad plains carved into sedimentary rock and broken by small mesas, buttes, and plateaus capped by hard sandstone beds or volcanic deposits that resist erosion.

When combined with the Mogollon Highlands to the south, the Colorado Plateau joins the Tibetan Plateau in Asia as the two largest upland masses in the world. The Colorado and Tibetan plateaus are believed to contribute greatly to the earth's current climatic conditions. With elevations ranging well above 1,500 m, the Colorado Plateau is relatively cool, but the rugged landscape and conspicuous elevation differences make it difficult to characterize the entire province accurately. Although temperatures frequently exceed 100°F in some areas, the overall average during the warmest month is only in the high eighties. Similarly, the coldest winter month can produce frigid temperatures of −20°F or lower, but the average night-time temperature is a more tolerable 10°F. While a few high-altitude areas offer a mere ninety continuous days with temperatures above freezing, most parts of the Colorado Plateau experience a frost-free season of well over 120 days. This still leaves up to 240 days a

2.5 Landscapes of the Colorado Plateau include the arid San Juan Basin (top) and the comparatively moist Red Mesa Valley (bottom); exposed sandstone is everywhere.

year, however, during which a farmer's crops could experience a killing frost – temperatures can plunge below freezing as late as June or as early as September (Box 2.1).

Surprisingly few permanent streams are found on the Colorado Plateau. Rain and snow fall more heavily on higher elevations, where annual precipitation can exceed 500 mm. This water feeds a number of streams, such as the Zuni and Little Colorado "Rivers," which rapidly descend from the Colorado Plateau into the more substantial San Juan

---

Box 2.1   Why is farming so difficult in the Southwest?

Just like farmers today, pre-Contact Puebloan farmers faced a challenging environment in which to cultivate crops successfully. Maize, the most important domesticated plant, was originally a tropical grass not adapted to the conditions of the northern Southwest. Over many generations, Southwest farmers developed maize cultivars that could withstand the rigors of the arid and cool Colorado Plateau. While modern corn (the kind in the grocery store) requires up to 130 continuous frost-free days, some Southwest cultivars mature in ninety days or fewer. Productivity, however, is severely reduced by cool temperatures during early plant growth, and in fact optimal growth occurs at a steamy 86°F (Muenchrath and Salvador 1995).

Modern corn uses as much as 800 mm of water to mature, but the lower limit for some cultivars is considered to be around 150–250 mm without supplementary irrigation. This may not seem like much, but this lower figure assumes that all of this precipitation is available for the plant. If runoff is high, if evaporation is a problem, and, most importantly, if the rainfall is not available throughout the growing season, maize will fail to mature. Water is especially crucial during germination and early growth, as well as during silking, which directly determines the size of the crop (Muenchrath and Salvador 1995).

Of course, maize was not the only domesticated plant grown by indigenous inhabitants of the Southwest. Other crops, however, were even more demanding – cotton, beans, and even squash require longer growing seasons and more water and therefore were less frequently planted. Beans, for example, rarely appear in the archaeological record. Maize was already difficult enough to grow, and expending energy on more demanding crops was probably seen as wasteful in such a marginal environment.

and Colorado Rivers. Much of the province is located in rain shadows of north–south cordilleras, resulting in as little as 200 mm or less of annual precipitation.

The climatic and topographic variability that characterizes the Colorado Plateau creates a similarly diverse plant and animal environment. In the lower-elevation basins, plants adapted to the semi-arid climate thrive, including fragrant sagebrush, hardy saltbush, and various cacti, yuccas, and drought-tolerant grasses. Tablelands feature the classic Southwestern woodlands of scattered piñon and juniper trees interspersed with a thin understory of shrubs and grasses. Mixed conifer forests of ponderosa pine surrounded by oak, sumac, and mountain mahogany and an occasional stand of Douglas firs appear in the higher, better-watered elevations.

A variety of animals occupy these plant communities. Pronghorn antelope graze in the open grasslands, while mule deer prefer the protection of the piñon–juniper woodlands. Elk and bighorn sheep once enjoyed more extensive ranges across the higher elevations, but their numbers have decreased over the past several decades owing to habitat destruction and overhunting. Smaller mammals such as jackrabbits, cottontails, ground squirrels, and a host of other rodents, birds, and reptiles are found throughout the Colorado Plateau. Their populations are influenced by the amount of annual precipitation, which in turn affects the numbers of carnivores such as coyotes and foxes that prey on them.

Southern Rocky Mountains

One of the most diverse physiographic regions in the Southwest is the southern Rocky Mountain province, which extends from south-central Colorado well into northern New Mexico (Figure 2.6). This province is dominated by a series of uplifts that form the high elevations of the Sangre de Cristo Mountains, through which ice-age glaciation once scoured alpine valleys. To the west of these ranges are rift basins – depressions formed as deep geological faults move apart – including the extensive rift valley through which the northern Rio Grande flows. The southern Rocky Mountain province includes the remains of extensive volcanic activity, ranging from ancient basalt flows around the town of Taos through which the Rio Grande has cut a precipitous gorge, to the enormous caldera in the Jemez Mountains that formed 1.4 million years ago during eruptions so violent that ash rained down on what is now Kansas.

As might be expected given the name, the southern Rocky Mountains province has the highest altitudes in the entire American Southwest and thus the coldest climate. Night-time temperatures during the winter drop well below 10°F, while summer days average around 80°F. Accordingly,

2.6 Landscapes of the southern Rocky Mountains include the high meadows and snowy peaks of the Sangre de Cristo range (top) and the canyons cutting through the Pajarito Plateau as they empty into the Rio Grande (bottom).

the frost-free season in this region is very short, rarely lasting longer than 130 days and in the mountains averaging fewer than sixty continuous days. On the other hand, the summer orographic storms that the high elevations capture provide over 300 mm of precipitation, with some high elevations receiving 750 mm of snow and rain. As with all areas in the Southwest, however, annual precipitation in the mountains is completely unpredictable; in 1957, the modern town of Chama, New Mexico, suffered through a drought during which only 220 mm of precipitation were recorded; the very next year, over 800 mm of rain and snow fell.

The landscape of the southern Rocky Mountains is defined by rapid changes in elevation. The province's vegetation is therefore arrayed into different vertical zones. Expanses of grasses and sagebrush are found in some of the low basins, but woodlands and forests dominate the region's higher elevations. Between 1,700 and 2,300 m, fairly dense piñon and juniper woodlands are mixed with shrubby vegetation such as oak and sagebrush. From 2,300 to 3,000 m, these scrappy woodland species are replaced by dense stands of tall ponderosa pines and Douglas firs, broken by green meadows of fescue and bluegrass. Engelmann spruce and subalpine fir gradually replace the Douglas fir at elevations exceeding 3,000 m, with stands so dense that little understory can grow.

With so much of the province's biomass tied up in trees, and with such long and cold winters, few animal species thrive in the Rocky Mountains. Large animals that move long distances to find food, such as elk and bighorn sheep, historically occupied the province. Mule deer live at lower elevations among the piñons, junipers, and ponderosa pines. Black bears, mountain lions, and bobcats are also found in the mountain areas, although now in much smaller numbers than during the pre-Contact period as their habitats are encroached upon by ski areas and cattle.

Mogollon Highlands

The Mogollon Highlands form a rugged and heavily dissected physiographic province that runs from just west of the San Francisco Mountains in central Arizona to the edge of the Rio Grande basin in west-central New Mexico. The entire province was formed by volcanic activity 40–20 million years ago that left behind huge calderas, elevated domes, and flows of lava and volcanic mud. Splintering this expansive tableland of volcanic rock are several block-faulted ranges and prominent basins, including the San Augustin Plains in New Mexico that during the last Ice Age contained an enormous lake. Between these rugged geological features are elevated expanses such as Grasshopper Plateau in Arizona, which is bordered on its northeastern edge by the Mogollon Rim that climbs to the Colorado

Plateau. On the southwestern edge of the Mogollon Highlands are deep canyons incised by perennial streams through softer deposits; these join together to form the Gila and Salt Rivers.

With elevations generally ranging 2,000–3,300 m, the climate of the Mogollon Highlands is more moderate and wetter than that of the Colorado Plateau despite its location farther south (Figure 2.7). The hottest summer temperatures rarely surpass 100°F, and averages from the warmest month are only in the low to middle eighties. Winters are also moderate, with night-time temperatures during the coldest month regularly exceeding 15°F and rarely dropping below 0°F. Despite this comparatively moderate climate, freezing nights begin early in fall and linger late into spring, providing a short frost-free season of 90–120 days, except in the lower elevations to the south, which are warmed by heat rising from the Chihuahuan Desert.

The various ranges that break up the Mogollon Highlands capture a surprising amount of precipitation, especially during summer months when moisture flows northeast from the Pacific Ocean. Although the very southern edges of the province receive only 250 mm of annual precipitation, the amount of rain and snow increases rapidly once in the higher elevations, with yearly totals commonly 350–500 mm. The modern town of Deming, New Mexico, situated immediately south of the Mogollon Highlands, has an average of 225 mm of annual precipitation, while Silver City, located only 80 km to the northwest, receives over 400 mm of rain and snow.

This precipitation supports a fairly dense biomass. The lowest basins of the Mogollon Highlands are populated by shrubby plants adapted to drier conditions, including saltbush and sacaton. Most of the province, however, is dominated by well-watered piñon and juniper woodlands with a dense undergrowth of Gambel oak, mountain mahogany, and cliff rose. The higher elevations feature forests of ponderosa pine with the occasional Douglas fir; in fact, the largest continuous ponderosa pine forest in the United States runs almost the entire length of the province. Animal populations in many ways mirror those found on the Colorado Plateau, although the greater precipitation supports larger populations of mammals such as mule deer and rabbits.

Chihuahuan Desert

Technically, the remainder of the American Southwest is part of an immense physiographic province known as the Basin and Range, which extends all the way from north-central Mexico well into the state of Oregon. This province is defined by an undulating pattern of low-elevation,

2.7 The Mogollon Highlands zone is one of the best-watered areas in the American Southwest. It supports ponderosa pine forests in its higher elevations (bottom) and relatively green piñon and juniper forests in the valleys (top) that drain into the Chihuahuan and Sonoran Deserts.

north–south ranges that alternate with broad, shallow basins. For example, the Basin and Range province east of the Mogollon Highlands includes the broad Jornada del Muerto basin – named by Spanish explorers for its dry, inhospitable expanses – which on its east side is bordered by the 240 mile long San Andres Mountains. This narrow range itself is flanked on the east by the Tularosa Basin, followed by yet another north–south cordillera, the Sacramento Mountains. This landscape of alternating highlands and lowlands is typical of the Basin and Range province.

Because this province includes such a vast area, it is useful to divide it into smaller physiographic sections defined less by geology than by other environmental features. While much of Puebloan history does not occur directly within this province, two Basin and Range areas are important, especially during specific moments in time. The first of these is the Chihuahuan Desert (Figure 2.8). This region is characterized by low block-fault mountain ranges separated by wide basins that once held Ice Age lakes. Basalt flows, some of which are quite recent, extend across many of these basins. Permanent sources of groundwater are rare, although the Rio Grande rift valley does bisect the region as it flows toward the Gulf of Mexico. A number of small but important drainages emanate from the higher elevations, including the Mimbres River in New Mexico and the Rio Casas Grandes in the modern Mexican state of Chihuahua.

The highest portions of the Chihuahuan Desert are not particularly high – most elevations are 1,000–3,000 m. The lower elevations and southern location make this one of the warmer areas of the Southwest, with summer temperatures regularly above 95°F and the hottest days reaching 110°F. Winter temperatures rarely dip below 25°F. Frosts usually hit the area in late October and end by mid-April, providing a frost-free season of 180 days or more. With the excessive heat and few high mountains to catch summer moisture, however, most of this area has annual precipitation below 275 mm, with some portions barely getting 200 mm each year. Drought years with less than 75 mm of rain are not unheard of.

Except for in the higher elevations, most of the Chihuahuan Desert is sparsely covered by short grasses and shrubs. Creosote bush, acacia, saltbush, burrograss, and grama grass are some of the species adapted to the arid conditions, along with various cacti and yuccas scattered across the landscape. Some of the ranges feature small junipers and hardy mountain shrubs such as scrubby oak and sagebrush. Small numbers of desert-dwelling animals inhabit the region – in addition to the expected

2.8 The Chihuahuan Desert is part of the Basin and Range physiographic province, in which numerous steep mountain ranges are separated by flat and arid basins (bottom). The Chihuahuan Desert is sparsely vegetated with plants adapted to the harsh conditions, but pockets of piñon and juniper trees grow in some mountain ranges (top).

assortment of rabbits, rodents, and lizards, these include small white-tailed deer and collared peccary.

Sonoran Desert

The other relevant subarea of the Basin and Range physiographic province is the Sonoran Desert. Like the Chihuahuan Desert, this region does not figure as prominently in Puebloan history. The Sonoran Desert was home to the Hohokam, however, and through most of the pre-Contact period, these desert dwellers were close neighbors to many Puebloan groups. The Hohokam influenced, traded with, and no doubt intermixed with their neighbors, especially during the extensive migrations of the late pre-Contact period.

The Sonoran Desert features a topography characteristic of the Basin and Range province, but this region features the lowest elevations in the Southwest, with few mountain ranges exceeding 1,000 m. The Sonoran Desert also receives the least annual precipitation; few areas record more than 250 mm of rain and most suffer through a mere 200 mm or less. Average temperatures are so high that few nights dip below 32°F; the city of Phoenix enjoys a frost-free season of almost 360 days.

Two important characteristics make the Sonoran Desert unique. The first is a bimodal distribution of annual precipitation. Despite the small amounts of moisture, the rains come twice a year, during violent summer thunderstorms and as gentle winter systems moving in from the Pacific Ocean. Since the frost-free season is so long, the desert vegetation can reap the full benefit of this bimodal pattern of rainfall. The second important feature is that three major rivers flow through the desert, having originated in the highland provinces to the north and east. This includes the Salt and Gila Rivers, which ultimately feed the powerful Colorado River. These rivers provide year-round sources of water and comparatively lush riverine environments set in the otherwise arid desert.

The unusual distribution of water in the Sonoran Desert contributes to a surprisingly rich diversity of vegetation. While the creosote bush, acacia, saltbush, and yucca of the Chihuahuan Desert ecosystem appear in some areas, plants such as mesquite, paloverde, jojoba, agave, and the famous saguaro cactus are also common. The higher elevations accommodate semidesert grasslands and evergreens such as juniper, while the riverine environments nurture cottonwoods, willows, and various legumes. In all, over 250 plants in the Sonoran Desert are known to have served as food for indigenous inhabitants. Small animals such as jackrabbits, cottontails, and various rodents are common, while deer are found in the higher elevations. In some ways, calling this province a "desert" is a bit misleading because of its rich plant and animal population.

Why does this matter?

Anyone who has driven any distance through the American Southwest is well acquainted with the remarkable environmental diversity that makes the area an international playground. Hopefully, this brief summary of the different physiographic regions demonstrates that substantial topographic, climatic, and biotic variety can occur across very small distances. The importance of this quality of the Southwest environment cannot be overemphasized, for it had a profound impact on the pre-Contact occupation of the region.

As an example of the impact of this environmental diversity on human behavior, consider again the split of the Hopi village of Oraibi. In Bradfield's original analysis (1971) and a subsequent study by Jerrold Levy (1992), explanations for the 1906 crisis emphasize the highly diverse nature of the local environment. Both the variable distribution of soils adequate for farming as well as the irregular access to water sources of different types contributed to a highly diverse agricultural landscape. The best areas, with dependable sources of water and richest soils, were located along major floodplains, while more marginal but serviceable farmlands were only a short distance away on sand dunes and the slopes of small tributaries. Both Bradfield and Levy contend that this variable spatial distribution of croplands resulted in inequitable agricultural productivity among the different clans living at Oraibi, which in turn led to factionalism and the split of 1906. For both scholars, the unique spatial variability that characterizes the Southwestern environment was a critical factor in the social and cultural changes that culminated in the disintegration of Oraibi. This diversity across space is one important aspect of the Southwest landscape that both restricted and provided opportunities for Puebloan cultural change.

Diversity through time: paleoenvironmental changes

As Kenneth Petersen points out (1994), weather is the condition of the atmosphere at any particular time or place, while climate is a statistical composite of all weather events that have occurred over a lengthy period of time. In the previous discussion of the major physiographic provinces, depictions of climatic conditions were based on weather station data that go back no more than fifty years. This means that the average readings given for each physiographic province are misleading – just as the spatial distribution of environmental features across the American Southwest is remarkably uneven, the climate has also been extraordinarily variable over the lengthy period of human occupation. Because the region is so marginal for successful human occupation, a record of this temporal climatic variability is critical if we want to understand the context of changes in pre-Contact human society and culture.

The Oraibi split of 1906 again provides a good example of the impact of climate change on human behavior. Most scholars who have discussed the events leading up to the split acknowledge the importance of a series of droughts in the latter half of the nineteenth century. As summarized by Bradfield (1971), rain- and snowfall were below average from 1865 to 1904, with a severe drought devastating the region over thirteen years from 1892 and 1904. Although overall precipitation returned to normal levels in 1905, it fell in the winter and not in the summer when crops needed the moisture. By 1906, wells around Oraibi were running dry. A drought of such duration and severity exacerbated existing tensions in all Hopi villages, providing the context for incipient factionalism to become more severe. Clearly, the conflict in Oraibi cannot be adequately understood by simply relying on average climatic readings. Any discussion of pre-Contact behavior and cultural change in the Southwest therefore should take into account the detailed paleoclimatic record.

The Southwest paleoenvironmental record

The pre-Contact Southwest is marked by constant environmental change, and it has long been recognized that successful inquiry into the region's past requires an understanding of changing temperature and precipitation. Fortunately, in 1966, Thor Karlstrom of the US Geological Survey (USGS) invited archaeologists to investigate an area near Black Mesa where astronauts were training for the lunar landing. Thus began a lengthy collaboration between scholars from several disciplines that informally became known as the "Paleoenvironmental Project" (Gumerman 1988; see also Dean 1992). Through analysis of a variety of data sources, including floodplain sediments, packrat middens, palynological records, and dendroclimatic patterns, the group produced a 2,000-year record of environmental change (Figure 2.9). A number of environmental features important to pre-Contact people were emphasized in this reconstruction, including annual precipitation; changing patterns of erosion, which affect soil fertility and irrigation potential; and decreases and increases in water table levels, which impact soil moisture and spring flows.

Recognizing that changes in climate do not occur evenly or predictably, the Paleoenvironmental Group considered different patterns of

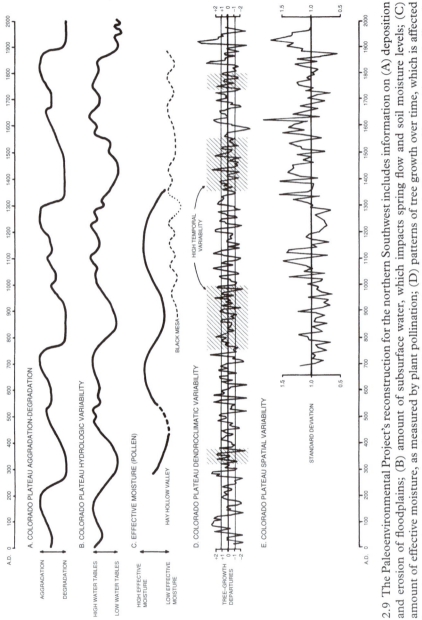

2.9 The Paleoenvironmental Project's reconstruction for the northern Southwest includes information on (A) deposition and erosion of floodplains; (B) amount of subsurface water, which impacts spring flow and soil moisture levels; (C) amount of effective moisture, as measured by plant pollination; (D) patterns of tree growth over time, which is affected by moisture and temperature; and (E) patterns of tree growth across space, an indication of how widespread climatic conditions are.

precipitation. During some years, for example, localized climatic conditions contribute to *high spatial variability*, with one part of the Southwest receiving above-average rainfall while an area a short distance away is suffering through a drought. In contrast, *low spatial variability* reflects an even distribution of precipitation across the entire Southwest. The researchers similarly acknowledged that differences in temporal variability in precipitation also are important. During a period of *high temporal variability*, the amount of rainfall from year to year is highly irregular and thus unpredictable; in contrast, periods of *low temporal variability* are more regular and predictable. These variables were considered separately from an overall characterization of precipitation. Over a certain period of time, for example, people might experience a minor drought with low and thus highly predictable temporal variability. In contrast, during another series of years, average conditions might prevail, but with such high temporal variability that one year people enjoy plenty of rain while the very next year virtually no rain falls at all.

Figure 2.9 illustrates the Paleoenvironmental Group's reconstruction, illustrating paleoclimatic periods that are of particular importance for discussion of late pre-Contact events in the Puebloan Southwest. The emergence of Chaco Canyon as an important cultural center, the starting point for this book, is associated with a generally moist period that began in approximately AD 925. This climatic regime also encouraged soil aggradation that built up floodplains. Alongside the wetter conditions, however, were increasing spatial variability and year-to-year instability, although the latter changed around AD 1000 with a shift to low temporal variability that lasted into the mid-1300s. The eleventh century was generally moist, but a moderately dry spell did hit the northern Southwest between AD 1030 and 1060, followed by especially wet years in the early AD 1100s.

The Paleoenvironmental Group's sequence identifies a modest but prolonged drought around AD 1130–80 that corresponds with the collapse of the important cultural centers in Chaco Canyon and the Mimbres drainage. This event was accompanied by increasing spatial uniformity in precipitation, such that all areas suffered equally from the lack of rainfall. The continuing drought also adversely impacted water tables and soil aggradation. Wetter conditions returned in the AD 1200s and combined with low temporal variability to provide relatively mesic conditions for most inhabitants of the Colorado Plateau during much of the thirteenth century.

The end of the thirteenth century marks a climatic period that Southwestern archaeologists often call "The Great Drought." From AD 1276 to AD 1299, according to the Paleoenvironmental Group's reconstruction, the region experienced a dramatic reduction in precipitation, a precipitous crash in water table levels, and rapid floodplain erosion that destroyed fertile soil deposits. High temporal variability combined with high spatial variability to add a high degree of unpredictability to the already marginal conditions. Although rainfall returned for a few decades in the early AD 1300s, conditions remained challenging until the latter half of the sixteenth century. It was at this critical juncture that the first Spanish explorers began to enter the Southwest, introducing new challenges for indigenous populations.

The important work of the Paleoenvironmental Group continues to guide our understanding of pre-Contact conditions across the Puebloan world. However, because of the original goals of this project, most of the data are from the Black Mesa area; whether the sequence is adequate for understanding human–environment interaction elsewhere in the Puebloan Southwest is unclear. A recent collaboration between Jeffrey Dean, Gary Funkhouser, and the late Donald Graybill provided insight into this issue (Dean 1996a). They examined dendroclimatological samples from twenty-seven locations across the Colorado Plateau, determined the sequences of precipitation for each, and employed statistical procedures to identify patterns in the data. The study produced a few interesting conclusions. First, the scholars found that the current division of the Southwest into two climatic zones, one characterized by a bimodal distribution of annual precipitation and the other featuring summer-dominant rainfall, has always existed (Figure 2.10). The boundaries of these zones have not been stable, however – between AD 739 and 838, the zone of bimodal precipitation included areas much farther to the southeast. After AD 966, this zone slowly shrank to its current size. Perhaps more importantly, during some periods, such as between the mid-1300s and mid-1400s, the geographic patterning completely broke down, with different localities experiencing a high degree of climatic independence.

The study by Dean and his colleagues demonstrates that the sequence produced by the Paleoenvironmental Group may not always adequately represent local environmental sequences at any given moment of the pre-Contact period. While the Black Mesa sequence is probably an effective representation of general paleoclimatic patterns in the Puebloan Southwest, it is also important to consider localized paleoenvironmental sequences. In their study of pre-Contact agriculture in southwestern Colorado, Gary Huckleberry and Brian Billman (1998) remind us that "no two streams are alike, and each has to be treated individually," concluding that local geology, topography, and climate interact in unique ways.

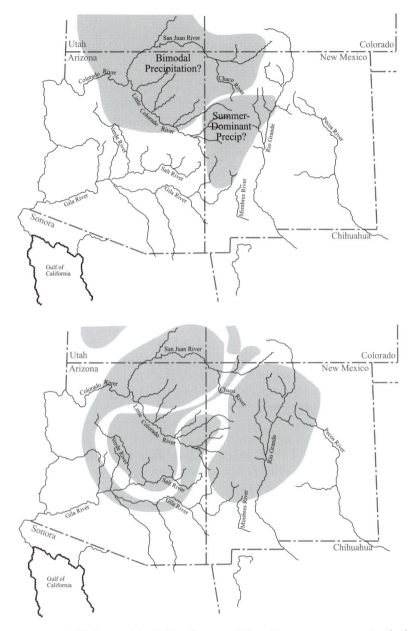

2.10 Research by Jeffrey Dean and his colleagues suggests not only that the boundary between zones of unimodal and bimodal precipitation has shifted through time, but that occasionally the boundary has completely broken down. The top figure separates two zones of distinctive tree growth patterns from AD 739 to 838; the bottom figure illustrates the breakdown of these zones between AD 1339 and 1438.

A Weather Channel into the past: localized paleoenvironmental sequences

Attempts to understand developments in the Puebloan world can obviously benefit from detailed paleoenvironmental sequences for local areas. Such efforts are time-consuming and costly, however; few of us have the resources to generate a sequence as thorough as that produced by the Paleoenvironmental Group. Nevertheless, such efforts are important and a number of attempts have been made. Discussing every local climatic record is well beyond the scope of this volume, but sequences for two areas important in the evolution of the Puebloan Southwest do merit further consideration.

Numerous well-known pre-Contact sites are located in the area north of the San Juan River and south of the San Juan Mountains in southwestern Colorado. Places like Mesa Verde, Chimney Rock, and Hovenweep are well known to both archaeologists and the traveling public, and they figure prominently in our understanding of Puebloan history. This portion of the Colorado Plateau – generally referred to as the "Mesa Verde region" – is environmentally distinct from areas farther south, and for this reason its paleoclimatic sequence is unlike that of Black Mesa. Fortunately, the efforts of several scholars have contributed to a localized sequence of paleoenvironmental change for this unique region.

Based on dendroclimatological and palynological analyses, Petersen (1987b, 1987c, 1994, 1996; see also Van West 1994a) describes some of the more important paleoclimatic patterns in the Mesa Verde region. Of particular interest are changes in temperature, which in this high-altitude northern area are probably more critical than overall rainfall, especially for farmers trying to bring their crops to maturity. Petersen's sequence (Figure 2.11) begins with a period lasting around AD 1–500, during which both precipitation levels and temperatures steadily decreased. Between AD 600 and 750, however, conditions improved, with both increased rain and higher temperatures. Patterns of precipitation shifted after AD 750, bringing more convectional storms in the summer but little moisture during the winter. Temperatures also changed, such that the frost-free season shortened and the amount of land available for dry farming decreased.

The years between roughly AD 950 and 1250 are known as the Medieval Warm Period, a climatic event with repercussions all over the world. As the name suggests, this period was characterized by mild temperatures in the Mesa Verde region, with the most pleasant conditions around AD 1100. Heavy spring rains and cool cloudy summers provided abundant moisture during the most critical months for growing crops.

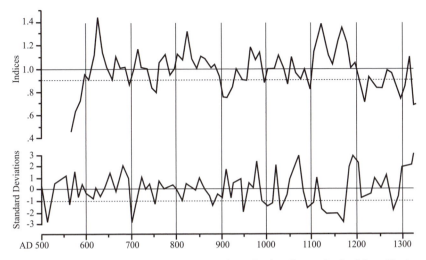

2.11 K. L. Petersen's reconstruction of paleoclimate in the Mesa Verde region of southwestern Colorado. The top sequence illustrates changing temperature, with the dashed line showing the point at which the frost-free season was shorter than 110 days. The bottom sequence displays changing precipitation, with the dashed line indicating one standard deviation below normal levels.

Petersen argues that the rains and mild temperatures created a farmable area that was twice as big as it is today and presumably enhanced wild plant growth as well.

Unfortunately for inhabitants of the Mesa Verde region, the conditions characterizing the Little Ice Age appeared around AD 1250, if not earlier. This climatic period may have been triggered by a series of enormous volcanic eruptions in the early and middle 1200s (Salzer 2000). Although occurring in parts of the world far from the Southwest, these eruptions are believed to have significantly impacted the earth's climate by producing gases that decreased solar radiation. Whatever the cause, the Little Ice Age was marked by a sequence of climatic changes that were increasingly unfavorable for people living in the Mesa Verde region. Beginning perhaps as early as the late AD 1100s, winter precipitation gradually decreased, leading to less snowpack and therefore drier soils during the spring. This pattern was soon joined by a trend for the monsoonal rains to arrive later in the summer and not last as long nor penetrate as far north as they had during the Medieval Warm Period. Finally, during the early thirteenth century, northern cold, dry air pushed farther south into the Southwest during the winter, and the frost-free season in the Mesa Verde area was

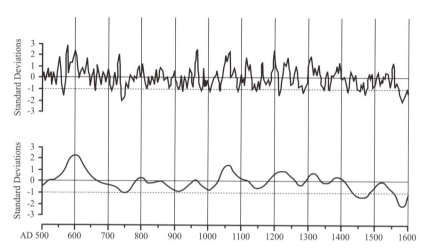

2.12 H. Grissino-Mayer's reconstruction of paleoclimate in the El Malpais area of west-central New Mexico. Short-term variability is illustrated at the top and long-term trends at the bottom; as in Figure 2.11, the dotted line represents one standard deviation below average precipitation.

radically shortened. Petersen (1994:264) contends that the perseverance of the Little Ice Age in this region explains why Anglo-European explorers in the middle 1800s described snow on the San Miguel Mountains in early August; today, the snowpack is gone an entire month earlier.

The Mesa Verde sequence shows that the applicability of the Paleoenvironmental Group's reconstruction to the entire Puebloan Southwest may be limited both by unique physiographic circumstances that affect local climatic conditions and by different concerns for the human inhabitants.

A different example is provided by the dendroclimatological sequence for the El Malpais area, located on the southernmost edge of the Colorado Plateau in west-central New Mexico. Developed by Henri Grissino-Mayer (1996; Grissino-Mayer et al. 1997), this reconstruction in many ways parallels the Black Mesa sequence, but a number of significant differences would have impacted pre-Contact residents of the El Malpais area in unique ways.

Grissino-Mayer based his 2,129-year reconstruction on tree-ring samples from Douglas fir and ponderosa pine stands and subfossil wood scattered among the lava flows of El Malpais. Two reconstructions were created, one emphasizing short-term variability and the second identifying long-term trends (Figure 2.12). Of particular interest is the 350-year period of mostly below-normal precipitation that occurred between

AD 661 and 1023. This was immediately followed by a few decades of relatively plentiful rain and snow until the early 1100s, when a short-lived and not especially severe drought impacted El Malpais. The region subsequently experienced two more cycles of above-normal followed by below-normal precipitation, and by AD 1400, severe drought was finally felt in this part of the Southwest, where it lasted until the early 1600s.

Grissino-Mayer's reconstruction (Figure 2.12) compares favorably with the Paleoenvironmental Group's sequence (Figure 2.9), but a few notable differences should be mentioned. In the El Malpais sequence, dry conditions lasting from the late 900s to the early 1000s were more severe than is recorded in the Black Mesa reconstruction, as was the drought in the early 1100s. Another difference is that, in the El Malpais area, their Great Drought arrived later and lingered longer. Grissino-Mayer's study illustrates how different portions of the Puebloan Southwest often experienced quite dissimilar environmental conditions. This is further demonstrated by a statistical analysis that Grissino-Mayer (1996:196) conducted that compared the El Malpais sequence with twenty-five other reconstructions from the Four Corners area. He found that his sequence was most similar to those from the area directly surrounding the San Juan Basin, and most dissimilar from sequences from Black Mesa, the Mesa Verde region, and the central Rio Grande drainage.

The local paleoclimatic reconstructions summarized here are only two of almost thirty sequences developed for the northern Southwest, including an extensive one for the northern Rio Grande area (Rose *et al.* 1981) and a recent sequence from the San Francisco Mountains (Salzer 2000). While these reconstructions are invaluable for understanding how human populations responded to environmental change during the pre-Contact period, we should also be aware that they are incomplete views of past conditions. Dendroclimatological studies are seductive, for they provide a fine-grained picture of past precipitation, but trees do not live on water alone. Temperatures, available nutrients, and diseases and insects also impact tree growth and have to be accounted for. For example, Richard Milo (1994:40) notes that two insect pests – white grub beetles and false wireworms – likely attacked Puebloan cornfields at various times, perhaps with devastating results. A dendroclimatological sequence also should not be confused with a full environmental reconstruction, which requires a consideration of landscape, plants, and animals. Nevertheless, sequences such as those generated by the Paleoenvironmental Group, Petersen, Grissino-Mayer, and others are providing archaeologists with critical insight into the experiences of Puebloan people, whose efforts to thrive in the marginal landscape of the Southwest substantially shaped their society and culture.

Concluding thoughts

When the Hopi village of Oraibi fissioned, its inhabitants had suffered through almost fifty years of below-normal rainfall and thirteen years of a severe drought. No analysis of the events of the summer of 1906 can deny the importance of the dire environmental situation, and scholars such as Bradfield focus on the drought as the primary cause for the factionalism that tore Oraibi apart. But humans are complex animals who do not simply respond to environmental stimuli. In recent decades, a number of anthropologists and archaeologists have reevaluated the circumstances surrounding the Oraibi split, inspired by questions such as "Why did the split occur well into the lengthy drought and not earlier?" and "Why didn't other Hopi villages, which were experiencing the same climatic conditions, also split?"

Anthropologists such as Peter Whiteley (1988), Jerrold Levy (1992), and Scott Rushforth and Steadman Upham (1992) propose their own explanations of the Oraibi split that see the environmental situation at the turn of the twentieth century as important, but not the only or even the direct cause of the events of 1906. Whiteley, for example, particularly objects to explanations suggesting that "the mindless Hopis, uncomprehending the conditions of their existence, responded like laboratory rats to randomly changed stimuli" (1988:251).

While these scholars are not in agreement as to what caused the Oraibi split, they do highlight important factors that an adaptationist view might overlook. Smallpox epidemics, Navajo raids, and Mormon encroachment added additional stresses that all Hopi villages had to confront. Perhaps most critical, however, was the incipient political factionalism that revolved around membership in clans with unequal access to land and power, combined with a village leadership that was founded upon traditional ritual authority. From this perspective, the climatic conditions are seen as *providing the context* for the sociopolitical intrigue underlying the Oraibi breakup. The community did not fall apart simply because it was no longer sustainable in the face of the drought. Instead, the drought intensified the underlying factionalism by exacerbating socioeconomic differences and undermining the religious authority that legitimized the status of the village's most prominent members. Whiteley argues that these traditional leaders, faced with threats to their status, actually precipitated the split themselves by refocusing blame for the crisis on the acceptance of Anglo-American customs by those Hopi most impacted by the drought.

Although not all scholars agree with this particular scenario for the dissolution of Oraibi, the important point is that environmental conditions only provide the context for human sociocultural behavior. For both groups and individuals, the environment offers opportunities or imposes constraints on behavioral options, which in turn are shaped by social and cultural considerations. In the following chapters, discussions are informed by this perspective, with paleoenvironmental conditions and changes regarded as playing a role in, but not directly determining, behavior and culture among pre-Contact Puebloan people of the Southwest.

3 Return to *Ánosin Téhuli*? The origins of Puebloan culture

The first world, *Ánosin Téhuli*, was too dark and small. So the Twin Children of the Sun made some grasses grow taller and more robust, creating a ladder upon which all creatures could climb into the second world, *K'ólin Téhuli*. Populations in *K'ólin Téhuli* again grew so rapidly that yet a third world, *Áwisho Téhuli*, was needed, but once again there were too many people. They therefore divided into different tribes, forming distinctions that became most apparent as they ascended into the fourth world, *Tépahaian Téhuli*. Eventually, the Twins led all the different nations and animals upward toward the light, into the current world, *Ték'ohaian Úlahnane*, the Daylight World (Cushing 1896).

According to the *chimik'yanakona penane*, the Zuni origin story, many different groups of people have existed since the beginning of time. Each made a similar journey through successive worlds in which they acted and looked differently, before migrating across the Daylight World and arriving at the spot where they live today. The Zuni accordingly recognize that their current world only makes sense in reference to this past history that shaped them (Ferguson and Hart 1985). In its own way, archaeology tells a very similar story, and its lessons are the same – any given moment in human history is the product of everything that came before. This chapter, then, establishes the foundations for our story of the Puebloan people.

Paleoindians: the earliest people of the Southwest

The earliest inhabitants of the American Southwest, whom archaeologists call the Paleoindians, lived in an environment utterly unlike that of the modern Southwest. The climate, the vegetation, the animals – every aspect of the late Ice Age was so different that we could, indeed, consider it to have been a different world (Elias 1997). The climate was moister and more stable than today – more rainfall fell and summer temperatures were lower, while winter temperatures were similar to or even warmer than today. Areas that are now deserts were grasslands, woodlands occurred at much lower elevations, the highest elevations were covered permanently with ice and snow, and surface water was more plentiful. Available game animals included "megafauna" such as mammoths, mastodons, giant sloths, and *Bison antiquus*, huge creatures perhaps half as large again as modern buffalo.

The timing of the initial movement of people into the New World is one of those interesting questions that for many years appeared to be answered, then underwent a major revision and was thought to be solved, and now is being questioned again (Dixon 1999; Feidel 1999, 2000). Although much of the available evidence is still consistent with the interpretation that Clovis people were the earliest inhabitants of the New World, a growing body of data casts serious doubt on that view. A number of meticulously excavated and carefully dated sites in both North and South America indicate pre-Clovis occupation dating to 20,000 years ago or even earlier. For the Southwest, however, the earliest widely accepted dates for Paleoindian begin about 13,000 years ago, and the Clovis people are still recognized as the earliest inhabitants of the region; no older tools have been found (e.g., Sanchez 2001; but see Chrisman *et al.* 1996).

The Paleoindians were highly mobile people adapted to the game-rich environment of the Southwest (Haynes 1980, 1991). They had the skill and technology to kill very large and dangerous animals (Figure 3.1), but they appear to have hunted herd animals such as camel and horses as well as other smaller species (Agenbroad 1990). They also undoubtedly collected plentiful plant resources such as cactus fruits and piñon nuts. Group size was small during most of the year, perhaps no more than forty people, although occasional gatherings of larger groups for feasting, trading, and exchanging information were important, both economically and socially. Based on analogy with similar ethnographic societies, leadership positions were based on seniority, kinship, and personal skill in activities such as hunting or curing. The decisions that a leader advocated would be weighed by the group according to his or her perceived skills and previous success at making good decisions.

As the ice sheets began to retreat to the north some 14,000 years ago, the climate in the Southwest grew drier and exhibited greater seasonality (Figure 3.2). Many of the largest game species, as well as horses and camels, became extinct. Perhaps this was because they could not adapt to the climate changes, but some researchers (Martin 1973; Martin *et al.* 1985) argue that Clovis hunters were also responsible for the megafauna extinctions. Meanwhile, more modestly sized game animals, such as bison, adapted by shifting their ranges farther north or east, moving beyond the boundaries of the Southwest.

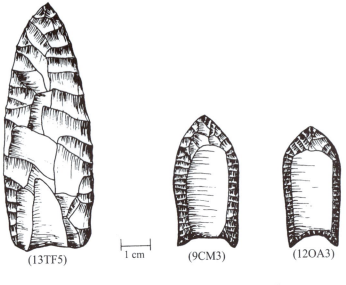

(13TF5)   1 cm   (9CM3)   (12OA3)

Clovis point   **Folsom points**

3.1 The size and workmanship of Paleoindian spear points make them easy to identify in the archaeological record; other food-gathering tools, such as those for gathering plants, are more elusive.

Because of this extinction and exodus of larger animals, Clovis culture faded as the large game disappeared. In the eastern parts of the Southwest, Clovis was followed by Folsom, Paleoindian people whose hunting strategies were focused on the now extinct *Bison antiquus,* and by later Paleoindian complexes that primarily hunted *Bison bison* and other still extant species. The latest Paleoindian complexes are most common in the northern Great Plains but are rare to nonexistent in most of the Southwest, where Holocene conditions no longer supported large herbivores.

The Archaic foraging adaptation

As the Holocene progressed and the Southwest environment changed, Paleoindian people no longer could rely on large herds of big game. For those people who did not follow these animals east on to the Plains, they had to change their diets, toolkits, and traditions to contend with the smaller animals and scattered stands of edible plants that took over the Southwestern landscape. By about 5500 BC, the region was occupied widely, though thinly, by people whose new lifeway is referred to as

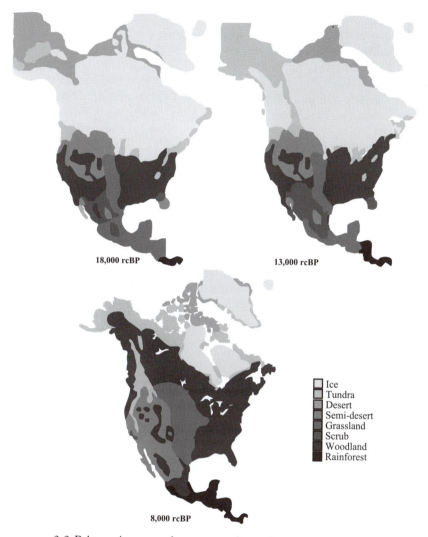

18,000 rcBP

13,000 rcBP

□ Ice
□ Tundra
□ Desert
□ Semi-desert
□ Grassland
□ Scrub
■ Woodland
■ Rainforest

8,000 rcBP

3.2 Paleoenvironmental reconstructions of the Pleistocene–Holocene transition, illustrating the rapid changes that contributed to the megafauna extinctions.

"Archaic." If stability is evidence of adaptive success, the Archaic people were the most successful people in the history of North America, for their way of life continued largely unchanged for at least 5,000 years. Indeed, in some places, the Archaic lifeway continued until European contact.

Sandwiched between the Paleoindians, with their beautiful spear points and exotic Ice Age game, and the pre-Contact Puebloans, with their aesthetically pleasing pottery and evocative ruins, the Archaic people have tended to be short-changed by archaeologists. Generally, the Archaic has been treated as if it constituted an extremely long prelude on the way to sedentary and more complex societies. Studies of Archaic cultures in the Southwest have most often focused on the origins of farming (e.g., Hogan 1994; Huckell 1995; Matson 1991) and the antecedents of the Anasazi, Mogollon, and Hohokam cultures (e.g., Irwin-Williams 1973; Sayles 1983; Sayles and Antevs 1941). Fortunately, a small but dedicated set of archaeologists have devoted considerable effort to studying the Archaic for its own sake (e.g., Huckell 1996; Irwin-Williams 1967).

Archaic people were hunters and gatherers whose specific adaptations depended on the nature of locally available resources. Botanical and faunal remains reveal a very broad diet and leave the impression that Archaic people made use of virtually every edible plant and animal in their environment, including some that we probably would not classify as "edible." Plant foods were a significant component of the diet, along with both small and large game animals. The Archaic toolkit was designed to be very flexible and adaptable, so that its users could find and process any and all edible parts of their landscape. Grinding stones for processing seeds and nuts, stone projectile points hafted to wooden shafts and thrown using a wooden spear-thrower, and a variety of chipped stone tools are common parts of the toolkit. Excavations in dry rockshelters, where normally perishable materials are often preserved, indicate that people also made a wide range of baskets, cordage, nets, and bone and hide items.

Archaic people were highly mobile, with frequent residential moves, relatively simple material culture, and generally ephemeral dwellings that left few remains in the archaeological record. As with the Paleoindians, day-to-day group size was small, and leadership positions were situational and based on skill as well as age and kinship. Periodic larger gatherings are likely, but archaeologists have yet to find any sites indicating sustained use by large social groups until after the advent of farming (Huckell 1996:351; Wills 1995:234–5). Archaic populations were very flexible, however, and groups combined and fissioned in response to opportunities and stresses in their social and physical environment. The combination of conservative material culture traditions, high mobility, and great time depth created complex patterns of interaction reflected in the Archaic archaeological record: although subtle regional trends in material culture can be identified (e.g., Geib 2000), Archaic people throughout the Southwest are characterized by a fair degree of homogeneity.

The introduction of cultivated plants to the Archaic diet

The beginning of the end for the Archaic way of life appeared in the form of a plant imported from the south as long ago as 2000 BC (Smiley 1994; Wills 1995). This domesticated version of a wild grass native to highland Mexico was a botanical oddity (Box 3.1). It was unable to grow and propagate itself with any degree of success, but if planted in fertile, well-watered ground, it yielded abundant edible seeds on a very dependable basis. Like so many events that in hindsight seem so momentous, maize probably did not seem like a big deal at the time. The ambivalence that Archaic people felt toward maize is reflected in the considerable length of time between its first introduction into the Southwest, its slow spread north by 1200 BC (e.g., Gilpin 1994), and the eventual emergence of a truly farming lifestyle several hundred years later. At first, Archaic people planted small plots of maize that they left alone while they continued their seasonal moves to collect wild foods. In the fall, they would perhaps return to see if there was anything to harvest, and they might store away the dried maize to use in case of emergency (Rocek 1995; Wills 1988, 1995).

Maize was no big thing. But the seductive part was, the more care and attention you gave it, the better it produced. Perhaps you might have a run of bad luck in hunting and gathering wild foods, and so you plant a little more maize in the spring. Worried about having another bad year, you dedicate more attention to your small garden, returning perhaps a few times during the growing season to care for it. You still prefer the taste of the wild game and gathered plants, but, in the unstable Southwestern climate, you might care more and more about the one food source you do have a little control over. Year after year, growing maize – and perhaps some squash, also borrowed from highland Mexico – takes up more of your time, with less left over to gather and hunt. By the turn of the millennium, people were constructing simple irrigation ditches in the southernmost parts of the Southwest, demonstrating their increasing investment in domesticated crops.

Toward the end of the Archaic period, people gradually expanded both into upland areas as well as down into the valleys and basins. On the Colorado Plateau, in locations ranging from the massive sandstone cliffs of Utah to the drainages below the San Juan Mountains, these people are known as "Anasazi Basketmaker" owing to their increasingly elaborate basketry and textiles. Farther to the south, in the Mogollon Highlands,

Box 3.1   Mesoamerica's domesticated plants

The first cultigens to enter the Southwest are collectively referred to as the Upper Sonoran Agricultural Complex, which consists of maize, beans, and squash. Over many generations, these plants were manipulated to exhibit traits desired by humans – more food energy and greater ease of harvesting – at the expense of their natural ability to prosper in the wild. By at least 6,000 years ago in what is now central Mexico, maize was "domesticated," with the other two plants following soon after. Soon, cultivation of these "three sisters" spread.

The timing of the appearance of these cultigens in the American Southwest is a topic still explored by researchers (Smiley 1994; Wills 1995). While maize found in the Sonoran Desert of southern Arizona dates back to at least 1500 BC, the oldest, best-dated maize in the Puebloan Southwest dates to 1400 BC, from Tornillo Rockshelter in the Chihuahuan Desert. In the Mogollon Highlands, maize remains dating to around 1300 BC were recovered from the oldest deposits of Bat Cave. The earliest cultigens found in northern parts of the Southwest include squash rinds from Chaco Canyon that date to 1000 BC. The evidence available so far suggests that maize first appeared in the Sonoran Desert and spread rapidly through the Southwest. Maize and squash were apparently introduced together in most areas, while the common bean entered later, perhaps before 300 BC.

The introduction of domesticated plants to the Southwest has been described as "a monumental nonevent with little immediate impact on native human populations" (Minnis 1985:310). The first maize cultivar to enter the Southwest was a Chapalote 12- to 14-rowed popcorn – the more rows, the smaller the kernels, and these kernels were hard, not unlike the popcorn kernels we know today. It was not very productive and did not contain the nutritious flour endosperms characteristic of later varieties. Furthermore, within a few centuries, the Chapalote maize introgressed with teosinte grass in the Sonoran Desert, resulting in an unpredictable hybrid. There is therefore no reason to assume that people eagerly became dependent upon this undependable and unproductive resource.

people known as the "Mogollon" pursued similar lifeways, relying on foraged foods but also planting some crops. Perhaps because of greater numbers of people, or perhaps because of the increased focus on farming, Basketmaker and early Mogollon populations moved around the landscape less and less. But were they truly sedentary? Did they live in villages as we think of them today, with full-time residence in permanent homes? And, most importantly, how did this impact their social interactions and political lives?

The beginnings of village life

Archaeologists identify subterranean pithouses as the first residential structures in the Southwest. Their appearance long pre-dates the introduction of maize. An Archaic-era pithouse on the Chama River in northern New Mexico, for example, may be as old as 3200 BC and was accompanied by ground stone and large pit hearths for roasting food. Several pithouses found in the lower Rio Grande drainage date as early as 2700 BC and two possible structures along the Rio San José in west-central New Mexico could date back to 2700 BC (Huckell 1996; Whalen 1994; Wills 1995). Pithouses were a successful adaptation to any environment and any season, for they provided protection from both heat and cold. Distinct clusters of a dozen or more pithouses are regarded by some archaeologists as the earliest "villages" in the Puebloan Southwest (Figure 3.3) (Dohm 1994).

But are these pithouse clusters really the earliest sedentary villages in the Southwest? To address this question, Patricia Gilman (1987) compiled data from pithouse dwellers around the world and concluded that most people residing in pithouses are seasonally mobile and subsist on a wide variety of foods. She further examined Basketmaker pithouses on Black Mesa and found that storage pits were usually located outside the structures, where they could be easily hidden when the pithouses were temporarily abandoned. Gilman therefore concluded that early pithouses were winter habitations built by groups with a relatively low dependence on farming. A similar study considered Shabik'eshchee Village in Chaco Canyon (Wills and Windes 1989), which consisted of two groups of pithouses separated by a wash. Investigation focused on the nineteen pithouses in the southern cluster. Some were superimposed on older dwellings, while others had been partially dismantled to obtain material for the new construction, indicating frequent use and abandonment of the "village." Surrounding the pithouses were over forty-five storage features. Researchers concluded that these were used for caching food supplies when the dwellings were seasonally abandoned. Basketmaker

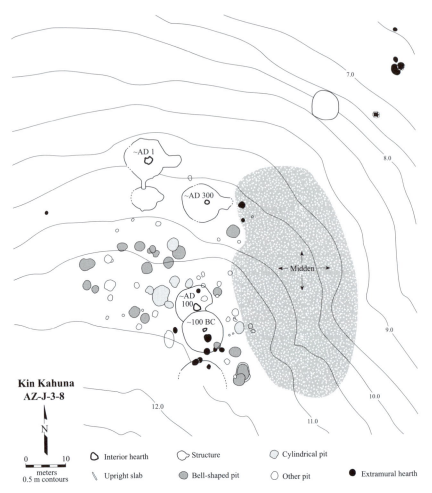

3.3 The Kin Kahuna site includes several pithouses and numerous hearths and storage pits that were used from 400 BC to AD 400; the site continues to the south, where archaeological investigation was not conducted.

and early Mogollon villages, therefore, were not the kind of "village" that we think of today. Instead, these were locations where a few families might gather during one or two seasons.

Sedentism and farming

By 1000 BC – probably earlier in the Mogollon Highlands and a few hundred years later on the Colorado Plateau – maize cultivation began significantly to impact the Archaic lifeway, creating a mixed farming/ foraging way of life that lasted into the early centuries of the new millennium. Investment in weeding, predator control, and other farming activities increased yield and dependability of maize, which then led to increased storage and increasing sedentism. Sedentism in turn limited the available range of wild plant resources, leading to increased dependence on maize horticulture. And increasing sedentism, combined with the availability of maize-based weaning foods, meant that less time was needed between births, which encouraged population increase – further increasing dependence on maize, the most productive resource. The feedback loop between sedentism, farming, and population growth led to remarkably rapid changes. Accelerating the process was the arrival of ceramic technology sometime during the last few centuries BC (Heidke 1999). Pottery made maize easier to prepare and securely store, and dried foods could be rendered edible through lengthy boiling (Crown and Wills 1995; Skibo and Blinman 1999).

The increasing sedentism at the turn of the millennium created the kind of regionalization that was *not* characteristic of earlier Archaic peoples. In southern Arizona, in the Mogollon Highlands, and on the Colorado Plateau, populations exhibited similar adaptations as they turned to farming, but they also began to develop more distinctive material culture. Pithouse forms differ from region to region, suggesting networks of exchange or perhaps even early ethnic boundaries. Changes in basketry and rock art suggest that people intentionally created designs that communicated their distinctive identities (Figure 3.4). A review of early Basketmaker rock art across the Four Corners, for example, revealed that headdresses on anthropomorphic imagery were distinctive, with different areas exhibiting their own unique decoration (Robins and Hays-Gilpin 2000). Similar studies show that the most elaborate basketry designs appear on bags and baskets, items that were readily visible during social interactions and therefore most effective at communicating social identity (e.g., Webster and Hays-Gilpin 1994). Early pottery is simple and undecorated, but beginning in the AD 500s elaborate designs paralleling those found on basketry began to be painted on pottery on the Colorado Plateau (Reed *et al.* 2000).

By the first few centuries AD, most of the larger pithouse clusters were sedentary villages, although some mobility is considered still to have been a necessary adaptation to the vagaries of Southwestern climate (Diehl and LeBlanc 2001). A sedentary lifestyle oriented around farming has a number of important consequences. People no longer could benefit from the flexibility of a foraging lifestyle, simply moving to a new location when local resources were used up. Although cultivated crops provided a consistent source of food during good times, farming always required a

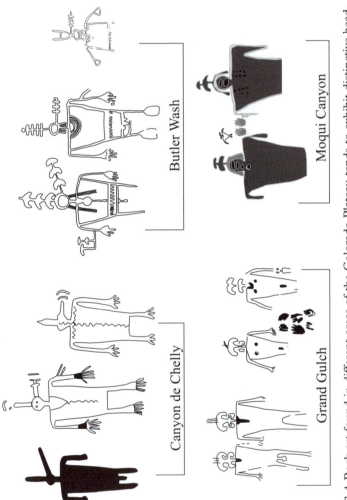

3.4 Rock art found in different areas of the Colorado Plateau tends to exhibit distinctive head-dresses.

considerable investment of labor. Most early farmers relied on rainfall – a technique known as "dry farming" – so if the rains failed to come, people had to work even harder, hand-carrying water to their crops. People in most parts of the Southwest soon learned that the key to success was to overproduce: plant as much as possible, perhaps in a number of fields, so that they would have at least some food come harvest time. Extra crops – especially maize, which could be dried – could be stored to help people get through tough times. Not surprisingly, then, pithouses became more elaborate, with antechambers and internal storage areas added. A row of large storage cists, many of which were room-sized and lined with stone, began to be built behind the pithouses to spirit away additional surpluses.

Life in a pithouse village

Most archaeologists agree that social and political organization in pit-house villages was becoming more elaborate as larger numbers of people began to live together year-round (Reed 2000). Successful farmers occasionally help one another, to share ideas, labor, and sometimes surpluses. Exceptionally large pitstructures found in some villages therefore are often interpreted as "integrative facilities," public architecture whose function included the accommodation of community-wide events. Found from the southern Mogollon into the northern Basketmaker areas, these large circular structures lack domestic features such as storage pits, but do feature benches lining the walls that allowed large numbers of people to sit at the same time, and a large firepit is usually found in the center of the floor (Nelson 1999:32; Wills 1989). Unusual artifacts are found in these structures, such as caches of old Archaic spear points and other odd stone items (Kearns et al. 2000). Ceremonial events attended by entire communities probably occurred in these public buildings. These events played an important role in affirming village ties, not just between community members but also with guests from other villages.

What kinds of ceremonies did pithouse dwellers organize? While we will never know for certain, tantalizing clues can be found in the archaeological record. During the Archaic and early pithouse times, when people were still fairly mobile and relying on wild foods, religious life was probably oriented around what anthropologists call "shamanism." Shamans, or medicine men, are individuals with purported supernatural gifts that provide them with some control over the spirit world. They are especially skilled at dealing with illnesses, especially those caused by witches or harm-causing spirits. Shamans in action appear to be represented in some Basketmaker-era rock art panels (Figure 3.5), and bird iconography

3.5 This Basketmaker pictograph from Canyon de Chelly has been interpreted as a shaman healing a woman, although alternative explanations include a puberty event.

may symbolize magical shamanic flight or bird spirit helpers (Robins and Hays-Gilpin 2000).

The emergence of a more settled way of life oriented around farming shifted attention away from shamanic ritual. Medicine men and individual healing never disappeared; they are still a part of indigenous Southwestern life even today. But people increasingly became concerned with favorable climatic conditions and communal well-being, both of which were needed to be successful sedentary farmers. Rock art, basketry, and pottery from this era often illustrate rows of people holding hands or engaged in ritual together, and animals associated with water, such as ducks and cranes, are more common than in earlier periods (Robins and Hays-Gilpin 2000). At this time, a rigid ceremonial calendar tied to the cycle of planting and harvesting may have emerged. With these changes, shamans were probably supplemented by priests, individuals with no supernatural power of their own, but rather authorities who kept track of the ceremonial calendar, who memorized the proper rituals, who supervised village-level decision-making, and who played important roles in guiding relationships beyond the village (Reyman 1987).

In a study of Puebloan pithouse villages, Kent Lightfoot and Gary Feinman (1982; Feinman *et al.* 2000) argue for the presence of authority-based community leaders by AD 600. They point to the larger size of some individual pithouses, as well as their greater storage capacity and inordinate quantities of non-local goods – at Shabik'eshchee (Figure 3.6), for example, the largest pithouse, located in front of the village's ceremonial pitstructure, contained a number of unusual artifacts, including turquoise (Roberts 1929:142, 153). According to this view, leaders occupying modestly larger pithouses were not able to command others to do their bidding, but rather did their best to persuade others to help them, relying on a combination of outright charisma, well-targeted gift-giving, the cooperation of their family and friends, and perhaps their roles as village priests. Known in anthropology as "Big Men," this kind of leadership was always a tenuous affair. Incipient leaders could, however, strengthen their authority by tying themselves to the ceremonial pitstructures, perhaps by mustering their supporters to build the structures or to sponsor ceremonial feasts, ostensibly to benefit the village as a whole but undoubtedly enhancing the sponsor's own status and prestige (Figure 3.6). Thus it is not surprising that in at least some of these early villages, the biggest pithouse homes were found near large public structures (e.g., Damp and Kotyk 2000:111; Feinman *et al.* 2000:462).

The weakness of authority-based leaders may be revealed by the post fences built around some of their purported residences (Damp and Kotyk 2000), perhaps a measure to protect the few goods that they were able to spirit away for themselves or that they were accumulating for a particularly ostentatious ceremony. On the other hand, some archaeologists refer to these as "palisades" that served as a defense against village raiding rather than a deterrent against pilfering by neighbors (e.g., Chenault and Motsinger 2000). An assessment of violence in the pre-Contact Southwest by Steven LeBlanc (1999) in fact concludes that many early Puebloan villages were placed in defensive settings and built to repel simple raids by other groups intent on stealing food, capturing women and children, or exacting revenge for some actual or perceived wrong. Before the modern era, such low-level endemic warfare was an occasional occurrence in small-scale societies all over the world, and it is often associated with the beginnings of village life and farming. It should therefore not be surprising to see evidence for it in the Puebloan Southwest. While this kind of conflict was infrequent, we can imagine that it affirmed the authority of aspiring leaders who played a role in organizing village-level responses to external threats. Perhaps a palisade around the home of a

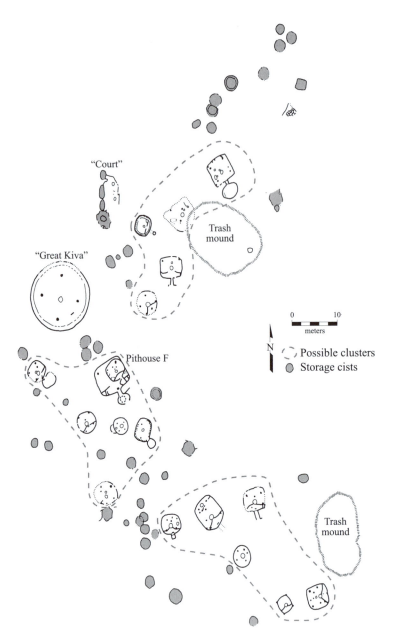

"Court"

"Great Kiva"

Trash mound

Pithouse F

0   10
meters

N

Possible clusters
Storage cists

Trash mound

3.6 In Shabik'eshchee Village, Pithouse F not only is the largest habitation, and not only is located close to the communal pit structure, but it also contained an inordinate quantity of rare artifacts, including turquoise. Different pithouse clusters likely represent episodic use by distinct semi-sedentary groups. About half of the village, located less than 50 m across a drainage to the north, is not mapped here.

priestly leader – and the privacy and status the fence provided – was seen as legitimate owing to the special ceremonial items that were stored there.

Villages and pueblos: the foundations of Puebloan culture

During the AD 600s, a highly productive variety of maize began to be grown that had a profound impact on pithouse village evolution in the Puebloan Southwest. This new variety, called Maiz de Ocho, featured larger kernels, fewer kernel rows, and earlier flowering. In marked contrast to the Chapalote popcorn that people first adopted from highland Mexico, Maiz de Ocho had more food energy owing to its floury endosperm, and it was easier to grind. For a long time, archaeologists believed that Maiz de Ocho developed in Mesoamerica and diffused into the Southwest, but rockshelter deposits in the southern Mogollon region show a gradual indigenous evolution from the earlier Chapalote to the Maiz de Ocho (Upham *et al.* 1987). This suggests that Southwest farmers consciously selected plants that produced larger kernels and flowered earlier. It is not too hard to figure out why they would do this – larger kernels are much easier to grind, especially for people who are relying more and more on dried and stored surpluses. Experimental data indicate that the selection of larger kernels also led to a decrease in kernel row number and earlier flowering. And in turn, earlier flowering allowed people living at higher, moister altitudes with shorter growing seasons to grow maize successfully. Clearly, Southwestern groups were becoming quite adept at manipulating cultivated plants to serve their needs, and other locally adapted varieties soon followed Maiz de Ocho.

Pueblo architecture emerges

The appearance of highly productive, drought-resistant, and early flowering maize varieties corresponds with rapid changes on the Colorado Plateau, where populations had tended to mirror trends set by the Mogollon groups to the south. With the development of new cultigens better suited to their environment, Basketmaker people began to set their own trends, and they started by constructing above-ground architecture – Mogollon people would not make this move for a few hundred more years. Initially fabricated of upright stone slabs and *jacal*, a wattle-and-daub construction technique, surface rooms were later built with dry-laid and unshaped masonry (Figure 3.7). This surface architecture replaced the row of stone-lined cists associated with earlier pithouses, suggesting that the shift to "pueblo" architecture was related to an increasing need for storage. In Patricia Gilman's study of world-wide architecture

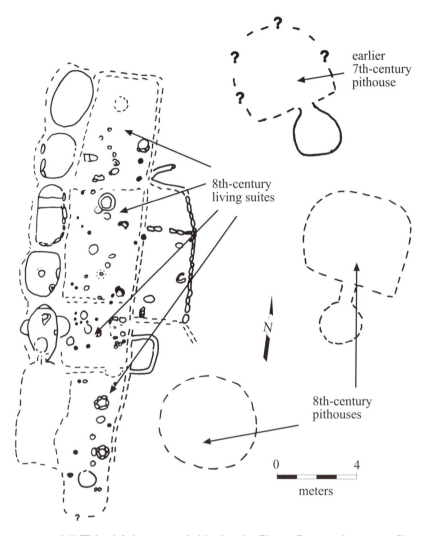

3.7 This eighth-century habitation in Chaco Canyon, known as Site 627, included two pithouses backed by an above-ground structure that featured a row of living rooms backed by a second row of storage rooms. Construction was primarily of *jacal*, or wattle-and-daub, in which walls are made of posts intertwined with brush and plastered with mud.

(Gilman 1987), she found that the shift from pithouse to above-ground structures in most societies was highly correlated with agricultural intensification and the production of surpluses requiring storage. In contrast to subsurface storage pits, foods stored in jacal or masonry rooms are less susceptible to moisture and vermin and can therefore be stored for longer. Above-ground storage facilities are also clear evidence of sedentism, for these rooms were vulnerable to pilfering if left unguarded for any length of time.

The increased need for storage was not just due to the appearance of productive varieties of maize. Beginning in the AD 700s, the Southwest experienced worsening climatic conditions (Grissino-Mayer *et al.* 1997; Gumerman 1988). Rain came less frequently, and springs began to dry up as water tables fell. When rains did come, they were often violent storms that eroded waterways and farmlands. And the precipitation was more unpredictable, both from season to season and from year to year. In the face of these problems, the best solution for farmers was to produce and store as much food as possible, ideally so that they could get through a year or two of poor crop yields. Large, dry surface rooms therefore were needed to store large quantities of surpluses safely.

We might expect that village dwellers would have moved into pueblo rooms alongside their storage facilities, but this did not happen right away. In fact, except during inclement weather, interior spaces were infrequently used throughout Southwest history. Imagine what these spaces were like. As you entered a pithouse or pueblo room, you would notice the lack of windows and the small, protected doorways. Once inside, the spaces were dark and stuffy, and lighting a torch or building a fire caused them to become smoky. Daily activities, therefore, from grinding maize to making stone tools to weaving clothing, most often occurred in the village's open plaza areas. During hot weather, people might take refuge under *ramadas*, open-walled structures with simple roofs built to provide shade. Cool winter weather or monsoonal summer rains might drive people into their pithouses, but even then you might prefer to bundle up and brave the weather rather than inhale the smoky air of the confined interior spaces.

During the AD 700s and 800s, people on the Colorado Plateau built their pithouses deeper into the ground and began to include fewer domestic features and more features used in ritual activity. Many pithouses were now more circular, and a ventilator shaft replaced the antechamber. Occasionally, a small hole was dug into the floor, which in modern Hopi society is known as a *sipapu*, a symbolic entrance to the spiritual world. Despite these arguably ceremonial features, however, many scholars believe that pithouses were probably still used for domestic activities (e.g., Lekson 1988). These small pitstructures with ceremonial features are therefore referred to as *protokivas* owing to their ambiguous nature, halfway between fully domestic pithouses and the subterranean ceremonial *kiva* still used by Pueblo people today. Surface rooms were typically built as a single-story arc behind the protokiva, forming what is often known as the "Prudden unit pueblo," named after T. M. Prudden, one of the fathers of Southwestern archaeology. The row of storage rooms was soon fronted by a second row of domestic quarters. Puebloan communities consisted of clusters of these roomblocks, often accompanied by one or more oversized pitstructures that continued as the locus of ceremonial and communal activities. The size and growth of these villages is unfortunately difficult for archaeologists to track; several studies have shown that the average Puebloan habitation was occupied for only thirty to fifty years (Varien 1999; Wilshusen and Ortman 1999), at which point people simply built a new home nearby, often using materials salvaged from their abandoned dwellings.

Pueblo households

What was life like in these early pueblo communities? When archaeologists consider earlier pithouse villages, the small size of the structures suggests that households were small, perhaps consisting of a classic nuclear family of mom, dad, and the kids (e.g., Diehl and LeBlanc 2001:117). As people became more sedentary, however, villages began to show distinct spatial organization indicating that related households were building their pithouses close to one another. At the Mogollon village of Old Town, for example, archaeologist Darrell Creel identified small groups of pithouses facing one another across a small open plaza (Nelson 1999:32; see also Diehl 1998:631). The development of pueblo architecture marks the clearest evidence for extended family households, which could include a few nuclear families from multiple generations – grandparents, their children and *their* spouses, and all of the grandchildren. At Duckfoot (Figure 3.8), an early pueblo site on the Colorado Plateau, archaeologists excavated four pithouses backed by two rows of rooms divided into three distinct sections, each probably used by an extended family (Lightfoot and Etzkorn 1993; Varien and Lightfoot 1989).

The growth in household size as people settled into a sedentary farming lifestyle provides insight into other aspects of their social organization. Scholars generally believe that the earlier mobile hunter-gatherers in the Southwest – as elsewhere in the world – were loosely oriented around patrilineal or ambilineal kin relationships in which one's kinship was determined either through the father's line or through both parents

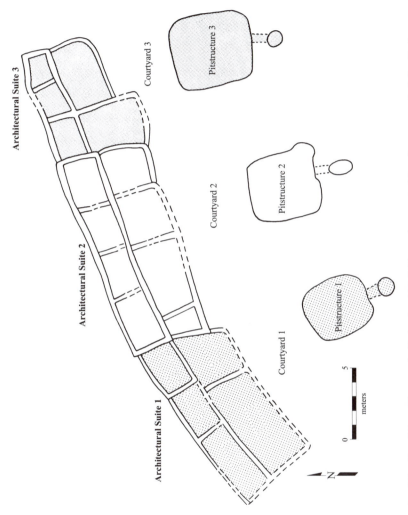

3.8 The Duckfoot Site was built in the AD 850s and occupied by three extended-family households, each with its own pithouse and section of pueblo rooms. A fourth pithouse was added in the AD 870s, before the entire habitation was abandoned around AD 880.

(Hunter-Anderson 1986). This kind of flexible organization is the hallmark of foraging societies, for it allows them to respond to unpredictable environmental conditions, quickly calling upon their many kin relationships with other groups. If a gender is favored at all, male kinship is typically privileged, and when a man is married, he might bring his new spouse to live with his relatives. This is thought to be a sensible strategy for people whose lifeway is oriented around lengthy hunting trips undertaken mostly by men – this despite the fact that the bulk of calories are provided by gathered plants and smaller animals, a task attributed to women. A typical foraging band therefore consists of a core group of related men and their spouses, as well as a number of other people who come from other groups, drawing on the web of kin relationships that ties many bands together.

Archaeologists believe that, when Puebloan people began to settle down into villages to farm their fields, the focus of organization shifted away from a loosely determined kinship structure to one that was more strictly organized. Some scholars argue that this happened as arable land became more important – there is not a lot of it in the Southwest, largely owing to the lack of permanent water, and so gaining and retaining access to it became imperative. Timothy Kohler (1992a), for example, suggests that small fieldhouses began to be built on farmlands to demonstrate ownership of valuable plots. And once your family had control over good land, the best way to retain it was to ensure that it passed along a single, well-defined family line, excluding as many claimants to the land as possible (Hunter-Anderson 1986:43).

Associated with greater control over land was an apparent shift from a male emphasis to a kin structure centered on women, one in which rights to land and other resources were passed along the female line. Why this would happen is not exactly clear. It may be that plant resources and knowledge of the lands that produced them had long been the venue of women, and as cultivated plants became increasingly central to the diet, kinship shifted from patrifocal to matrifocal. Another argument is that men were the more unsettled gender; they continued to emphasize hunting to obtain meat (Box 3.2), they undertook long-distance trading journeys, they engaged in occasional raids, and accordingly, they died more often (Peregrine 2001:38). Men also were apparently more involved in the elaborate ritual life of the community (e.g., Mobley-Tanaka 1997; Robins and Hays-Gilpin 2000). The crops required continual maintenance, and although men no doubt assisted in farming, women probably had the burden of responsibility to maintain the fields. And women were responsible for managing the surpluses, especially for determining when and with whom to share extra food. Whatever the exact reasons, the

Box 3.2   Domesticated animals in the Southwest

None of the indigenous fauna of the Southwest ever was domesticated. Perhaps animals such as deer, antelope, and rabbits were not amenable to the confinement and selective breeding that led to animal domestication in other parts of the world. The only domesticated animals that appear in the Southwest archaeological record are dogs and turkeys, both of which were probably introduced to the region.

Although debated, the evidence suggests that no wild turkeys existed in the Southwest prior to the first millennium AD. Charmion McKusick (1986:3) argues that the first turkeys to enter were a small breed that was domesticated along coastal eastern Mexico. It was highly dependent on humans and not capable of surviving on its own. By AD 500, a larger turkey – also already domesticated – appeared in the Southwest, perhaps from the east. Some became feral, establishing the wild population of Merriam's Wild Turkey seen in the region today. As Puebloan people became more sedentary, both the small and large domestic breeds were kept in pens, and the wild turkeys were hunted. Anecdotal evidence suggests that turkeys – particularly the smaller breed – were raised for their feathers to make robes, and McKusick (2001) also argues that they were sacrificed and ceremonially buried in times of crisis. Later, after the tenth century, both the larger domestic breed and wild turkeys were used more frequently for food and making bone tools. Turkeys also were useful for managing insects that could damage crops, such as grasshoppers (McKusick 1986:9).

Dog remains are ubiquitous in archaeological sites across the Puebloan world. A number of breeds have been identified, including the Small Indian Dog and the longer-limbed Plains Indian Dog. Evidence of formal dog burial is seen at least back into the Archaic period, and burials dating to 8,500 years ago are found in other parts of the Americas. This preferential mortuary treatment suggests that dogs held a unique value to early Puebloan people, and no doubt they were used in a broad range of tasks, from hunting to guarding crops. Interestingly, however, formal dog burials decrease after AD 1200, and Richard Lang and Arthur Harris (1984:90) argue that the decline of hunting at that time diminished the value of dogs. At about this same time, dog remains appear in contexts and exhibit damage indicating that they were occasionally eaten (Olsen 1990:166). When Europeans first arrived, they described in detail the great flocks of turkeys kept by Pueblo people, but only passing mention is made of the small dogs that reportedly were kept in "underground huts."

appearance of household clustering, first in pithouse villages and then later in pueblo architecture, is seen by many archaeologists as a shift from a somewhat loosely organized patrifocal society to a matrifocal society in which kin ties were becoming much more important and carefully monitored.

Although research on the internal organization of these communities is still in its infancy, a picture of early pueblo life is emerging. We can imagine a village with a couple of dozen pithouses, many clustered together as seen at Duckfoot and backed by one or two rows of pueblo rooms. Each cluster is a small neighborhood occupied by a matrilineal kin group oriented around a core of related women; their husbands came from elsewhere, perhaps even from outside the village. Different kin groups in the community probably share a number of bonds: the family lines of the women might cross, or at the very least some of the men from one kin group might all be married into another lineage.

And the pueblo village might include recent immigrants. The mobility of earlier times never went away. Even full-time farmers might find it necessary to pack up and abandon their homes, moving to new areas where they have distant relatives or where they might be welcomed as strangers. Many archaeologists note the variability of material culture in both late pithouse and early pueblo communities, with some suggesting that this reflects the immigration of families from different ethnic traditions (see summary in Vivian 2000). The distribution of ceramic designs in some areas shows abrupt spatial boundaries suggestive of strong ethnic symboling. In the Mesa Verde area, for example, Richard Wilshusen and Scott Ortman (1999) identified two different ethnic groups that maintained clear boundaries on either side of the Dolores River, with those on the west side exhibiting greater social and political inequities – as well as evidence of violent death. Farther south, in contrast, interethnic mixing appears even within single villages, suggesting a high degree of mobility for farmers in some regions (e.g., Reed and Wilcox 2000). This is a topic that still needs much archaeological research, but the general picture is that ethnic boundaries became more intensively symboled as the pueblo era began.

Early pueblo politics

Archaeologists debate how decision-making and leadership were organized in early pueblo villages, but few studies have directly addressed the issue. We might expect that the trends identified for earlier pithouse villages continued into the pueblo era. Leaders were probably those authority figures – especially those religious authorities – who established their fragile hold over decision-making through acts that enhanced their status and prestige, from making effective decisions to judiciously giving gifts to others who could help them achieve and maintain their positions. Decision-making was probably tied to the ceremonial structure of society, with authority figures perhaps gaining legitimacy through their roles in ritual, which provided a public venue for gaining individual and group prestige and influencing social and political relationships (e.g., Schachner 2001).

Two changes discussed above no doubt impacted the structure of leadership. First, the increasing focus on overproduction and the generation of surpluses provided aspiring leaders with the material means to expand their authority (Kantner 1999a; Sebastian 1992). Surpluses could be "loaned" to other community members, who then would become indebted. The surpluses also could be used to organize trading expeditions to other areas, where new alliances could be established and valuable items exchanged. Rare red-slipped pottery made by a few specialized producers in the Mesa Verde area (Hegmon *et al.* 1997), turquoise from discrete sources such as the Cerrillos area on the Rio Grande (Mathien 2001), and shell from the Gulfs of California and Mexico (Mathien 1997) were some of the items traded long distances that played roles in gift-giving and symboling prestige. And surpluses – as well as social debts – also could be invested in the construction of facilities, such as ceremonial structures, that would further enhance one's prestige, thereby positioning them to both influence and benefit from important community decisions.

Eric Blinman's analysis (1989) of McPhee Village in the Mesa Verde area illustrates this elaboration of status differences. This community consisted of twenty-one contemporaneous pueblo dwellings of varying sizes, as well as accompanying pitstructures, the largest of which contained features indicating use for communal rituals. Archaeologists recovered unusually high numbers of serving vessels and food remains – especially jackrabbit bones – suggesting that feasting activities occurred near the communal pitstructures (Potter 1997). But what was perhaps even more interesting was that the communal architecture was located near the larger households – so large, in fact, that they formed distinctive U-shapes as the rooms wrapped around the plaza areas containing the pitstructures. Not only did these households apparently control community ritual, they also exhibited the greatest quantities of imported trade goods, such as red-slipped pottery. Archaeologists further noted that access to some of the communal pitstructures was controlled by walls that closed off plazas (Hegmon *et al.* 2000:68–69), and the structures themselves were too small to accommodate many people (Schachner 2001). For most members of McPhee Village, then, access to important ritual areas did not come easily, even though evidence of community-wide preparation indicates that the feasts themselves were "potluck" affairs (Potter 2000).

The shift to more tightly integrated matrilineal kin groups is the second change that impacted leadership in early pueblo villages. While we might expect that women became more empowered by this transition, the evidence suggests little gender difference in status prior to or immediately after the emergence of pueblo architecture (see contributions in Crown 2000b). The closer control over farmlands that this kinship form provided, however, necessarily introduced new inequities into pueblo village life, for those kin groups established in prime farming spots enjoyed advantages over others. Their better lands produced more food, they probably had ready access to good water sources, and they could more easily ride out a bad drought or other crisis. More recent immigrants, on the other hand, would be relegated to less productive lands, and they might therefore find themselves in debt more often, owing food, labor, and favors to the more established lineages in the village. In fact, the promise of such inequities may have encouraged the older kin groups – or at least the leaders who guided them – to accept immigrants desperate enough to take on lower-status roles.

These early pueblo villages were dynamic places. Occupied by a few dozen to a few hundred people, they were not simple farming hamlets. On one hand, village life was inextricably oriented to cultivating maize, squash, and other crops such as beans and, later, cotton. Ceremonies were organized to encourage rainfall, kin groups stayed together to preserve land, and people banded together in times of scarcity. On the other hand, the social and political life of the village was complex. People came and went from the village, drawing on extensive family relations spread over the landscape, often to escape from inequitable sociopolitical situations. Matrilineal kin groups broke apart, often over real or perceived injustices, while others banded together to promote the success of their charismatic priest. Periodic ritual events were especially exciting, with visitors coming from distant villages to trade exotic goods, arrange marriages, establish alliances, and engage in political intrigue. Life in these pueblo villages was not so unlike our lives today.

The end of the millennium: a new beginning

Driving north from Albuquerque along US Highway 550, the traveler first skirts the western edge of the Jemez Mountains, formed by explosive volcanic action ending about one million years ago. Near the small town of Cuba, the road veers to the northwest, leaving the mountains

3.9 The immense San Juan Basin, one of the least hospitable environments in the American Southwest, is surrounded on all four sides by higher elevations. In this photograph, Lobo Mesa is visible on the southern horizon, 50 km from Pueblo del Arroyo in Chaco Canyon.

behind as it crosses the San Juan Basin, one of the more desolate basins in the Southwest. This vast, high-altitude, semi-arid region is surrounded on all four sides by mountains (Figure 3.9): the Jemez Mountains to the east, the San Juan Mountains to the north, the Chuska Mountains to the west, and, to the south, the Dutton Plateau and the San Mateo and Zuni Mountains.

Turning west just outside of the tiny town of Nageezi, the traveler embarks on a bumpy journey across nearly 30 km of dusty road that can be impassable after a summer storm. On a clear day – and most are – you can see the mountains in all four directions as you race across the scrubby landscape, occasionally passing antelope and braking for the rabbits that dart across the road. Until 1996, the dirt road took you right to the steep edge of a shallow, broad drainage known as Chaco Canyon. These days, the road has been rerouted so that you hardly know you have entered the canyon. If it is spring or early summer, you might notice a narrow, muddy trickle of water as you drive along the deep wash in the center of the canyon, the first water of any type you have seen since crossing the Rio Grande near Albuquerque.

3.10 Pueblo Bonito, containing 500 rooms and standing at least four stories tall, provides a stunning contrast with the isolation and aridity of Chaco Canyon.

And then you see the buildings. Against the north side of Chaco Canyon, arrayed along the steep sandstone cliffs, massive Puebloan structures with hundreds of rooms still stand up to four stories tall – archaeologists call them "great houses." Made of intricately shaped and placed masonry and roofed using beams from the mountains off on the horizon, the architecture is simply awesome (Figure 3.10). No one can visit Chaco Canyon and not wonder, "Why here?" And what you see still standing today is only a sample of what existed in the canyon 1,000 years ago, when hundreds of smaller pueblo homes and pithouses were clustered on the valley floor alongside the great houses, when roadways crisscrossed the landscape, and when intricate field systems captured the scanty amounts of available rainwater.

The first monumental architecture

What you see in Chaco Canyon today is the culmination of centuries of human activity – it did not just all spring up overnight. To understand how it all happened, we have to go back to a time when the Puebloan Southwest was covered with small pithouse villages. Our story begins just before AD 700, when dozens of pithouse sites such as Shabik'eshchee were arrayed along the floor of Chaco Canyon, occupied perhaps for a season, perhaps for longer, depending on the amount of rainfall and its impact on both wild and domesticated food resources. Farmers living in Shabik'eshchee were able to take advantage of the creek flowing nearby, but they also had to worry about the short growing season, for Chaco Canyon is at an elevation of about 2,000 m and can get quite cold.

People in Chaco Canyon, like everywhere else in the Southwest, had to contend with drought conditions that started in the AD 700s. Many parts of the canyon were abandoned, but people eventually did come back to farm as intensively as possible, storing their surpluses in jacal and masonry rooms. By AD 800, large clusters of pithouses and pueblo rooms sprang up in key locations on the canyon floor where side drainages channel runoff into the Chaco Wash (Windes 2001). Not a lot is known about these pueblo villages, for later developments largely obliterated them, leaving behind only a few structures and ceramics to indicate that they ever existed (Vivian 1990:153–8). One example was revealed during archaeological work around Fajada Gap, one of those areas in the canyon where multiple drainages converge. Archaeologists identified a loosely clustered community containing over fifty habitations and at least one large ceremonial pitstructure. The village was spatially divided into five smaller "neighborhoods," some of which contained one or two dwellings larger than the others (Windes 1993:337–82).

Sometime in the middle of the AD 800s, people in at least three Chaco Canyon villages constructed a new kind of building. Where this happened first is unclear, although the best evidence from tree-ring dating suggests that the people living around what is now Pueblo Bonito started the trend by the AD 860s. Here, a structure with fewer than a dozen rooms was built using a masonry style known as core-veneer, in which a rubble core is faced with a veneer of shaped stones (Windes and Ford 1996). The early core-veneer style was fairly crude, especially compared to later forms, but the walls were thick, the rooms spacious, and the structure large compared to regular houses such as Site 724. Fronting the shallow arc of southeast-facing surface rooms at Pueblo Bonito were two large pitstructures, but little is known about them. The assumption is that they served ritual rather than domestic functions since a third pitstructure built a few decades later was devoid of any features, not unlike the ceremonial pitstructures found in other pueblo villages.

Pueblo Bonito was not the only such structure built in ninth-century Chaco Canyon (Lekson 1984). Approximately 5 km upstream, near another cluster of pueblo homes, residents built Una Vida, another early great house (Figure 3.11). And 5 km in the opposite direction, downstream from Pueblo Bonito, the first rooms of Peñasco Blanco were

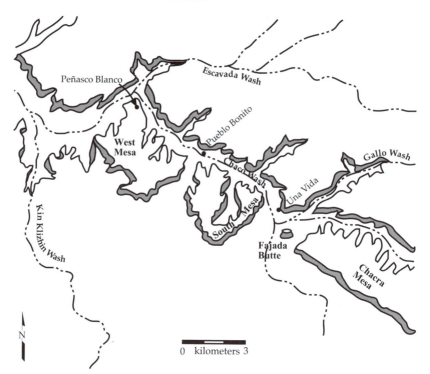

3.11 The first great houses built in Chaco Canyon were established at locations where side canyons drain into the main wash.

constructed (Box 3.3). Una Vida appears to have started as six rooms and a pitstructure built in the early AD 860s, while construction of possibly thirty-three rooms in two rows occurred at Peñasco Blanco perhaps a few years later. Over the next several decades, all three structures were gradually expanded with new rows of rooms, new wings, and additional stories. By the early AD 900s, each great house included a few dozen rooms, dwarfing the typical habitations found in Chaco Canyon (Figure 3.12). At least one new great house was also built in the early AD 900s, the East Community great house, located well upstream from Pueblo Bonito (Windes 1993:459–63; Windes *et al.* 2000). This new structure was a harbinger of things to come in the tenth and eleventh centuries in the northern Southwest.

We will probably never know exactly what happened in the first rooms built at Pueblo Bonito, nor will we know exactly why it was constructed. Over 200 years of additions and modifications to Pueblo Bonito make it difficult to reconstruct its earliest uses. Further complicating our

Box 3.3   Lake-front property in Chaco Canyon?

In 2002, Eric Force and several colleagues published the results of an intensive study of the Chaco Wash that combined information on the sedimentary geology of the canyon with its archaeology. They determined that a large wind-blown dune at the mouth of Chaco Canyon – just below the Peñasco Blanco great house – impacted the flow of Chaco Wash. During periods when water flow was low, this dune formed a dam, backing water up the canyon and creating a shallow lake; in contrast, during wetter periods when more water flowed through the canyon, the dune was breached and soils deposited by the lake were eroded.

Force and his colleagues (2002) estimate that the lake was present for several centuries prior to the AD 900s, with its increasingly saline waters backing up the valley for at least one kilometer. The first three great houses in Chaco Canyon were built during this period, which probably explains why Peñasco Blanco was constructed on the rim above the canyon rather than on its floor – the lake covered the canyon below it. Not long before AD 900, the dune was breached owing to a combination of increasing rainfall and lake sedimentation. For residents of Chaco Canyon, this event was a problem, not because the salty lake waters were useful, but because the lake inhibited soil erosion. With the dam breached, the stream channel cut into the canyon floor, lowering the water table, eroding side canyons, and making it difficult to control water and soil for farming. Interestingly, this era saw very little great house construction.

After AD 1025, Chaco Canyon again experienced soil deposition and channels filled up again. The dune dam may have re-formed, but it also seems likely that Chaco's residents took matters into their own hands – a massive masonry dam apparently was built at this time. This corresponds with the establishment of a number of water-control features used for farming, and great house construction again increased. It was at this point in the Puebloan history of Chaco Canyon that it enjoyed its greatest influence. This new sedimentary history suggests that the development of surpluses and the resulting inequities in Chaco Canyon were not possible without the favorable farming conditions provided by the "Chaco Lake."

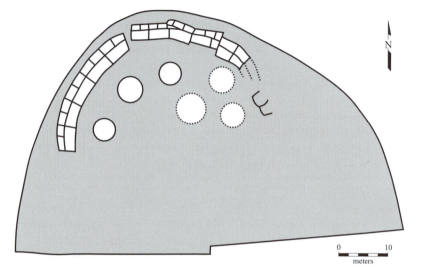

3.12 Unlike the massive structure seen today, Pueblo Bonito only had a few dozen rooms by the early AD 900s. Part of the northern wing was constructed first, probably in the middle AD 800s, and the western wing was added not long after. The dates of kiva construction are less certain.

understanding of the great house is its lengthy history of investigation, including excavations that date to the dawn of American archaeology. Scholars still debate whether great houses were residential, used for storage, the focus of village ceremonial activity, or all of the above. Did the entire community pitch in to build them, or was their construction funded by ambitious leaders eager to promote their own interests? These topics will be taken up in the next chapter, when we consider the height of developments in Chaco Canyon. Two clues, however, serve as a teaser for that discussion. First, the appearance of great houses corresponds with a gradual improvement in climatic conditions. Second, by this time, people were intensely dependent on farmed foods. An analysis by Paul Minnis (1989) of preserved human fecal matter – known as "coprolites" – from tenth-century sites in the San Juan Basin found that an average of 85 percent of each sample was composed of maize. Very few wild foods were identified.

The first apartment buildings

Over 350 km south of Chaco Canyon, the Mimbres River drainage provides a stunning contrast to the San Juan Basin (Figure 3.13). Draining

3.13 The upper reaches of the Mimbres River Valley are relatively well watered, but as the drainage descends toward the south and the flood-plain widens, the cottonwood trees and other riparian plants are replaced by flora better adapted to dry conditions.

from the continental divide that bisects the rugged Mogollon Mountains, the Mimbres River and its branches meander southeast through green pine forests, passing rich alluvial plains but quickly descending into the arid Chihuahuan Desert. To the west, the Gila and San Francisco Rivers drop off the other side of the divide, draining their waters into what is now Arizona. As described in chapter 2, this is a land of contrasts, with wet and cool mountains only a short distance from hot and dry deserts. Farming was difficult in this setting, but compared to Chaco Canyon the perennial streams and ecological diversity created a rich environment with a variety of resources.

Mogollon people living in the Mimbres area were among the first in the Southwest to build pithouses, moving seasonally to take advantage of the easy access to different ecological zones (Diehl and LeBlanc 2001). They were also among the first to experiment with farming, adding maize and squash to their diet, perhaps as an emergency supply to back up more desirable wild resources (Minnis 1985; Wills 1988). Eventually, the Mogollon dedicated their subsistence efforts to farming, perhaps by AD 200 (Akins *et al.* 1999; Buzon and Grauer 2002; Wills 1995), although some scholars argue that the transition was not complete until much later (e.g., Gilman 1995). A study of groundstone tools, for example, found that the size and shape of Mogollon *manos* and *metates* – used to grind hard seeds – changed after the AD 600s, becoming bigger and better designed to accommodate the larger kernels of Maiz de Ocho maize (Diehl 1996). Around the same time, people stopped building their pithouses on hills and ridges and moved down on to river terraces, near prime farmlands. During this transition, about a dozen large villages popped up along the Mimbres Valley, each oriented around large ceremonial pitstructures that were occasionally burned and rebuilt (Creel and Anyon 2003).

Demographic studies of the Mimbres area suggest a greater than four-fold increase in population from the AD 700s through 900s, with the pace of growth especially rapid in the tenth and eleventh centuries (Blake *et al.* 1986; Nelson 1999:37). This translates to a growth rate of 0.3 percent per year, which is high for a pre-modern society. Even conservative revisions of this rate suggest abnormally high population growth (Cordell *et al.* 1994:126–7; Nelson *et al.* 1994:119). Archaeologists debate the causes of such a rapid increase, and probably a number of factors were involved. The adoption of farming and sedentism is always a stimulus for growth, but another cause may have been immigration inspired by worsening climatic conditions in the AD 700s. As people fled lower-elevation areas in search of food and water, the upland river valleys were especially attractive – and remember that the Mogollon Highlands were a virtual oasis compared to the surrounding Chihuahuan Desert. Researchers have identified considerable variability in ceramic designs and mortuary practices during this era (e.g., Powell 1996), perhaps reflecting a concern with group identity as populations grew and as new immigrants introduced their own cultural practices. New residents also may explain the expansion of habitation into the less desirable secondary drainages during this era as well as the influx of some trade goods from distant sources, especially shell ornaments and perhaps pottery coming from Hohokam people to the west (Bradley 2000; Nelson 1999:33).

Surprisingly, above-ground architecture was a late phenomenon in the Mimbres region. Even during the period of rapid population growth, and even after groups on the Colorado Plateau began to build pueblo architecture, Mogollon people continued to live in pithouses, using underground cists to store surpluses. Why they resisted a move to surface rooms is something of a mystery. Perhaps they continued to rely on a flexible strategy that included considerable mobility, although their dedication to cultivated foods would suggest otherwise. Another possibility is that they were not as geared to overproduction and the storage of vast surpluses as were people to the north. This seems a more likely explanation, as the rivers draining the Mogollon Highlands were more dependable than the ephemeral washes and springs that supplied water to dry-farmers living

3.14 Mimbres architecture is not visually exciting, both because the walls of rounded cobbles collapsed long ago and because the sites have been heavily pothunted. This aerial photograph of Old Town reveals the hundreds of pothunter holes that have all but destroyed the site.

on the Colorado Plateau. The Mogollon placed their fields in floodplains where water tables were high and the rivers close enough to feed small irrigation canals, perhaps making it unnecessary to accumulate vast stores of surpluses to last through multiyear droughts. The diversity of arrowhead forms and animal remains also suggests that a wide range of game and other wild resources was available to Mogollon villagers (Nelson 1996).

The resistance to surface architecture faded during the AD 900s, corresponding with a peak in cultural diversity – perhaps representing a surge in immigration and population aggregation. Similar to what happened in the AD 700s on the Colorado Plateau, the Mogollon first built pueblo rooms to store small food surpluses, but soon residential rooms were also constructed. Overhunting and excessive foraging in areas surrounding the villages may have also inspired greater investment in farming and the production of surpluses (Cannon 2000; Spielmann and Angstadt-Leto 1996). The new architecture was constructed of river cobbles held together with copious amounts of mud (Figure 3.14), making the walls less stable – and perhaps less aesthetically pleasing – compared with the nicely shaped sandstone masonry used in most areas of the Colorado Plateau. Also, unlike the clusters of "Prudden units" seen to the north, buildings in the Mimbres region continually grew; as kin groups expanded through birth and marriage, they simply kept adding on more rooms rather than constructing separate residences. By AD 1000, these structures were getting quite large, rivaling the scale of the ceremonial great houses in the San Juan Basin. And people living in the Mimbres area started making the beautiful pottery that would make them famous.

4 The wrong Middle Places? Chaco Canyon and the Mimbres Mogollon

The Hopi speak of *Palatkwapi*, while the Zuni relate the tale of *Hán'hlipink'ya* and the Acoma talk of "White House." Each describes a place in their ancestors' journeys where people strayed from the proper way of living. At *Palatkwapi*, things were good – the rains fell, the river was always full, and there was plenty of game to hunt. The older people knew that the Hopi had to continue their journey to the "Middle Place," where they would meet up with other wandering clans. But *Palatkwapi* grew, people rejected the proper way of living, and evil and corruption emerged. Instead of gathering in the kivas, people gambled, harassed the elders, and neglected their ritual obligations. Only complete destruction of the village – a massive flood or choking fumes, depending on the story – reminded people of the journey they were obligated to continue (Courlander 1971; Cushing 1896; Parsons 1939).

Do the Pueblo histories refer to real places, sites that we can visit today? On one hand, the stories are parables that teach people the consequences of unethical behavior, and whether they are real places is not important. But archaeologists have identified a time in Puebloan history when selfish behavior may have troubled society – a time of plenty, but also a time of inequities, with a few people exerting more control over others and the fruits of their labor.

The Chaco tradition

After several generations of poor rainfall, people living on the Colorado Plateau were completely dependent on farming – it was the only source of food that they had any chance of controlling and one that could produce surpluses to save for bad years. Fortunately, after 150 years of little rain, conditions in the northern Southwest gradually improved, beginning at the turn of the tenth century (Dean 1992; Windes 1993:44). This is not to say that water was plentiful, for the improvement was nearly imperceptible in human terms, and climatic instability continued to cause plenty of trouble. But things were slowly turning for the better, with some years of high rainfall that yielded surpluses not seen in a number of lifetimes. It is in this context that the first great houses, puny as they were, were constructed in Chaco Canyon communities in the late AD 800s.

Architectural elaborations

After the first flurry of great house construction, relatively little happened in Chaco Canyon during the AD 900s (Lekson 1984; Windes and Ford 1996). Both Pueblo Bonito and Una Vida were expanded during the middle of the century, but the additions were somewhat haphazard and continued to use the same crude, albeit massive, masonry style. After AD 1020, however, construction activity in the canyon took on a quite different flavor. The new great houses of Chetro Ketl, Hungo Pavi, and Pueblo Alto were all built near Pueblo Bonito, creating a true architectural center inside Chaco Canyon (Lekson 1984). These buildings differed from the earlier work – the great houses were more linear, seemingly more planned, and built using a new labor-intensive masonry style. Each was simply two straight rows of large square rooms facing two pitstructures, contrasting sharply with the organic, curvilinear appearance of the first great houses (Figure 4.1).

A few decades later, in the mid-eleventh century, the real frenzy of construction began (Lekson 1984). All of the canyon's great houses were substantially expanded, with new stories and entire wings added, but the great houses in the Pueblo Bonito area received the most attention. This marks the appearance of the first "blocked-in kivas," largely ceremonial pitstructures built into the blocks of rooms as opposed to in the open plaza area. Most additions were rectilinear, while the irregular wall alignments of early Pueblo Bonito construction were fixed by adding a nicely arcing row of rooms to its back wall. Even more intensive masonry work was used, creating a beautiful veneer that, strangely enough, was then covered with plaster. A few hundred meters from Pueblo Bonito, construction began on a new great house, Pueblo del Arroyo. By the AD 1070s, the architecture of Chaco Canyon had been massively expanded, creating a dense concentration of monumental buildings centered on Pueblo Bonito. Each had hundreds of rooms, and later additions would make them still larger (Figure 4.2).

The great houses were not the only architectural form elaborated by Chaco people. Oversized pitstructures that had been built for centuries by Puebloan people to accommodate their ceremonies became more formalized, consistently featuring a masonry bench along the interior wall, four massive posts to hold up a roof weighing tons, two unusual floor

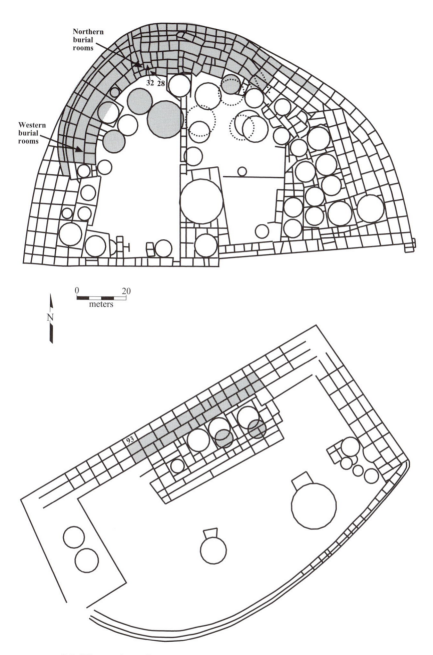

4.1 These plans show both the maximum extents of Pueblo Bonito and Chetro Ketl and the amount of architecture completed by around AD 1040 (shaded). Note that the early great houses faced southeast; Pueblo Bonito was not reoriented to face south until the AD 1080s. Room numbers referred to in the text are also indicated.

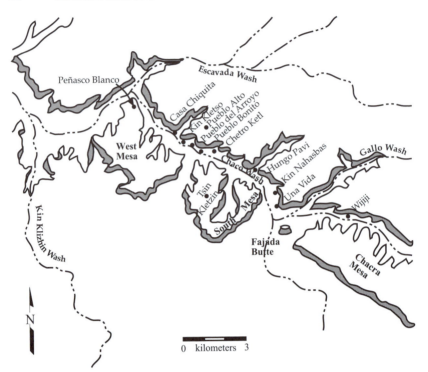

4.2 By the beginning of the twelfth century, "downtown" Chaco Canyon was filled with massive great houses containing hundreds of rooms each.

vaults whose function is still debated, and a raised fire box and deflector (Vivian and Reiter 1960). Most also had at least one antechamber providing entrance to the subterranean space. Archaeologists refer to these formal structures as "great kivas," distinguishing the Chacoan version from its more variable antecedents (Figure 4.3).

Although great house and great kiva construction increased during the eleventh century, some of the smaller habitations in Chaco Canyon apparently were abandoned. In the Fajada Gap community, for example, the number of houses decreased from a high of forty during the AD 900s to thirty during the AD 1000s (Windes 1993:361). This occupational hiatus correlates with environmental degradation that may have inspired some population reorganization throughout the San Juan Basin. However, research also indicates that none of the earlier canyon villages was fully abandoned. In fact, in some of these communities, new great kivas were constructed during the late AD 1000s, such as Casa Rinconada,

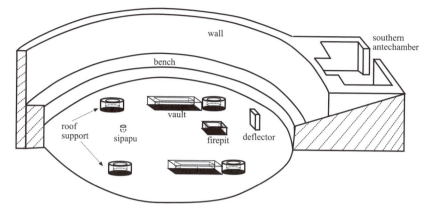

4.3 Stylized features of a typical Chaco Anasazi great kiva.

built among exceptionally large homes across the canyon from Pueblo Bonito (Windes 1993:358–60).

All this construction exacted a steep price on the local environment. It is hard to imagine, but the amount of water needed just to make plaster was substantial for farmers in such an arid climate, especially considering that the buildings had to be regularly recoated. Roofs required a tremendous quantity of trees of all sizes, from the enormous ones needed to span a great kiva to the multitude of small saplings used between the beams. As people used up local ponderosa pine, which happened as early as the AD 910s (Windes and McKenna 2001), they had to go much farther away to find appropriate timbers (Box 4.1). During the mid-1000s, thousands of beams were spruce and fir, species only available from higher elevations located in the mountains as far as 75 km away (Betancourt *et al.* 1986; Windes and Ford 1996).

What were great houses?

No question has haunted archaeologists more than how the great houses were used. Despite all the attention that Chaco Canyon's great houses have received, interpretations are confounded by a number of problems. First, most excavations took place when archaeology was still in its infancy and modern techniques for recovering information were not available. Recent excavations have occurred only at Pueblo Alto, one of the more atypical great houses located on the canyon rim rather than on the canyon floor.

Also challenging our ability to interpret the function of great houses is what Steadman Upham (1987) calls the "tyranny of the ethnographic

Box 4.1   Where did the beams come from?

Wood used in the earliest structures built in Chaco Canyon came from local stands of short piñon and juniper trees, taller cottonwoods from the wash, and ponderosa pines available farther up the canyon. The earliest great house architecture of the ninth century used these same sources, but by the eleventh century up to 93 percent of the timber in great house construction was non-local. Thousands of spruce and fir – neither of which was locally available – and ponderosa pines were imported into "downtown" Chaco Canyon. Some scholars estimate that over 200,000 trees were brought into the canyon (Betancourt *et al.* 1986; but see Windes and McKenna 2001:122–3).

Where did these trees come from? Because the San Juan Basin is largely treeless, the only forests that could supply that many trees are in the higher elevations surrounding the San Juan Basin, at least 50 km from Chaco Canyon. Attempts to determine specific sources have considered two kinds of evidence. First, archaeologists look in these distant forests for evidence of large-scale tree-cutting activities. The Chuska Mountains 75 km to the west, for example, are reportedly covered with axes and choppers (Windes and McKenna 2001:122), while unusual concentrations of small fieldhouses are found in ponderosa pine forests on Lobo Mesa, 50 km to the south. The second approach to trace the source of timber is more experimental, in which rare chemical elements found in great house beams are used as "fingerprints" to tie them to particular forests with unique soil chemistries (Durand *et al.* 1999; English *et al.* 2001). These studies are still in their early stages, but results so far confirm that forests in the Chuska Mountains, as well as around Mount Taylor 90 km to the southeast, provided timber for roofing the hundreds of great house rooms and kivas in Chaco Canyon.

record." Many scholars have looked at great houses and seen historic Pueblo architecture (e.g., Judd 1954; Kluckhohn and Reiter 1939). The similarity with the well-known "apartment buildings" of Taos Pueblo is particularly striking, leading many visitors to Chaco's great houses to assume that they were entirely residential, each filled with hundreds of people. But these similarities are mostly superficial, and the structures are separated by 1,000 years. Scholars now realize that uncritically imposing the ethnographic record on the archaeological record is inappropriate, and that is certainly true for Chaco Canyon.

Challenges to the hypothesis that great houses were residential came in the 1980s. Thomas Windes (1984) searched old excavation records of Pueblo Bonito to determine hearth locations. His argument was that each cooking hearth represented a single family, and therefore archaeologists simply needed to count the hearths to find out how many people lived in the great house. Windes concluded that no more than 100 people ever lived in the structure, far below earlier estimates that assumed the structure was residential. His conclusions are confirmed by a recent analysis (Bernardini 1999) showing that no more than a dozen families ever lived in Pueblo Bonito at one time and that this residential use ended in the eleventh century. Investigations of the 133-room Pueblo Alto similarly reveal a small residential population, perhaps only twenty-five to fifty people (Windes 1987). Many long-standing mysteries of Chaco Canyon – such as the absence of burials in or near great houses – are not so mysterious if indeed few people lived in these monumental structures.

If great houses were not simply massive apartment buildings, what were they? Their unusual design and contents provide some clues. Great house rooms are spacious, but the rooms are devoid of features and access to them is restricted, prompting some researchers to suggest that they were used for storage (Bustard 1996). We might imagine that Chaco people, geared toward overproduction and storing surpluses, built the structures as massive food warehouses. But the large quantities of broken storage vessels and spilled maize that might confirm this suspicion have yet to be identified.

Another idea is that at least some rooms were used as guest quarters, perhaps to accommodate pilgrims visiting Chaco Canyon from distant villages (Lekson et al. 1988; Windes 1991). Pueblo Alto, one of the rectilinear structures built in the eleventh century, provides some support for this hypothesis. Excavations in the main structure revealed little, but archaeologists did identify large ovens for cooking, a spacious walled plaza to the east of the great house itself, and an enormous mound believed to be a trash midden. Trenches carefully excavated through the mound revealed layer after layer of deposits containing a surprising number of broken pots and unusual quantities of food remains. Researchers concluded that occasional feasts occurred at Pueblo Alto, perhaps including the ritual destruction of pottery (Toll 1991). This research adds fuel to the idea that pilgrims swarmed to the Chaco Canyon great houses during episodic ceremonial events. The debate continues, however – a recent reanalysis of the Pueblo Alto archaeology challenges the conventional wisdom on the alleged trash mound, instead arguing that it is piled-up construction debris (Wills 2001). And most rooms in Pueblo Alto were devoid of features, even those that pilgrims might need to spend the night.

4.4 A variety of unusual artifacts were recovered from Pueblo Bonito, such as the turquoise-encrusted vessel, imported ceramic pitcher, and deer bone spatula with inlaid jet and turquoise shown here.

While great houses were clearly designed to be seen, and public events occurred around them, their interiors were not readily accessible to everyone. In fact, hundreds of unusual artifacts were carefully hidden away inside them (Durand 2003). Intricately carved wooden objects, vessels covered with mosaics of turquoise, copper bells imported from Mesoamerica, shell trumpets from the Gulf of California, and effigy pottery shaped as humans or animals come from excavated great houses in quantities unrivaled anywhere else in North America (Figure 4.4). Estimates are that somewhere around four times as much turquoise was recovered from Pueblo Bonito than from all other Southwestern pre-Contact contexts combined (Snow 1973). Even unusual animals were part of the great house menagerie – live macaws brought from north-ern Mexico were kept in several rooms in Pueblo Bonito. Rare items often were kept together in specific rooms. Over 110 unusually shaped "cylinder jars" were cached in Room 28 of Pueblo Bonito (Judd 1954), while Room 32 contained 375 painted and carved sticks as well as two sandstone balls (Pepper 1920:369–70). In Room 93 of Chetro Ketl, more than 200 painted wood artifacts were revealed by excavations, including parts of headdresses and altars (Vivian *et al.* 1978).

Kathy Roler Durand's (2003) recent assessment of great house function concludes that the structures were used for ceremonial activity, especially during the height of their expansion in the mid-1000s. She bases this conclusion on the many unusual artifacts of suspected ritual function, the massive size of the architecture, and the close association with great kivas – the ceremonial buildings of earlier times – as well as other nonfunctional features. Durand is not alone in coming to this conclusion. Several scholars argue that eleventh-century great houses were the destinations for pilgrims coming from throughout the northern Southwest to revel in the grandeur of Chaco Canyon, to see the massive buildings with their hidden secrets, including interior kivas to which access was restricted; to see priests covered with turquoise, shell, copper bells, and macaw feathers; and to participate in feasts and ceremonies that they would never forget (Judge 1993; Malville and Malville 2001).

What kinds of ceremonial events occurred at great houses? We will never know for sure, but some intriguing evidence suggests that astronomical observations, especially those related to solar events, were an integral part of Chacoan ritual. Unusual architectural features in structures such as Pueblo Bonito and the Casa Rinconada great kiva appear to mark solstices and equinoxes, and the famous "Sun Dagger" on Fajada Butte may further identify unusual lunar events (Box 4.2) (Carlson and Judge 1987; Malville 1994; Sofaer and Sinclair 1987). John Fritz (1987) and Dennis Doxtater (1991, 2002) argue that the architectural layouts of great houses served as metaphors for Chacoan concepts of ideology and order, especially regarding symmetry and duality. Andrew Fowler and John Stein (1992) propose that the architecture served as symbols conveying ideological meaning through time and across space. While these suggestions are difficult to confirm archaeologically, they do suggest that great houses and the ceremonies they accommodated were tied both to time – the cyclical farming calendar – and to space – the ideologically charged landscape within and surrounding Chaco Canyon.

Who built the great houses?

Construction of so much architecture in Chaco Canyon required a substantial labor investment. However, it was not all constructed at once, a point that Stephen Lekson (1984:257–63) emphasized in his analysis

Box 4.2   The Sun Dagger

Fajada Butte is an impressive geological feature that stands alone where a side canyon enters Chaco Canyon and the southern cliffs open to the south (Figure 4.2). Late in June 1977, artist Anna Sofaer was on the butte recording rock art when she noticed that a dagger of light bisected a spiral pecked on to the sandstone cliff. She had discovered the famous "Sun Dagger" (Sofaer 1997).

The Sun Dagger consists of three vertical sandstone slabs that fell in a side-by-side arrangement against Fajada Butte's cliff face. At some point – and when this happened is debated – Puebloans pecked two spirals into the sandstone wall behind the slabs in precise locations such that slivers of light pass between the stone slabs and on to the spirals during solstices and equinoxes. At the summer equinox, for example, the larger of the two spirals is perfectly bisected by noon sunlight, while the smaller spiral is bisected only during an equinox event. Some archaeoastronomers claim that the Sun Dagger also identifies lunar "standstills," when the moon remains in the same position in the sky for several days, an event that occurs once every nineteen years (Malville and Putnam 1993:32–3).

Some archaeologists are skeptical about the importance of the Sun Dagger. Unlike other well-known solar observatories created by Puebloan people, the Sun Dagger cannot predict solar events since the "dagger" appears about a month before the solstice but then barely moves position on the spiral – Pueblo "sunwatchers" traditionally use this kind of movement to determine the actual day of the solstice. The Sun Dagger is also difficult to get to, leading Michael Zeilik (1987; see also Carlson 1987) to propose that it was a sun shrine that simply took advantage of fortuitous rock fall. Other scholars argue that the Sun Dagger post-dates the height of the Chaco tradition. Despite these caveats, however, the Sun Dagger is just one of many suspected archaeoastronomical features in Chaco Canyon, illustrating how important the heavens – and particularly the path of the sun – were to the canyon's Puebloan inhabitants.

of Chacoan architecture. Nor, as Lynne Sebastian points out (1992), was construction of great houses a constant background activity. Instead, great houses were built in spurts. Early construction events were relatively modest, at a scale that could be accomplished by 100 people over a few days. Later efforts, however, required perhaps ten times more labor, and different great houses often were under construction at the same time. Dendrochronological evidence suggests that Chaco people began to stockpile materials for major construction events several years in advance, especially as timber came from farther away. Some clues nevertheless reveal that great house builders were not especially concerned with labor costs. During the late AD 1000s, for example, the reuse of beams from abandoned rooms stopped and the great quantities of imported lumber even included prefabricated lintels assembled elsewhere (Windes and McKenna 2001). Canyon builders apparently did not rely on their own labor for great house construction.

What social and political context promoted the construction of such massive ceremonial architecture? Sebastian (1992) identifies an interesting pattern that provides insight into this question. On the basis of detailed dendroclimatological records from Chaco Canyon, she developed a computer simulation that estimated yearly maize production. In some years, her simulated farmers harvested more than enough maize to live on, allowing them to spirit away some reserves. Other years were not so good, and they had to dip into their stores.

Coming out of the lean years of the AD 700s and 800s, Sebastian found that her simulated farmers had to overproduce, ideally putting away enough surplus food to get them through three lean years – a pattern consistent with ethnographic evidence from historic Pueblo people. During the relatively moister AD 900s and 1000s, the great house era, Sebastian's farmers did better, producing enough food to allow them to take a few days off here and there to work on great houses. But, oddly enough, when Sebastian correlated her sequence of surplus production with the timing of early construction events, she found that great houses were built or expanded when times were bad – when surpluses were the most severely stressed (Figure 4.5). This pattern suggested to Sebastian that the development of great houses was ultimately not a purely communal event, for not everyone was equally positioned to expend their efforts on major construction events (Sebastian 1992:111–28).

Imagine that you have a friend who frequently loans you money or allows you to borrow his car. If this keeps happening, you find yourself increasingly indebted to him. When he in turn asks you for a favor – moving furniture or assisting in preparations for a party – you cannot so easily spurn him. This, according to Sebastian, is analogous to what was happening in Chaco Canyon. It was no mistake that the first great houses were built in prime horticultural locations. Sebastian proposes that inequities emerged as the improving climate especially favored those on good lands, while continued instability continued to haunt those in less productive areas. New immigrants into the canyon, perhaps coming

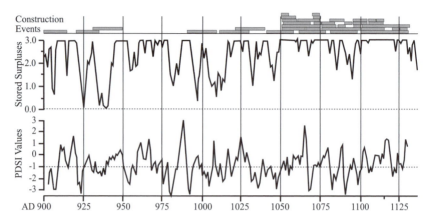

4.5 The top sequence shows great house construction activity in Chaco Canyon, with each bar representing a building phase at one great house. The middle sequence indicates the number of years' worth of stored maize, according to Sebastian's simulation. The bottom sequence shows yearly precipitation in the San Juan Basin based on a three-year running mean of the Palmer Drought Severity Index; the value of −1 is average for this region.

from the San Juan drainage to the north (Wilshusen and Ortman 1999), may have also found themselves indebted to locals as they settled more marginal lands. As some people acquired more and more social debt, they turned it into labor, directing it toward a variety of tasks – including building great houses. Initially, these structures may have been used as residences by the more fortunate farmers, and the earliest great houses do look like most regular houses in Chaco Canyon, just bigger (Bernardini 1999).

But social debt is not the same as social power, and jealousy and resentment might have encouraged these emerging elites to turn the great houses into public architecture, ceremonial features that took on some of the functions of earlier great kivas (Kantner 1996). The well-to-do farmers still benefited, for directing their resources toward public buildings would have been seen as a generous act, one that garnered more respect and perhaps more latitude as their prestige grew. Further promoting an arena for sociopolitical inequities, friendly competition between the villages in Chaco Canyon probably revolved around the great house that each was building and the ceremonial events that they accommodated. Sebastian (1992:122) suggests that the successes of the most fortunate farmers may have been seen as a sign of supernatural support, providing these people with a source of religious legitimation that could be highlighted in the construction of great houses and the ceremonies the elites sponsored there.

Sebastian (1992:120–6) proposes that the tenor of great house activity changed in the early AD 1000s. This period was marked by especially favorable conditions for producing surplus food, and it was also a time of frequent construction events that were mostly uncorrelated with climate changes. Building occurred at existing great houses, with Pueblo Bonito and Hungo Pavi quadrupling in size and Peñasco Blanco tripling in size. Foundations for an enormous extension east of Pueblo Bonito were built in the early AD 1070s, but this project was never completed (Lekson 1984). Sebastian argues that by this time, the economic inequities that had provided a foundation for social differences in the AD 900s became crystallized into more permanent sociopolitical ranking between kin groups, a ranking probably enforced by the ceremonial authority of the most successful families. The more powerful groups no longer needed to build up social debt before initiating new construction, but instead could call for labor and materials nearly at will, perhaps tying these efforts to the ceremonial calendar.

What is the evidence for the social and political differences in Sebastian's scenario? The data to address this question, unfortunately, are incomplete owing to the rudimentary nature of early archaeology in Chaco Canyon. A well-known study of both great house and "small house" burials by Nancy Akins (1986, updated in Akins 2001) found evidence for hereditary positions of authority, particularly among two burial locations in Pueblo Bonito known by scholars as the "northern burial rooms" and the "western burial rooms." The overall wealth of these two mortuary contexts is unparalleled in the Southwest. The richest burials are of two men found in the northern burial rooms who were interred in an elaborate tomb with vast amounts of turquoise, shell, and other valuables. Another dozen or so individuals, perhaps intentionally disarticulated, apparently were included as part of the mortuary ritual. The intuition that these were highly respected leaders is compromised by the fact that one of the men – a 25-year-old whose burial was the most elaborate – apparently was killed by blows to both sides of his head and to his left leg (Akins 2001:172).

Osteological research by Akins (1986) and Ann Palkovich (1984) found that individuals interred in Pueblo Bonito were healthier than those buried in domestic structures. Not only were these purported elites taller by 4.6 cm, but they also suffered fewer pathologies, a pattern indicating that hereditary inequalities affected access to nutritious foods or simply that people with access to the most productive lands, and thus the healthiest diets, achieved high status in Chacoan society (Akins 1986:135–6).

Morphometric analyses suggest that the two burial clusters in Pueblo Bonito are genetically distinct, perhaps representing two separate kin groups. Especially intriguing are possible biological connections between these burial groups and habitation clusters elsewhere in the canyon: the western burial rooms' remains are osteologically most similar to burials in the Fajada Butte community, while the northern burial rooms are quite unique, sharing a weak link with people living around the Casa Rinconada great kiva (Akins 1986:75; Schillaci et al. 2001, Schillaci and Stojanowski 2002; but see Akins 2001:185).

Was Pueblo Bonito used by two different groups living in distinct parts of the canyon, and, if so, did they share use of the great house, or did one group succeed the other as the custodians of the massive structure? Archaeologists continue to explore these issues. One problem, however, is that archaeologists have little understanding of when these burials took place. Both burial groups are in the older parts of Pueblo Bonito, but the pottery found with the remains is from all time periods, perhaps indicating continuous use of the cemeteries throughout the history of Chaco Canyon. Complicating matters are reports by excavators that many of the burial rooms appeared to have been "violated," with skeletons thrown about and perhaps items removed. Osteological evidence reveals that some of the burials were disturbed not long after interment (Akins 2001:181–2).

Overall, Sebastian's complex yet compelling scenario for the development of Chaco Canyon and the use of great houses fits the available climatic, architectural, and mortuary evidence. New studies, however, are refining some of the basic details. For example, the National Park Service is undertaking a major reassessment of the tree-ring dates from the canyon's great houses (Windes and Ford 1996; Windes and McKenna 2001), while an upcoming publication on the sophisticated water-control and farming techniques of Chacoan people promises to shake up our understanding of the canyon's horticultural development. Questions also are being directed at the methods Sebastian used for reconstructing surplus production (Mills 2002:75). For the time being, Sebastian's model is promising but in need of further evaluation.

A number of scholars argue that the emergence of great houses was a communal rather than competitive process. W. H. Wills (2000; see also Saitta 1997), for example, suggests that great houses were cooperatively built to establish rights over farmlands, while the process of building the structures was itself a ritual that affirmed social ties, promoted solidarity, and repressed competition. Although Wills denies a role for leadership or other inequities in his model, his scenario is not incompatible with competition-oriented models (Kantner 1996, 1999a; Sebastian 1992), which acknowledge that inequities emerging in egalitarian societies must be couched in communalism and solidarity. No aspiring leader can step forward one day, declare himself king, and start commanding people to do his bidding. What is ultimately at debate is whether the process is driven by intentional individual behavior or adaptive group behavior – or some combination thereof (Kantner 2003a). This level of archaeological inquiry is complex and requires resolution of many of the poorly understood aspects of Chacoan development.

Chaco's far-reaching influence

At some point after great houses began to be built in Chaco Canyon, related developments appeared in other parts of the San Juan Basin. Communities that were in other ways typical of any tenth-century Puebloan village began to construct new architectural features – great houses and great kivas – similar to those found in the central canyon. These villages are known as "outliers," "great house communities," or "Chacoan communities" (Judge 1991; Kantner and Mahoney 2000; Marshall *et al.* 1979; Powers *et al.* 1983). Unlike the dominating structures still standing in Chaco Canyon, great houses in outlying communities are difficult to identify, especially since most are now mounds of rubble with obscured architectural characteristics (Figure 4.6). Archaeologists tend to define outlying great houses as masonry structures larger than the surrounding houses, although, as Fowler and his colleagues (1987:80) point out, "[great house size] is largely an illusion: exceptionally massive, yet smaller in plan than other forms of contemporaneous Anasazi buildings." The ambiguity has led Lekson (1991:36) to conclude, "the deciding criterion is this: is the candidate great house a significantly bigger 'bump' than other contemporaneous bumps in its vicinity?"

Part of the problem in defining and understanding great house communities outside of Chaco Canyon is that research on these sites is still in its infancy. Although early investigations acknowledged the connection between outlying great houses and Chaco Canyon, most archaeologists were not fully cognizant of how widespread these features were until archaeologists conducted several large surveys in the 1970s (e.g., Marshall *et al.* 1979; Powers *et al.* 1983). Since that time, a handful of comprehensive studies in outlying communities have been conducted, although many are still unpublished (see discussions in Kantner and Mahoney 2000). The rapidity with which our knowledge of great house communities is changing is exemplified by the number that are recognized: in 1980, perhaps thirty or forty outlying great houses were known in the published literature (Marshall *et al.* 1979; Powers *et al.*

4.6 This digital reconstruction shows what Edge of the Cedars, a great house in southeastern Utah, may have looked like. Like most "outliers," it is much more diminutive than the great houses of Chaco Canyon.

1983); today, more than 200 have been identified (Figure 4.7), and the search continues (Kantner 2003b).

What do we know about outlying great houses? The evidence so far suggests that approximately thirty of these structures were built in communities outside of Chaco Canyon during the AD 900s. The majority are located in the central, southern, and western portions of the San Juan Basin as well as in the Red Mesa Valley just to the south of the basin – arguably none was established north of the canyon until the eleventh century. These early great houses and perhaps a Chaco-style great kiva were built in previously established communities, many of which had been occupied at least since the AD 700s.

The AD 1000s saw the greatest expansion of Chacoan influence, especially after the AD 1040s. While tenth-century great house villages continued to be occupied, over eighty new great houses also emerged at this time, with most appearing in villages in the Mesa Verde area to the north or along the Chuska Mountains and Rio Puerco to the west. Great houses appeared in distant areas, well into what is now Arizona, Utah, and Colorado. A few new great houses built in outlying villages were inordinately large, such as the 175-room Salmon Ruin along the San Juan River

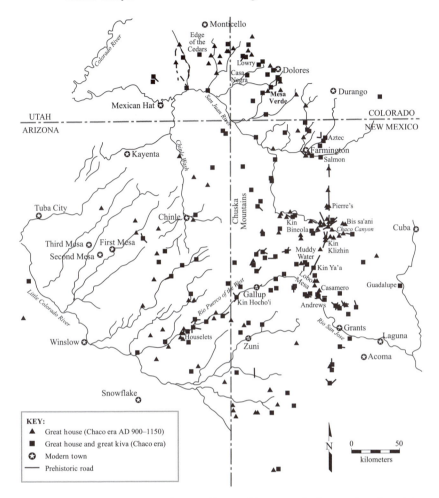

4.7 Great house and great kiva architecture similar to that found in Chaco Canyon has been identified over much of the northern South-west. Pre-Contact roadways emanate from many of these Chacoan architectural features. Named great houses are referred to in the text.

(Irwin-Williams and Shelley 1980) and Kin Bineola near Chaco Canyon, which ultimately grew to 230 rooms. While outlying great houses established in this period were usually built in preexisting communities, this was not always the case – a handful of new great houses were not associated with any community, such as Casa Estrella, a small structure strategically placed right in between two large great house communities (Kantner

1997). Others are completely new great house communities, including Bis sa'ani, which was fully investigated in 1980 (Breternitz *et al.* 1982). Archaeologists concluded that the two great houses elevated on a mesa, as well as the surrounding small village, were rapidly built together after AD 1050.

The big mystery is why these Chaco-style great houses were built outside the canyon. Some scholars argue that Chaco Canyon became an imperialistic state, sending armies across the San Juan Basin to subjugate outlying communities (Wilcox 1993, 1999a). Others prefer a gentler view, proposing that the canyon sent out missionaries who built great houses and converted local populations to Chacoan religion (Eddy 1975; Kane 1993). Yet another scenario regards the regional "system" as having developed to expedite the movement of surpluses from areas with excess production to villages temporarily in need of food (Judge 1979; Lekson 1999a:45; Schelberg 1992). A growing body of scholars argue for a more complex interaction between powerful kin groups in Chaco Canyon and their peers in outlying villages, one that stimulated competition, the exchange of valuable goods, and the construction of great houses by locals trying to emulate the apparent successes of Chaco's leaders (Kantner and Mahoney 2000). All models of regional development draw upon three primary sources of evidence for support: the outlying great house architecture, the famous road system, and the flow of material culture.

At first glance, the outlying great houses are mirror images of their better-known counterparts inside Chaco Canyon. Similarly massive masonry styles, the use of blocked-in kivas, multiple stories, and oversized rooms characterize great houses wherever they are found. But were they built by the same people, perhaps by missionaries or architects sent out by Chacoan leaders? This is a difficult question to address, but Winston Hurst (2000) and Ruth Van Dyke (2000, 2003) independently evaluated the issue by distinguishing external from "hidden" architectural elements. External features are those that any casual observer of a great house would know about, such as its overall size and layout. Hidden elements, however, are structural features such as foundation design and wall construction details that could be known only to the architect or builder. Guided by these criteria, Hurst argues that hidden details identified at the Edge of the Cedars Ruin in Utah suggest involvement by Chacoan architects. Van Dyke comes to a different conclusion in her study of Red Mesa Valley architecture. She proposes that variability in how great houses were expressed indicates that local architects copied a general architectural canon; individual builders in fact may have never even seen a great house, instead only hearing about the magnificent architecture through other visitors (Figure 4.8). These contradictory results suggest

Upper Kin Nizhoni

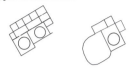

Lower Kin Nizhoni

LA 16508

LA 16509

LA 16515

Pierre's

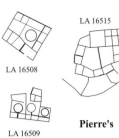

Kin Klizhin

Casamero

Andrews

Guadalupe

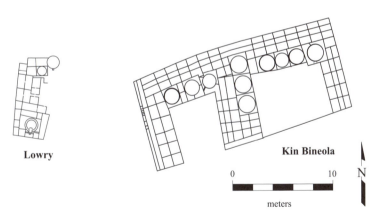

Lowry

Kin Bineola

0   10   N

meters

4.8 The architecture of great houses outside of Chaco Canyon is quite variable, suggesting that design and construction were handled locally. In some cases, local builders may have known a lot about Chacoan great house style; in other cases, they probably just copied the basic architectural canon.

that both emulation and direct involvement by Chaco guided great house construction in different parts of the "Chaco world."

Much of our understanding of the relationship between Chaco Canyon and great house communities comes from the famous Chacoan roadways (Figure 4.7), which are found all over the San Juan Basin and beyond (Till and Hurst 2002; Vivian 1997a, 1997b). A common interpretation is that these roads connected great houses into a network that facilitated the flow of resources into and out of Chaco Canyon (Powers *et al.* 1983:342; Schelberg 1992:67–8; Snygg and Windes 1998; Tainter and Plog 1994:171–2). Other analyses, however, are challenging this interpretation, and a consensus is emerging that two kinds of roads existed (Kantner 1997; Nials *et al.* 1987; Roney 1992). The first type includes at least two lengthy roads that emanate from Chaco Canyon: the South and North Roads. Although these were once thought to have connected the canyon with distant villages, further investigation reveals that they symbolically articulate with prominent geological features – the South Road travels 55 km from the canyon to the highly visible Hosta Butte, while the North Road heads about the same distance in the opposite direction before dropping into Kutz Canyon. This is not to say that no one ever traveled on these roads, but rather that their design was not primarily guided by a desire to integrate communities physically together.

A much greater number of roadways are actually short segments that extend away from local great houses or great kivas (Figure 4.7). This has led some scholars to suggest that roads were constructed to focus attention on the local ceremonial landscape, rather than connecting communities with one another (Kantner 1997; Roney 1992). Many of these small roadways, not unlike the longer North and South Roads, are aligned with prominent features on the landscape. The impression one gets from these smaller roads is that they functioned in much the same way as the lengthy roads emanating from Chaco Canyon – symbolically articulating with important features on the landscape – but on a much smaller scale. Van Dyke (2003) notes that this pattern is most common farther from Chaco Canyon, almost as if those people most distant from the central canyon were more likely to emulate the canyon not only by building local versions of great house architecture, but also by including small roads; they were trying to create their own "mini-Chacos."

The flow of commodities among outlying great house villages and between them and Chaco Canyon provides an additional source of data for understanding the Chaco "phenomenon." Archaeologists have known for some time that all kinds of material was pouring into the canyon (Mathien 1993). Non-local pottery, for example, consistently accounts for over 30 percent and up to 50 percent of ceramic collections recovered

4.9 Unusual vessel forms such as these "cylinder jars" were found in Pueblo Bonito – with 111 coming from a single room in this great house. Like most pottery in Chaco Canyon, these cylinder vessels may have been produced elsewhere and imported.

from Chaco Canyon great houses (Figure 4.9). The sources of this pottery change over time, beginning in the south, moving to the west (Box 4.3), and ending with a diminishing flow of goods from the north (Toll 1991, 2001). This pattern once fueled models of the canyon as a major storage facility for surpluses that were then redistributed back to outlying villages during times of need. However, although pottery flowed into Chaco Canyon, it never was redistributed back out to outlying areas – investigations in distant great house communities identify very low amounts of imported pottery (Kantner *et al.* 2000; Stoltman 1999; Umberger *et al.* 2002; Van Dyke 1997). Studies of stone tools produce similar results (Cameron 1984, 2001), suggesting that most great house communities exchanged everyday goods over small areas, perhaps only with a handful of neighboring villages with which they established relations of reciprocity.

The movement of more valuable items through the northern Southwest was also dominated by Chaco Canyon. As mentioned earlier, vast quantities of turquoise were recovered from canyon great houses, as were shell and exotic materials from Mesoamerica (Mathien 1993). Most of these items are typically found in small amounts throughout

Box 4.3   What's so great about Chuska pottery?

Although areas to the north and south produced pots consumed by Chaco Canyon, vessels produced to the west in the Chuska Mountains were especially numerous. Prior to Chaco's emergence as an influential center, less than 4 percent of all pottery in the canyon came from the Chuskas, but after AD 1040, over 30 percent of vessels were produced there. The majority of imported Chuskan pottery was grayware – the undecorated vessels used for preparing foods. In fact, almost 50 percent of all grayware pots found in Chaco Canyon after AD 1040 were produced in the Chuskas (Toll and McKenna 1997:130–1).

Why was Chuskan pottery consumed in such quantities? Scholars consider three possible explanations. First, the pottery may have been especially desirable for cooking. Chuska pottery was made with a distinctive temper, a volcanic rock called "trachyte" that probably prevented the vessels from breaking during cooking (Hensler 1999). Another reason that Chuskan pottery appears in large quantities is perhaps because Chaco Canyon enjoyed a strong relationship with villages in the Chuska region. Several large great house communities were located near trachyte outcrops (Mills *et al.* 1997), and they were also the source of other goods imported to the canyon, such as raw material for making stone tools and perhaps even game animals (Akins 1985; Cameron 2001).

A third reason why the frequency of Chuskan pottery is so high in Chaco Canyon may be due to the ease with which it can be identified. Trachyte temper is very easy to see, and the natural outcrops of trachyte are well known (Mills *et al.* 1997). In contrast, the temper used in the majority of pottery found in Chaco was "grog" – crushed pieces of old pottery – and sand or ground sandstone. These tempering agents were used by potters both inside and outside of the canyon, and tracing the trade of vessels made with such common material is difficult. Some archaeologists, however, argue that most imported pottery in Chaco Canyon was made with these tempers (Warren 1980). This could mean that as much as 37 percent of pottery in the canyon was imported from distant producers who tempered with grog and sandstone – more than the proportion of Chuskan imports (Toll and McKenna 1997:136–7).

Chuskan grayware pottery was probably favored in Chaco Canyon, perhaps because of its qualities when heated. But other parts of the Chaco world provided comparable quantities of pottery, particularly decorated vessels. Chaco Canyon was a consumer, and it consumed the best products available from each outlying area.

the pre-Contact Southwest, but Chaco Canyon accumulated much more than its fair share. What makes this especially unusual is the distance of the canyon from any source of rare goods. The closest turquoise quarry is almost 200 km away on the opposite side of the Jemez Mountains (Mathien 2001; Windes 1992). Shells from the Gulfs of California and Mexico are common in the canyon, including whole conch horns, despite the hundreds of kilometers such exotics traveled to get there. Much of this material arrived in the canyon in its raw form, and F. Joan Mathien (2001) describes workshops where finished turquoise artifacts such as beads and pendants were produced. Finished copper bells and exotic birds from Mesoamerica, however, are also found in the larger great houses in Chaco Canyon, especially in Pueblo Bonito. Like pottery, all these valuables were entering Chaco Canyon in appreciable quantities, but whether they were redistributed outside of the canyon is not known.

So, then, what was Chaco?

Chaco Canyon was a consumer – all kinds of goods were going into the canyon, and seemingly little was going back out. Many archaeologists argue that the canyon also "consumed" labor, drawing people from far-flung villages to assist in construction projects. Not only did they build great houses, but their labor was also needed for great kivas, roads, irrigation works, and other features, making the desolate canyon a place of nearly constant activity. Chaco Canyon clearly depended on outlying villages to fuel its growth, for it needed everything from timber to pottery to the rare goods that had to pass through distant communities. None of this was locally available – in fact, very little was locally available. Chaco Canyon has few unique resources, and it is located in a particularly harsh environment. The question, then, is how did the canyon manage to become so dominant that not only were people in outlying areas copying Chacoan architecture, but they were also willing to contribute commodities, valuables, and even labor to help develop the canyon into, as Lekson (1999a:26) describes it, the "800-pound gorilla of Anasazi archaeology."

The likely answer to this question stems from Sebastian's model (1992) for the emergence of great houses within the canyon. The inequities that she argues developed during the tenth and eleventh centuries must have inspired greater competition between the great house communities found within Chaco Canyon, with the kin groups controlling the earliest great houses competing with one another for prestige. Such "peer-polity competition" promoted the growth and elaboration of ceremonial infrastructure as a way to impress people further both within and out-side of the canyon and to draw in the resources and labor needed to fuel the rivalries. Immigration probably further exacerbated the compet-itive atmosphere as village leaders sought to attract more residents who could provide not only additional labor, but also connections with other populations on the Colorado Plateau. The predictable result of this kind of contest was the centralization of the canyon's population, most likely around the kin groups and ceremonial leaders that controlled Pueblo Bonito and its surrounding ceremonial infrastructure.

Many scholars contend that eleventh-century Chaco Canyon became a pilgrimage center, a location of intense ceremonial activity drawing people from long distances away (Judge 1989; Malville and Malville 2001; Renfrew 2001). Why come to the canyon? Like any pilgrimage center, different people came for different reasons. Grandiose ceremo-nial events focused on awe-inspiring infrastructure attracted some folk, while the unusual astronomical observatories built in the canyon no doubt impressed farmers whose own techniques for tracking seasonal changes were simple in comparison – if perhaps not less accurate. The power of Chaco's priestly leaders also was emphasized by the long, hot journey across the desolate San Juan Basin to the relative oasis of Chaco Canyon – certainly, a pilgrim would reason, anyone who could build such an extrav-agant center in the middle of the high desert must be especially adept at influencing the supernatural world. During the mid-eleventh century, a number of short-lived droughts could have been turned to the advan-tage of Chaco's leaders when good conditions were quickly restored, enforcing their ritual authority. The AD 1054 supernova that created the Crab Nebula, arguably recorded in a pictograph below Peñasco Blanco (Malville and Putnam 1993:36), perhaps served as an omen of Chaco's power (Figure 4.10). And, like any pilgrimage center, the reputation enjoyed by the canyon fed itself as more and more people came to Chaco Canyon bearing gifts of valuable materials and crafts, needed food and pottery, and muscle and sweat.

The influence of Chaco Canyon, however, probably did not equate to control over outlying villages. Current research in great house communi-ties reveals that people on the edges of the San Juan Basin – as well as the immediate neighbors of Chaco Canyon inside the San Juan Basin – were closely tied to the central canyon. These villages tend to have the largest great houses, built most closely to Chacoan standards (Van Dyke 1999, 2003), and it is from these villages that many of the goods found in Chaco Canyon originated (e.g., English *et al.* 2001; Toll and McKenna 1997). The edge of the basin also marks the extent of the North and South

4.10 This pictograph, located under a sandstone overhang near Peñasco Blanco, shows a large star near a crescent moon. The size of the star and the location of the moon relative to the star have led archaeoastronomers to propose that this represents the Crab Nebula of AD 1054.

Roads. As one moves out of the San Juan Basin, however, the fidelity to Chacoan patterns becomes less clear, with the evidence suggesting that these villages copied some of the impressive features of Chaco Canyon, but on a much more modest scale (Meyer 1999; Van Dyke 2003). Kantner (1996) found that the configuration of great house architecture in these distant communities reflected local social and political concerns, as if the authority of Chaco Canyon was called upon to legitimize the local leadership. This was probably true of many outlying communities – ties with the leadership of the pilgrimage center were negotiated in the context of village competition for positions of status and authority. In essence, Chaco Canyon traded a powerful ideology for the materials it needed to build and sustain that ideology.

Life in Chaco Canyon

Of course, inhabitants of Chaco Canyon were not so Machiavellian as to scheme all day about how to manipulate more resources out of outlying villages. People were still farmers, spending much of their lives tending their crops, preparing meals or maintaining their houses, and teaching their children the proper way of living.

Several archaeologists have suggested that "small house" grinding groups were an important social and political unit for Chacoan society, especially for the women in what was an increasingly patriarchal and hierarchical society (Hegmon *et al.* 2000; Neitzel 2000). As suggested in the last chapter, the transition to farming villages across the Puebloan Southwest led to a social, political, and economic focus on kin groups whose membership was determined through the maternal line. In Chaco Canyon, however, this may have changed during the eleventh century. John Ware (2001; but see Peregrine 2001) argues that these property-holding matrilineages slowly disappeared, to be replaced by a system in which descent was bilateral – reckoned through both parents – making the formation of large kin groups nearly impossible. He further argues that male-centered moieties dominated social and political interaction. Unlike lineages, moiety organization results in large social groups that accommodate more permanent hierarchical organization and generate substantial labor forces. Some evidence supports this proposed shift in Chacoan organization. The two morphologically distinctive burial groups in Pueblo Bonito, for example, are consistent with the existence of dual moieties. The cemeteries also appear to be composed of closely related males, while the female skeletal remains exhibit greater variability, perhaps indicating a switch toward a male-focused society (Schillaci and Stojanowski 2002). Another clue is the addition of a dividing wall after AD 1080 that effectively split Pueblo Bonito in half, each side featuring its own great kiva (Lekson 1984).

It is perhaps surprising that this suspected shift to a more patriarchal society occurred during a relatively peaceful period in Southwestern history. Lekson (1999a:63–4, 2002; see also LeBlanc 1999) contends that the tenth and eleventh centuries represent a "Pax Chaco," a time of little obvious violence on the Colorado Plateau. Archaeologists debate the reasons for this, with many agreeing that devotion to Chaco Canyon and the ideology it represented trumped any antagonism that people felt for one another. Other scholars, however, contend that the benign atmosphere was a veneer hiding a more sinister reality in which Chacoan leaders occasionally maintained their positions through carefully exacted and purposefully severe violence (e.g., Kantner 1999b; LeBlanc 1999; Turner and Turner 1999). Both views are likely to be correct, with the Pax Chaco sporadically broken by targeted political violence designed to send a message to potential troublemakers.

The Mimbres tradition

Today, visitors to the Southwest flock to the famous Anasazi ruins scattered over the Colorado Plateau. The stunning architecture feeds the imagination, giving people a feel for what life was like almost 1,000 years ago. Few tourists, on the other hand, make their way to southern New Mexico to visit the ruins of the Mimbres tradition. To modern sensibilities, the buildings are not impressive, having been constructed with unshaped river cobbles held together with generous amounts of adobe mortar – an unstable technique that one archaeologist referred to as "stacking ball-bearings." This construction technique made it difficult to build structures with many stories, and standing walls collapsed long ago. Most Mimbres sites also have been heavily damaged – if not completely obliterated – by illegal digging by criminals eager to get their hands on valuable antiquities. As a result, what were once thriving communities are now low cobble mounds pockmarked with unsightly craters left by "pothunters."

"Stacks of ball-bearings": Mimbres architecture

Above-ground architecture was a relative late-comer for people living in and around the southern Mogollon Highlands (Figure 4.11). By AD 1000, a cultural period known by archaeologists as the "Classic Mimbres," typical residences consisted of blocks of contiguous rooms that grew accretionally – a building might start with a handful of rooms to which others were added over many years. Mimbres architecture did not follow a set floorplan. Instead, a number of roomblocks clustered together, facing a common plaza area, and as they grew they merged into a single building. The resulting aggregated pueblo accommodated up to 300 people. Swarts Ruin, located along the Mimbres River, provides a good example of this architectural growth (Figure 4.12). The site started in the tenth century as a pithouse village, but after a couple of generations, six small blocks of surface rooms were built on top of the abandoned pitstructures. Over the next two centuries, rooms were added to these original structures, which eventually merged into two large roomblocks arrayed around open plazas (LeBlanc 1983:108–11).

Unlike the Chacoan great houses to the north, Mimbres buildings were indisputably residential, exhibiting a variety of storage, living, and cooking rooms. A few larger rooms with unique "dual-hearths" were established as ceremonial "shrines," which were occasionally burned and rebuilt (Figure 4.13). Patricia Gilman (1989) suggests that as each

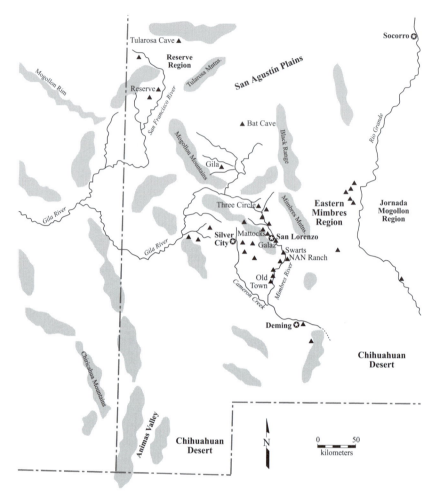

4.11 The Mogollon Highlands includes a number of mountain ranges that primarily feed the San Francisco, Gila, and Mimbres rivers. Most of the best-known Mimbres sites are in the Mimbres Valley itself, although additional sites are also found in several small drainages in the Eastern Mimbres region.

roomblock grew, older residential rooms in the core of the structure were converted into a ritual center serving a particular kin group. On the other hand, the oversized pitstructures of earlier times – often called "great kivas" owing to their similarity with Anasazi structures of the same name – were no longer constructed after AD 1050. Instead, plaza areas created by surrounding roomblocks served as community-wide ritual centers (Creel

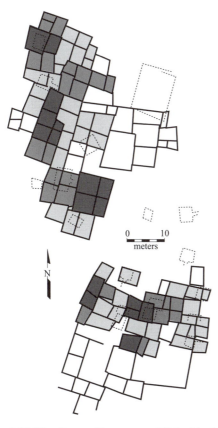

4.12 The Swarts Site was established in the tenth century with the construction of several pitstructures (dashed lines). In the eleventh century,
six small masonry roomblocks were built over the earlier structures (solid
lines). Over the next century, they were added to, until they formed two
large roomblocks. The darkest rooms represent the first stage of construction, with increasingly lighter fills indicating subsequent additions.

and Anyon 2003). At the Mattocks Site, archaeologists discovered that
the space between two roomblocks was partially surfaced with flagstone
and surrounded by a low wall, which they interpreted as an open ceremonial area (LeBlanc 1983:86–8). Small unroofed rooms hidden inside
the roomblocks of the Galaz Site also probably served as open spaces for
ritual activity (Anyon and LeBlanc 1984:140).

Although most southern Mogollon people lived in these large "apartment buildings" during the Mimbres period, the majority of *sites* were
actually small, consisting of fewer than ten rooms (Lekson 1992; Nelson

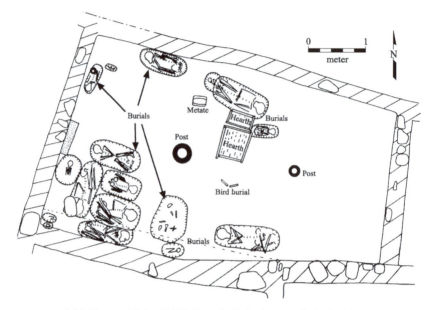

4.13 Room 12 in NAN Ranch Ruin is a typical dual-hearth room. Owing to its unusual features and its use as cemetery space, some scholars believe such rooms were ceremonial spaces.

1999:38). In fact, only about fifteen large roomblock villages existed along the Mimbres drainage, with several more west of the southern Rio Grande and a handful in the upper Gila drainage (Hegmon *et al.* 1999). The remaining small structures were temporary shelters for farmers and residences for people who chose not to (or were not allowed to) tie themselves closely with the main villages. At the site known as NAN 15, for example, a modest twenty-five-room pueblo was built around AD 1080 along a tributary of the Mimbres River; a generation later, the residents left their home and moved somewhere else (Shafer 1999b:125). Residences like NAN 15 may have been occupied by recent immigrants, judging by the evidence for substantial population growth from the Late Pithouse to the Classic Mimbres periods (Nelson 1999:37; Nelson *et al.* 1994:119).

What's the deal with Mimbres pottery?

The highlight – and perhaps the curse – of Mimbres archaeology is the stunning pottery produced during the AD 1000s (Figure 4.14). Technologically, the pottery is neither flawless nor unique, and the colors used are no different than are found in most other parts of the Southwest at

4.14 Mimbres pottery is most famous for its pictorial bowls, which feature humans engaged in various activities as well as animals such as the stylized fish featured on this vessel.

this time. But the iconography decorating the vessels, as well as the contexts from which they are recovered, make Mimbres pottery highly sought after on the illegal antiquities market. This has resulted in the rampant destruction of archaeological sites as "grave robbers" hack through ruins in search of pots, compromising our ability to reconstruct what Mimbres life was like 1,000 years ago.

A number of pottery styles were produced during the Mimbres era, but the most famous is a "black-on-white" type – black paint applied over a white slip – that developed out of the Mogollon brownware tradition (Hegmon 2002:329). Hohokam people to the west probably influenced the Mimbres designs (Brody 1977:89; LeBlanc 1989:186), although representational designs also suggest influence from Mesoamerican people. Naturalistic imagery such as rabbits, fish, and birds are complemented by depictions of humans engaged in a variety of activities, from giving birth to beheading one another. More fanciful creatures combining human and animal attributes are also painted on the vessels, including representations of humans wearing masks of the horned serpent, a common Mesoamerican motif (Young 1989). Despite these parallels with nearby traditions, many researchers believe that the development of Mimbres designs was mostly indigenous, with parallels between Mimbres and Mesoamerican iconography largely based on convergent views of the world rather than direct diffusion (e.g., Brody 1977:77–8; Shafer 1999a:104).

As might be expected considering the compelling designs, many studies concentrate on the iconography. In his assessment of over 2,000 motifs, Marc Thompson (2000) concludes that bowls were used in mortuary contexts since supernatural figures and the underworld are frequently depicted. He also suggests that the vessels played roles in rituals, especially those during which myths were narrated. Flower motifs are also painted on many of the vessels, often in combination with other imagery suggestive of the underworld. Kelley Hays-Gilpin and Jane Hill (1999) propose that this imagery is reminiscent of the "Flower World," the place where the deceased go, according to ethnographic accounts from Mesoamerica and the historic Southwest. Another area of special interest in Mimbres iconography is the representation of gender roles (e.g., Munson 2000; Shaffer et al. 1999). Researchers are finding that males are most often portrayed as actively hunting or engaged in ritual activities, while females are represented in more static poses related to child care and domestic tasks. Most of these patterns are intriguing but difficult to assign meaning – for example, women are more often associated with macaw and parrot imagery.

How was Mimbres pottery produced? Archaeologists believe it was made by a relatively small number of part-time specialists, individuals who probably learned the craft from a skilled relative but who spent most of their time engaged in other domestic pursuits (Hegmon 2002:330; Shafer 1999b:128). Many of the vessels are technologically imperfect, indicating that many of the part-time potters were not highly skilled nor were they dedicating all their time to carefully forming the pots. Chemical analyses of the pottery show that production occurred in many if not all of the sizeable villages, with potters drawing upon a wide variety of sources for their raw materials (Creel et al. 2002; Gilman et al. 1994). The consensus is that primarily women constructed the vessels and painted the designs, although an interesting debate on this subject has emerged, including discussions of how the accuracy of birthing scenes on the pottery may or may not indicate which gender painted them (Hegmon and Trevathan 1996; Shaffer et al. 1997).

One reason why Classic Mimbres pottery is so well known is its use as a mortuary offering – the vessels were more or less intact when placed in graves, unlike the discarded and broken materials that archaeologists

4.15 A few Mimbres bowls appear to show ceremonial events, such as this possible processional or dance.

typically find. Unfortunately, the ability to recover whole bowls with their stunning designs makes Mimbres vessels especially valuable on the international antiquities market, even though disturbing cemeteries is now illegal. Adding to the mystique of Mimbres vessels is *how* they were interred: mourners often punched a small "kill" hole through the bottom of the bowl and placed the inverted vessel over the face of the deceased, which some scholars argue was intended to channel the spirit of the dead appropriately (Thompson 2000).

Mimbres bowls were not produced just to be used as mortuary offerings – archaeologists also find them in other contexts, and even vessels used in burials show wear from regular use. Food preparation and serving were likely common tasks in which bowls were used, although some scholars argue that they were especially reserved for ceremonial events (Shafer 1999a:102), a few of which are actually depicted on the pottery (Figure 4.15). Mimbres vessels may have been similar to the "good china" displayed when guests were in town. However, some guests apparently took pottery home as gifts, for items show up in small residences located considerable distances from where they were produced, comprising as much as 10 percent of ceramics recovered in the Chihuahuan Desert

(Creel *et al.* 2002). Steven LeBlanc (2000:43) notes that frequencies of the valuable pots decrease the farther from the Mimbres Valley one goes, a "fall-off" distribution that archaeologists associate with casual exchange from a central source. Despite this low-level trade, Classic Mimbres people imported little pottery from anywhere else, providing an interesting contrast with the pattern of exchange seen at Chaco Canyon, in which everything came into the canyon from distant sources.

The organization of Mimbres society

When looking for clues to Mimbres social and political life, most archaeologists turn to their architecture. LeBlanc (1983), for example, sees each roomblock as the residence for a corporate kin group which worked common fields and pooled its surpluses. A number of scholars (e.g., Shafer 1982) point to the stability of the core rooms in a typical Mimbres roomblock, suggesting that the established membership of the kin group permanently resided there – for up to six generations – while peripheral rooms were added and abandoned as fringe members came and went. This resulted in a large building in which few of the rooms were permanently occupied. One possibility is that these fringe rooms and small, isolated residences were occupied by immigrants whose social and political ties with the village's central kin groups were weak, marginalizing them both socially and spatially. Correlations of dendroclimatological reconstructions with construction sequences show that during good years more people joined the roomblocks, perhaps abandoning their dispersed farmsteads to move on to the better lands surrounding the largest villages (Shafer 1999b). At the NAN Ruin (Figure 4.16), for example, new construction tended to occur after a couple years of good rainfall, and Harry Shafer (1999b:125) suggests that the increased labor pool allowed for both construction and the use of irrigation systems. He further proposes that during bad years, these families, with no claims to the best food-producing lands "owned" by core households, dispersed back to poorer but uncontested farmlands. Some people even may have retreated to the Chihuahuan Desert to live off wild foods.

Some scholars believe that Classic Mimbres villages were divided into two moieties, similar to claims made for late Chaco Canyon social organization. A common pattern, identified by Lekson (1982), is for roomblock clusters to be separated into northern and southern groups. At the handful of villages where macaw remains have been recovered, for example, birds were buried on the north side of the community while only bowls bearing macaw iconography were recovered from southern

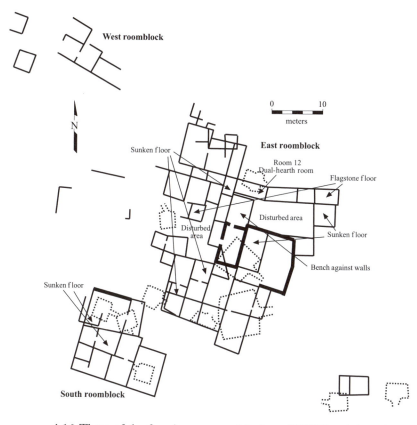

4.16 Three of the four known roomblocks at NAN Ranch have been excavated. The largest, built over earlier pitstructures, includes dual-hearth rooms, flagstone and sunken floors, built-in benches, and a few walls with two or more courses of masonry.

households (Nelson 1999:39). If indeed Mimbres society organized into large moieties, how can this be reconciled with the evidence for small, corporate kin groups with their own dual-hearth ceremonial rooms? Perhaps Mimbres organization was undergoing change from the smaller kin groups of earlier times toward larger social divisions, leaving archaeologists with mixed patterns that are hard to interpret.

How were moiety or community decisions made if society was divided at a number of different levels? Shafer (1999b:123) proposes that public rituals in open plazas helped to organize people in the absence of strong leadership, but how this would actually happen in practice is a mystery – *someone* had to manage the scheduling and preparations for the rituals and guide decision-making in some way. To address the question of Mimbres status and leadership, Gilman (1990) analyzed goods recovered from inhumations and found no evidence of hereditary status differences. Imported valuables and other ornaments do not seem to have been as important to Mimbres people as they were for the Anasazi to the north. Even the nearby turquoise sources were not used very much (Lekson 1999a:67). Perhaps because Mimbres people had fairly direct access to items such as macaws, shell, and copper bells (Creel and McKusick 1994; Wilcox 1999a:116), these goods were not as useful for building status differences, and in fact they may simply have been traded northward to feed the demand by Chacoan people.

Black-on-white bowls, another candidate for an item of value, were present in almost 68 percent of all graves, hardly the proportion expected if the vessels were only used in high-status interments. On the other hand, relatively few people were interred with more than one bowl, and Gilman (1990) notes slight differences in materials associated with different kin groups. Other non-material clues also reveal that not everyone was treated equally in Mimbres society. An inordinate number of eleventh-century burials at NAN Ruin, for example, are inhumations below the floors of dual-hearth ceremonial rooms, but 10 percent of individuals, especially males, were buried outside with few mortuary goods. Another 10 percent of the NAN Ruin burials are cremations placed in plaza areas (Shafer 1999b:123–8). Confounding the picture of mortuary differences is Burial 18 from Old Town, an adult male inhumation in front of an unusual earthen platform that itself was situated between two abandoned great kivas (Creel and Anyon 2003:82–3). These data suggest that the style and location of one's interment might reveal more about status than what one was buried with.

Cremations represent around 1.5 percent of all Classic Mimbres burials and received the most special treatment. Not only was there greater investment in mortuary preparations for these individuals – cremation is more labor-intensive than inhumation – but the interments also included nearly twice the quantities of mortuary goods, including arrowheads, imported obsidian, and multiple bowls (Creel 1989). It is tempting to interpret these cremated individuals as high-status members of Mimbres society. This mortuary treatment became more common in the twelfth century, leading some scholars to suggest that a new religious tradition was emerging, one that increasingly emphasized community-wide ritual events in open plazas (Woodson *et al.* 1999). Perhaps earlier cremations were reserved for practitioners of this new religion. Unfortunately, all that can be concluded from these ambiguous data is that modest social differences were present in Mimbres villages. How this reflects inequities in status or leadership is still a mystery, but the presence of some burials with more elaborate mortuary treatments, as well as their placement in ceremonial locations in specific roomblocks, suggests that individuals in some kin groups were able to achieve higher levels of status (Hegmon 2002:336–7).

Unlike the situation seen on the Colorado Plateau, where Chaco Canyon dominated the human landscape, Mimbres communities were autonomous (Hegmon 2002:337; but see Creel and Anyon 2003). Villages were roughly the same size and spaced evenly along the major drainages. Ties between villages did exist, and both commodities such as pottery and a few exotic items such as macaws were traded. Margaret Nelson (1999:44) suggests that larger villages may have established trading networks with one another to take advantage of environmental variability – surpluses produced by one pueblo might be distributed to others that would then reciprocate later. Archaeologists identify slight differences in ceramic styles produced in each major drainage, and perhaps these variations symbolized membership in specific communities or social groups (Gilman et al. 1994:705–6). Despite these modest differences, relationships between villages seem to have been equitable, with no regional hierarchy across the Mimbres world and no sharp boundaries in the distribution of material culture that might reflect rigid political borders (LeBlanc 2000). If any inequities in the Mimbres region existed, they were between the large aggregated villages and the dispersed and seemingly more marginalized residences that revolved around the core roomblocks (Box 4.4).

The Mimbres tradition contrasts with the Chaco tradition owing to the paucity of social and political differences in the former. Assuming that further archaeological research confirms this pattern, we might ask why fewer inequities emerged among Mimbres people. One potential answer may lie in the context of Mimbres villages. Recall that the working model for the evolution of Chaco Canyon relies upon inequities that arose when people lived on lands with different productive capabilities at the same time that climatic instability challenged farming success. In this context, farmers on the best lands turned their relatively high productivity into social debt and enhanced status, which led to social and political disparities. Mimbres villages, on the other hand, were built in equivalent settings along drainages that were more dependable than the Chaco Wash, arguably making inequities difficult to establish – even though the desire to do so probably existed, particularly among the core-roomblock kin groups. The climate in the Mimbres area was also more favorable for farming compared with the Chacoan experience (Shafer 1999b:124–5), making it difficult to accumulate significant

Box 4.4 Mimbres irrigation and sociopolitical inequity

Archaeologists believe that many Mimbres villages relied upon simple irrigation systems to capture water from the rivers for their crops, as farmers in the area do today. Some estimates suggest that the population size was too large to support without the larger crop yields of irrigation farming (e.g., LeBlanc 1983:154). A few canals have been identified, although associating them with the Mimbres occupation of the area has not been easy (Creel and Anyon 2003:85–6; Shafer 1999a:99). Assuming that the Mimbres people did irrigate their fields, however, has implications for understanding their social and political lives. Even simple irrigation systems provide crop yields that contrast with the returns from rainfall farming, providing opportunities for some social groups to produce surpluses and achieve higher levels of status – they provide for the unequal production that can lead to sociopolitical inequities. Such a scenario is consistent with the evidence for core kin groups that variously attracted socially peripheral residents to their roomblocks.

Irrigation farming also requires a fair degree of management, for people need to be mobilized to confront changes in river flow and to clean out canals. This can promote the emergence of managerial leaders within the social groups engaged in irrigation farming. Whether this happened in the case of the Mimbres is not clear, and certainly the small scale of the canals identified so far did not require a complex managerial bureaucracy to maintain. Another factor complicating the development of inequities based on irrigation farming is the unstable nature of river flows in the Mimbres drainage (Shafer 1999a:99). River discharge can vary more dramatically than rainfall, and in some years irrigation farmers may have been worse off than rainfall farmers, particularly if floods destroyed the gates that connected canals with natural waterways. In the end, farming was probably equally unpredictable for everyone, making it difficult for inequities to grow within and among the Mimbres towns.

social debt or build other inequities, except perhaps between the villages' inhabitants and those more marginal groups living in side canyons or in the Chihuahuan Desert. Even these folk, however, apparently were not beholden to the larger villages – if the situation became uncomfortable, they simply retreated back to their isolated homesteads.

The beginning of the end

In the grand scheme of environmental change in the Southwest, the tenth and eleventh centuries were characterized by decent rainfall for farming societies, as described in chapter 2. Certainly there were numerous ups and downs, and, as discussed in this chapter, this instability probably contributed to the unique developments of Chaco and Mimbres society. Not until the twelfth century did the climate more dramatically worsen. In the Mimbres region, the year AD 1130 was the driest since AD 1035, and although the climate briefly rebounded, an even more devastating drought hit in the late AD 1130s (Hegmon 2002:321; Shafer 1999b:124–5). The next several years were actually quite good, but something about the experiences of the AD 1130s profoundly impacted Mimbres society.

To the north, Chacoan people experienced similar climatic fluctuations (Dean 1992; Grissino-Mayer 1996). After decades of decent conditions for farming in the late AD 1000s, inhabitants of the San Juan Basin were hit by a drought in the last few years of the century. A rebound in the early twelfth century similar to that in the southern Mogollon area lasted for about a decade, but the mid-1100s were particularly dry. Conditions were not as bad as the droughts of earlier centuries, nor were they nearly as severe as what Puebloan people would experience in the late AD 1200s. But it was a sustained drought, lasting a couple of decades, and the conditions stifled developments in Chaco Canyon. A return of modest levels of rainfall in the late AD 1100s was apparently too late to restore the canyon to the preeminence it once enjoyed.

5 The migrations continue: the end of Chaco and Mimbres

According to Hopi oral history, the decadent behavior at *Palatkwapi* was recognized as a problem by both the *kikmongwi*, the village chief, and the clan leaders. Kivas no longer were used for ceremonies and introspection, but instead were filled with men and women playing games. Fields were neglected, and *pahos* were no longer offered to the gods. So the village leaders dressed a young man in a costume to resemble *Tsaveyo*, the fearsome monster with horns, huge eyes, a long jaw filled with sharp teeth, and a huge stone ax. The *Tsaveyo* impersonator admonished the people of the village for their corrupt and evil ways, but everyone laughed at him and returned to the kivas to gamble. Another year passed, and the decadent ways became so pervasive that even the *kikmongwi's* wife succumbed to the temptations. Summoning his nephew, the leader again ordered him to frighten the villagers, which worked so well that they killed and buried him, hoping that this would allow them to return to their gambling. Four days later, however, the sun rose intensely red, and rumbling could be heard in the distance. Soon, rain poured down so fiercely that water gushed out of the fireplaces. And where the *kikmongwi's* nephew was buried, the great water serpent *Balolokong* emerged, thrashing about as people struggled to escape the flood.

The survivors of *Palatkwapi* gathered on the rocks above the ruined village. The leaders said, "Our village is a ruin and cursed place that will be haunted until the end of time by the evil deeds committed there. Again we will journey, each clan on its own migration following the signs that are known to it. Somewhere is a place where our people will find one another again. Let us begin" (Courlander 1971:56–65).

Chaco Canyon in the early twelfth century: down but not out?

Archaeologists are skilled at identifying beginnings. We are not, however, as good at reconstructing endings. When a cultural tradition emerges, we see it in the archaeological record, for people begin building the buildings and making the artifacts that define the new cultural trajectory. But when things end, the picture is more complex. Except in very unusual circumstances, the buildings do not just disappear, and neither do the people. The material culture – the buildings and artifacts – instead may be used differently, while some people may leave, some may stay, and other new folk may enter the scene. The archaeological record becomes messy, requiring all of the skills that archaeologists can muster. The end of the Chaco Anasazi tradition is a good case in point.

Changes in Chaco Canyon

As the AD 1100s began, the nearly continuous great house construction in Chaco Canyon quickly tapered off. At the older great houses, the massive additions typical of the eleventh century ended, with new efforts dedicated to small-scale remodeling, including the addition of narrow arcs of rooms that closed off the plazas (Lekson 1984; Roney 1996; Windes and Ford 1996). Tree-ring dates from Chetro Ketl illustrate this change (Wills 2000:26): between AD 1050 and 1070, around 8,000 imported beams were used for its construction, but in the following years, only 800 more were added. On the other hand, some brand-new great houses were built in the early AD 1100s. Wijiji, a 200-room building resembling earlier great houses, was rapidly assembled between AD 1110 and 1115, while unusual great houses known as "McElmo structures" also were built. Unlike the older great houses built around large plazas and made of finely shaped masonry, McElmo structures are solid blocks of small rooms constructed of roughly pecked stones (Figure 5.1). No great kivas were built alongside McElmo structures – instead, these great houses typically feature a couple of blocked-in kivas hidden deep in the roomblock. These small great houses were comparatively cheap to build, requiring a fraction of the materials and labor that were invested in the plaza-oriented great house–great kiva complexes.

After the AD 1110s, even this reduced level of construction ceased. And these efforts apparently did not pay off, for evidence indicates that the new buildings were not used much. After Wijiji was constructed, for example, it was never occupied, as revealed by the nearly complete absence of any artifacts (Durand 1992). Stephen Lekson (1984), however, proposes that McElmo structures were designed solely for storing surpluses and that therefore no evidence of residential use should be expected. This may be true, for the early AD 1100s were quite good for farming (Sebastian 1992). On the other hand, the construction of these new buildings some distance from the older great houses is curious. One McElmo structure, Tsin Kletzin, is built on the mesa-top opposite Pueblo

5.1 Kin Kletso is typical of great house construction in the early twelfth century. These new great houses are often referred to as "McElmo structures" because their masonry style is reminiscent of stonework seen along McElmo Creek far to the north, above the San Juan River.

Alto, a good hike from any other buildings in the canyon. Its placement, in fact, seems to have been to provide line-of-sight to other great houses, not to facilitate easy storage of surpluses (Lekson 1984:231). Whatever the intended function of these new great houses, most saw limited use.

The end of major construction projects was accompanied by substantial changes in the imported goods coming into Chaco Canyon – and people stopped depositing material on the large canyon middens (Toll 2001). Activity at most older great houses faded around this time. The quantities of ceramics deposited at Una Vida, for example, steadily decreased after AD 1050 (Mathien and Windes 1988), suggesting declining use. Obsidian, a valuable stone material that produces exceptionally sharp edges, no longer was imported to Chaco Canyon as finished tools from outlying communities to the south. Now only raw material entered the canyon, and this came from a source far to the east that Chaco people had to visit themselves (Cameron 2001). Similarly, exotic materials such as turquoise declined in quantity, while a change in the species of shell imported into the canyon suggests that the trade routes used earlier by Chaco people were no longer available (Mathien 1984, 1997). It seems as if most people stopped visiting Chaco Canyon, and the goods they brought – as well as the labor they provided – were no longer available to the canyon's inhabitants.

Not all evidence, however, points to an abrupt end for Chaco Canyon. Instead, some consolidation apparently occurred around the time the McElmo structures were being built (Wills 2000:30). Thomas Windes (1987:403, 2001:43) suggests that people left the more far-flung canyon communities and moved closer to Pueblo Bonito, making it the focal point of all canyon activity. Workshops for producing turquoise goods, for example, occurred in and around Pueblo Bonito (Mathien 2001:106). This concentration of people and activity has led some archaeologists to propose that the early AD 1100s represent the height of Chacoan development, with the physical centralization representing a reconstituted social and political leadership (e.g., Stein and Fowler 1996). Other scholars, however, point to the fading control over resources and labor and suggest that the consolidation was a tyrannical last gasp of a fading system (Sebastian 1992:138).

Life continues outside the canyon

Even as Chaco Canyon's authority was waning in the early AD 1100s, Chacoan influence achieved its greatest extent (Figure 4.7). More than 200 communities located throughout the Colorado Plateau now included their own great houses (Kantner 2003c). Expansion of Chacoan traits particularly pushed far to the north of the central Canyon, where great house construction accelerated at the very end of the AD 1000s and into the early twelfth century. Frequently accompanied by great kivas, great houses were established in communities arrayed along the side drainages feeding the San Juan River. Visitors today can visit Salmon, a large great house located on the San Juan River that was built between AD 1088 and 1106 (Figure 5.2). Even farther to the north, in Sand Canyon, a more modest great house known as Casa Negra was built in a community dating back at least into the tenth century. Several kilometers away, a similar structure was built in the Goodman Point community. A roadway connected these two great houses together (Adler 1994; Varien 1999:147).

Influence from Chaco Canyon was not felt equally everywhere. The Rio Grande drainage to the east, for example, never attracted large numbers of residents, and those people that did live there tended to be fairly mobile (Spielmann 1996). Even here, however, Chaco's reach was felt, especially around the Cerrillos turquoise mines, a likely source for turquoise imported into Chaco Canyon during the eleventh century. Ceramics from

5.2 The Salmon great house was constructed quickly, from AD 1088 to 1106, to include almost 200 rooms in two stories, a large blocked-in kiva, and a great kiva in the plaza area. Later post-Chaco occupants added over a dozen more kivas and remodeled the rooms for domestic use. Most of the excavations at Salmon have been "backfilled" to protect the architecture.

the San Juan Basin as well as local "knock-offs" of Chacoan pottery have been found north of the city of Santa Fe at a site where a great kiva similar to those found in Chaco Canyon was also identified (Stubbs 1954; see also Dick *et al.* 1999:87–9) No great houses have been found, perhaps owing to the transitory nature of Rio Grande basin communities, but

Chaco influenced developments here even as the central canyon began to fall apart.

The influence of Chaco Canyon during the late eleventh and twelfth centuries can be misleading. Certainly, by the first decade of the AD 1100s, "Chacoesque" material culture was seemingly everywhere in the Puebloan world, and many scholars interpret this as meaning that Chaco Canyon controlled these areas (e.g., Lekson 1999a:46–8). In recent years, however, archaeologists have been finding evidence for considerable autonomy in many areas where Chaco's influence was felt. John Roney (1996:162) describes how pottery from Cebolleta Mesa – an area south of Chaco Canyon where several great houses were built – reveals influence from Chaco while also reflecting unique local styles, indicating that the most meaningful political systems were small and localized. A study of trace elements in materials used to produce pottery on either side of Lobo Mesa shows that few vessels moved between the San Juan Basin and areas to the south (Kantner et al. 2000). And to the north of Chaco, Mark Varien (1999:174–7) demonstrates considerable variability in the spatial relationships between great houses and associated residential clusters, with diverse patterns among the many great house communities. These studies indicate that at a time when Chaco's influence was at its greatest extent, most areas were autonomous, emphasizing social and political relationships with their immediate neighbors rather than strong bonds with Chaco Canyon (Kantner 1996; Wilcox 1996).

The farther one goes from Chaco Canyon at the turn of the twelfth century, the weaker the evidence of direct influence. Around Chinle Wash and Black Mesa in what is now Arizona, unusual structures were built that superficially resemble great houses simply because they differ from typical domestic architecture. Their small size, however, and the absence of Chacoan masonry styles or blocked-in kivas, have led many archaeologists to refer to them as "great houselets" or "good houses" – they do not quite qualify to be *great* houses (Figure 5.3). One example, West Great Houselet, contains only five rooms, although it is made of substantial masonry, surrounded by a berm, and accessed by a roadway (Gilpin 1995). Scholars argue that people living in this region simply adopted some styles from Chaco Canyon, perhaps having heard stories about the pilgrimage center that were passed from village to village (Adams 1996; Dean 1996b). Even the Mimbres area far to the south may have been impacted by Chaco – Lekson (1999a:42–3) claims that structures like Woodrow Ruin were great houses made of cobbles rather than the finely shaped sandstone used in the north. In all of these cases, the great-house-like structures almost certainly did not symbolize direct connection with

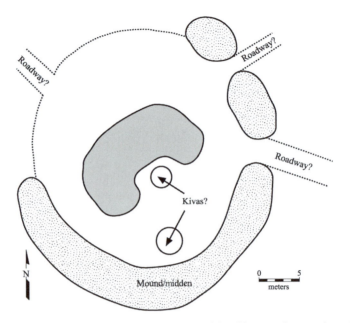

5.3 Small great houses lacking many of the Chacoan features have been referred to as "good houses." Navajo North, illustrated here, does feature possible roadways and encircling mounds, but the "good house" is small, lacks a second story, and has no blocked-in kivas.

Chaco Canyon, nor did they necessarily reflect the same cultural processes that were impacting the canyon.

Why would people living in distant areas far from Chaco Canyon adopt Chacoan features in the first place? Sarah Herr's research (2001; Mills *et al.* 1999) along the Mogollon Rim provides some insight into this issue. Great houses were never built there, but residents constructed great kivas in the early AD 1100s. Many of these great kivas are exceptionally large, up to 25 m in diameter, and at least some were unroofed. A common feature is that these great kivas were entered along a wide ramp (Figure 5.4), differing considerably from Chaco Canyon great kivas that had restricted entrances through antechambers. The overall impression is that Mogollon Rim people used the idea of a Chacoan great kiva, but invested less labor and provided greater public access to their interior spaces. Herr (2001:94) suggests that the structures were built to host ceremonies that increased the status of the builders and attracted valuable migrant labor, in a manner similar to how great houses in Chaco Canyon probably were used. In other words, Mogollon Rim great kivas

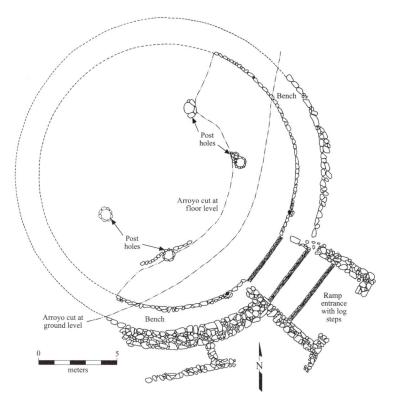

5.4 The great kiva at Tla Kii Pueblo was probably constructed and used in the first few decades of the AD 1100s. It was entered by a wide stairway and may have been only partially roofed, providing ready access and views to activities occurring within.

served in local social and political machinations, borrowing some of the styles and perhaps aspects of the ceremonies found in Chaco Canyon to attract people familiar with these symbols. But the structures were also adapted to fit the local sociopolitical landscape, including an emphasis on public space rather than the restricted space of great houses. Herr (2001) interestingly suggests that these great kivas were inspired by an influx of immigrants coming from areas close to Chaco Canyon – people who knew the grandeur of Chaco – but she also notes that there is no evidence that people in the area regularly interacted with the influential canyon.

While people in distant regions continued to use knowledge of Chaco Canyon to serve local ends, areas closer to the canyon ran into trouble by

5.5 The tower kiva at Kin Ya'a still stands two stories above the surrounding great house ruins; the entire structure once stood four stories tall. Although the great house itself may have been built as early as the AD 1020s, tree-ring dates from the tower kiva suggest that it was built in the AD 1080s.

the late AD 1000s. In Muddy Water, a large community at the southern edge of the San Juan Basin, a large great house was abandoned and two small ones were built in its place. John Kantner (1996) interprets this as evidence for increasing factionalism between disparate social elements. Not long after, the community was largely abandoned. A few kilometers away, one of the best-known outlying great houses, Kin Ya'a, was modified to include a tower kiva projecting above the rest of the structure (Figure 5.5). Once thought to have facilitated regional communication, a recent study suggests that the feature was built so that more people could see the great house (Kantner and Hobgood 2003). The structure was burned and the great house abandoned not long after. But why? As described in the previous chapter, many communities within the San Juan Basin were closely tied to Chaco Canyon, with local leaders probably legitimizing their own status through their relationships with canyon leaders. It is therefore not surprising that signs of dissent in these outlying communities – including burning great houses, the symbols of Chaco – occurred at the same time that imports into the canyon were waning and its residents entrenched themselves around Pueblo Bonito.

Meanwhile, up in the San Juan River drainage, a new great house was built that rivaled the scale of architecture seen in Chaco Canyon. Today, the ruins are known as "Aztec," since nineteenth-century Anglo-European visitors thought they were too monumental to have been built by Southwestern Indians. As many as six great houses were ultimately built here. One of the buildings, known as Aztec East, is mostly unexcavated and not well known, but its tree-ring dates are spread from the early to mid-1200s, long after Chaco Canyon was abandoned. Its neighbor, Aztec West, was fully excavated and can be visited today (Figure 5.6). Containing 437 rooms arrayed around a plaza and an impressive great kiva, Aztec West was built rapidly in two construction episodes in AD 1113 and 1119 (Windes and McKenna 2001). Containing substantial quantities of imports and rich burials, Aztec West has no peers among the over 200 outlying great houses recorded so far. Its size, layout, and masonry work make it a nearly perfect replica of the largest Chaco Canyon great houses, but it is associated with additional features not typically found in the canyon, including an unusual "tri-wall structure" (Box 5.1). It is unlikely to be a coincidence that the Aztec complex appears in the Mesa Verde region at the same time that Chaco Canyon's preeminence was fading.

So, what did happen to Chaco Canyon?

The picture presented so far shows the once-influential Chaco Canyon in a state of crisis by the early AD 1100s. What could possibly have happened to undermine this magnificent center? Most explanations turn to the ever-important climatic conditions that impacted the canyon, with the most compelling scenarios proposing a combination of human-induced and natural environmental changes as the reason for Chaco's demise. Analysis of packrat middens, for example, reveals that over the course of Chaco Canyon's development, the surrounding landscape was largely denuded, with most woodland gone by the AD 1100s (Kohler 1992b). It is not hard to imagine why: Chaco was a busy place. Great volumes of trees, brush, and even grasses were needed for roofing the canyon architecture. The constant need for firewood had an astounding impact as well, for hundreds of families for over 200 years cooked and kept themselves warm. Studies of firewood found in great houses show an increasing use of inferior cottonwood and ponderosa pine from distant sources (Windes and Ford 1996; Windes and McKenna 2001). These

5.6 The architecture of Aztec West is identical in mass and scale to the largest great houses in Chaco Canyon. It includes intriguing details, such as this band of green stone that – as at all great houses – would have been covered by adobe plaster, hiding the intricate masonry work from view.

Box 5.1   What is a "tri-wall structure"?

The Hubbard Site, situated 60 m from the Aztec West great house, is one of the best-known tri-wall structures (Figure 5.7). Built on top of older residences and a small kiva that had been dismantled, the Hubbard tri-wall consists of a small, underground kiva surrounded by twenty-two small masonry rooms arrayed in two concentric rows. Because of the site's complex history, and because the tri-wall structure was reoccupied later in time, archaeologists disagree as to when the Hubbard tri-wall was built. The original assessments placed its construction after AD 1150, but Lekson's reanalysis (1983) suggested an earlier date, perhaps the first decade of the twelfth century.

A second unexcavated tri-wall structure lies between the Aztec West and Aztec East great houses, and other tri-wall structures – as well as similar "bi-wall" structures – are scattered across the Puebloan world (Lekson 1983). A single tri-wall was built at Pueblo del Arroyo, a great house located near Pueblo Bonito in Chaco Canyon. A tree-ring date of AD 1109 makes it perhaps earlier than its northern counterparts. At this tri-wall structure, however, the central space was not a kiva, but instead was a space paved with sandstone slabs. All of the surrounding rooms were devoid of any features. At some point, this tri-wall structure was razed (Lekson 1984:223).

How were these unusual structures used? Various ideas have been proposed, including the possibility that they were residences for priestly leaders. Unfortunately, because they were reoccupied in some cases and destroyed in others, establishing their function will probably require new excavations. One intriguing aspect of the tri-wall structures, however, is their accessibility – while rooms in each concentric ring opened into one another, doorways connecting rings to one another are rare. And the central spaces had no obvious means of access. Like the McElmo structures, the tri-wall structures reflect a trend at the end of the Chaco era toward increasingly restricted access to sacred spaces.

human-induced changes to the landscape no doubt made life increasingly difficult in Chaco Canyon.

Many archaeologists also point to the changing climatic conditions of the early AD 1100s. As described in chapter 2, a series of dry years hit at the turn of the century, with the first occurring in the AD 1090s, followed by a sustained drought around AD 1130 that lasted at least two decades (Grissino-Mayer 1996). What is most interesting about this sequence is

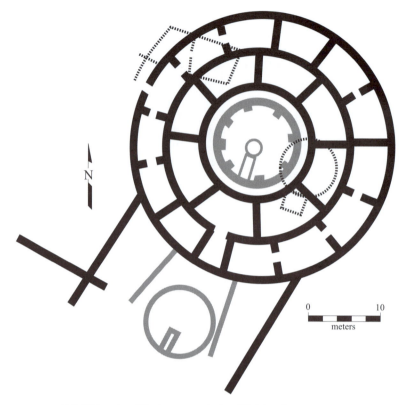

5.7 This simplified map of the Hubbard tri-wall kiva shows the earlier adobe household (dashed lines), which was razed when the above-ground tri-wall architecture was built. The gray walls represent subterranean kiva spaces.

that the beginning of Chaco's demise is most closely correlated with the earlier drought, one that was minor compared to prior droughts in the canyon and one that was followed by a nice rebound in precipitation. Even the poor conditions of the AD 1130s were not unprecedented – a similar drought had hit the area at the turn of the eleventh century. This suggests that climate changes do not tell the whole story of what happened to the Chaco Anasazi.

As proposed in the last chapter, Chaco Canyon emerged as a prominent pilgrimage center that largely developed and was run by leaders whose status was tied to their kin group's economic advantages as well as their own religious authority. As their influence evolved and expanded beyond the canyon's walls, religious success was the primary resource fueling Chaco's growth – the ceremonial function of great houses and the ideologically charged artifacts found in these structures underscore this conclusion. For people across the Southwest, the primary concern was the weather, and no doubt Chaco's religious authority was tied to the benign conditions of the tenth and eleventh centuries. Leaders probably sustained their positions based on their perceived influence on climate and their esoteric knowledge and control of the ritual calendar (Malville 1994; Reyman 1987). Occasional short-lived droughts not only fueled economic inequities within the canyon, but could have played to the advantage of the canyon's leaders since good conditions always quickly returned.

The droughts at the turn of the twelfth century occurred within this context. While relatively minor, dry conditions like those of the AD 1090s had not been experienced in a couple of generations. The drought also followed upon the heels of one of the most ambitious construction phases seen in Chaco Canyon, with not only an expansion of most great houses but also the establishment of many of the major roadways. It was also a time when the canyon needed more and more imported resources as its inhabitants placed increasing demands on the local environment. In other words, just as Chaco Canyon was extracting more labor and goods from people living in outlying areas, the drought hit. For a sociopolitical system built on religious influence over the climate, the timing of the AD 1090s drought could not have been worse. It is no coincidence that this marks a cessation in construction and a decline in canyon imports. And the effect snowballed. Dean Saitta (2000:159), for example, points out that many of the exotic goods brought to the canyon probably were distributed by Chaco's leaders as payments to ensure the loyalty of allies both inside and outside of the canyon. The loss of these imports ended the distribution of these gifts as well as cutting off access to items such as macaw feathers and turquoise that served as material symbols of Chaco's authority.

For the permanent residents of Chaco Canyon, who were dependent on the utilitarian materials – and probably even food – brought to the canyon by pilgrims, the waning authority of their pilgrimage center was devastating. Disgruntlement with religious authorities of Chaco Canyon may even have led to the suspected assassination victim whose ornate burial was found in Pueblo Bonito, although the timing of this burial is poorly understood (Akins 2001). Researchers have also identified other cases of unusually violent deaths that occurred around this time (e.g., Billman *et al.* 2000; LeBlanc 1999, 2000; Turner and Turner 1999). While most of these are not from Chaco Canyon, they reveal unrest that emerged as the era of "Pax Chaco" ended (Box 5.2).

Box 5.2   Cannibalism and Chaco Canyon

In 1999, Christy and Jacqueline Turner published a widely read book summarizing two decades of research on highly fragmentary human remains recovered from the Puebloan Southwest. Based on forensic analyses, they conclude that the remains exhibit a combination of systematic bone breakage, cut marks made by stone knives, and intentional burning that suggests that the individuals had been cannibalized. Brian Billman and his colleagues (2000) report a similarly fragmented assemblage of human bones associated with preserved human fecal matter containing human proteins – proteins that only could have got there through the ingestion of human muscle.

Although the Turners' best-documented cases, as well as the site examined by Billman and his colleagues, were not from Chaco Canyon, most are from late in the Chaco era (see also LeBlanc 1999, 2000). This led the Turners to suggest that Chaco Canyon was emerging as the center of a new cannibalistic cult, perhaps introduced by Mesoamerican immigrants. In contrast, other scholars argue that these cases of cannibalism were the result of increasing starvation caused by drought in the early AD 1100s (White 1992).

In a reanalysis of most earlier work on Puebloan cannibalism, Kantner (1999b) comes to a different conclusion. Noting the rarity of these violent acts as well as their increasing frequency toward the end of the Chaco era, he argues that these were politically motivated episodes of extreme vitriol. He proposes that the highly charged political atmosphere at the end of the Chaco era resulted in factional violence that included excessive mutilation – and perhaps the rare act of cannibalism – intended to influence local social and political conflicts. Kantner argues that as the Chacoan belief system was challenged, those who had benefited from it either engaged in excessive violence in a last gasp attempt to maintain their status, or themselves were victims of violence as disgruntled members of society attempted to overturn the old system. In the final analysis, such behavior was rare and short-lived – and still today, Pueblo people consider only the most evil witches to be capable of such violence, and they reserve severe punishments for such witches in case they should ever appear again (Darling 1998:737).

When climatic conditions improved in the AD 1110s, Chaco Canyon may have tried to reassert its authority. This is the time when the smaller and boxy McElmo structures were built. Requiring less labor to build, these were probably a response to the loss of pilgrim labor. Some scholars, however, note that the McElmo structures – especially the masonry work – are reminiscent of an architectural style from the Mesa Verde region (e.g., Vivian and Mathews 1965). One possibility is that Chaco's attempted resurgence focused on influencing people in this area, which until then had not contributed much material to Chaco's cause. Ceramic evidence does show an increase in imports from the north in the AD 1100s (Toll 1991), and a new ceramic style exhibiting the carbon paint and designs of the Mesa Verde area appeared in the canyon. Chaco's leaders may have been reaching out to the last people who could save them.

But Chaco Canyon's magic had been irreparably undermined. And people, just as fickle then as they are today, turned their attentions elsewhere. David Wilcox (1999a) suggests that, by the late eleventh century, competing political systems emerged in outlying areas. Perhaps once allied with Chaco Canyon's leaders and locally empowered by such connections, these polities eventually may have asserted their autonomy and competed to draw the attention of the Puebloan populace. The violence referred to above perhaps was stimulated by this competition. The most compelling candidate for one of these new political centers is Aztec, as previously described. Lekson (1999a) goes so far as to propose that it was built by people who abandoned Chaco Canyon and moved north to find greener pastures – both literally and figuratively. Unfortunately, little convincing evidence for the existence of separate polities during the late Chaco era or the migration of people from Chaco to Aztec currently exists, although this is a promising area for future research (Wilcox 1999a; and see Kantner 1997).

The last construction beam used in Pueblo Bonito was cut in AD 1129 (Windes and Ford 1996), the last piece of datable firewood in Pueblo Alto was collected in AD 1132 (Windes 1987:213), and the last fire was burned in Pueblo del Arroyo in the mid-1100s (Lekson 1984:223). The more sustained drought beginning at this time was the final *coup de grâce* for Chaco. The era of great house construction in the San Juan Basin was over, and the exodus from Chaco Canyon accelerated. Not everyone left right away, however. At least some "small houses" were used well into the middle of the twelfth century. Excavations at the Eleventh Hour Site, located near Fajada Butte, exposed a residence established in the AD 900s that was occupied on and off until the mid-1100s (Mathien 1991). At that point, however, even this structure was abandoned.

Mimbres at the turn of the century: abandonment or mobility?

The brief span of time from about AD 1120 to 1150 has been the subject of debate among archaeologists working in the southern Mogollon Highlands (e.g., Creel 1999:107; Hegmon 2002:327–8). Some scholars argue that the Mimbres tradition collapsed and the area was abandoned, not unlike what was happening at the same time in the San Juan Basin (e.g., Shafer 1999b). An alternative view is that the Mimbres people never left but instead underwent a significant cultural transformation that makes it seem as if they disappeared (e.g., Nelson 1999). The conflicting opinions are largely based on different ways that the evidence is interpreted – everyone recognizes the substantial changes in Mimbres material culture during the twelfth century but, as in the case of Chaco Canyon, archaeologists are finding that reconstructing the end of this cultural tradition is much more challenging than identifying its origins.

The end of Mimbres villages

In technical terms, the early AD 1100s marks the end of the "Classic Mimbres" period, described in the last chapter, and the beginning of the "Postclassic" period (Hegmon 2002:312–13). This transition is marked by notable settlement pattern changes, the most significant of which is the apparent depopulation of the big towns, especially those in the Mimbres Valley. People left the towns fairly rapidly, perhaps on the order of a single generation, with higher-elevation towns vacated first. The large roomblocks in the lower Mimbres drainage, however, experienced a surge in occupation early in this period, perhaps filling with immigrants descending from upper valleys. This growth was temporary, and by the middle of the twelfth century, even populations in these towns were decreasing (Creel 1999:118–19).

Until recently, debate revolved around the degree to which Mimbres towns were fully abandoned. Harry Shafer (1999b) and LeBlanc (1989) argued for an abrupt exodus during which the Mimbres area was vacated, only to be reoccupied fifty to seventy-five years later by people from a different cultural tradition. Both scholars pointed to the disappearance of the Classic Mimbres black-on-white pottery and related mortuary behaviors. Whereas a few cremations received inordinately favorable treatment before about AD 1100, the pattern was reversed in the twelfth century, with inhumations receiving elaborate mortuary treatment and cremations becoming more widespread (Woodson et al. 1999:75–7). Later occupants of the area also did not build large masonry roomblocks but

---

Box 5.3   Dental evidence and the fate of the Mimbres

One method to reconstruct pre-Contact relationships – including migrations – is to compare skeletal populations to determine how closely related they are to one another. Osteologists focus their analyses on distinctive skeletal traits that are strongly shaped by genes and relatively unaffected by environment. Human dentition offers a number of such characteristics, including the number of cusps and roots found on molars and the shape of incisors.

One such study, conducted by Turner (1993, 1999), examined twenty-nine dental traits on over 4,600 skeletal remains from seventy-five different living and pre-Contact populations in the American Southwest, including groups living on the fringes of the Mesoamerican world to the south. One of the many questions that Turner addressed with these data was whether Mimbres people were more closely related to groups farther south in what is now Mexico, or whether they were biologically affiliated with people living to the northwest, along the Mogollon Rim. His results showed that the Mimbres dentition at NAN Ranch was most closely related to the dentition of remains from the southern Sonoran and Chihuahuan Deserts, including those recovered from the important center of Casas Grandes. Because the Mimbres dentition was compared primarily with groups from later in time, the results of Turner's analysis may indicate that as the Mimbres tradition faded, at least some people moved toward the south – where they had pre-existing cultural and perhaps kinship connections – and contributed to the emergence of the Casas Grandes trading center.

---

instead favored architecture made of coursed adobe mud. Proponents of abandonment proposed that the Mimbres area was used occasionally by Jornada people moving up from the Chihuahuan Desert to live temporarily on land vacated by Mimbres people. They attributed any residual Mimbres patterns to this short-term sedentism by people who long had been influenced by the neighboring Mimbres tradition. But they argued that the vast majority of Mimbres people moved away, probably to the southern deserts (Box 5.3).

In the last few years, several archaeologists have argued convincingly against large-scale abandonment of the Mimbres region (e.g., Creel 1999; Hegmon et al. 1999; Nelson 1999; Nelson and Hegmon 2001; Wilcox 1999a:122). They instead argue that people became more mobile, with most families leaving large villages and moving frequently within and between the valleys draining the southern Mogollon Highlands (e.g., Nelson and Anyon 1996). To support this position, they emphasize the evidence for continuity. At NAN Ruin, for example, artifacts representing both the Mimbres and Postclassic traditions are intermingled in contexts dating to around AD 1125. Similar mixing is found elsewhere, including at Galaz where Postclassic pottery is found in mortuary contexts that are otherwise identical to Classic Mimbres burials – the bowls are even "killed" in the same way. Many of the cultural traits associated with the Postclassic actually do have precedents earlier in the Mimbres era, including the coursed adobe building technique, which is occasionally found in structures dating as far back as AD 900 (Creel 1999:116). Advocates of continuity acknowledge that substantial cultural changes did take place during the Classic Mimbres to Postclassic transition, but that the new traditions emerged among Mimbres people rather than being introduced by new immigrants filling the voids left by regional abandonment.

Recent archaeological work on some of the smaller architectural features in the Mimbres region supports the idea of continuity. Margaret Nelson and Michelle Hegmon (2001; Nelson 1999), for example, examined some of the "fieldhouses" in the eastern Mimbres region and identified evidence for uninterrupted use. During the Classic Mimbres period, these diminutive structures with few domestic features were built around the big towns and used as temporary shelters near horticultural fields as well as physical symbols of claims over those lands (e.g., Kohler 1992a). During the early to mid-twelfth century, many fieldhouses were expanded into residential hamlets and occupied on a more permanent basis (Figure 5.8). Because the fieldhouses were remodeled while still standing, and because no break in their deposits can be identified, Nelson and Hegmon (2001:229–30; Nelson 1999:139) argue that people were moving out of Mimbres towns and into these expanded hamlets. Here they focused on farming maize and gathering immediately available resources, occasionally moving to other hamlets to take advantage of new opportunities. In many ways, the Mimbres turned to the strategy of mobility that had served their pithouse-dwelling ancestors so well.

But why leave the towns?

No matter which model for the end of Classic Mimbres one supports, clearly substantial changes did occur. By the mid-1100s, the landscape was no longer dominated by aggregated villages consisting of large roomblocks and surrounded by a network of ephemeral fieldhouses.

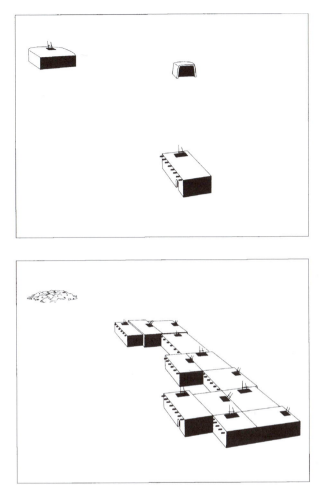

5.8 As illustrated in this artist's reconstruction, many Classic Mimbres fieldhouses were expanded for more substantial domestic use during the Postclassic period.

Instead, the sizeable villages were largely if not entirely abandoned, and life in the Mimbres area revolved around scattered small hamlets occupied by residentially mobile farmer-foragers. The question is, "why such a radical change?"

For the Mimbres, just as for Chaco Canyon, the usual suspect implicated for culture change is the challenging climate. The end of the eleventh century was marked by increasing instability in the pattern of rainfall, and Nelson (1999:41) points to evidence that people were already relying on an increasing diversity of wild plants and animals as the richer floodplains became overstressed. Although adequate precipitation continued into the early AD 1100s, the year AD 1130 was quite bad, and it was the harbinger of a more sustained drought at the end of the decade (Hegmon 2002:321; Shafer 1999b). For most minor dry spells, Mimbres people could rely on the rivers, perhaps digging their irrigation canals a bit deeper to accommodate dropping water levels. A prolonged drought, however, was more of a problem. And, to make matters worse, the one at the end of the AD 1130s occurred at a time of rapid population growth, which Mimbres people were responding to by clearing more land for fields, including marginal lands farther from the rivers (LeBlanc 1989; Minnis 1985). Cultivating more land made erosion more of a problem, further exacerbating the already tenuous situation.

Recall that the large Mimbres towns grew around core households during good times but that many residents dispersed when the climate worsened or when sociopolitical conditions became untenable for the more marginal families who depended on the core families for access to land. This pattern resulted in a continual ebb and flow of people moving into and out of the roomblocks. With the sustained drought of the mid-1100s, however, emigration from the major towns persisted. Hegmon and her colleagues (1998:148) propose that these conditions led to increasingly stringent social control; at the same time, the sustained environmental crisis probably undermined the strength of ancestral ties to the land that underlay the core groups' authority and status (Shafer 1999b:131). The resulting collapse of town organization in turn jeopardized region-wide relationships that once allowed people to share food during minor crises (Nelson 1999). As these networks fell apart, people could not rely on distant alliances or easily move long distances, so they instead scattered near the increasingly vacated towns (Nelson 1999:44–5). Shafer argues that this led to the end of the black-on-white pottery tradition and some of the accompanying mortuary traditions.

The evidence reveals that climate change was an important component but not solely responsible for the end of the Mimbres tradition. Creel (1999:119) notes that some of the depopulations, such as in towns of the upper Mimbres Valley, do not have clear roots in the drought since those areas remained wet enough to sustain the same horticultural lifestyle. But these towns were largely vacated, never to be resettled again. One possibility is that people moved to lower elevations where increasingly valuable cotton crops grew better (LeBlanc 1983). In her discussion of textiles in the Southwest, Lynn Teague (2000:433–8) proposes that, after AD 1100, status became associated with sleeveless cotton shirts

5.9 This representation on a Mimbres bowl appears to show a woman wearing a sleeveless cotton tunic. The labor investment in cotton fabrics suggests not only that they were used in ceremonial contexts, but also that they served as a display of wealth.

that required the skill and labor of a specialized craftsperson to produce (Figure 5.9). Cotton clothing is portrayed in iconography showing that it was used during ceremonies, and it also is recovered in archaeological contexts suggesting that it was openly displayed by higher-status individuals, perhaps by religious authorities from those core families which controlled cotton-producing lands.

As in Chaco Canyon, cultural developments in the southern Mogollon Highlands apparently had stimulated early stages of social and political inequities by the turn of the twelfth century. Mimbres towns were established around core families, and it seems likely that their status influenced the growth of roomblocks and the accompanying material culture. In this context, an extended drought was a major crisis, not so much for the people – there is no evidence for a massive famine – but rather for the sustainability of a cultural tradition increasingly rooted in differences of status and authority. Those individuals enjoying higher status probably suffered the most radical change to their way of life. They may have hung around the Mimbres towns longer, but their authority and ability to attract labor for farming and for ceremonies was probably at an end. A sign of this change is the move away from exclusive cremations with comparatively elaborate mortuary treatments toward a more equitable pattern in which 25 percent of the deceased were cremated and inhumations had only a slight edge in quantities of burial goods (Woodson *et al.* 1999:74–7).

The late AD 1100s

Archaeologists are often asked what mysteries of Puebloan history still remain unsolved. To most casual observers of Southwest archaeology, it appears as if every inch of the region has been investigated, and they wonder how it could be possible for any questions to be unanswered. Most archaeologists, however, will point out that "the more you know, the more you realize you don't know." This is especially true for the period from AD 1150 to 1250, the era immediately following the collapse of the Chaco and Mimbres traditions when Puebloan people were moving frequently – perhaps migrating vast distances, merging with other groups, and adopting and developing a variety of cultural traits. For archaeologists, such moving targets are difficult to deal with, but it makes for exciting and challenging research.

Picking up the pieces after Chaco

Although popular accounts of Chaco Canyon speak of the "disappearance of the Anasazi," people did come back after the mid-1100s drought ended (Mathien 1991:343–5). Who they were is unclear, although the artifacts they left behind are most similar to the material culture of the Mesa Verde area. What is known is that they moved into abandoned Chaco-era buildings, especially great houses, remodeling them to serve residential functions. The new residents added walls to subdivide overly large rooms, put in new doors and sealed old ones, and built hearths and other domestic features (Roney 1996:156; Wilcox 1999a:120–1). Some of the old rooms were used for depositing trash and burials. Blocked-in kivas were remodeled to reflect new styles, while additional kivas were placed outside of the great houses. Even the Eleventh Hour Site, the small house described earlier, was reoccupied by a family or two who buried four of their members and left behind pottery decorated with designs commonly found to the north (Mathien 1991).

Elsewhere in the San Juan Basin, people took refuge in the few well-watered refuges available, including on Chaco Mesa east of the central canyon. Most communities that had arisen and thrived in the shadow of Chaco Canyon, such as Muddy Water and Kin Ya'a, were abandoned and never again reoccupied until Athapaskan people moved in hundreds of years later (Roney 1996). Other great house communities farther from Chaco experienced a more gradual decline. At the Guadalupe community, for example, the number of domestic structures decreased gradually throughout the twelfth century (Durand and Durand 2000). This was accompanied by a decrease in the quality of locally made pottery as well as a loss of stylistic cohesion – in other words, pottery was increasingly just a container rather than a symbol of status or identity to be proudly displayed during feasts and ceremonies. The great house itself was remodeled for domestic use (Figure 5.10), a pattern seen in many of the old great house communities outside of Chaco Canyon (Pippin 1987; see also Adler and Varien 1994:88).

Meanwhile, outside the San Juan Basin, great house communities once influenced by Chaco Canyon began to follow divergent paths. The new sociocultural patterns that emerged are so distinctive that Lekson (1999a:19) calls this a period of "Balkanization," with the development of numerous independent polities that may or may not have been on friendly terms with one another. Communities whose original connections with Chaco were weak persevered relatively unscathed, especially those in moister locations where they could ride out the mid-twelfth-century drought. In many of these villages, populations actually increased, probably as groups abandoning the San Juan Basin sought refuge in higher elevations with more rainfall. The same process probably led to the formation of new villages, such as those south of Guadalupe that started appearing in the AD 1150s. Interestingly, structures similar to great houses were constructed in these new communities, but unlike their Chacoan predecessors, they were apparently residential (Roney 1996:148). A similar trend occurred in the Cibola area around the modern Pueblo of Zuni. There, Chaco-era great houses were abandoned, but residents built new ones within elaborate landscapes composed of earthworks, great kivas, and other unusual features (Figure 5.11). Roadways often connected these new community centers with their abandoned predecessors (Kintigh 1996; Kintigh et al. 1996; Stein and Fowler 1996). Was this an attempt to draw upon the authority of the older Chaco religion, or could this even represent the movement of people from Chaco

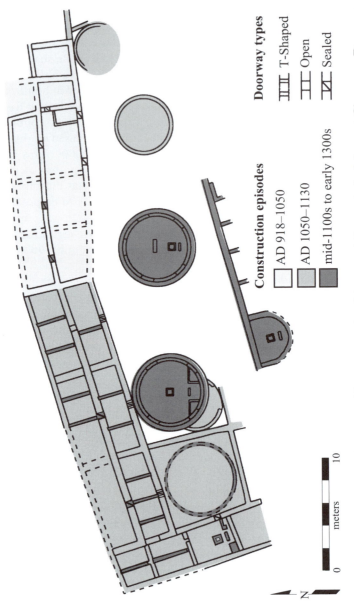

Construction episodes

AD 918–1050

AD 1050–1130

mid-1100s to early 1300s

Doorway types

T-Shaped

Open

Sealed

N

0   10

meters

5.10 The Guadalupe great house provides an example of the remodeling typical of the post-Chaco era. Doorways were filled, new dividing walls constructed, and additional kiva spaces added, and a wide variety of storage bins, hearths, and niches were built into the rooms.

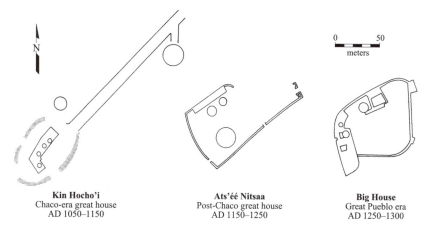

Kin Hocho'i
Chaco-era great house
AD 1050–1150

Ats'éé Nitsaa
Post-Chaco great house
AD 1150–1250

Big House
Great Pueblo era
AD 1250–1300

5.11 In Manuelito Canyon, located in the Cibola region, the Chaco-era great house was vacated in the mid-twelfth century and Ats'éé Nitsaa was constructed a few kilometers away. The canyon's residents built a roadway to connect the two structures. Later, Big House was built even farther up the canyon.

Canyon into the Cibola area, where they tried to regain the glory of the eleventh century? Research on these questions is just beginning.

Although "Chacoesque" architecture continued to be built in areas far removed from Chaco Canyon, the structures were changed in ways that reflect not just a loss of influence but perhaps an intentional reaction against Chaco. The use of ceremonial features accessible by a larger public, for example, becomes widespread. This includes the construction of enormous unroofed kivas that are reminiscent of amphitheaters. Keith Kintigh (1994) identifies them in the Cibola area, where they measure up to 33 m across and are built alongside post-Chaco "great houses." Far to the north, in the Mesa Verde region, two large circular enclosures were built in the Sand Canyon and Goodman Point communities (Adler 1994:99). Kintigh (1996:132) notes that "not coincidentally, these oversized, unroofed great kivas were constructed in such a way that ritual events taking place within them could have been witnessed by a much larger number of people than could have been accommodated in the largest Chacoan great kivas." The concern seems to have been to ensure that the entire community could access and view all activities taking place within the ceremonial precincts. Even the inequities in access to turquoise and other ideologically charged imports appear to ameliorate in most areas during the post-Chaco period (Kantner 2003a).

5.12 The architecture of Wupatki is not unlike the great houses of the earlier Chaco era. And like the great houses of Chaco Canyon, Wupatki was able to attract considerable quantities of exotic trade items, including over forty macaws, the largest concentration found north of Casas Grandes.

Kintigh (1996) proposes that the communities of the late twelfth century were largely self-sufficient, building check dams, reservoirs, and canals that allowed them to maximize their farming pursuits. This helped communities maintain a fair degree of autonomy, and larger villages may have even emerged as the centers of "peer polities," small political entities that competed with similarly sized neighbors for status and resources. These arguments are supported by a study by Eric Blinman and Dean Wilson (1993) that shows an overall decrease in long-distance exchange and a corresponding focus on interaction with immediate neighbors. Unfortunately, little is known about the organization of these late twelfth-century communities, such as whether relationships were structured around moieties or smaller kin groups, or whether inequities in decision-making or wealth were present.

Wupatki, a fascinating community found far to the west of Chaco Canyon, provides some insight into the unique developments of the late twelfth century (Figure 5.12). Located in Arizona near the modern town of Flagstaff, this community emerged in the middle of the AD 1100s and became the center of a small political system. Developments at Wupatki

Box 5.4   Who were the Sinagua?

The Sinagua tradition emerged in a fairly small region centered on the modern town of Flagstaff, Arizona, situated between Puebloan populations to the east and Hohokam groups living to the south. The development of the Sinagua reveals a diversity of influences. They made brownware pottery using a paddle-and-anvil technique reminiscent of the Hohokam ceramic tradition, while their pithouses were similar to those made by Mogollon groups to the southeast. Living on a mixture of cultivated and wild foods, the Sinagua also traded with other Puebloan people and with Hohokam groups. Sinagua villages were modest in size, but some centered on unusually large pitstructures that probably accommodated community-wide events.

After Sunset Crater erupted, the Sinagua tradition experienced changes that archaeologists continue to debate. Some scholars propose that immigrants flowed into the area, introducing new traditions and ideas, from Hohokam ballcourts to Puebloan masonry architecture. The attraction may have been the improved farming conditions made possible by volcanic ash deposits, or perhaps immigrants regarded the volcano as an incredible supernatural force whose power they sought (Reid and Whittlesey 1997:217). Peter Pilles (1996), in contrast, argues that it was not immigrants that drove the cultural changes in the Sinagua region, but rather an increase in external trade and interaction. Perhaps improved farming techniques combined with the volcanic mulches to generate unprecedented surpluses – and eventually allow the cultivation of cotton (e.g., Hunter 1997), a demanding crop from which much-desired cloth was produced. Associated with this era of Sinagua development is the so-called "magician's burial," a man whose mortuary treatment included over 600 grave goods, from exotic jewelry and trade items to beautifully carved wooden "wands" (McGregor 1943). Pueblo consultants recognized this extraordinarily rich burial as that of a powerful leader, perhaps reflecting the influence and wealth that the Sinagua were able to wield during the late twelfth century.

were probably stimulated by a number of historical factors. First, in the winter of AD 1064–65, nearby Sunset Crater came to life, spewing ash and cinders into the air and driving the "Sinagua" people living in the area from their homes (Box 5.4). When the volcano finally quieted down enough for people to return – with a watchful eye on the still active volcano – they found that the water-retaining qualities of these ash deposits were beneficial for farming, and populations grew as they built check dams and gridded fields for growing maize and cotton. By the early AD 1100s, even with sporadic volcanic activity from Sunset Crater, an influx of immigrants came from the east, consisting of Kayenta Anasazi people either fleeing the collapse of Chaco or leaving lower elevations as the twelfth-century droughts continued (Sullivan 1994). Other people probably came from the west, as well as from the south, where Hohokam communities in the Arizona Desert were undergoing their own transformations.

This melding of cultural traditions inspired the emergence of a unique center dominated by Wupatki. Meaning "big (or tall) house" in the Hopi language, Wupatki still stands three stories tall and once contained over 100 rooms, all built on a prominent point. The architectural style is strongly reminiscent of eleventh-century great houses, reflecting the residual influence of Chaco Canyon. A large, open structure resembling an unroofed great kiva was built downhill from the impressive ruin. And, perhaps most unusual of all, a ballcourt was constructed nearby (Figure 5.13). Similar to the ballcourts common in the Hohokam area, the Wupatki version used masonry walls typical of Puebloan architecture. Archaeological investigations have found surprisingly large quantities of turquoise, shell, and copper bells, and the greatest number of macaws ever found in the northern Southwest (Neitzel 1989). Wilcox (1999a:137) proposes that powerful religious leaders controlled the center, guiding the production of cotton cloth that was then traded with neighboring groups. Although Wilcox (1996, 1999a) argues that Wupatki grew alongside Chaco Canyon, the powerful community is most probably a contemporary of the diverse small and autonomous post-Chaco polities that sprung up all over the Colorado Plateau, filling the power vacuum left by Chaco's demise.

The post-Chaco era is characterized by a great deal of variability. After Chaco Canyon's importance faded, different areas that had once exhibited Chacoan influence responded in a number of ways, ranging from complete abandonment all the way to rapid population growth. Accordingly, no single description can capture all of the patterns exhibited during the late twelfth and early thirteenth centuries. In general, however, we see a retention of some Chacoan traits. Roadways, great houses, and great kivas appear in varying combinations in post-Chaco contexts, undoubtedly drawing upon the residual authority that these features represented. The evidence suggests, however, that Chacoan religion itself did not persevere unscathed, and some people even converted the once sacred great houses into residences. New religious infrastructure mostly

5.13 The ballcourt at Wupatki reflects influence from the Hohokam region, although the masonry work is typical of Puebloan architecture. Whether the ballcourt was used in the same way as those built by the Hohokam is unknown, but it and others like it in the Sinagua region may reflect immigration from the south.

lacked the monumentality and organizational consistency of earlier great house complexes. Instead of the clean, predictable ritual landscapes of Chacoan times, later contexts either were "busy" – crowded with a mix of buildings, kivas, mounds, and roadways – or were purged of all features associated with Chaco Canyon.

Scaling back in the Mimbres region

Uncertainty about the end of the Mimbres tradition taints our understanding of the late twelfth century in the southern Mogollon Highlands. No one doubts that people were here during this era. What is unresolved is who these people were and how intensively they used the Mimbres and Gila drainages. This late Postclassic phase is characterized by mixed use by a number of disparate groups, many of which migrated to the area from long distances away. This may explain why material culture in the Gila and Mimbres valleys becomes so much more variable in the late twelfth and early thirteenth centuries. Masonry construction reminiscent of earlier Mimbres times, for example, was used alongside structures whose walls are made of puddled adobe mud (Creel 1999:108). The distribution of these diverse styles argues against wholesale migrations of entire communities and is instead more consistent with numerous small groups moving through the area and setting up short-term residences (Nelson 1999; Nelson and Hegmon 2001).

The diversity of pottery styles is perhaps the best indicator of how complex the sociocultural landscape was at the end of this Postclassic phase. Earlier Classic Mimbres forms are used, brand-new styles develop, and styles from adjoining regions pop up in increasing quantities (e.g., Hegmon *et al.* 1998). Archaeologists recognize two possible explanations for why styles common to distant regions appear in the southern Mogollon region: either entire pots entered the area through exchange or in the hands of immigrants, or people living in the Gila and Mimbres valleys were reproducing the foreign styles on locally made pottery. Compositional analyses that can identify where pots were made surprisingly support both explanations – some of this pottery is indeed foreign and probably was introduced to the area as migrants moved in, while other vessels were made with local clays but then decorated with foreign motifs, perhaps by immigrants trying to replicate the styles of their homelands. An examination of ceramics from the eastern Mimbres area, for example, focused on vessels bearing distinctive styles found far to the northwest (Ennes 1999; Hegmon *et al.* 2000; see also Creel *et al.* 2002). The researchers discovered that some vessels were actually carried into the area by migrants from the Reserve area, but once these people settled down, they also reproduced these styles using local materials. Locals also attempted to make these northern styles, resulting in crudely made pots bearing Reserve styles. Because all these patterns were identified in the same contexts, the investigators concluded that immigrants were joining local hamlets, perhaps through intermarriage.

Nelson (1999:177–84) believes that dispersed hamlets of the late AD 1100s, with their diverse material culture, participated in a wide regional network fed by the arrival of so many different people. All of this interaction, according to Nelson, was fueled by intermarriage between locals and newcomers. We can envision a woman of an immigrant group marrying into a local Mimbres family, where she is required to produce the local style. But she only knows the ceramic style and technology of her homeland, and so her execution of the local designs is unskilled at first – she also only knows how to make pottery the way she learned, not the way her in-laws do it. The result is a vessel exhibiting all of these competing influences. It is this kind of material culture that is common in the southern Mogollon area at the end of the twelfth century.

Although evidence indicates that some Mimbres people stayed in the Gila and Mimbres drainages during the Postclassic, not everyone did. Some had maintained relationships with distant villages in other regions, providing them with potential refuges as the Mimbres towns were abandoned. One example is the Convento Site, located in the Chihuahuan Desert of northern Mexico. At this site, which dates somewhere between AD 1000 and 1200, around 75 percent of the non-local pottery is from the Mimbres area (Douglas 2000). As the Mimbres tradition fell apart, some families may have chosen to take advantage of this relationship and headed south. This kind of interaction was apparently widespread, and by the end of the AD 1100s, large adobe roomblocks built in the Chihuahuan Desert of southwest New Mexico probably represent migrants from the Mimbres region (Nelson 1999:182). This influx from the north contributed to the emergence of a new center at the turn of the thirteenth century whose influence was comparable to the earlier reach of Chaco Canyon. Known as Casas Grandes or Paquimé, this development is discussed in the next chapter.

The migrations continue

The Chaco and Mimbres traditions are often touted as the height of Puebloan developments in the pre-Contact Southwest. While this is a debatable proposition – and one contingent on how one defines "height" – the archaeological evidence does indicate that social and political relationships reached a new level of complexity during the eleventh century. At the very least, the flow of valuable materials across the Southwest was unprecedented, and clearly not everyone participated equally in this exchange, for turquoise, shell, copper bells, live macaws, and fine textiles were not equitably distributed. Few people received the elaborate burials seen in Pueblo Bonito, and not everyone belonged to a prestigious core family of a Mimbres roomblock. Perhaps it was these inequities that led to the collapse of these influential traditions – the increasing decadence of the elite leadership surpassed their tenuous authority, especially when challenged by the droughts as the AD 1100s began.

In both the Mimbres and Chaco heartlands, it is not surprising that people dispersed during the twelfth century. And while some of the cultural features of Mimbres and Chaco were retained, none remained unmodified, as exemplified by the roofless great kivas now open to the entire public. For populations fed up with the political machinations and economic demands of the previous era, two solutions probably seemed attractive. The first was an ethos of communalism, one illustrated by the unprecedented aggregations and more accessible public architecture that appear in the AD 1100s. For others, an emphasis on autonomy probably seemed attractive. The return to residentially mobile hamlets occupied by extended families and the movement of people to new areas are an indication of this autonomy, one that persevered even as environmental conditions improved. It is these two patterns that characterize the Puebloan Southwest as the AD 1200s began.

6   The AD 1200s: the Great Pueblo period

During the journey of the clans in search of the Middle Place, the ancestral Zuni came upon the *Kianakwe* people who lived in large towns in the highlands and cliffs. As related in oral traditions, the inhabitants of these places were successful farmers who could command the waters to their fields without the need for rain, and they had many possessions. And so the ancients, the *Áshiwi*, hungry from long wandering, attacked. But aided by *Kúyapalitsa* the deathless Ancient Warrior Woman, the enemy could not be defeated. Rain fell, stretching the sinew of the *Áshiwi* bows, and many were captured. By evening of the third day, the *Kianakwe* had captured four *Áshiwi* gods, and prospects for success were dim. Then it was learned that *Kúyapalitsa* carried her heart in her rattle, and the *Áshiwi* devised new bows of yucca fibers that were impervious to rain. So on the fourth day, *Kúyapalitsa* was slain, the town taken, and the *Áshiwi* captives freed. The surviving *Kianakwe* were spared owing to the knowledge they could provide. "Thereby our fathers gained much knowledge, even of their own powers and possessions . . . Growing wiser in the ways of living, they learned to cherish their corn more, discovering they might have life and abundance rather than cause death and hunger" (Wright 1988:90–1).

The Great Pueblos of the north

As the AD 1200s began, the Puebloan Southwest was experiencing a remarkable transition as the reverberations of Chaco's and Mimbres's disintegration continued to be felt and people moved toward new forms of organization. Interestingly, while large concentrations of households faded in the Mimbres and Chaco areas, large communities emerged in other areas. In the Cibola area south of the San Juan Basin, in the Kayenta region to the west, and even in the Chihuahuan Desert, new aggregations formed as people clustered more and more closely together. Although this phenomenon occurred in many populations – and not in others – our understanding of these new aggregations is best known from the

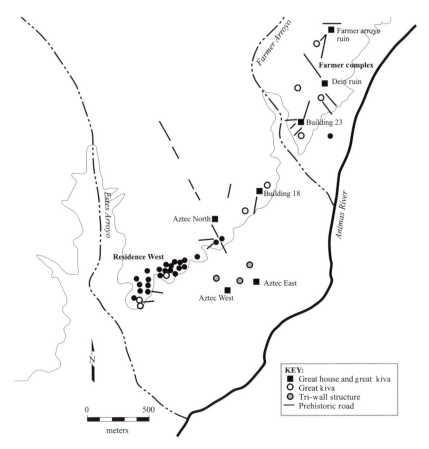

6.1 The well-known Aztec West great house is only one of possibly seven great houses found in the greater Aztec community. While recent agricultural activity and pothunting make it difficult to reconstruct the layout and use of the community, Aztec was clearly important during the twelfth and thirteenth centuries.

Mesa Verde area located north of the San Juan River and south of the precipitous and snow-covered San Juan Mountains.

Will it ever go away? Aztec clings to the Chaco tradition

Aztec was the last bastion of the Chaco tradition, gaining prominence as Chaco Canyon faded in importance (Figure 6.1). Its great houses rival the size of places such as Pueblo Bonito, and most of Aztec's Chacoan features continued to be used well into the AD 1200s, including its great kivas and roadways. The surrounding community was quite large, and elaborate burials from the one excavated great house indicate inequities in wealth and status comparable to that seen in Chaco. Aztec, however, did not have the same impact as Chaco did during its height. Areas distant from Aztec appear to have given up on the Chaco tradition, and most great houses built in the late eleventh century fell into disuse or were remodeled to serve other purposes. This is illustrated in Woods Canyon, some 100 km north of Aztec. Here, the Albert Porter great house was an important community center through the AD 1100s, but by the early thirteenth century, the focus of the community shifted away from the great house – even though Aztec was still going strong (Lipe and Varien 1999:300).

Other evidence also points to the limited scope of Aztec's influence. During the era of Chaco Canyon's preeminence, a small but steady flow of imported pottery came into the Mesa Verde region, no doubt a benefit of the increased interaction afforded by Chaco's far-reaching and unifying religion. As Chaco Canyon was deserted, however, villagers in the Mesa Verde region were apparently unable to sustain these long-distance connections, and the proportion of imported pottery in most communities dropped from 20 percent in AD 1100 to 2–7 percent by AD 1200 (Blinman and Wilson 1993:80–3). Aztec was unable to inspire the same level of interaction seen late in the eleventh century.

The last tree-ring dates from Aztec are in the AD 1230s to 1250s. What happened to Aztec remains a mystery (Box 6.1), but people probably lost interest in the center, perhaps because the extravagance of its leaders did not match the benefits that local populations received. As at Woods Canyon, attention simply shifted away from Aztec as they found more beneficial social and political arrangements. Aztec, like many great houses, was eventually reoccupied in the late 1200s by people who remodeled the buildings for their own uses. But by then the great houses were purely residential and the power of Chacoan architecture just a memory.

People, people, everywhere

Several archaeologists are dedicating considerable effort to reconstructing the complex population dynamics of the Mesa Verde region. They are finding that until AD 1150 annual population growth, including through immigration, was extremely high, in some instances nearly 1 percent a year (Adler 1994:90–3; Duff and Wilshusen 2000; Mahoney et al. 2000). The result is that Mesa Verde was densely populated by the AD 1100s. The late twelfth century, however, experienced no evident

Box 6.1 The Chaco Meridian and the fate of Aztec

Stephen Lekson (1999a) suggests that the establishment of Aztec and the fate of its residents were ultimately tied to Chaco Canyon. He argues that residents of the canyon's great houses were powerful elites who sought to reestablish themselves elsewhere as drought impacted Chaco Canyon's success. Eyeing the San Juan River region, these elites established a presence to the north, first building the North Road out of Chaco Canyon and then the Salmon great house along the river. Finally, according to Lekson, they left the canyon and constructed the Aztec great houses along the Animas River. In Lekson's model, these elites attempted to draw upon the influence of Chaco Canyon as a sacred location by establishing Aztec along the same north–south meridian. Lekson refers to this as "positional legitimation."

Lekson (1999a) argues that Aztec became the new center for Chacoan elites through the thirteenth century and that they established control over much of the Mesa Verde area. As the climate continued to change, however, and the "Great Drought" of the late AD 1200s approached, these elites decided to move once more. With the inhospitable San Juan Mountains to the north, their only choice was to head south. According to Lekson, they traveled along the same north–south meridian, passing through Chaco Canyon, through the Cibola region, and through the highlands surrounding the Mimbres homeland, ultimately settling along the Rio Casas Grandes, 720 km south of Aztec. Lekson proposes that this was the only inhabitable location at that time, assuming that they constrained themselves to the same meridian as Chaco Canyon and Aztec. Here they called upon the same "positional legitimation" to establish their third major center, Casas Grandes.

Lekson's model (1999a) is controversial among Southwestern archaeologists, who tend not to look at patterning at such a large scale. Lekson marshals a variety of supporting evidence, including shared cultural features between Chaco Canyon and Casas Grandes and the fact that all three locations lie close to the same meridian line. He also notes that Pueblo oral histories relate how their ancestors divided into two groups, one traveling south to the "Land of Everlasting Sunshine." Many archaeologists, however, dispute details of Lekson's model, challenging specific interpretations of evidence or questioning aspects of the model (Phillips 2000). At the very least, Lekson encourages us to look at larger scales than we are accustomed to, and it has already inspired the identification of other episodes of long-distance migration in the pre-Contact Southwest.

growth – almost no new construction can be seen anywhere in Mesa Verde villages – and some scholars suspect that declining precipitation made life more difficult (Varien 1999:132–6, 190). Several lines of evidence also suggest that people already were leaving the region by the late AD 1100s (Duff and Wilshusen 2000; Varien 1999:148; Varien *et al.* 1996).

By AD 1200, the trend reversed, and populations again grew and bunched ever more closely together (Mahoney *et al.* 2000). Three major changes mark this transition: first, people moved their homes closer to one another, forming increasingly dense clusters of residences; second, people moved away from older mesa-top villages to the more limited spaces along the edges of canyons; and, third, typical residential structures became larger, perhaps accommodating a few related families as opposed to just one or two (Adler 1996; Varien 1999). This all happened very quickly, perhaps even over a single generation, and by AD 1225 the character of settlement in the Mesa Verde area was completely different.

This remarkable transition is epitomized by cliff dwellings, the best known of which are found in the steep-walled canyons draining Mesa Verde. Early occupation of the mesa included communities such as Mummy Lake, where thirty-six mesa-top residences surrounding an artificial reservoir housed between 200 and 400 people during the tenth century. By the mid-1100s, some Mesa Verdeans were already taking advantage of the protection afforded by cliff overhangs and alcoves in the sandstone canyons. In Johnson Canyon, for example, construction started at Hoy House and Lion House, small cliff dwellings that grew to sixty and forty-six rooms, respectively. But the population shifts of the early thirteenth century led to the most intensive occupation of the canyon walls. The best-known cliff dwellings of the AD 1200s are places like Cliff Palace, which eventually included 220 rooms and twenty-three kivas. Most are like Mug House, where ninety-four rooms and eight kivas accommodated as many as 100 people (Figure 6.2). To get all of those people into a small alcove, Mug House's builders maximized space in every way they could. Archaeologists identified several living "suites," each consisting of a few rooms for daily activities, sleeping, and storage arrayed around a small kiva, the roof of which served as a tiny courtyard (Rohn 1971:37–9).

Not all people living in the Mesa Verde region during the early AD 1200s lived in cliff dwellings, for natural alcoves do not form in the Dakota sandstone walls that line most of the region's canyons. The majority therefore aggregated into large multi-family structures rambling along canyon rims and slopes. In these less constrictive spaces, buildings grew to unprecedented sizes as more and more people moved in, inspiring archaeologists to label the thirteenth century "The Great Pueblo Period."

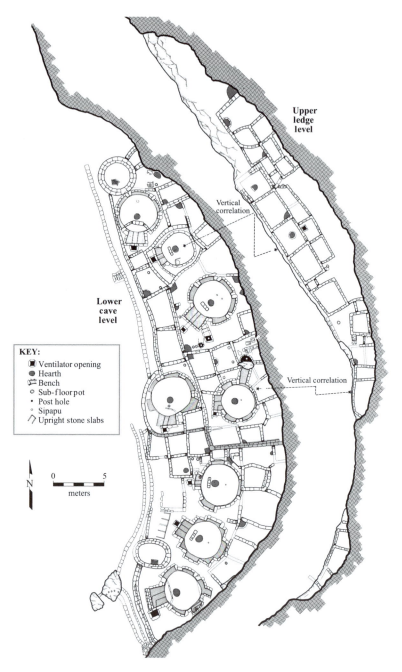

Upper ledge level

Vertical correlation

Lower cave level

Vertical correlation

KEY:
■ Ventilator opening
● Hearth
⌒ Bench
○ Sub-floor pot
• Post hole
○ Sipapu
⌒ Upright stone slabs

0   5
meters

N

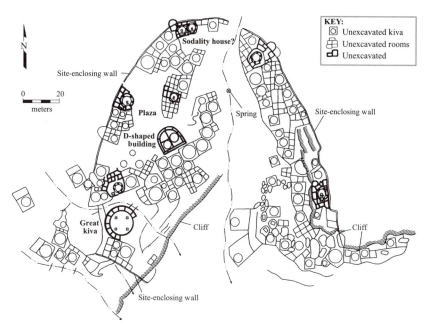

6.3 Sand Canyon Pueblo was established around AD 1250 with the construction of the community's enclosing wall. Over the next few decades,
over 400 rooms and 90 kivas were built, including a D-shaped ceremonial structure, a great kiva, and at least one possible block of rooms used
by a sodality.

Perhaps the most intensively studied aggregation of this type is found in
Sand Canyon, a shallow drainage not far from the modern Four Corners
(Varien 1999). Since the AD 900s, people had lived in small households scattered both within and outside of the canyon – Michael Adler
(1996:359–60) estimates a local population of no more than 250 people
by the mid-eleventh century. By AD 1200, people were clustering more
closely together, culminating with the establishment of Sand Canyon
Pueblo around AD 1250 (Figure 6.3). One of the first construction

6.2 Mug House was built in an open rockshelter around AD 1250 from
materials left behind from earlier use of the shelter and other nearby
sites. Situated above a reservoir that provided water, the village was large
enough to accommodate as many as twenty households. Archaeologists
suggest that a moiety organization was present at Mug House, owing to
the lack of access between two halves of the structure indicated by the
gray wall.

projects at this site was a low wall enclosing the head of the canyon and the permanent spring found there – a task that took thirty to forty people about two months to complete, demonstrating both the planning dedicated to this new community center as well as the builder's concern with defense (Kenzle 1997). Over the next thirty years, twenty separate roomblocks containing a total of 420 rooms, fourteen towers, and ninety kivas were built on either side of the spring and the creek it fed. The western half of the town was probably its ceremonial heart, for it is here that an open plaza area, a great kiva, an unusual D-shaped building, and a number of featureless roomblocks were built (Bradley 1993; Lipe and Varien 1999:335; Ortman and Bradley 2002). Perhaps 500 people lived in Sand Canyon Pueblo, and even more lived outside of the town's walls, continuing to reside in small houses scattered around the pueblo (Mahoney et al. 2000:82–3).

By the late AD 1200s, the landscape extending from Mesa Verde to southeastern Utah was dominated by over seventy aggregated pueblo towns, each consisting of more than fifty rooms and many having at least 250 rooms (Adler 1996:361; Varien 1999:163). Some scholars estimate that around half of the population continued to live outside of the aggregated pueblos (Lipe and Varien 1999:326–7), but even for these people, their social, political, and economic lives were tied to the large pueblo towns. Mark Varien's research (1999) suggests that each aggregated town – and the dispersed households orbiting around it – was spaced 2–7 km from its neighbors, providing each with its own landscape for fulfilling its subsistence needs. Living in these seemingly autonomous communities were around 13,000 people (Duff and Wilshusen 2000; Wilshusen 2002).

Why put up with nosy (and possibly infected) neighbors?

For Mesa Verde people of the thirteenth century, abandoning small extended-family households to move into large pueblos with dozens if not hundreds of other people was probably traumatic. Few of the cultural traditions and rules that today allow us to deal with dense populations existed for Puebloan people accustomed to household autonomy and the ability to move around the landscape almost at will. And, besides the awkwardness of having to share walls with neighbors, living in aggregated pueblos introduced other problems. For people in cliff dwellings, hauling water, wood, and food to their homes was a major chore. The stress on local resources, especially the firewood needed daily for cooking and warmth, was particularly intense (Kohler and Matthews 1988). Conditions in aggregated pueblos also were not very sanitary. Constant contact with other people and their waste provided ideal conditions for parasites and contagious diseases. An examination of coprolites – preserved fecal matter – from Hoy House and Lion House found pinworm remains in every sample analyzed (Cummings 1994). More a nuisance than a danger, the pinworm is the most common parasite in the world today owing to the ease with which it spreads among people living in close quarters.

Given all the disadvantages of living in aggregated towns, why did people in the thirteenth century move into these closely packed roomblocks? For transitions of such suddenness, archaeologists consider two general explanations: either people were "pulled" toward aggregated towns, or they were "pushed" into them. So-called "pull models" propose that living together provided benefits that drew families together, while "push models" argue that some external threat or crisis forced people to aggregate. While not mutually exclusive, the two kinds of models do advocate different perspectives on why change takes place in human societies. In the case of the Mesa Verde aggregations of the AD 1200s, most archaeologists agree that it must have been some "push" – or a combination of "pushes" – that forced people to live together.

Population growth is considered to be a particularly influential "push." After several generations of population growth, people packed the landscape in densities so high that aggregated pueblos may have been a necessary outcome. Around Sand Canyon, for example, populations grew from 5–12 people/km^2 in the tenth century to as many as 30–50/km^2 by the AD 1200s (Adler 1996:354; Adler et al. 1996:395–6; Wilshusen 2002:114). As densities increased, domestic architecture became larger, culminating in aggregated roomblocks (Adler 1994:94–5). Some scholars expand on this idea by emphasizing a corresponding need for arable land to feed growing numbers of people; construction of small check dams, reservoirs, terraces, and fieldhouses indicates that farmers were intensifying their efforts during the AD 1200s (Figure 6.4). Competition for good farmland also may have prompted people to bond together to assert rights over the best fields, as illustrated by the case of Sand Canyon, where people still living in small residences outside of the growing pueblo were increasingly relegated to poorer-quality lands (Adler 1996:354–5). Living in aggregated pueblos probably also helped to pass land rights along kinship lines from generation to generation, something especially important if people were investing in agricultural infrastructure to squeeze out every bit of food possible – you would not want to build all those check dams and terraces if passing that land on to your children was not assured (Adler 1994:95, 1996:358).

Another important "push" was the onset of the Little Ice Age, a climatic phenomenon that led to cooler temperatures in the northern hemisphere. Although the height of the Little Ice Age was still around the corner, some

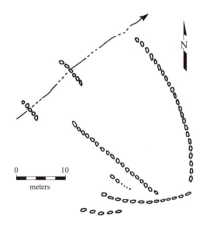

6.4 Site 1398, located on Mesa Verde, consists of a series of check dams that captured up to a meter of soil and contour terraces that spread water on to fields. Such basic strategies were effective ways to increase farming productivity.

evidence suggests that temperatures were falling during the thirteenth century. The environmental changes associated with this transition are not fully understood, but people living closest to the San Juan Mountains were affected first. Growing food at these elevations was always difficult, not because of the lack of water, but because of the short growing season. As the Little Ice Age progressed, farmers probably moved their fields to lower elevations, but that infringed on lands of other farmers. As stores of maize were depleted, farmers faced few choices: either form alliances with neighbors in an attempt to free up good lands and work them together, or try to drive people off their land or steal their food. Whatever particular solution people chose in the thirteenth century, dropping temperatures probably contributed to the aggregations, and archaeologists identify a corresponding shift in populations toward the south and west, away from higher elevations (Lipe and Varien 1999:322).

In the face of all of these "pushes," people in the Mesa Verde area had yet another reason to move into aggregated villages: the need for greater cooperation. Sharing and cooperation were almost certainly part of early Puebloan life, even for people living in largely independent single-household residences scattered across the landscape. Archaeologists find that even the most isolated residences during the eleventh and twelfth centuries still obtained some pottery, and probably food, from some distance away, while major ceremonial events at Chaco-era great kivas and great houses were opportunities for sharing food and crafts. Scholars believe that this cooperation allowed people to contend with a patchy environment in which precipitation and other resources varied across the landscape. Such "spatiotemporal heterogeneity" is thought to promote sharing. If you produce a lot of extra food one year, you might trade it for pottery made by a distant ally who is having difficulty with crops – and the next year, the flow of goods might go in the opposite direction. In the challenging environment of the northern Southwest, such flexible interactions were advantageous to everyone.

All of this appears to have changed in the thirteenth century, when the climate became more spatially homogeneous at the same time that temporal heterogeneity continued. In other words, the climate was unpredictable and could be good or bad for farming, but in any given year, everyone across the Colorado Plateau was equally affected (Adler *et al.* 1996:387, 390–3). No longer was it helpful to share widely. Instead, the most sensible thing would be to combine your efforts with those living near you to produce as much food as possible. Pooling labor and surpluses with neighbors was easier to do if everyone lived together rather than in scattered households, and thus aggregated towns were a sensible arrangement. In an analysis that draws on "rational choice" models popular in microeconomics, Timothy Kohler and Carla Van West (1996) found that in the mid-1200s, the self-interested thing to do was to cooperate – pooling labor and surpluses together ensured that everyone did just fine, and aggregated pueblos helped to make that possible. Kohler and Van West also point out that living in close quarters near stored surpluses deterred "cheaters," people who might try to get out of their responsibilities to help farm the fields but then still benefit from the harvest. Various sources of evidence support these arguments. For example, analyses of the clays in thirteenth-century pottery show that some vessels were traded up to 45 km from their source (Glowacki *et al.* 1998, 2002), but this whiteware exchange was minimal compared with earlier periods (Wilson and Blinman 1995:77), reflecting the increasing focus on local cooperation rather than widespread sharing.

One final "push" explanation for the Mesa Verde aggregations deserves consideration: violence. As described in chapter 5, while the end of Chaco Canyon was associated with a few exceptionally violent episodes (Kantner 1999b), in general, little conflict is seen in either the demise of Chaco or the fading of Mimbres towns (Martin 1997:47; Nelson 2000:327). This all changes in the AD 1200s (Box 6.2). Evidence for conflict is nearly ubiquitous across the northern Southwest, but it is especially common in the Mesa Verde area. At Salmon, an old Chaco-era great house reoccupied in the thirteenth century, 45–55 individuals, mostly children, were burned in the central tower kiva around AD 1263 (Irwin-Williams

Box 6.2   Violence in the thirteenth century

John Kantner (1999b), Steven LeBlanc (1999), and Stephen Lekson (2002) suggest that the nature of violence was different in the AD 1200s than during the preceding century. Kantner (1999b), for example, conducted a statistical analysis of skeletal data from the Chaco era through the early 1200s and found that violence during the early AD 1100s was characterized by exceptional levels of mutilation – it is this era that has the strongest evidence for cannibalism (e.g., Billman *et al.* 2000; Marlar *et al.* 2000; White 1992). Violence during the following decades, however, was of a different nature. While mutilation still occurred, it was nowhere near the level seen earlier. And the nature of traumatic injuries, the manner with which the dead were treated, and the overall context in which violence occurred suggested to Kantner (1999b) that raiding for resources and warfare to displace populations was common during the thirteenth century.

Sand Canyon Pueblo provides an example of this new trend in violence (Kuckelman 2000; Kuckelman *et al.* 2002; Lightfoot and Kuckelman 2001). Archaeologists recovered human remains with head wounds in the fill of the town's kivas, and weathering of the bones and evidence of animal gnawing showed that the bodies were left exposed after death. Many of these kivas had been burned, while the recovery of intact artifacts suggests that residents left in a hurry, presumably under duress. Other scholars, however, propose that the burning was a formal way to "close down" structures (Walker 2002), and they note that the use of abandoned pitstructures for burials has a long history in the region (e.g., Martin and Akins 2001:228). Nevertheless, the combination of evidence indicates that Sand Canyon Pueblo was abandoned after a round of attacks – as were many others during the AD 1200s.

A different view of thirteenth-century violence is provided by Debra Martin's and Nancy Akins's study (2001) of skeletal material from the La Plata region bordering the San Juan River. Collections analyzed from this area date from AD 1100 to AD 1300, and their sample included twenty-nine individuals. None of the skeletons exhibited clear evidence of violent death, but many had healed traumas, and several of them – almost all from the thirteenth century – were not buried in prepared graves. Young females were especially prone to this treatment, and many had healed "depression fractures" on their skulls – the kinds of wounds caused by being struck with blunt objects. These females also exhibited poor health. Although Martin and Akins are cautious in their interpretations, one possible explanation is that these young females were captured or displaced by raids, and they suffered domestic violence and other inequities in their new homes. Neither males nor children exhibited this kind of treatment among the La Plata skeletal samples.

and Shelley 1980). Castle Rock Pueblo, built against a small, precipitous butte, was burned down on top of forty-one people, many of whom had suffered violent blows (Kuckelman *et al.* 2002). Although archaeologists debate whether the increasingly common masonry towers and enclosing walls were defensive or served some other purpose, many scholars believe that violence encouraged people to group together into defensive towns (Adler *et al.* 1996:388–90; Kenzle 1997).

Why did Puebloan people living in the thirteenth century experience so much violence? Desperate times lead to desperate actions, and perhaps as cooler temperatures drove people away from the San Juan Mountains, they allied with one another to drive farmers from lands that were still arable or seize their surpluses. Many of the violent episodes do appear to result in the survivors leaving, for the attacked and burned structures are rarely reoccupied. Such violence would have promoted even larger aggregations in defensible locations. It is probably no coincidence that the most defensive thirteenth-century towns in the Mesa Verde region grew around springs, providing inhabitants with a protected water source. Increasingly regular spacing between communities also indicates the establishment of "no man's lands," buffers created as people left vulnerable farming hamlets and retreated to defensive towns (Wilcox and Haas 1994). Although conflict was not a daily occurrence, the evidence indicates that violence shaped occupation of the Mesa Verde region in the AD 1200s. And a concern with conflict is reflected in artwork – a petroglyph panel at Castle Rock Pueblo shows individuals facing off with bows-and-arrows (Figure 6.5).

Life in an aggregated town

For people who once lived in small, extended-family residences, moving into the close quarters of aggregated pueblos undoubtedly led to many changes. One of the most important consequences was the loss of mobility as an important option for adapting to changes in the social or physical environment. In earlier times, the ability periodically to abandon one's home and simply move elsewhere, even if it was just a few hundred meters away, was a powerful form of independence. And many

6.5 A rock art panel on the butte above Castle Rock Pueblo seems to show three figures with shields firing bows and arrows.

people had maintained long-distance relationships, inspired by long journeys for raw materials or ceremonial events, that allowed people to move
longer distances if they felt it was needed. Conditions in the thirteenth
century changed all that, and people living in Puebloan towns lost some
of this flexibility.

Archaeologists contend that these new circumstances prompted
momentous changes to Mesa Verde sociocultural systems. A shift from a
focus on women as the core kinship unit to a social life increasingly dominated by men is one possible change. In the face of increasing violence and
agricultural intensification, core groups of related men could more readily
join together to protect key resources. This would have been difficult to do
if related males married outside of their kin group and ended up scattered
across the landscape. Some evidence supports this shift to patrifocal organization. For example, Michael Schillaci and Christopher Stojanowski
(2002) analyzed skeletal material associated with the thirteenth-century
reuse of Aztec and found that males shared more osteological features
while females were more diverse. The pattern was not strong, but it also
was not what would be expected if post-marital residence was matrilocal,
leading the researchers to conclude that a new couple either moved in with
the husband's family or chose which family they wished to reside with.
Martin and Akins (2001) came to a similar conclusion in their assessment of gender-biased violence in the La Plata drainage north of the San
Juan River. In this study, the high incidence of violence against females is
suspected to indicate that women were strangers in their marital homes,
perhaps even immigrants or captives. In general, skeletal analyses show
that women's health deteriorated more rapidly than that of men, and they
suffered more work-related pathologies (Martin and Akins 2001:241–3),
indicating an overall decrease in women's status during the AD 1200s.

Another suspected change to the social structure of Mesa Verde towns is the introduction of moiety organization, in which society was divided into two parts, with every individual assigned to the moiety of one of his or her parents. Some scholars argue that moiety organization was already developing at Chaco Canyon at the turn of the twelfth century, and they point to dual divisions in the architecture of buildings such as Pueblo Bonito (Vivian 1990:298–9). It is not until the AD 1200s in the Mesa Verde area, however, that this kind of architectural duality became more widespread. An architectural study of Mug House (Figure 6.2), for example, suggested that the structure was divided into two distinct sections (Rohn 1971:39–40), and recent investigations have identified walls at other cliff dwellings that divide them in half (Lipe and Varien 1999:320). In aggregated towns in less precipitous contexts, such as at Sand Canyon Pueblo, community architecture is typically bisected by a creek, providing at least the impression of duality.

What was the advantage of moiety organization? Anthropologists point to several possible reasons for dual divisions to emerge. In confusing social settings, such as might be expected in the thirteenth century, moieties provide some cohesion – it is easier to track social membership when two divisions are predominant than it is to track kinship among a bunch of families that are thrown together into aggregated towns. Perhaps more importantly, moiety divisions create large groups of people that can be mobilized for large-scale activities such as warfare or intensive farming. Instead of having to negotiate with lots of unrelated or weakly allied families to harvest crops or build terraces, moieties create an instant social identity that makes cooperative endeavors easier. Similarly, moieties encourage a more centralized decision-making structure, with senior moiety members providing efficient political leadership. All of these features were beneficial for aggregated Mesa Verde towns, and moiety organization probably grew out of existing alliances and kinship relationships as people moved in together.

Making the whole greater than the sum of the parts

While the thirteenth-century aggregations impacted many aspects of Puebloan life, some things were slow to change. Small pitstructures remained the most common form of ceremonial architecture, and in the Mesa Verde region these kivas actually became more standardized, with a consistent southerly orientation and a regular set of features including a southern recess and six pilaster roof supports (Lipe and Varien 1999:319). As people clustered together, the kiva's function and the social unit it served apparently did not change. For example, at Sand Canyon

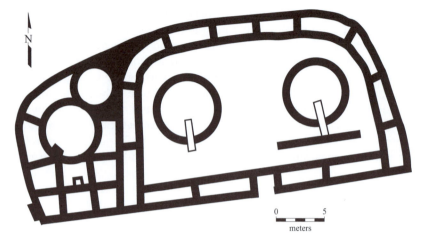

N

0   5
meters

6.6 Sun Temple is an example of one of the unusual D-shaped structures that appeared in the Mesa Verde area during the thirteenth century. Construction at Sun Temple started in AD 1275 and the walls were built up to 4 meters high. The next year, however, construction stopped, and the building was never roofed.

Pueblo, the ratio of rooms to kivas is 5:1, the same ratio seen in dispersed residences during earlier centuries (Bernardini 1996:391–2). Ceremonial activity still revolved around small kivas and the households that used them.

No one who had directly experienced Chaco Canyon's power was still living by the thirteenth century, and therefore the Chaco tradition was remembered only in oral histories. However, Aztec, the last bastion of Chacoan ideology, did persevere until the early AD 1200s, and everywhere people were still surrounded by great house ruins. Such lingering influences apparently promoted the retention of some Chacoan features in new religious infrastructure. Great kivas continued to be built, for example, even though they were larger and unroofed. D-shaped buildings reminiscent of earlier tri-wall structures also were established in many towns, including one at Sand Canyon Pueblo and Sun Temple on Mesa Verde (Figure 6.6). Bruce Bradley (1996) proposes that these forms represent a resurgence of interest in Chaco-era religious traditions.

But this "Chaco revival cult," as Bradley calls it, was short-lived, and the religious landscape across the northern Southwest slowly changed as people aggregated in dense town settings. A diversity of new religious features appeared in northern communities. Tall masonry towers, often argued to be defensive but also occasionally exhibiting domestic use, were curiously connected to kivas with tunnels. Small plazas surrounded by roomblocks and often partially covered by roofs also appeared. Each Mesa Verde town exhibited its own unique combination of old and new ceremonial features, suggesting that people were experimenting with a variety of religious forms as they searched for ways to establish bonds above the level of the simple household kiva (Lipe and Varien 1999:319).

The continuing use of small kivas and the experimentation with more integrative religious forms reveal an apparent paradox in the organization of Mesa Verde aggregated towns – people were clustering together to gain the advantages of living in large groups, but they apparently had trouble developing unifying sociopolitical institutions. The diversity of ceremonial architecture may in fact represent attempts to establish town theocracies. At Sand Canyon Pueblo (Figure 6.3), one unique roomblock consisting of three kivas and a handful of rooms is suspected to have been a complex used by an emerging association of religious authorities – what anthropologists call a "sodality" (Lipe 2002). The building and nearby great kiva featured unusually large bowls, high bowl-to-jar ratios, and large quantities of deer remains, suggesting that large groups of people gathered at these locations (Lipe and Varien 1999:336–8, Potter 2000:478–9). However, the appearance of several different forms of public architecture in Sand Canyon Pueblo and the presence of over eighty small kivas suggest that any emerging religious sodalities or moiety divisions were weak.

In general, Mesa Verde households enjoyed considerable autonomy that they were reluctant to give up, and this is further reflected in the absence of identifiable inequities in the aggregated towns. At Sand Canyon Pueblo, three pieces of turquoise and eighteen of shell are virtually the only exotic trade items recovered, and any unusual concentrations of food remains were associated with religious structures rather than particular households (Lipe 2002). If any social differences existed in the thirteenth century, it was between the aggregated towns and the small dispersed residences found outside the towns' walls (Adler et al. 1996:424–5; Lipe and Varien 1999:336–7). But within the towns, strict "leveling mechanisms" designed to ensure that no single individual or family got ahead in life may have been commonly employed to ensure the equitable distribution of resources. A similar degree of independence characterized interactions between many of the towns as well, as indicated by their fairly regular spacing and the lack of a regional hierarchy (Lipe 2002:218–19; Varien 1999:168–9). Perhaps memories of the excesses of Chaco Canyon and Aztec were still fresh, and people were hesitant to become involved in any political system that could possibly compromise their autonomy. As several scholars have suggested (e.g., Bernardini

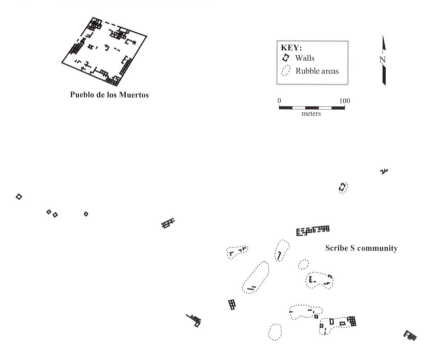

Pueblo de los Muertos

KEY:
Walls
Rubble areas

N

0   100
meters

Scribe S community

6.7 The Scribe S community, consisting of several separate roomblocks containing hundreds of rooms, was established in the middle of the thirteenth century. Later, between AD 1279 and 1284, the residents quickly built Pueblo de los Muertos, a more defensible aggregated town.

1996), this stubborn independence probably contributed to the troubles of the late thirteenth century, a topic considered in the next chapter.

Great Pueblos elsewhere in the Puebloan Southwest

The trend toward aggregation was not confined to the Mesa Verde region – large towns began popping up all over the Puebloan Southwest. In the Cibola region, for example, people established new communities and gravitated toward large residential buildings (Kintigh 1985, 1996). The formation of these aggregations is similar to how Mesa Verde towns grew: at the turn of the thirteenth century, once dispersed households moved into modest-sized roomblocks of fewer than sixty rooms clustered around public architecture similar to Chaco-era great houses and great kivas. As time passed, these aggregations grew denser and the public architecture was abandoned, resulting in communities such as at Scribe S (Figure 6.7), where several roomblocks totaling almost 500 rooms were

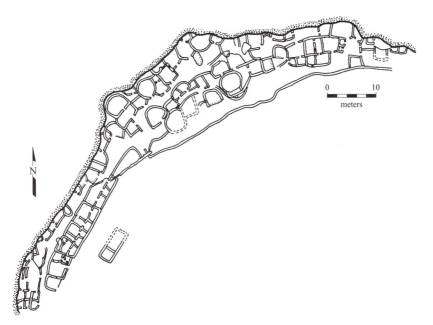

6.8 Established in the late AD 1240s, Kiet Siel grew to include twelve room suites by AD 1271. One generation later, the villages had swelled to include over 150 rooms as small groups of immigrants took up residence in the alcove. By the AD 1290s, Kiet Siel was largely abandoned.

established in the mid-1200s (Cordell *et al.* 1994:129; Kintigh 1994:132, 1996:136). Unlike the Mesa Verde area, however, Cibola towns included few kivas of any size. The reasons for aggregation are also unknown, for perfectly good sections of the landscape were still unoccupied, suggesting that if people had wanted to retain the old ways of dispersed living, they could have (Kintigh 1996:139). Immigrants probably contributed to these new towns, but despite tensions expected when disparate groups come together, thirteenth-century Cibola towns were largely peaceful – Keith Kintigh (1996:140) sees little evidence of violence.

Kayenta consolidation

Farther to the west, in what is now Arizona, the Kayenta region was undergoing similar transitions. As the AD 1100s ended, people abandoned dispersed, largely autonomous residences and joined large roomblocks built near dependable water sources and decent farmland (Dean 1996a:34–5). By the mid-1200s, these dense towns were the focus of habitation. One such place is Kiet Siel (Figure 6.8). Situated in a large sandstone alcove with its own spring, this small town was established by a few households in the late AD 1240s. By AD 1271, twelve room suites had been built, each with its own living, storage, and mealing rooms arranged around a courtyard. More people moved in over the next few years, and a retaining wall was built to expand the alcove's floor area, new room suites were added, and new kivas were built. Perhaps 150 people lived in Kiet Siel at its height. Like at Scribe S far to the east, Kiet Siel was probably abandoned in the late AD 1280s – the last remodeling took place in AD 1286 (Dean 1970:161).

Kayenta towns apparently had concerns similar to those in the Mesa Verde region. Jonathan Haas's and Winifred Creamer's work (1993, 1996) in Long House Valley found that as people left small residences scattered along the valley floor around AD 1250, they chose elevated and defensible locations for their new towns. What is especially interesting about the sites they selected is that many of them are intervisible – the new towns were situated so they could see one another. That this was intentional is revealed by the fact that they actually cut a notch out of the ridge of a mesa to ensure line-of-sight between two towns. Haas and Creamer argue that this allowed communication among Long House Valley communities, especially warnings about impending raids or other threats (also see LeBlanc 1999:226–7).

And who is the enemy that inspired such drastic defensive measures? The most likely candidates were other Kayenta people living in more marginal parts of this arid landscape who were seeking better farmlands, although raiders coming from even longer distances in search of food or valuables may have represented another danger. A trickle of immigrants coming from the north and west was also beginning, a flow that increased as the Little Ice Age progressed and families began to flee from cooler elevations and drier lands. Perhaps Kayenta towns feared this influx of foreigners and responded by aggregating in defensive locations. Their fear apparently exceeded the actual dangers, however, as little evidence of violence is found at Kayenta sites (LeBlanc 1999:311).

Northern Rio Grande growth

Until the AD 1000s, not many people lived in the northern Rio Grande drainage. With much of the area situated at fairly high elevations and surrounded by mountains that funnel cold air into the arable basins, this part of the Colorado Plateau suffers from a perilously short growing season. People dwelling here tended to favor pithouse habitations

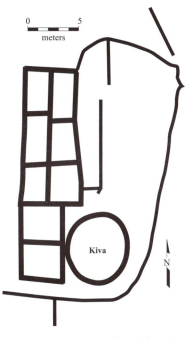

6.9 LA 3852 is a small residential structure dating to the late twelfth century on the Pajarito Plateau.

and a fairly mobile and flexible lifestyle. Even the height of Chaco Canyon's influence failed to have much impact on the settlement of this landscape.

As Chaco and its most closely allied communities were abandoned in the AD 1100s, some refugees fled toward the east, an area they knew because it had been a source of obsidian and turquoise. Their journey may not have been without peril – residents of the Gallina Highlands, situated between the San Juan Basin and the Rio Grande, built towers and strongholds, perhaps in reaction to these movements. As these migrants entered the Rio Grande drainage, they contributed to modest population growth, first in the Galisteo Basin southeast of the city of Santa Fe during the AD 1100s, and later in the early AD 1200s on the Pajarito Plateau to the north of Santa Fe (Crown *et al.* 1996:195–9). Once there, household residences and great kivas with vaults not unlike those seen in Chaco were built (Figure 6.9).

The trend toward aggregation seen everywhere occurred in the thirteenth century in the northern Rio Grande. Many households moved into buildings consisting of twenty to thirty rooms, and a few of these roomblocks occasionally were arrayed around open plazas. By the latter half of the AD 1200s, some of these roomblocks were growing together into a single mass of architecture, resulting in large villages of up to 250 rooms (Cordell *et al.* 1994:115). And, just as in the Mesa Verde area, the growth of these communities occurred alongside other changes, including the dedication of a considerable amount of energy to building agricultural infrastructure such as terraces, dams, and fieldhouses.

Communities also became more insular – Michael Walsh (1998) analyzed the distribution of raw lithic material and finished tools in the region and found that access to good stone was becoming more difficult, suggesting increasing territoriality and circumscription as the towns grew larger and more powerful.

But not here . . .

Not everyone was aggregating in the AD 1250s. In the San Juan Basin, for example, people continued to live in dispersed households and even in remodeled great houses. Some areas that had been largely abandoned experienced a minor rebound in population, and many dispersed communities grew larger as more small residences were built (Roney 1996:165). Even Chaco Canyon saw continuing use – Hillside Ruin probably was built between the ruins of Pueblo Bonito and Chetro Ketl at this time (Stein and Fowler 1996:120). Most new growth occurred on the edges of the former Chaco world, especially to the east and southeast. At Guadalupe, a great house community during the tenth and eleventh centuries, the old Chaco structure was remodeled for domestic use and eighty-two different sites, including scattered residences, continued to be used during the thirteenth century (Stein and Fowler 1996:149).

Farther to the south, the former Mimbres area continued to be occupied by people who built adobe-walled structures of twenty-five to forty rooms that were loosely arrayed around plazas (Lekson 1996:173). Meanwhile, the lower Rio Grande drainage experienced increasing use by a variety of groups. The diversity of thirteenth-century architecture found there, including pithouses, jacal buildings, and masonry and adobe pueblos, represents locals who were moving toward year-round sedentism as well as immigrants from surrounding areas (Spielmann 1996:182–3). While archaeologists regard the AD 1200s as the "Great Pueblo Period" owing to the large towns that appeared in so many areas, these aggregations were unique responses to particular contexts and were not a

6.10 The Chihuahuan Desert around Casas Grandes includes grassland and desert scrub plant communities that in the modern era have been impacted by grazing, as seen here. The Sierra Madre range, in contrast, includes various woodland communities.

universal phenomenon in the Puebloan Southwest. And no better example of the diversity of cultural behavior exists than the emergence of a new influential center far to the south: Casas Grandes.

Casas Grandes: the Puebloan tradition in the Chihuahuan Desert?

The name "Chihuahuan Desert" evokes an image of a vast and arid plain devoid of much in the way of plant and animal life – and a few corners of this physiographic zone live up to this reputation (Figure 6.10). This generalization, however, glosses over environmental diversity of the so-called "International Four Corners," where two Mexican and two US states meet. Driving west along Mexico's Route 2 from Juarez reveals this variability – you pass through the low desert and its dried playas, but the road gradually climbs out of the scrub and into patchy grasslands. Soon the Sierra Madre looms ahead. This mountain range runs roughly north–south along the entire western edge of Mexico, and its high elevations capture precipitation coming from the Pacific Ocean, watering forests of fir, spruce, and pine, and feeding several drainages. Much of the runoff

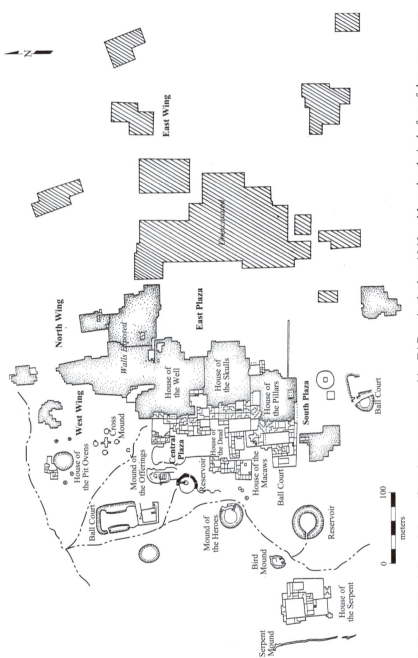

N

North Wing

West Wing

East Wing

Walls Exposed

Cross
Mound

House of
the Pit Ovens

Mound of
the Offerings

Central
Plaza

House of
the Well

House of
the Skulls

East Plaza

Unexcavated

Reservoir

House of
the Dead

House of
the Macaws

House of
the Pillars

South Plaza

Ball Court

Ball Court

Ball Court

Mound of
the Heroes

Bird
Mound

Reservoir

House of
the Serpent

Serpent
Mound

0   100

meters

6.11 The West Wing of Casas Grandes was excavated by Di Peso in the late 1960s, although relatively few of the rooms were fully exposed. The configuration of the East Wing is not well understood, but both wings may have contained as many as 2,000 rooms. Dates from Casas Grandes suggest that construction began around AD 1200.

works its way west, back to the Pacific, but some also drains toward the east, ultimately evaporating in the low deserts.

At the point where the mountain creeks settle on to the Chihuahuan grasslands, surprisingly rich environments have developed. The largest of these drainages is the Rio Casas Grandes. Flowing out of the Sierra Madre and heading north into the Chihuahuan Desert, this "river" is little more than a seasonal trickle of water today. But it was once an important waterway lined with marshes and river woodlands, and a rich archaeological record surrounds it. It is here that tourists can visit the ruins whose Spanish name is "Casas Grandes" and whose Náhuatl name is "Paquimé" – meaning "big houses" in both languages.

What is so unique about Casas Grandes?

As its name suggests, Casas Grandes features huge pueblo build-ings surrounded by a multitude of unusual features, including sev-eral Mesoamerican-style ballcourts and platform mounds (Figure 6.11). Although the ruins have been described by explorers and archaeologists for over a century, only recently was it determined that construction of Casas Grandes was initiated around AD 1200 (Dean and Raves-loot 1993). The total size and configuration of the major structures are still debated (e.g., Lekson 1999a; Wilcox 1999b). Most reports describe Casas Grandes as a massive terraced building arrayed around three sides of a plaza, and excavations in the west wing conducted by Charles Di Peso between 1958 and 1961 exposed 950 rooms arranged in a complex floorplan. Di Peso (1974) also identified numerous T-shaped doorways, alcoves containing elevated platforms, and thick adobe walls that still stand 10 m high in some places. Casas Grandes may have included 2,000 rooms, but the rest of the ruin has not been excavated, and some archae-ologists question the existence of the alleged eastern wing, which is not readily visible today owing to modern habitation.

Whether or not the controversial wing exists, Casas Grandes is impres-sive. It was built using a coursed-adobe technique that has antecedents dating to the tenth century in the Mimbres area (Creel 1999:116), and Di Peso estimated that the entire structure was built in a single generation. The variation in design and construction, on the other hand, suggests that many different people were involved in Casas Grandes's creation (Whalen and Minnis 2000:171). With large-scale facilities for preparing food grouped on the north edge of the site, including vast ovens, it is easy to imagine a steady flow of workers coming from considerable distances away to help construct the adobe buildings and engage in grand feasts and ceremonies. Perhaps an additional attraction was the presence of several large ballcourts that could accommodate large numbers of spectators (Box 6.3).

More spectacular than the ruins themselves are the remains from extensive trading activities centered at Casas Grandes. Over 4 million pieces of shell have been recovered from the excavated areas, with most from huge caches found in a handful of rooms (Bradley 2000:180). Unmodified shell apparently entered the town, and initially archaeologists thought that centralized shell-production workshops were busily crafting beads, pendants, rings, bracelets, and other ornaments that were then traded over much of the Southwest. Further investigation, however, has revealed that craft activity was distributed over the entire Casas Grandes region, suggesting a more dispersed production in which different kin groups maintained their own small-scale workshops (Whalen and Minnis 2000:175). This conclusion does not lessen Casas Grandes's primacy in the shell trade – Ronna Bradley's research (1999:224–5) demonstrates that the diversity of shell artifacts found in Puebloan sites to the north increased with the emergence of Casas Grandes, replacing the Hohokam as the major provider of these valuables.

Shell was not the only commodity driving Casas Grandes's trade. Over 300 macaw skeletons and numerous eggshells have been recovered from the ruins, as have adobe "cages" for keeping these birds (Figure 6.12). The uniquely shaped stones used for cage doors are found not only in Casas Grandes, but also in smaller sites surrounding the major ruins, suggesting that they too participated in the macaw trade. Most archaeologists believe that any live macaws and macaw feathers that made their way north into other Puebloan areas must have passed through Casas Grandes.

Less well understood is the pottery style associated with Casas Grandes. Ramos Polychrome is found over a large area of the Chihuahuan Desert, and it also appears in the Sonoran Desert to the west and in trace amounts in the Mogollon Highlands to the north. At first, scholars argued that this pottery was produced in Casas Grandes and then traded over considerable distances. Recent compositional analyses of Ramos pottery, however, suggest that vessels produced at Casas Grandes are found no farther than 80 km away – vessels exhibiting the Ramos style beyond this range were apparently copies of the style replicated on locally made vessels (Woosley and Olinger 1993). Why would people living far from Casas Grandes copy their styles? Many scholars believe that one of the most influential "exports" from Casas Grandes was its religious tradition, or at least some aspects of it, and people living far away represented these beliefs by copying some of the styles and iconography from Ramos Polychrome vessels (Whalen and Minnis 2001b:54–5).

Box 6.3   How were ballcourts used?

Archaeologists have known for some time about the elliptical earthen ballcourts of the Hohokam people of southern Arizona, which suggest influence from Mesoamerican societies far to the south. Archaeologists are also familiar with the I-shaped ballcourts constructed at Casas Grandes, inspiring interpretations that it was a Mesoamerican trading outpost. Within the past decade, however, large-scale surveys have identified even more ballcourts in the Chihuahuan Desert around Casas Grandes. They are providing us with a more complete picture of the significance of these unique features.

Michael Whalen and Paul Minnis (1996) examined twenty-one of the ballcourts in northern Mexico, including the three at Casas Grandes and eleven more from the lowland Chihuahuan Desert. Their research identified three styles of ballcourts. The classic I-shaped ballcourt, like those found at Casas Grandes itself, is completely ringed by earthen embankments, with the enclosed area wider at both ends. Like all ballcourts, this style tends to be oriented north–south. T-shaped ballcourts are similar, but they are open on the southern end. The third style is perhaps more appropriately called a "playing field" than a ballcourt, for it has the simplest construction – a row of stones that delineate the court area. Whalen and Minnis note that the more elaborate ballcourts appear later in the Chihuahuan sequence, which mirrors the pattern identified farther south in northwest Mesoamerica.

How were ballcourts used? As with their Mesoamerican counterparts, the Chihuahuan ballcourts probably served a number of functions. The ballgame was not merely a sport, but a ritual event full of symbolism relating to calendrical and agricultural events. Many scholars point to ballcourt events as providing opportunities for regional participants to exchange goods and information, while other archaeologists emphasize the role of the ballgame in negotiating social and political relationships both within and among communities. In the case of the Chihuahuan ballcourts, little direct evidence regarding their function is available, but Whalen and Minnis (1996, 2001a) do identify relevant patterns. Noting the low frequency of Chihuahuan ballcourts and their clustering around Casas Grandes, they propose that ballcourt activities were driven by factional rivalries. The games themselves, as well as the construction and augmentation of the ballcourts, were probably driven by competition among peer groups – not unlike today's sports competitions, in which both the team's success and the magnificence of the venue reflect on the community they represent.

6.12 Adobe "cages" were used for keeping macaws at Casas Grandes. Their distinctive stone doors remain even after the cages themselves have eroded away, making it easy for archaeologists to identify which sites were involved in the macaw trade.

While many items were exported from Casas Grandes, some goods were imported as well. Copper craft items, especially bells, are found in the ruins, and it was once believed they were crafted there. The evidence, however, shows that the town was a consumer of copper goods manufactured farther south (Vargas 1995). And since few of these items were traded to the north, Casas Grandes apparently did not serve as a "middleman" in the exchange of copper goods. An assessment of turquoise artifacts from the ruins reveals a similar pattern – Casas Grandes was the consumer of a small amount (a mere 2.6 pounds total, although a large cache could still be in unexcavated rooms) of poor-quality turquoise that was primarily used as offerings in domestic contexts. Coming from the north, small quantities of obsidian as well as pottery from the Mimbres region made their way into Casas Grandes, perhaps as trade items given in exchange for shell (Schaafsma and Riley 1999:247).

Beyond Casas Grandes

Surrounding Casas Grandes is a landscape packed with hundreds of adobe mounds, the majority of which are the remains of one-story residences. These settlements fill the valleys and extend up on to the

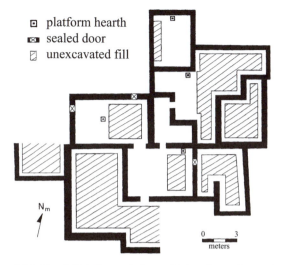

platform hearth
sealed door
unexcavated fill

6.13 Site 242 is located about 26 km from Casas Grandes, within the "inner zone" where the center enjoyed its greatest influence. Site 242 is unique for the number of Casas Grandes features found there, including thick adobe walls, a complex floor plan, T-shaped doors, an I-shaped ballcourt, and macaw cage doors.

piedmont zone and into the Sierra Madre. The sizes of the mounds vary considerably, and archaeologists have found it nearly impossible to reconstruct what these roomblocks looked like without excavating them. What they do know is that most were built alone, while occasionally two or three residences clustered together. Closer to Casas Grandes, however, up to eleven roomblocks were often placed next to one another, forming sizeable settlements. In fact, Whalen and Minnis (2001b:173, 194) believe that the area within 30 km of Casas Grandes – what they call the "inner zone" – exhibits a hierarchical pattern of settlement, with the larger roomblock clusters evenly spaced from one another and readily accessible from smaller sites with less elaborate architecture.

Settlements in the inner zone exhibit more than just regular spacing – the features and artifacts found at the most substantial clusters are surprisingly similar to those seen at Casas Grandes itself. Ballcourts and large ovens have been recorded in this zone, as have various imported items (Whalen and Minnis 2001b:173). One of these settlements is Site 242 (Figure 6.13), an unusually elaborate roomblock found about 26 km from Casas Grandes and excavated by Whalen and Minnis (2001b:661–3). Built of especially thick adobe walls, the floorplan of Site 242 is modestly sized but complex in design, with T-shaped doors and alcoves housing platforms with hearths and vents, all features reminiscent of Casas

Grandes architecture. An enormous ballcourt in the distinctive "I" shape and the only platform mound outside of Casas Grandes are also associated with Site 242, and unusual artifacts such as macaw cage doors and a stone ground into a phallus were found there. Site 242 is seemingly a miniature version of Casas Grandes.

Most ballcourts and other unusual features are located no farther than 30 km from Casas Grandes, but they are also not found any closer than 15 km – only residential mounds occupy this core area. If ballcourts were indeed expressions of factional competition (Box 6.3), their absence in settlements closest to Casas Grandes suggests that those people were sociopolitically tied to the center, while populations living farther away participated in a multitude of small political systems that arose in the shadow of Casas Grandes (Minnis *et al.* 1993; Whalen and Minnis 1996, 1999:61, 2000:175–7). Those living even farther away, outside of the 30 km "inner zone," arguably are the most autonomous, for they built only a handful of ballcourts and diminutive ovens, and they apparently did not keep macaws. Even the shell crafts they produced were crudely worked from readily available species (Whalen and Minnis 2001b:191).

Like Chaco Canyon before it, the fidelity of Casas Grandes features – and the direct control and influence they represent – fades the farther from the center one goes. This makes it difficult for archaeologists to draw boundaries that define a discrete political system. Scholars once thought that Casas Grandes lorded over a huge area extending well into what is now the USA (Di Peso 1974). Some now argue that direct control did not extend any farther than the 15 km core area, and certainly no more distant than the 30 km inner zone (Whalen and Minnis 2001b). Beyond that, the influence of Casas Grandes was not strong, but it was extensive and included Black Mountain sites in the Mogollon areas and Animas sites of the northwestern Chihuahuan Desert (Box 6.4), reflecting likely corridors of trade into the northern Southwest (Fish and Fish 1999:38–40; Schaafsma and Riley 1999:241–2). In other areas, in contrast, the impact of Casas Grandes was much weaker (Whalen and Minnis 1999:60–61). Research at Villa Ahumada, for example, some 40 km to the northeast of the center, suggests that people there were more closely tied to the Jornada Mogollon tradition than to the Casas Grandes system (Cruz Antillón and Maxwell 1999).

Where did Casas Grandes come from?

One reason that Casas Grandes has fascinated visitors for so long is because it is an enormous site that seems to have suddenly popped up in the middle of nowhere. Adding to its mystique is the combination of

Box 6.4 The Animas tradition

The Animas area, centered in what is now southwestern New Mexico, has played an important role in defining the scale of Casas Grandes's influence and authority. Because Animas archaeological sites share material culture with Casas Grandes, early interpretations considered this the northern frontier of Casas Grandes territory (e.g., Di Peso 1974). The identification of small "ballcourts" in the Animas area has encouraged this view, although these courts are simple rows of stones delineating a playing field rather than the Casas Grandes-style I-shaped ballcourts (Whalen and Minnis 1996).

A number of archaeologists suggest that this interpretation of the Animas area as subservient to the Casas Grandes political system is inaccurate. John Douglas (1995), for example, reviews the evidence for Casas Grandes dominance at Animas sites and finds little empirical support. He suggests that the distance and resulting interaction costs were too great for the center to have exerted much control, and he instead proposes a more dynamic model in which Animas people consumed some of the goods from Casas Grandes, but in small quantities that were procured indirectly. A similar conclusion is reached by Paul Fish and Suzanne Fish (1999:38–9). They note that while some polychrome pottery *styles* are shared between Casas Grandes and Animas sites, the two areas are separated by a region in which different pottery was produced, confirming that Casas Grandes was not a monolithic political entity controlling vast regions. And many of the Animas polychromes exhibiting Casas Grandes styles were locally made – they are copies of the Ramos style, not the result of direct exchange (Woosley and Olinger 1993).

An illustration of Animas archaeology is provided by the Joyce Well Site, located 130 km northwest of Casas Grandes (Skibo *et al.* 2002). The site consists of a 200-room pueblo built of coursed adobe mud around a plaza. Occupied from the thirteenth through fifteenth centuries, the Joyce Well Site was contemporaneous with Casas Grandes, and it features a simple ballcourt defined by two rows of rocks, locally produced pottery decorated with Casas Grandes styles, and shell ornaments and jewelry. Based on the configuration of architecture and artifacts, William Walker and James Skibo (2002) conclude that residents of the Joyce Well Site participated in a common religious system focused on Casas Grandes, and although they may have gone there on pilgrimages, they were not ruled by the influential center.

Puebloan features similar to those seen to the north with Mesoamerican traits commonly found to the south. These characteristics have inspired a variety of explanations for the emergence of Casas Grandes, few of which can be easily dismissed owing to the relatively unexplored and poorly understood archaeology of the ruins and surrounding area.

Di Peso (1974) originally proposed that Casas Grandes was a Mesoamerican outpost established to facilitate trade with Puebloan societies to the north. On the basis of an inaccurate chronology that put the ruins over 150 years too early, Di Peso argued that the outpost was established by Toltecs who subjugated Chihuahuan locals and traded with Hohokam and Chacoan people. A new chronology, however, reveals that Casas Grandes was not built until the turn of the thirteenth century, after both the Toltec and Chaco traditions had faded from prominence. Although some scholars still contend that the center was part of a Mesoamerican mercantile system, perhaps established by the Aztlán ancestors of the later Aztecs (e.g., Kelley 1993), the evidence indicates a more limited exchange economy at Casas Grandes and a smaller sphere of regular interaction.

An alternative view agrees that Casas Grandes was founded by immigrants who established control over local inhabitants but argues that these newcomers were Chacoan elites fleeing from the north. This model is proposed by Lekson (1999a), who points out that Chaco Canyon, Aztec, and Casas Grandes not only are on virtually the same north–south alignment – what Lekson calls the "Chaco Meridian" – but also appeared sequentially (Box 6.1). Architectural similarities, such as T-shaped doors and elevated platforms, are offered as evidence of this connection (Figure 6.14). Lekson (1999a) constructs a comprehensive argument for why and how the leading families of Chaco Canyon were compelled to flee first to Aztec and then more than 600 km south to Casas Grandes. According to the model, the Casas Grandes area was only sparsely inhabited, allowing the Chacoan refugees to establish a center that reflected both their own traditions and those of the Mesoamerican frontier.

While most archaeologists welcome Lekson's consideration of large-scale spatial and temporal patterns, a few scholars have challenged the details of his Chaco Meridian model (e.g., Phillips 2000; Whalen and Minnis 2003; Wilcox 1999b:98). Perhaps most problematic for any explanation that sees Casas Grandes as an imported phenomenon is the growing body of evidence suggesting that it was an indigenous development. This evidence is emerging from new research on the "Viejo Period," which lasted from AD 700 until Casas Grandes itself emerged around AD 1200. Viejo sites are not well known, owing to a lack of extensive research as well as the likelihood that many lie beneath sites of the later

6.14 Several features found at Casas Grandes, such as the T-shaped door illustrated here, also characterize the great house architecture of Chaco Canyon and Aztec. Some scholars therefore suggest a direct link – perhaps even a migration – between the two areas.

"Medio Period," the era of Casas Grandes. What is known about the Viejo Period is that the earliest sites formed pithouse villages not unlike the Mogollon villages to the north – they even clustered around larger semi-subterranean "community houses." As time passed, Viejo people began building above-ground buildings made of jacal, just like other Puebloan people (Whalen and Minnis 2001b:136–7, 197).

What makes the Viejo Period so important is that many of these early cultural patterns foreshadow features most commonly associated with the Medio Period. Viejo pottery, for example, includes brown- and redwares whose styles and vessel forms exhibit continuity with Casas Grandes polychromes (Schaafsma and Riley 1999:245–6). Furthermore, after about AD 1000, Viejo sites grew into large farming communities that expanded into the same piedmont areas where later Medio sites are found. Viejo people even started importing exotic pottery, marine shell, and pieces of copper (Whalen and Minnis 2001b:197), a trade that fueled increasing differences in wealth and perhaps decision-making authority among Viejo people.

This evidence of continuity between the Viejo and Medio Periods has led a number of scholars to conclude that Casas Grandes was an indigenous development. Whalen and Minnis (1996, 1999, 2001b, 2003) believe that the center emerged largely for the same reasons proposed for the development of Chaco Canyon several generations earlier. They argue that the comparatively rich riverine waterways draining the Sierra Madre fueled competition among kin-based social groups in different communities. This competition was rarely overt, instead occurring within the acceptable domain of ballcourt games, religious rituals, and feasting events. The more grandiose the events sponsored by your social group, the more impressive the venue, and the greater the apparent successes of the ceremonies, the more that people would acquiesce to the authority of your group and its leaders and the more willing they would be to help you arrange the next feast or ceremony. And your success would be measured not just by how much food you could muster, but also by the number of exotic items that you displayed. Archaeologists recognize that such "peer-polity competition" can rapidly drive communities toward more complex social, political, and economic relationships.

Whalen and Minnis (2001b) believe that Casas Grandes had advantages afforded by its unusually abundant arable land. Over time, this allowed its inhabitants to develop a political system whose control was concentrated within a 15 km radius of the center. Beyond this area, competition continued between peripheral communities, leading to the persistent density of ballcourts found up to 30 km from Casas Grandes. At various points in time, the leading groups of Casas Grandes probably maintained alliances with communities beyond the core zone. These alliances provided the necessary conduits for a modest "prestige goods" economy in which exotic craft items were traded both into and out of Casas Grandes, fueling development not only of the center but also of peripheral communities (Bradley 2000:181). Whalen and Minnis (2001b:185) further argue that Casas Grandes probably used these alliances to provision the center with basic commodities, such as food.

If Casas Grandes was as successful as Whalen and Minnis propose, why was it unable to unify a larger area? One suggestion is that Casas Grandes was not yet centralized enough, for a number of competing social groups apparently lived at the center, even at its height. This explains the decentralized production of shell crafts, with the major residential kin groups producing their own goods, perhaps guided but not directly controlled by leading kin members (Whalen and Minnis 2001b:184–5). Each group striving to outdo the others drove the vibrant prestige goods economy responsible for Casas Grandes's growth. Such competition also probably inspired awe-inspiring ceremonial displays that no doubt attracted visitors from long distances away, perhaps making Casas Grandes a pilgrimage destination not unlike Chaco Canyon had been over a century earlier (e.g., Fish and Fish 1999). But the lack of a single cohesive political entity at Casas Grandes made territorial consolidation difficult to sustain beyond fleeting alliances with neighboring communities.

This model explains the curious mortuary patterns identified at Casas Grandes. Di Peso recovered almost 500 interments, of which 42.5 percent had burial goods – half of those consisted of simple offerings of locally produced pottery, while another 42 percent included small quantities of shell, copper, and other jewelry items. John Ravesloot's (1988) statistical analysis of the mortuary data identified about a dozen people, including adults and adolescents, who had been afforded elaborate "secondary" burials in which their decomposed bodies were reinterred in either the Mound of Offerings or the House of the Dead. These burials included rare accompaniments like ceramic hand drums and bone flutes. Ravesloot concluded that this was evidence for ascriptive ranking at Casas Grandes, through which the most elite families retained their wealth and authority from generation to generation. The fact that the rarest burial goods were musical instruments probably used in ceremonies further suggests that the highest status was held by religious leaders, positions that may have been retained from generation to generation, as revealed by the layered interments in subfloor tombs in the House of the Dead (Whalen and Minnis 2001b:187).

Ravesloot's analysis identified a mere thirteen people who fit the highest category of mortuary treatment, suggesting they held positions at the pinnacle of Casas Grandes society. However, he could only associate fourteen people with his next lower category – primary interments in which a modest variety of mortuary goods were included. And only forty burials fit in his third category of minimal mortuary treatment. So, while fewer than 3 percent of all 447 identified interments at Casas Grandes fit in the elite level of mortuary treatment, this is misleading since only sixty-seven burials positively fit in *any* of Ravesloot's statistically derived categories. This means that, in fact, a surprising 19 percent of his positively identified sample received the highest level of treatment. The mortuary patterns therefore suggest that the highest status at Casas Grandes was achieved by a fairly sizeable portion of the population. And certainly, from a cross-cultural perspective, the amount of wealth invested in the highest-tier burials was modest (Whalen and Minnis 2000:173). All of this is consistent with an interpretation of Casas Grandes as a weakly centralized political system that was driven by social and ceremonial competition.

Assuming that Whalen and Minnis are correct and Casas Grandes was an indigenous development, one might wonder why the center exhibits so many cultural features typically associated with Mesoamerican and Puebloan societies. Answering this requires a consideration of the kind of prestige-oriented ceremonial competition proposed for Casas Grandes. As different social groups try to outdo one another, enhance their prestige, and attract new followers, one effective method is to appropriate symbols from more powerful traditions, particularly those that are distant in space and even time. At Casas Grandes, aspiring religious authorities may have looked toward Mesoamerica and Chaco Canyon for such symbols. People living in the Chihuahuan desert knew about the powerful religious traditions of both areas, a mystique that leaders could use to their advantage (Whalen and Minnis 2001b:187–8). To the north, the fact that Chaco was so distant in space and already fading in time made it a perfect source of powerful symbols, and immigrants from the Mimbres area and even from the Chaco region could have introduced ideas such as T-shaped doors and coursed adobe architecture. Meanwhile, Mesoamerican influences introduced ballcourt competitions, platform mound ceremonies, and symbols such as the plumed water serpent. All of this fed into Casas Grandes competition, producing a unique mix of cultural features. By the end of the thirteenth century, this suite of symbols and rituals had coalesced and began to reverberate across the desert and back into the northern Puebloan world at a time when the Southwest was undergoing substantial changes.

7　The Great Abandonment

Hopi oral traditions tell of the travels of those who survived the destruction of the corrupt village of *Palatkwapi*. People separated into several groups, each heading out in a different direction – some clans traveled alone, while others banded together. Those who went to the south were never seen again. The rest, however, walked for many years, encountering other tribes, some of which were friendly and others which were not. Some Hopi clans disappeared, while others filled their ranks with strangers they met during their journey.

Moving from place to place, building villages along the way, many of the clans converged on *Homol'ovi*, where they established two settlements. In the smaller one, people of the Water and Sand clans lived, while the larger structure housed members of the Tobacco, Rabbit, Sun, Eagle, Hawk, Turkey, and Moon clans. Some time later, villagers at *Homol'ovi* were joined by the Badger clan and a group calling itself the Reed clan. Other groups arrived, including the Fox and Fire clans from the east. And from time to time, still more people drifted in from different directions. "Thus *Homol'ovi* grew large and populous" (Courlander 1971:70–3).

Perhaps the Pueblo oral histories recall the decades at the end of the thirteenth century and beginning of the fourteenth century, a period that is often referred to as the "Great Abandonment" since Puebloan people depopulated large portions of the Colorado Plateau. This has often erroneously been labeled the "disappearance of the Anasazi" and presented as one of the unsolved "mysteries" of Southwest pre-Contact history, but archaeologists have made considerable progress in reconstructing and explaining the massive population movements that took place at this time. As related in the oral histories, the Puebloan people did not disappear – they simply moved, sometimes covering hundreds of kilometers during their migrations. And, for many Pueblo people today, the places they left even today are considered sacred homelands, their points of origin.

From where? People leave the north

The so-called "abandonments" – the depopulations and migrations – did not happen all at once. In some regions, emigration had been going on for some time. The Virgin Anasazi on the far northwestern frontier of the Southwest, for example, left their homelands by the late AD 1100s (Figure 7.1), moving west and east, probably impacted by the same drought that undermined the Chacoan tradition. After first aggregating along the Colorado River, the Virgin Anasazi vacated this area too by the early AD 1200s and probably moved southeast into the Kayenta region (Lyneis 1996:25–6).

The most remarkable abandonments, however, occurred in the late thirteenth century, particularly in the Mesa Verde region. As many as 15,000 people lived there in the early AD 1200s – by AD 1250s, perhaps seventy towns packed the region around Mesa Verde (Varien *et al.* 1996:104). Although archaeologists have a difficult time reconstructing depopulation, one approach is to track the numbers of tree-ring dates from each year, knowing that peaks in the numbers of dates probably represent peaks in construction, while the absence of new dates indicates a lack of expansion. Lipe's assessment of tree-ring data found that tree-cutting in southeastern Utah all but ceased after the AD 1260s, while no new dates are found on Mesa Verde after AD 1280. By this time, as few as 7,000 people remained, and they also soon left (Lipe and Varien 1999:325–7; Varien *et al.* 1996).

Research in Sand Canyon provides a specific case study of depopulation in the Mesa Verde region. Throughout the drainage, the aggregated town of Sand Canyon Pueblo and the dispersed households surrounding it continued to grow through the early part of the AD 1200s, but no new construction occurred after AD 1277, and even minor remodeling ceased after the AD 1290s. The trash deposits in the midden show that the initial abandonment was gradual, with perhaps a family or two leaving every once in a while, but the final exodus was more rapid – so rapid that they actually left behind many intact vessels and perfectly good stone tools (Lipe 1995). Whether the process of abandonment in Sand Canyon characterizes other Mesa Verde communities is unknown at this point, but it does suggest that depopulation started as a trickle of families left, and ended with a more precipitous abandonment by the last two decades of the thirteenth century (Duff and Wilshusen 2000; Wilshusen 2002).

Farther south, the Kayenta region also experienced depopulation, but the record there is more complicated. As outlined in the last chapter, this region experienced a modest amount of immigration from the north and west as early as the late AD 1100s. This was accompanied by the contraction of local populations, as marginal areas such as Monument

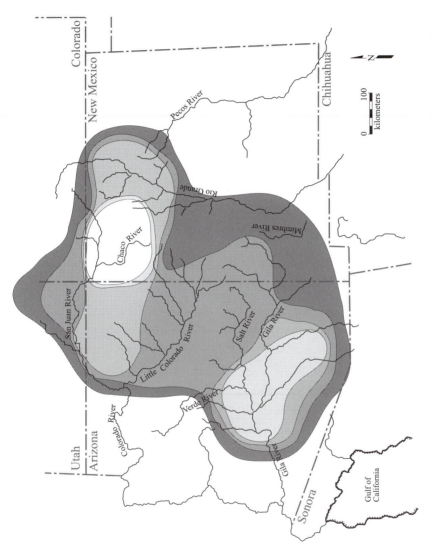

7.1 Farming populations in the early AD 1200s were concentrated in the Four Corners area of the Colorado Plateau and along the Gila and Salt rivers. Lighter shading represents larger populations.

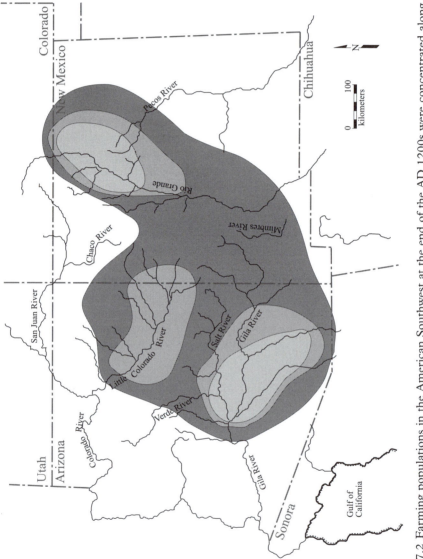

7.2 Farming populations in the American Southwest at the end of the AD 1200s were concentrated along the upper Rio Grande drainage and the Gila and Salt Rivers; people also clustered in the Little Colorado River drainage. Lighter shading represents larger populations.

Valley and side canyons feeding the San Juan and Colorado Rivers were abandoned and people aggregated in plaza-centered towns along the upper reaches of smaller drainages amenable to intensive farming. Jeffrey Dean (1996b:35–9), for example, estimates that as many as 700 people established at least twenty of these towns in Tsegi Canyon between AD 1250 and 1286. But in a brief period between about AD 1290 and 1300, even these aggregated sites were abandoned in an orderly fashion, with residents sealing doors to their homes and taking portable tools with them (Fish *et al*. 1994:149).

To the east, in the San Juan Basin and surrounding drainages, a similar surge of population growth was followed by a similarly precipitous abandonment. The brief reoccupation of Chaco Canyon that occurred in the early AD 1200s ended, and people aggregated in wetter highlands, building defensible roomblocks. In the eastern San Juan Basin, these communities persevered for a few decades, but depopulation began around AD 1275 and was complete a few decades later (Roney 1996:156–7). And just beyond the southern margins of the Basin, the same process occurred. On Cebolleta Mesa, near the present-day Pueblo of Acoma, dispersed populations briefly came together to form two very large, defensive towns that soon were abandoned (Roney 1996:162–5). To the northeast, in the Gallina Highlands, people built towers well into the late AD 1200s, and evidence of violent death and burned sites suggests upheaval – over 40 percent of skeletal remains from this area exhibit traumatic injuries (Martin 1994:104; Wilcox and Haas 1994:216). By AD 1300, this region too was empty (Crown *et al*. 1996:193–4).

The trend of abandonment across the northern Southwest is clear, and although it was more rapid during the late thirteenth century, the exodus began much earlier. Puebloan people in the northernmost regions gradually moved south, beginning in the late AD 1100s. This started first as the contraction of populations into aggregated villages, but even these too were depopulated. And as northern populations flowed south, they contributed to new aggregations, both as some locals accepted refugees into their growing towns and as others clustered to defend themselves against the expanding tide of immigrants. By the AD 1290s, the northern San Juan River area was largely empty of Puebloan people, and by the AD 1300s, so too were the Kayenta region and San Juan Basin (Figure 7.2).

Why the big hurry to leave?

Explaining the "Great Abandonment" has proven to be a challenge. The earliest explanations blamed the exodus on the appearance of new

nomadic groups who pressured Puebloan people through raids and warfare (e.g., Gladwin 1957). This proposal was based on historic episodes
of hostility between Puebloan people and Athapaskans and Utes, relative
newcomers to the Southwest who moved in from the north. The evidence
for warfare, the widespread abandonments, and the subsequent settling
of vacated regions by these nomadic peoples were considered to be compelling evidence. The arguments, however, have not held up to scrutiny.
Archaeological evidence indicates that Athapaskan people did not arrive
in the Southwest much earlier than the late AD 1400s (Towner and Dean
1996:13–14). While some scholars argue for an earlier appearance, in the
late AD 1300s, even this would be too late to explain Puebloan abandonments. The movement of the Ute into the Southwest, on the other hand, is
more poorly understood (Brugge 1996:259), and they could have arrived
in the AD 1200s. But for either of these nomadic groups, no direct evidence of their role in the Puebloan abandonments has been identified.

The Great Drought

Today, most archaeologists see environmental change as having played a
substantial role in the Puebloan abandonments. Chapter 2 surveys the
evidence for the so-called "Great Drought," a precipitous drop in rainfall the likes of which had no precedent in the region's human history.
Starting in the northern Colorado Plateau in the last two decades of the
thirteenth century, challenging conditions persisted for many years. It
was not, however, identical across the entire Southwest, and in fact it
seems to have crept from north to south – the El Malpais of central New
Mexico, for example, experienced drought most acutely in the late AD
1300s, almost a century after it hit Mesa Verde (Grissino-Mayer 1996;
Grissino-Mayer et al. 1997). Since this seems to parallel the movement
of people toward the south, the temptation is to regard the drought as
driving people before it as their crops failed and they literally sought
greener pastures. But why would entire regions have been so thoroughly
abandoned? Some waterways, such as the San Juan River and the side
drainages feeding it, continued to flow even during the height of the
drought, so certainly it was possible for people to make a living there.
But these areas too were left vacant.

No one doubts that the Great Drought severely impacted people living
in the Southwest. Two bits of evidence, however, suggest that a simple
cause–effect relationship cannot fully explain what prompted abandonment. First, the correlation between the onset of the drought and the
beginning of the exodus is not particularly strong. People living in the
western Mesa Verde region, for example, began to leave a few decades

before the drought hit, and even around Mesa Verde, emigration was occurring earlier in the thirteenth century. Second, evidence suggests that, even as people were leaving, enough rainfall was falling to accommodate substantial populations. Carla Van West (1994a, 1994b) simulated the impact of the Great Drought on farming productivity and discovered that even with the decrease in rainfall, people in the Mesa Verde region could have produced enough food as long as no other social or political factors prevented equal access to farmlands. Michael Adler (1994:91; see also Varien et al. 2000:59) similarly describes how nearly twice as much arable land was available as was needed by thirteenth-century populations.

When describing climatic changes of the late AD 1200s, however, simply looking at annual rainfall is probably not adequate. Equally important was the decreasing predictability of rainfall, especially during the critical summer months when crops were maturing. Kenneth Petersen (1994) points to a shift in the thirteenth century toward unpredictable summer rainfall and drought conditions during winter months. Some evidence also suggests that erosion was an increasing problem, leading to arroyo cutting and the degradation of soil fertility (Fish et al. 1994:148). The cold of the Little Ice Age, which does predate the Great Drought by a few decades, perhaps had the most significant impact for people in higher elevations where a short growing season was probably more of a concern for farmers than was the amount of rainfall (Petersen 1994, 1996).

All of these climatic factors combined to stress farmers of the northern Southwest (Figure 7.3). But were they sufficient to force people to leave? Mark Varien and his colleagues (1996:104) provide anecdotal evidence that climatic change is an insufficient explanation for the thirteenth-century exodus. They describe the summer of 1989 as one of the driest on record in southwest Colorado – tree-rings from this year show a substantial impact on growth (Cook 2000; Grissino-Mayer 1996). However, commercial farmers were still able to obtain at least partial crops. All of this evidence suggests that other factors contributed to the "Great Abandonment," perhaps even playing greater roles than the climatic changes.

The human impact

One possible reason that everyone left was severe human-induced environmental degradation that, when combined with the climatic changes, made staying in the Mesa Verde area that much less palatable. Aggregated towns of the AD 1200s had a more substantial impact on the landscape

7.3 In addition to the unpredictable summer rainfall, winter drought conditions, and increasing erosion impacting people in the Mesa Verde area, the growing season may also have shortened because of the cold of the Little Ice Age.

than did dispersed households of earlier periods. Such dense populations were hard on local wild resources, and archaeologists have identified decreasing frequencies of large game and increasing quantities of smaller animals such as cottontail, jackrabbit, and domesticated turkeys in later Mesa Verde sites (Driver 2002; Muir and Driver 2002). Alongside these changes is a decrease in the number of arrowheads found – at Wallace Ruin, a twelfth-century great house, one point was found for every fifty-seven decorated sherds recovered, but at Long House, a thirteenth-century cliff dwelling, only one point for every 1,200 decorated sherds was identified (Lipe and Varien 1999:317). This suggests a decrease in the amount of bow-and-arrow hunting during the thirteenth century and may be symptomatic of environmental degradation. It may also reflect reduced access to prime hunting areas as the larger towns asserted their control over discrete territories (Driver 2002:158–9).

Extensive farming activity around the aggregated towns probably also caused problems, although the evidence for this is equivocal. Macrofloral analyses reveal a modest decrease in tree cover and an increase in shrubs that grow in deforested areas, a pattern indicating that forests were being cleared for farmland and firewood (Lipe and Varien 1999:330). Karen Adams and Vandy Bowyer (2002) note that an increase in weedy species and lower-ranked plant foods in archaeological sites of the AD 1200s may reflect problems with farming, but the trend is not very strong, and the continued use of maize cobs for fuel rather than for food is evidence against any severe crisis in farming productivity – in historic times, cobs served as a backup food source. Since people were mostly dry farming, soil exhaustion also could have become a problem, but the Mesa Verde region is covered by a silty loam that is not very susceptible to fertility depletion.

What do the bones tell us?

Since many models for depopulation of the northern Southwest are based on climate- or human-induced environmental degradation, one way to evaluate them is to look at human health during the thirteenth century. Since the human skeleton records information about diet, disease, and nutritional stress, it provides a window to understanding what people were actually feeling about their situation.

Several studies have assessed Puebloan health in the AD 1200s through the analysis of human skeletal material (e.g., Martin 1994; Nelson et al. 1994). What they found is that the typical person living in the Mesa Verde region suffered from a variety of ailments. Infants had a 15 percent chance of dying before the age of 1, and even more deaths occurred at the age of weaning, between the ages of 2 and 3. Before the age of 5, frequent stresses caused by diet or disease were severe enough to disrupt growth of tooth enamel and long bones. Although not directly fatal, anemia brought on by poor diet or chronic diarrhea impacted the cranial bones in about 50 percent of children. The mortality rate was also severe for youths between 15 and 25, perhaps owing more to violence than to diet or disease – 41 percent of skeletal remains from the Gallina area exhibit traumatic lesions. Overall, life expectancy for a newborn was a bit over 18 owing to the high rate of infant mortality; surviving to puberty increased your life expectancy to around 30 years of age (Stodder 1987).

Despite this poor picture of health, people in the Mesa Verde region were actually better off than many of their peers elsewhere in the Southwest. And while their ailments might seem severe, few were fatal, and in fact populations grew at a steady rate during the twelfth and thirteenth centuries. People may not have always felt great, but in general their health was not really any worse than anywhere else in the world at this time – newborn life expectancy in medieval Europe was only in the mid-twenties.

As the thirteenth century progressed and aggregations grew larger, people did experience a modest decrease in overall health. Ann Stodder's comparison (1987) of Mesa Verde people before and after AD 975, for example, found that anemia chronic enough to impact bone afflicted 72 percent of children above the age of 3 in the early population, but that 69 percent of the lesions exhibited healing. In the late population, about the same number of children exhibited lesions, but only 46 percent showed any healing (Box 7.1). In Stodder's late sample, infant and child mortality was minimally higher than for the early sample, and evidence for episodic stress impacting the skeleton was also slightly more common, a trend also exhibited by the thirteenth-century population at Salmon Ruins (Berry 1983). Skeletal analyses identify a substantial increase in dental problems; cavities are typically found in less than 25 percent of individuals before the AD 1200s but climb to as high as 85 percent in some thirteenth-century populations, suggesting a much greater reliance on starchy farming produce than on nutritious wild foods (Martin 1994:104).

Despite these trends, differences between the early and late Mesa Verde samples are not extreme enough to suggest that people were faced with severe food shortages. In fact, many of these changes may be the result of the denser living conditions in aggregated towns, where poor sanitation probably encouraged transmission of intestinal and respiratory disorders. Aggregated towns also perhaps relied more on farmed foods, especially maize, as they impacted wild resources in their territories and their mobility became restricted by neighboring communities. Whether these changes reflect food crises severe enough to force complete regional abandonment seems unlikely.

The social crisis

The environmental degradation of the late thirteenth century was apparently not severe enough to have made abandonment the only solution. Certainly, some of the traditional Puebloan solutions to climatic stress, such as an increase in mobility and population dispersal, would have been difficult as populations grew (Van West 1996:219; Varien 1999). But other solutions were probably possible, such as more intensive farming strategies, more centralized decision-making, or the emigration of smaller numbers of people. Some of these strategies were in fact important for later populations living along the upper Rio Grande drainage

Box 7.1 The Dan Canyon child

Discovered in 1990 along the edge of Lake Powell in southeastern Utah, the Dan Canyon burial provides a glimpse of life and death on the fringe of the Puebloan world. In the late AD 1200s, the burial had been placed in a simple pit underneath an overhanging cliff face. Archaeologists, who consulted Hopi Pueblo representatives during their investigations, discovered that the burial had been damaged by the reservoir, and they excavated it to prevent further destruction (Dominguez *et al.* 1994).

The Dan Canyon burial consisted of the remains of a young child who was interred with several items, including a ceramic canteen placed near the child's head, a leather bag containing rice grass seeds, three baskets made of yucca, spoons made of cottonwood, an Amazonstone pendant, and several other wild plant foods. The burial contained a few seeds of domesticated squash. This configuration of items was common in Puebloan burials of this era, although archaeologists were surprised at the relative paucity of domesticated food. One other unusual discovery in the burial was coprolites – desiccated fecal matter that apparently survived in this arid climate (Dominguez *et al.* 1994).

From the skeletal remains, investigators determined that the child was about 3 or 4 years old when he or she died. Microscopic examination of the teeth found them to be healthy, with no indication of severe dietary stress. Radiographic studies of the child's leg bones, however, did identify three "Harris lines," disruptions of bone growth caused by an episode of nutritional stress – they are not uncommon among pre-Contact populations. Study of the coprolites revealed that the child's last few meals were primarily ground seeds from wild grasses. No parasites were identified. Evidence did show, however, that the child was probably consuming Mormon tea (Dominguez *et al.* 1994), a local plant with medicinal properties especially valued for alleviating respiratory problems.

The Dan Canyon child is only a single case of premature death in the thirteenth century, but provides a snapshot of what life was like. The recovery of wild plant foods is not surprising in this part of the Puebloan world, where farming was always a challenge, particularly in the late AD 1200s. The child indeed had suffered episodes of dietary stress, but the skeleton was otherwise in remarkably good health. Obviously, however, some ailment had taken his or her very young life. Was it a respiratory ailment that spread among people living in close quarters with one another?

in similar environmental circumstances, as will be discussed in the next chapter. So why did thirteenth-century groups in the northern Southwest not pursue alternative solutions to the crises they faced?

One possible explanation is that the aggregated towns simply lacked social cohesion and effective decision-making mechanisms (Adler 1994:95; Adler and Varien 1994:83). Recall from the last chapter that thirteenth-century towns such as Sand Canyon Pueblo were largely composed of disparate social groups who came together out of necessity. Various sources of evidence suggest that households maintained a substantial degree of autonomy within these new towns, and centralized leadership was avoided (Lipe 2002). People were probably still leery of powerful leaders after experiences of the Chaco era, and no doubt a number of social mechanisms were employed to ensure that no single person or group could achieve an uncomfortable level of status and authority. Perhaps by this time, many of the morality tales that Pueblo people still tell today were developed to instill an egalitarian ethos.

These were therefore towns only in the sense that many people lived closely together and occasionally acted in concert to face a common threat, particularly for defense against a definable mutual enemy. But their internal ties were tenuous, and it may be that they were not sustainable when the problems were more nebulous and when the solutions required new social and political mechanisms. The lack of centralized control made it difficult to effect large-scale social or technological solutions requiring the cooperation of many different social groups. At the same time, as the Oraibi example of chapter 2 demonstrates, political machinations in the context of an egalitarian ethos can lead to the kind of factionalism and the potential for violence and fissioning increasingly seen in the archaeological record of the AD 1200s. And, in addition to the internal stresses and detrimental climatic changes, the disruptions of this period included increased raiding and warfare, further splintering the fragile social and political relationships within each town.

As tensions such as this grew in the towns of the northern Southwest, many families simply packed up their belongings and left. Doing so was perhaps a difficult decision, for while Puebloan people traditionally maintained long-distance contacts, aggregations of the AD 1200s probably broke many of these ties. This meant that any family setting out on their own could not be assured of their destination or whether or not they would be welcome once they got there. The fact that people did leave northern towns is testament to how uncomfortable life had become. As each family or kin group migrated south, tensions in the towns they left may have been alleviated for a while, but the town lost some of its labor force and defensive capacity with each person that fled. It is perhaps for this reason that the abandonment started as a trickle but ended as a flood. Continuing climatic degradation no doubt contributed to the exodus and may in fact explain why the entire northern Southwest was abandoned so completely and permanently – by the mid-1300s, no Puebloan people were left.

Where did everyone go?

On the face of it, abandonment was simple – people moved south, away from the cold and the dysfunctional towns of the Mesa Verde region and into warmer areas with arable lands and dependable water sources, where they joined locals and other migrant groups in increasingly multi-ethnic communities. The details of these migrations are fairly complex, however, for the destinations of migrants were quite varied. Tracking these movements is not one of the traditional strengths of archaeology, which works best when people stay in one spot and generate lots of trash for us to recover and analyze. Migrants, in contrast, leave little for us to use to reconstruct their movements, and when they do find a place to settle down, they are likely to blend in with the local populace. This makes the late thirteenth and early fourteenth centuries an exciting archaeological challenge, leading to some exceptionally innovative research.

The Kayenta–Tusayan fusion

One of the first areas impacted by refugees from the north was the Kayenta region in what is now northeastern Arizona. As described earlier, this region was undergoing changes as early as the late AD 1100s with the immigration of Virgin Anasazi groups from the northwest. Not long after, people coming from the Mesa Verde region appeared, funneling into Kayenta via the north–south corridor of Chinle Wash. These newcomers introduced distinctive pottery styles, and even Mesa Verde masonry techniques can be identified, such as in one of the granaries at Kiet Siel (Dean 1996b:35; Dean et al. 1994:59–61). As these immigrants flowed into the Kayenta area, local inhabitants responded in a number of ways. Some welcomed the newcomers, while others retreated to defensive locations. Still others apparently decided that it was time for them to move. Dean (1996b:35) notes that the Chinle drainage, once the setting for Kayenta–Mesa Verde interaction, was so inundated with Mesa Verde people that evidence of Kayenta material culture becomes hard to find.

Some Kayenta people apparently fled the growing onslaught by moving south into what is now central Arizona, which archaeologists consider to be the domain of the Tusayan tradition. Kayenta and Tusayan people

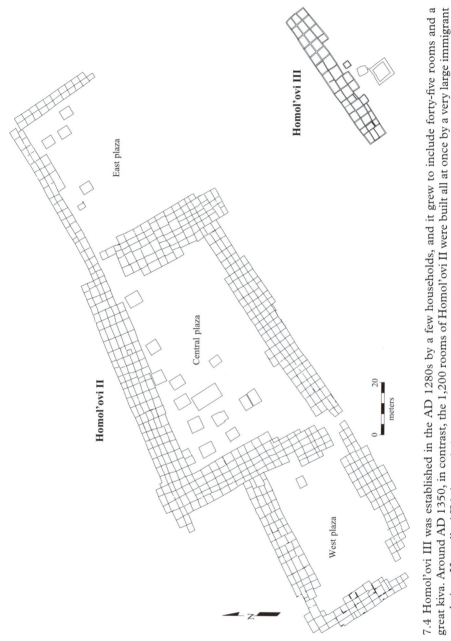

Homol'ovi III

Homol'ovi II

East plaza

Central plaza

West plaza

N

0   20
meters

7.4 Homol'ovi III was established in the AD 1280s by a few households, and it grew to include forty-five rooms and a great kiva. Around AD 1350, in contrast, the 1,200 rooms of Homol'ovi II were built all at once by a very large immigrant population. Homol'ovi II is located about 2 km east of Homol'ovi III, on the opposite side of the Little Colorado River.

long had maintained close connections, and extensive trade between the regions goes back to the twelfth century. After AD 1250, as Kayenta people retreated south, designs typical of their pottery appeared on vessels produced using Tusayan techniques and materials, reflecting a fusion of the two traditions. By the AD 1280s, additional influences from the east further impacted the ceramic styles, as did the use of coal for firing pottery, creating unique ceramic styles reflecting the cultural sharing typical of this era.

This melding of different traditions occurred in aggregated settlements built near springs along the Hopi Mesas and the Little Colorado River. The Hopi Mesa area became a melting pot for people from the north, west, and east, while the Little Colorado towns experienced the greatest influx of populations from the north and south. In all Kayenta–Tusayan towns, people built roomblocks around enclosed plazas, which E. Charles Adams (1996) argues became the ceremonial spaces of the late AD 1200s, supplanting the round and square kivas of earlier times. By AD 1350, these towns were 500 percent larger than they had been 100 years earlier, a pattern most clearly identified in the Little Colorado drainage (Adams 1996). Homol'ovi III, for example, is a forty-five-room pueblo and great kiva occupied from AD 1275 to 1300. By AD 1350, Homol'ovi II was built, consisting of 1,200 rooms arranged around three enclosed plazas (Figure 7.4). This new town included several square kiva rooms, but no great kiva (Adams 2002).

Multi-ethnic towns of the Mogollon Rim

As in the Hopi Mesas and Little Colorado drainage, places in the highlands along the Mogollon Rim also received an influx of immigrants. This took place somewhat later than in the Kayenta–Tusayan region, as illustrated in the Silver Creek drainage, located just north of the Mogollon Rim. Here, modest settlements of over twenty rooms were common through the late thirteenth century, with a few, such as Pottery Hill, containing around fifty rooms. By AD 1300, however, increasing immigration and the aggregation of the local population created much larger settlements, including the 200-room Bailey Ruin. This in turn was abandoned by AD 1325 in favor of the 500-room Fourmile Ruin (Mills 1999:505).

Who were the immigrants flowing into Silver Creek towns? Pottery again provides some clues. Ceramic vessels dating to the late AD 1200s exhibit styles from the Tusayan area as well as Kayenta vessel forms, but they are made with the same materials as the local pottery (e.g., Zedeño 1994:129). Because these northern-style pots also exhibit northern pottery-making techniques, archaeologists conclude that at least some of

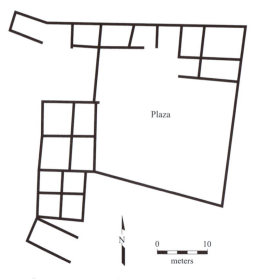

Plaza

N

0   10

meters

7.5 Construction at Chodistaas Pueblo began in AD 1263 with seven rooms and it grew to eighteen rooms by the end of the century. When it was abandoned around AD 1300, its residents established their own roomblock at Grasshopper Pueblo.

the thirteenth-century immigrants were Kayenta–Tusayan people. And they apparently brought more than just their pottery-making techniques – forms of northern ritual architecture also appear in new Mogollon Rim towns, including D-shaped kivas and Kayenta-style plaza kivas.

South of the Mogollon Rim, the Grasshopper Plateau was also a destination for migrants by the end of the thirteenth century. These newcomers joined a small and fairly mobile local population to form larger and larger towns. At the site of Chodistaas (Figure 7.5), for example, initial construction in AD 1263 created a small, seven-room structure that was seasonally occupied by locals. Between AD 1280 and 1285, another small block of eight rooms was constructed and inhabited year-round. Eventually, the modest settlement grew to eighteen rooms surrounding an enclosed plaza. When Chodistaas was abandoned around AD 1300, its residents moved to the then-diminutive Grasshopper Pueblo, where Chodistaas people established their own roomblock next to rooms inhabited by Grasshopper's founders (Reid and Whittlesey 1999:38; Riggs 2001). H. David Tuggle and J. Jefferson Reid (2001:93) suggest that Chodistaas's abandonment may have been under duress, for the structure was burned to the ground.

Like in the Silver Creek drainage, many immigrants to Grasshopper Plateau came from the north – in fact, ceramic evidence suggests that

Grasshopper received immigrants from Silver Creek itself (Mills 1999:508), continuing the domino-like cascade of immigrants forcing or encouraging locals to become migrants themselves. Other refugees arrived from desert areas to the south, from populations whose cultural ties were closer to the Hohokam. Skeletal remains at Grasshopper Pueblo help to confirm these suspicions. Most of the nearly 700 burials recovered from the site exhibit the style of intentional cranial modification – perhaps a sign of beauty and social identity – that is typical of Mogollon populations. However, at least twenty-eight individuals display cranial modification most common to Anasazi populations to the north, while yet a third group of eight people includes no cranial modification, perhaps representing the suspected southern immigrants (Whittlesey and Reid 2001:78).

Grasshopper Pueblo grew to 500 rooms divided into several roomblocks, some of which were contiguous (Figure 7.6). Different sections apparently were occupied by different social groups with varying ethnic backgrounds. Many of the suspected Anasazi people, for example, were interred in Roomblock 5, a structure built with Anasazi architectural details, including T-shaped doorways. A study of skeletal material by Joseph Ezzo (1993; Ezzo and Price 2002) reveals additional details of this social patterning. Ezzo reconstructed dietary habits of the residents in each roomblock by analyzing the elemental composition of their bones. In Roomblock 1, in which both Anasazi and southern immigrants lived (Reid and Whittlesey 1999:118), most people were consuming an unusually high quantity of wild foods. The Mogollon inhabitants of Roomblock 3, in contrast, had a diet high in cultivated foods, while the diet of people living in Roomblock 2 fell between the other two. These differences may reflect dietary preferences for each ethnic group, but also may indicate which resources each group had rights to use; this intriguing pattern will be discussed in more detail below.

Northern migrants moved even farther south, into the traditional heartland of mountain Mogollon people, such as at Point of Pines. Originally constructed at the end of the AD 1200s, this site underwent several expansions until it included approximately 800 rooms. At one point, an L-shaped roomblock with a D-shaped kiva was built by a large group of Kayenta or Tusayan immigrants who made their traditional Tsegi-style orange pottery (Zedeño 2002). They only stayed for a couple of decades, however, before their rooms were burned and abandoned, perhaps hurriedly – rooms full of surplus food were left behind (Haury 1958). Similar events occurred to the west, in the San Pedro Valley, where two Kayenta groups came together and built the thirty-five-room Goat Hill Site in the AD 1290s. Oriented around a central plaza and a D-shaped kiva, perhaps sixty-five people lived at Goat Hill until the AD 1310s, when

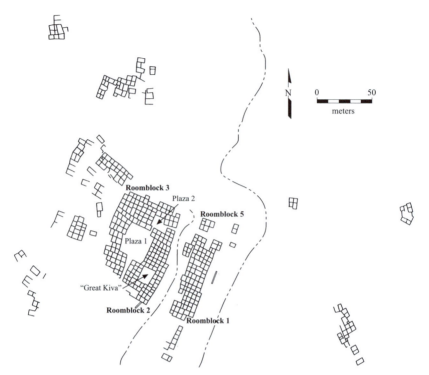

7.6 Starting as a small structure in the thirteenth century, Grasshopper Pueblo grew to include several roomblocks containing a total of 500 rooms. Much of this growth was fueled by immigrants, many of whom built their own roomblocks and maintained some of their own traditions.

the kiva and several rooms were burned and the people left (Woodson 1999).

Newcomers probably were attracted to the higher moisture and more dependable streams and springs of the Mogollon Rim region, although the cooler temperatures of the higher elevations were more challenging for farmers. As northern refugees entered the area in the late AD 1200s, new towns were built on defensible hilltops and ridges. Barbara Mills (1999:507) notes that nearly as much emigration as immigration reveals the instability of the late AD 1200s. By the AD 1300s, however, these trends reversed as unprecedented numbers of people moved into enormous towns, which were now constructed in less defensible locations – the mere size of these aggregations was enough of a deterrent for anyone contemplating a raid.

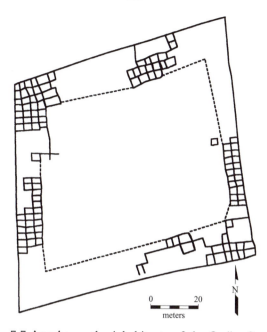

7.7 Attacks on the inhabitants of the Scribe S community probably drove them to build Pueblo de los Muertos quickly, a readily defensible town established between AD 1279 and AD 1284.

The Cibolan "cities"

To the east, in the Cibola highlands of west-central New Mexico, enormous towns also appeared as northern regions were abandoned. Starting in the mid-thirteenth century, people living in small, dispersed residences moved into dense roomblock clusters, but soon these settlements also were abandoned in favor of huge towns of up to 1,400 rooms surrounding central plazas (Cordell *et al.* 1994:129; Kintigh 1996). Most archaeologists believe that these preplanned buildings were constructed all at one time as several smaller settlements were vacated (Kintigh *et al.* 1996:136). Early versions of these towns feature large, open great kivas built outside pueblo walls, but in later towns, no great kivas were built and ceremonial activity instead focused on plaza areas.

The Scribe S site introduced in the last chapter exemplifies these changes. This community originally consisted of several roomblocks with a combined total of 500 rooms (Figure 6.7). Steven LeBlanc (2001:30) argues that attacks forced its inhabitants to construct the defensible Pueblo de los Muertos between AD 1279 and 1284 (Figure 7.7). The

7.8 Atsinna is one of the El Morro Valley towns built in the late thirteenth century. Set high upon a mesa, standing up to three stories tall, and protected by a substantial outer wall with no entrances, Atsinna was designed for defense.

builders were in such a hurry to get the new building up that they used a "ladder" construction technique in which the shell of the structure was first erected; interior divisions were made later. Instead of collecting new materials for the town, they salvaged stone and timber from their old homes. To ensure that residents stayed out of harm's way, the builders diverted a small stream to the only opening in the town's outer wall (LeBlanc 2001:31–4).

By AD 1300, small dispersed residences were gone from the Cibolan landscape and everyone lived in the large towns. In the El Morro Valley, three towns containing 500–1,000 rooms were built after AD 1280, and Andrew Duff (2000:77) estimates that fifteen towns with a combined 7,000 rooms clustered in the area of today's Zuni Pueblo (Figure 7.8). Although archaeologists suspect that immigrants contributed to the large Cibolan towns, the evidence is not nearly as compelling as in the Kayenta–Tusayan and Mogollon Rim towns to the west. Much of the growth of Cibolan towns instead may have been fueled by local population contraction. Since these towns tend to be contiguous roomblocks surrounding single plazas, residents probably shared a more common identity than in contemporaneous aggregations along the Mogollon Rim.

7.9 The Rio Grande drainage increasingly attracted immigrants during the late pre-Contact era, perhaps owing to the ready source of water provided by the river and its tributaries. This photograph shows the Rio Grande riverine area, with the Sandia Mountains in the background.

Keith Kintigh (1996) argues that most Cibolan towns were occupied for only a few generations – some for perhaps only twenty-five years – before they were abandoned. People did not leave, however, but simply built new plaza-centered towns nearby. These movements were probably motivated by a search for dependable water, as later Cibolan towns tend to be built right next to permanent springs. Kintigh also suggests that the lack of social and political mechanisms allowing so many people to live together also contributed to the towns falling apart rather quickly.

The Rio Grande drainage

People abandoning portions of the northern Southwest also flowed into the Rio Grande drainage (Figure 7.9). Although many of these immigrants came from the north, the diversity of cultural features that pop up along the Rio Grande suggest that newcomers came from all over. The

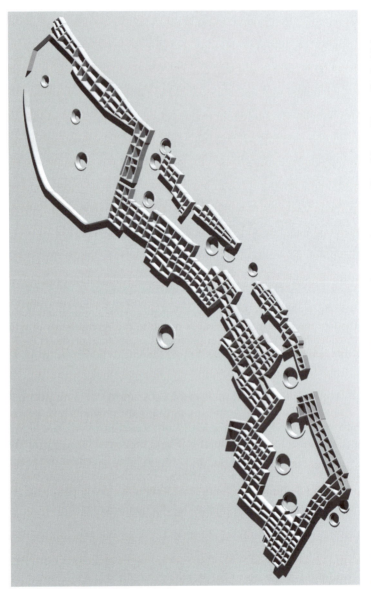

7.10 Tsiping features six plazas, as many as 400 rooms, and over a dozen small and large kivas, all of which were built on a steep volcanic mesa in the Jemez Mountains.

variety of thirteenth-century ceremonial architecture provides just one example of this ethnic diversity – residents of the Rio Grande region built round kivas, keyhole-shaped kivas, D-shaped rooms, square rooms, and great kivas, each representative of different parts of the Southwest.

The northernmost areas of the Rio Grande drainage were inhabited by very few permanent residents prior to the AD 1200s, although people had hunted in these highlands and collected wild foods and raw stone material for many centuries. The Chama and Jemez watersheds, for example, were largely vacant until the late thirteenth century, when newcomers built small residences of twenty to a hundred rooms focused on enclosed plazas. One unusually large settlement is Tsiping, which features six plazas surrounded by as many as 400 rooms and over a dozen small and large kivas (Figure 7.10). Built on a steep escarpment with a complex entryway, the builders of Tsiping were prepared to defend themselves (Haas and Creamer 1996:206). The origin of these immigrants is unresolved. Some may have come down from the Gallina area to the north, but some of the architecture is reminiscent of the northern San Juan drainage and even the San Juan Basin to the west.

Other parts of the Rio Grande drainage were inhabited by indigenous populations prior to the AD 1200s. Far to the northeast, near the modern town of Taos, a small local population living in dispersed households came together by AD 1250 to live in settlements containing hundreds of rooms. These new towns were composed of separate roomblocks, each containing ten to thirty-five rooms and small kivas, that were clustered around open plaza areas. At the well-studied town of Pot Creek, a trickle of immigrants after AD 1270 probably contributed to growth (Figure 7.11), but researchers consider a rapid influx of new groups as responsible for a burst of construction between AD 1310 and 1320 – the settlement almost instantly grew over 30 percent, enclosing the plaza. During this expansion, a large kiva akin to the "great kivas" of the west was constructed, but the entire town was soon abandoned and the kiva never used (Crown and Kohler 1994:104–11). Interestingly, while most immigrants to Pot Creek are thought to have come from the northwest, perhaps from the Mesa Verde area, some of the newcomers probably came from the east as well, from the Cimarron region adjacent to the Plains.

The Pajarito Plateau, where the modern town of Los Alamos is located, was settled by a trickle of refugees over much of the twelfth and thirteenth centuries, but it too saw an explosion of immigration at the turn of the fourteenth century, probably by people moving down from the north along the Chama River (Crown et al. 1996:196). Large settlements were built around three or four sides of plaza areas as newcomers arrived and locals and earlier migrants aggregated in good farming locations. Other

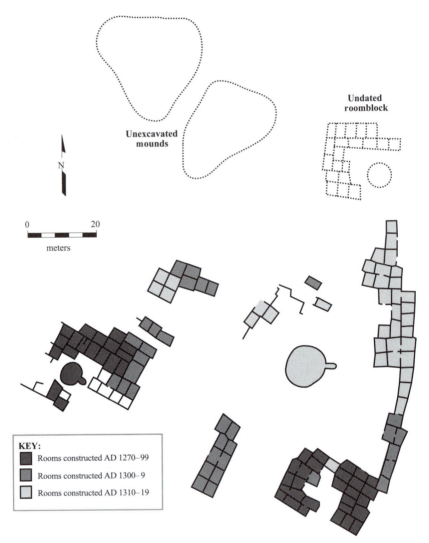

7.11 Growth of Pot Creek Pueblo started slowly between AD 1270 and 1300, but a burst of construction in the AD 1310s increased its size by 30 percent. The new additions – including a large kiva in the plaza – are attributed to immigrants.

residents lived in small, dispersed roomblocks, and these varying residential patterns may reflect ethnic differences. The larger towns established clearly defined territories, and as social and political relationships were negotiated, the insular nature of the earliest communities ended and regional exchange became more common (Walsh 1998).

Similar developments occurred in the Galisteo Basin south of Santa Fe, where a rapid increase in the use of timber can only be explained by immigration (Crown et al. 1996:198–9). By the AD 1300s, between 80 and 90 percent of the population lived in large towns, some of which were established so suddenly that archaeologists suspect that entire groups of refugees arrived en masse. And this pattern of immigration and aggregation is seen even farther south along the Rio Grande (e.g., Lekson et al. 2002). Up until the AD 1250s, people there had resided in a variety of buildings, from pithouses and jacal rooms to masonry and adobe structures, reflecting their varied backgrounds. But by AD 1300, numerous towns of more than 100 rooms were built from the Sacramento Mountains near the modern town of Roswell all the way north to the town of Las Vegas (Spielmann 1996:182–3). Even the Mimbres region far to the southwest, which had been largely depopulated by the late twelfth century, experienced population growth as Mogollon people moved south away from the pressures of northern immigrants (Dean et al. 1994:67). No part of the Puebloan Southwest remained unchanged during the fourteenth century.

Life in a multi-ethnic Puebloan community

The decades at the end of the thirteenth century and beginning of the fourteenth were unusual times. Instead of short-distance movements of small groups of people, which had been the traditional response to stressful times, Puebloan people traveled considerable distances, often in sizeable groups. As these populations moved steadily southward, they not only ran into one another, they also encountered local residents. In some cases, newcomers enjoyed prior relationships with locals, perhaps established in earlier times through trade, and they intentionally migrated toward these acquaintances hoping for a friendly reception. In most situations, however, locals were probably unprepared for the influx of these foreigners, and they responded in different ways, with some aggressively defending their lands and others accepting immigrants with open arms. No matter the specific response, the result was undoubtedly an uneasy relationship between locals and immigrants, one that required new forms of social and political organization that could accommodate the human landscape of the AD 1300s.

The newcomers: nothing but trouble or a great opportunity?

As a leading member of the local population, one whose opinion matters a great deal, what would your options be in the face of all these newcomers? Certainly, one reaction would be to try to discourage immigrant groups from taking up residence in your area, and the archaeological evidence does show that establishing a defensive and unfriendly stance was a common response (e.g., Haas and Creamer 1993). The wise leader, however, might try to avoid costly conflict and resolve the situation so that everyone – but particularly the local population – benefited in some way. As the Great Drought continued, few landscapes were open in which migrating groups could readily take up residence, and few of the refugees were in any position to demand access to scarce land and water sources (e.g., Adams 1996:55). For these people, then, accepting lower-status roles in local settlements may well have been the best option. For locals, resisting newcomers was probably not sustainable, for eventually immigrating populations would become desperate – and then deterring them would be even more difficult.

Welcoming at least some refugee groups moving into your landscape was beneficial in a number of ways. Newcomers could be encouraged to establish their own roomblocks in more vulnerable locations, providing a protective barrier around the main settlement where locals resided. Such "guard villages" served as a first line of defense against raids – as in the case of the historic village of Hano, a community established among the Hopi people by Tewa refugees retreating from Spanish intrusion into the Rio Grande (Wilcox and Haas 1994:222). Landless immigrants also might have been invited to settle among local residents because of particular skills they possessed. At Bailey Ruin in the Silver Creek drainage (Figure 7.12), for example, remains from the intensive production of shell ornaments were found alongside pottery exhibiting northern styles but made of local clays, suggesting the presence of immigrant craftspeople (Mills 1999:509). One roomblock at Grasshopper Pueblo included households specializing in the production of turquoise pendants (Neitzel 1999:211). Skilled refugees and their families were likely to be more readily welcomed, although their crafts may have been managed by locals.

No matter how welcome immigrants were as they entered new settings, this period was ripe for the development of inequities. Local kin groups were unlikely to relinquish their rights over prime resources, particularly in the face of continuing environmental degradation. And in those few areas where brand-new settlements were established by refugee groups, the "first-comers" – the first migrants to establish the village – were certain

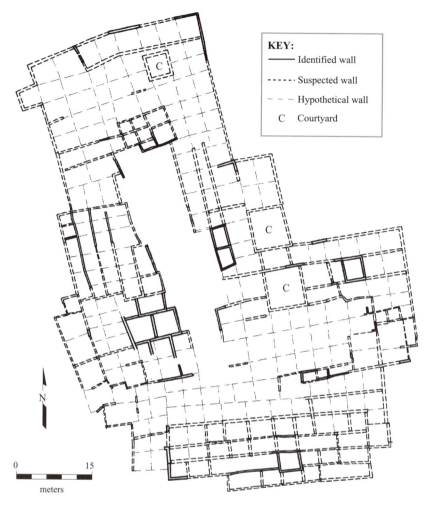

7.12 Bailey Ruin, which rises two stories in some areas, grew to at least 250 rooms. It probably started in the late AD 1200s as several distinct roomblocks that gradually grew to enclose the plaza by the early AD 1300s.

to claim the best lands and water supplies. This afforded the original families more security while making life for later arrivals a bit more difficult. Over time, such inequities could have built into greater disadvantages for newcomers and more status and authority for the original inhabitants. At Pueblo de los Muertos in the Cibola region, James Potter and Elizabeth Perry (2000:70–1) found that the remains of deer and antelope were unevenly distributed between households; perhaps status differences determined who received sought-after game.

Grasshopper Pueblo provides another well-studied case where incipient inequalities emerged as local and immigrant ethnic groups came together. Ezzo's analysis (1993) of diets in the different roomblocks revealed that not all residents had access to the same foods. As described earlier, Anasazi newcomers in Roomblock 1 were eating more wild food, suggesting that they had less access to lands suitable for farming (Ezzo 1993:84). This is consistent with Jill Neitzel's (1999:212) discovery that older households in the town were larger and had proportionally more equipment, including tools needed for successful farming. And in the ceremonial plaza of Roomblock 2, the original structure inhabited by local Mogollon people, one of the most elaborate burials ever found by Southwest archaeologists was recovered (Box 7.2).

Even though local people accepted immigrants at various times and places, the archaeological evidence indicates that violence did erupt on occasion. Its occurrence was relatively infrequent and probably was more often the result of raids rather than internal conflict (Fish *et al.* 1994:158; Martin 1997:49). At Grasshopper Pueblo, whose size made it a formidable opponent, only a handful of the hundreds of burials found there exhibit violent wounds – two males were scalped and a female had been struck in the head and then scalped (Allen *et al.* 1985). On the other hand, the frequent abandonments of entire sections of these large multiethnic towns suggests that, just like in today's world, throwing different people together in a confined setting did not always work out, particularly as such large populations stressed the surrounding landscape.

Ethnic melting pots?

While interactions between immigrants and locals were not always friendly, and even though locals probably took advantage of newcomers at certain times and places, contact between the two usually led to substantial cultural sharing. Thrown together in large towns and perhaps distrustful of neighboring communities, local people and the refugees they welcomed became dependent on one another, farming together, sharing surpluses with one another, defending their town side by side, and intermarrying. As the fourteenth century progressed, these large multiethnic towns gradually became more culturally integrated.

Much of the evidence for this ethnic melding comes from analyses of pottery. Case studies from Grasshopper Pueblo show that local Mogollon potters learned how to make designs typical of the Cibola area to the northeast, most likely from immigrants (Triadan 1997; Van Keuren

Box 7.2 Burial 140, the leader of Grasshopper Pueblo?

Debates over the structure of pre-Contact Puebloan political organization often focus on the identification of actual leaders in the archaeological record. Such evidence has proven elusive, which is perhaps not surprising considering the tenuous nature of authority proposed for much of Puebloan history. Burial 140 at Grasshopper Pueblo is therefore a particularly interesting case of an individual who clearly was an important person during his lifetime (Reid and Whittlesey 1999:130–2).

Archaeologists found Burial 140 in the so-called "Great Kiva" of Grasshopper Pueblo, a modestly sized, covered plaza bordered by roomblocks (Figure 7.14). The burial was of a male, 40–50 years of age, whose unusual interment was covered with a pole roof. A layer of grave goods was placed with the body, while a second layer was found on the grave's roof. In all, an astonishing thirty-six ceramic vessels accompanied the burial. Eight shell bracelets graced his upper left arm, while several decorated bone hairpins, including one with a turquoise and shell mosaic handle, were scattered where his hair once was. Also featured were an elaborately incised and painted wand made from a grizzly bear femur, 130 arrowheads, and a decorated quiver found at his right shoulder that contained a bone rasp. Few other burials in the Southwest parallel the wealth interred with Burial 140.

Owing to his distinctive cranial deformation – flattening of the back of the head caused by the specific method of cradleboarding – researchers concluded that Burial 140 was a member of the dominant Mogollon ethnic group (Reid and Whittlesey 1999:118). The inclusion of arrows and bone hairpins suggests that this man was a member – and probably the leader – of religious sodalities identified at Grasshopper Pueblo (see Box 7.3), and researchers concluded that his authority and status derived from the multiple roles he played in the town's ceremonial life (Reid and Whittlesey 1999:132). Unlike at Pueblo Bonito in Chaco Canyon, however, none of the richest burials at Grasshopper Pueblo enjoyed better health than those people with more modest interments. Leadership was tied to ceremonial authority, and it clearly provided advantages in wealth, but these advantages were apparently achieved later in life and such success was not transferred to one's progeny.

1999:50; Zedeño 2002:82–3). However, they were not able to replicate the exact steps of production used by Cibolan potters, instead relying on techniques they had learned for making their own ceramics. Farther to the north, in the Silver Creek drainage, the mixing of different refugee groups as well as continuing exchange with far-flung areas initially led to a great diversity of ceramic types in each town. As the thirteenth century ended, however, the light-slipped pottery faded from prominence as trading across the fragmented landscape became more challenging and as people found it difficult to produce white colors using available clays. By the AD 1300s, locally produced redware ceramics exhibiting a standardized style were predominant (Mills 1999:510; Triadan *et al.* 2002; Zedeño and Triadan 2000:224–9). This trend – particularly noticeable in towns of the Mogollon Rim – occurred alongside the emergence of a new religious tradition, a topic considered in more detail at the end of this chapter.

New ways to organize relatives

A comparison of early thirteenth-century settlements in the Mesa Verde area with late thirteenth-century Kayenta towns reveals an intriguing difference – very few kivas were built at the later aggregated sites. The residents of 155-room Kiet Siel, for example, built only six kivas, while the earlier 420-room Sand Canyon Pueblo included around ninety kivas, an astounding number even when the larger size of Sand Canyon is considered. What might explain this apparent discrepancy? One possibility may be gradual changes in the structure of kinship organization that accompanied the population movements of the late AD 1200s and the subsequent formation of large towns composed of disparate ethnic groups.

As described earlier, some scholars believe that thirteenth-century Mesa Verde populations maintained considerable household autonomy even as they aggregated into larger communities. Each household therefore was likely to build its own kiva to fulfill its domestic and ceremonial needs, resulting in large numbers of these structures (Adler 1994:97). In contrast, several archaeologists suggest that later towns accommodated social units substantially larger than a handful of related households, resulting in the need for fewer kivas (e.g., Adams 2002:179–81; Dean 1996b:41–2; Steward 1937). These scholars believe that the social and cultural changes of the thirteenth and fourteenth centuries led to the formation of clans, social units based on descent from a shared, perhaps mythical ancestor. Membership in a clan is determined in the same way as one might trace their family lineage, but because the common ancestor defining each clan is from the remote past, clan groups can become quite sizeable. The result is that society is composed of fewer social units.

What would have inspired the development of this new form of organization? One important factor was the migration of large numbers of people as the Little Ice Age impacted the region and the Great Drought began. As families abandoned their homelands and traveled together in disparate groups, they almost certainly adopted a shared identity, one that probably had roots in their common places of origin. Because they were unlikely all to be close kin, particularly as other refugees joined them, their sense of kinship had to be flexible and accommodative. Clan organization provides all these features. Perhaps most importantly, the larger scale of clans allows for more effective decision-making, particularly since the focus on lines of descent can guide the selection of leaders (e.g., Crown and Kohler 1994:111–13; Potter and Perry 2000). Instead of many families, each with its own concerns, the clan provides a unified front, an important advantage both during the migrations and in the context of large, multiethnic towns (Figure 7.13). In the face of marginal conditions for farming, the clan also could pool labor and surpluses, providing an advantage over autonomous households (e.g., Hegmon 1996).

Archaeologists have not been able specifically to identify the formation of clan organization during the late AD 1200s and early AD 1300s, but large social groups are visible at many sites. One good example can be seen at Betatakin, a settlement established in the Kayenta region around AD 1267. Initially a small residential structure built in an alcove, Betatakin was rapidly expanded between AD 1275 and AD 1277. Curiously, construction material had slowly been stockpiled since AD 1269, as if the final structure of 135 rooms and two kivas was planned in anticipation of a sizeable group moving in (Dean 1970:158–9). The small number of kivas built at Betatakin suggests that either people were organized in larger social units or their ceremonial lives were not as entwined in the kiva – or both.

Religion and ceremony: new forms, old consequences

Fewer formal kivas were built in the era of depopulation and migration, but this does not mean that religious activity became less important. In fact, the evidence indicates that ceremonial activity continued to be an integral part of daily life. At Grasshopper Pueblo, archaeologists have identified an apparent hierarchy in religious architecture (Whittlesey and Reid 2001:69). Every three households shared a modest ceremonial room that was nearly indistinguishable from normal domestic rooms. At the next level, every six households maintained a formal rectangular kiva,

KEY:

| Sandstone wall |
| Adobe wall |
| Suspected wall |

Spinal
roomblocks

East
plaza

West
plaza

Southeast
plaza

Spinal
roomblocks

South
plaza

N

Little Colorado River

0   15

meters

7.13 Homol'ovi I was established at around the same time as Homol'ovi
III, between AD 1280 and 1290, and it would ultimately grow to include
1,100 rooms by the late AD 1300s. It started, however, as four "spinal"
roomblocks, each two stories tall, each with its own ceremonial structure, and each probably occupied by a different lineage or clan.

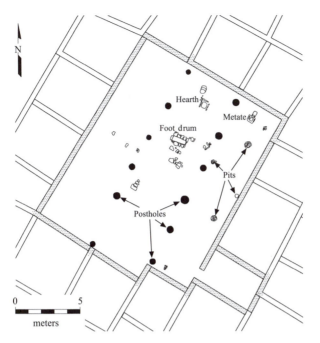

7.14 The "Great Kiva" at Grasshopper Pueblo is a plaza area walled in by surrounding roomblocks over which a roof was built in AD 1330, after it already had served as an open ceremonial plaza. Like similar structures found at other fourteenth-century towns, the Great Kiva at Grasshopper Pueblo was entered from a room to the east and included a foot drum and a fire pit.

complete with masonry benches. And the whole town used plaza spaces for large-scale ceremonial events, including one plaza called the "great kiva" because it was roofed (Figure 7.14). Ceremonial activity therefore occurred at a number of scales, from personal rituals in which everyone regularly engaged to larger ceremonies attended not only by the entire community, but even by guests visiting from other towns.

Perhaps as a consequence of the larger kin groups, or perhaps as an attempt to unify disparate people coming together to form new communities, an increasing scale of ceremonial interaction was a defining characteristic of many fourteenth-century towns. In the Salinas area of the middle Rio Grande drainage, southeast of the city of Albuquerque, the large town of Gran Quivira hosted impressive gatherings that included large feasts. These events were apparently so regular that a much greater number of ceramic bowls was thrown away at Gran Quivira than at neighboring towns (Graves and Spielmann 2000:54–5). To the west, El Morro Valley towns in the Cibola region show the same trend. Potter (2000) analyzed evidence for sizeable feasts in these communities and found that the nicer Cibolan pottery was made in two sizes: big ones for serving large volumes of food and small bowls for regular household use. Intriguingly, he also discovered that faunal remains in the plaza trash piles were less thoroughly processed than those bones found in the everyday household trash. Potter attributes this to the use of plazas for multi-town ceremonial feasts. Special communal grinding areas with easy access to the plazas also were probably set up to accommodate these events.

The larger scale of ceremonial activity seen at the turn of the fourteenth century developed alongside other changes in Puebloan religion. Perhaps the earliest of these new trends was the so-called "Southwestern Cult," defined by a style of redware pottery whose popularity swept across much of the Puebloan Southwest. The origins of this ceremonial tradition and its system of beliefs are not well understood (Crown 1994, 1995). What is known is that the associated ceramic style, known as "Salado Polychrome," developed in the AD 1270s among Kayenta–Tusayan immigrants in towns along the Mogollon Rim (Figure 7.15). It is characterized by a melding of the Cibola pottery tradition with new decorative elements, such as parrots, horned serpents, and sun and star symbols. Although this iconography is reminiscent of the earlier Mimbres tradition, Salado Polychrome vessels were not part of mortuary ritual. Some decorative motifs instead may reflect influence from Casas Grandes far to the south (Crary et al. 2001), and in fact this trading center continued to feed the Puebloan appetite for macaws, shell, and copper bells through the fourteenth century. Some scholars argue that the configuration of elements selected for use on Salado Polychrome vessels reflects a concern with fertility and weather control, and it seems likely that the ceremonial activities of the Southwestern Cult were directed at the poor farming conditions of this period.

The iconography of the Southwestern Cult spread rapidly, suggesting that the belief system also did. By AD 1300, the pottery style was found across most of the western Puebloan world, where it most commonly was painted on small bowls used in domestic contexts. These vessels show normal wear, indicating that they were used like any other painted bowl, and analyses of the clays and potting techniques reveal that Salado Polychrome was produced in almost every village – the Southwestern Cult was not a strongly centralized religion in which ritual pottery was produced and distributed by specialists. Instead, the vessels were made

7.15 This Salado Polychrome jar from the Tonto National Monument in Arizona dates to the fourteenth century. The motif seen on this vessel is probably a representation of the horned serpent, which appears in rock art along the southern Rio Grande as well as on earlier Mimbres pottery; the motif is also common in Mesoamerica.

locally by people who were participating in a loosely shared symbolic and ideological system (e.g., Crown 1994).

By AD 1325, pottery associated with the Southwestern Cult began to change (Crown 1994:217–21). Larger bowls for serving sizeable quantities of food became more common, and masked human-like figures frequently appear on the vessels. Design elements can be more readily traced to Casas Grandes, which at that time was reaching its zenith. Other intriguing changes include the concentration of iconography on the insides of Salado Polychrome bowls and an increased use of newly made vessels as burial goods. More controversial is the proposal that the pottery was changing from a symbol of participation in a belief system and instead becoming a status symbol. Scott Van Keuren (2000:93–4) suggests that because the newer styles required greater expertise to produce, it was no longer possible for everyone to make their own vessels. This created an opportunity for the production of these vessels to be centralized and thus controlled, leading to greater inequities among participants in the belief system.

Adams (1991, 2002) believes that intertwined with the emergence of the largely ideological Southwestern Cult was the more specific development of a Kachina Cult similar to that practiced by many Pueblo people today. He proposes that this tradition appeared along the Upper Little Colorado drainage at about the same time as the Southwestern Cult, but that the Kachina Cult provided an explicit ceremonial structure for integrating different immigrant groups converging in late thirteenth- and fourteenth-century towns. He ties the iconographic elements of Salado Polychrome with the new focus on community-wide, plaza-oriented ritual and the emergence of religious sodalities – ceremonial groups that cross-cut kinship organization, providing a structure that both integrated people and guided community decision-making (Box 7.3). According to Adams, as masked figures became prominent iconographic elements on

---

Box 7.3   Sodalities at Grasshopper Pueblo

Identifying sodalities is a challenge, for they transcend other forms of social and political organization that are usually easier to see in the archaeological record, such as households and kin groups. As described in the previous chapter, some researchers believe that sodalities existed in thirteenth-century villages of the Mesa Verde region. Evidence for this, however, is based primarily on unique architectural features that could have served other functions. In other words, only the *context* for possible sodality activity has been identified instead of direct evidence for cross-cutting ceremonial membership.

The analysis of the mortuary remains from Grasshopper Pueblo, in contrast, provides a more compelling case of sodality organization. A total of 674 burials were identified at this fourteenth-century town, and many were interred with items presumably reflecting each individual's identity. Analysis of these mortuary goods led researchers to conclude that at least four ceremonial sodalities existed at Grasshopper. One such group was labeled the "shell pendant society," identified by a *Glycymeris* shell recovered near the waist of the interred, suggesting that it adorned a belt or loincloth. The "shell tinkler society" included burials with *Conus* shells, which apparently were attached to clothing or quivers. Shaped and polished bone implements found near some burials' heads, as if they once held knots of hair in place, defined the "bone hairpin society." And clusters of arrowheads arrayed near a burial's shoulder, as if they once tipped arrow shafts placed in a now-decomposed quiver, identified the "arrow society" (Whittlesey and Reid 2001:78–81).

All four of the proposed sodalities consisted only of males, and the first three were mutually exclusive – no one interred with shell tinklers also had bone hairpins, for example. And both the Mogollon and Anasazi styles of cranial deformation were represented in the first three groups. The exception to these patterns was the Arrow Society. All seven males in this inferred sodality were Mogollon, and all seven possessed items from *all four* of the sodalities, including shell tinklers that once adorned their elaborate quivers. Burial 140 (Box 7.2) was a member of this group. Researchers concluded that the Arrow Society, representing about 10 percent of the male burial population, was a particularly exclusive sodality whose members had a hand in all of Grasshopper Pueblo's ceremonial organizations (Whittlesey and Reid 2001:78–81).

The mortuary analysis at Grasshopper Pueblo identified one final group: males and females with shell bracelets. Possession of these items was not as exclusive as the other items, and some of the individuals with bone hairpins also had bracelets, as did members of the Arrow Society. Shell bracelets therefore probably represented another form of identity, perhaps a sign of wealth or a symbol of one of the town's kin groups. In this respect, it is interesting that Burial 140 wore eight bracelets on his arm.

---

pottery and rock art in the early AD 1300s, the activities of the Kachina Cult increasingly emphasized control over weather. Ultimately, this religious tradition expanded into the Hopi area and east toward the Rio Grande, encompassing the Southwestern Cult both ideologically and geographically.

The larger ceremonial scale of these new religious forms had a number of important consequences for Puebloan society. Complex ceremonial events attended by many people impact social and political relationships. Large ceremonies require organization, the mobilization of labor, and the pooling of surplus foods and other resources, and this necessitates centralized direction and an ability to influence many people. By the early AD 1400s, large groups – whether clans, sodalities, or both – provided the social context and political structure to host and organize sizeable events of this nature. In many towns, however, several of these groups existed side by side, and of course a number of similar communities were scattered across each region. This probably resulted in the kind of competitive ceremonialism that is a hallmark of human social behavior and that accompanies communal aspects of ceremonial activity. Sometimes friendly, and other times confrontational, this competition develops as different groups attempt to outdo one another in the scale and grandiosity of events they host. When tied to kinship and subtle differences in ideology, such competition can become quite intense, perhaps even including the distribution of lavish gifts to guests with the hope of attaining greater levels of prestige for your clan and authority for your sodality.

Archaeological evidence indicates that the advent of large-scale ceremonial feasting had a ripple effect across the Puebloan Southwest. On one hand, it provided an incentive to intensify both food production and the trade of exotic items. Potter (2000:483–4) suggests that feasting prompted people to rear greater numbers of turkeys, an animal that was not a favorite food but one whose production could be manipulated. He found that turkey consumption doubled as these new towns formed, with some communities killing hundreds of turkeys each year. The scale of ceremonial activity probably promoted greater inequities between groups and perhaps even individuals, as those capable of mobilizing people and food gained increased prestige and status compared with smaller immigrant groups and villages relegated to less productive lands. Gran Quivira provides an example of this, for unusually high quantities of food preparation and serving vessels were recovered from the town (Graves and Spielmann 2000:51–5). Imported ceramics and other exotic goods also flowed into Gran Quivira in greater frequencies compared with neighboring towns.

Not all archaeologists would agree with these conclusions, noting that the fact that these events took place in each town's central plaza reflects a communal ethos, as does the emergence of sodalities that mitigate kinship divisions (e.g., Potter 2000:480). The locus of an event, however, may belie its cause. It is hard to imagine that the larger scale of ceremonialism during the fourteenth century would not have led to differences among social groups found in the more populous towns. The resulting inequities may have been unintentional, but they also could have been knowingly promoted within the context of communal activity. After all, Grasshopper Pueblo, which exhibits some of the best evidence for social and political inequities during this era, is built around a number of large plazas. The latter half of the fourteenth century in the Puebloan Southwest is perhaps illustrative of human behavior seen at other times and in other places – the emergence of an egalitarian ethos that helped to glue together disparate and potentially destructive elements of society but that at the same time disguised inequities brewing below the surface.

8   Finding *Posi*: the protohistoric Puebloan world

According to the Tewa people of San Juan Pueblo, their ancestors originally lived below *Ohange pokwinge*, Sand Lake, together with all creatures. One of the men was asked by Blue Corn (Summer) Mother and White Corn (Winter) Mother to search for a way to leave the lake, and on one of his journeys, he met the *tsiwi* – predatory animals and carrion-eating birds – who accepted him as the first of the Made People. He became the Hunt Chief and assigned two more Made People: Summer Chief and Winter Chief. The chiefs tried to lead people out of the lake, but four times they had to return and create more Made People, including the *Ke* medicine man, the *Kossa* and *Kwirana* clowns, the Scalp Chief, and the *Kwiyoh* Women's Society.

Finally, the ancestors left the lake and traveled south, with the Summer Chief and his people following mountains on the west side of the Rio Grande and the Winter Chief and his followers following mountains to the east. The Summer People farmed and ate wild plant foods, while the Winter People hunted, with each stopping and building villages eleven times. At the twelfth stop, the two groups rejoined at *Posi*, until an epidemic struck and they abandoned the village, splitting into six new groups. Each included both Winter and Summer People and representatives of all Made People, and each set out to found new villages. These are the six villages in which the Tewa still live today (Ortiz 1969:13–16; Parsons 1926:9–15).

For archaeologists, the "protohistoric" era – the century or so prior to European Contact – presents unique challenges. Continuing migrations make it difficult to reconstruct fifteenth- and early sixteenth-century Puebloan behavior. Because many sites from this period are valuable to living Pueblo people as sacred parts of their landscapes, archaeologists have to be judicious in the research in which they engage. And, of course, many "sites" of the protohistoric period continue to be lived in today (Box 8.1). Despite these challenges, this chapter discusses changes of the AD 1400s and early AD 1500s, emphasizing how pre-Contact Puebloan

Box 8.1   Introducing the Pueblo people of the ethnographic present

The descendants of pre-Contact Puebloans can be found throughout the world today, but the majority still live on over twenty reservations in New Mexico, Arizona, and Texas (Figure 8.1). Several of these are known as the "Western Pueblos" owing to their location west of the Rio Grande. In Arizona, the Hopi live in about a dozen villages, most of which are on the Hopi Mesas jutting off the southern edge of Black Mesa. Many of the communities on the Hopi Reservation date well back into the pre-Contact era. Similarly, the Zuni Reservation in west-central New Mexico is centered on the pre-Contact town of Halona: wa, today known as Zuni Pueblo; several other communities are also found on the reservation. The Keresan Pueblos of Acoma and Laguna, both located in central New Mexico, are also considered to be Western Pueblos. Each Keresan reservation is focused on its namesake town, although other villages are also inhabited.

The Eastern Pueblos are arrayed along the Rio Grande from Taos in northern New Mexico all the way down to El Paso, Texas – most are north of Albuquerque. Between Albuquerque and Santa Fe are the five Rio Grande Keresan Pueblos, which include Zia, Santa Ana, Cochiti, Santo Domingo, and San Felipe. They separate two groups of Tanoan Pueblos, which are grouped according to their language. Taos and Picuris Pueblos comprise the northernmost speakers of Tiwa, while Tewa speakers live on six reservations around Española: Tesuque, Nambe, Pojoaque, San Ildefonso, Santa Clara, and San Juan. Jemez Pueblo, located west of Santa Fe, is the only Towa-speaking group to retain its autonomy past the nineteenth century. Tanoan Pueblos south of the Keresan reservations include Sandia and Isleta, whose residents are Tiwa speakers. Much farther to the south, near El Paso, Texas, is Tigua Pueblo. Unlike all other Pueblo Reservations, which occupy the same landscapes as their pre-Contact ancestors, Tigua Pueblo was founded in the AD 1680s by Tiwa-speaking refugees who joined the Spanish when the Pueblo Revolt drove them out of the northern Southwest.

Although scholars often refer to a certain Pueblo as "speaking" a particular language, in fact many descendants of the Contact-era Pueblos no longer speak their native tongues. Some Pueblos are more traditional, practicing the ceremonies and traditions of their ancestors, while others are less engaged in their cultural heritage – they may be Catholics or Protestants and perhaps more involved in mainstream

American culture. Anthropologists therefore find it useful to distinguish the current cultural practices of any indigenous group from the "ethnographic present," a more normative understanding of what cultural traditions were like prior to the post-Contact era of forced or voluntary enculturation. The boxes in this chapter present summaries of Contact-era Pueblo cultural behavior from the perspective of the ethnographic present, acknowledging that today Pueblo people enjoy a rich and complex cultural heritage that reflects centuries of interaction with one another and with innumerable other traditions.

people became the Pueblo villages recorded by the first Spanish explorers to enter the Southwest.

Dispersal and contraction: the migrations continue

As the fourteenth century came to a close, the cycle of mobility intermixed with short episodes of aggregation continued in the Puebloan world (Figure 8.2). Even with the unifying influence of the Kachina Cult, villages experienced a constant ebb and flow of population as families, kin groups, or even an entire populace left to join other communities or establish their own villages. Many possible motivations inspired these movements – families were banished for real or imagined indiscretions, kin groups left to seek better farmland, political factionalism led to village fissioning, or firewood supplies simply ran out. In the west, unusually dry weather desiccated crops around AD 1350 and again in the AD 1390s. Along the Rio Grande, droughts hit in the late AD 1350s, the AD 1380s, and severely in the AD 1420s (Cordell *et al.* 1994:118). This climatic instability continually undermined ceremonial leaders and challenged fragile bonds holding communities together.

This process is illustrated on Grasshopper Plateau. People living at Grasshopper Pueblo began to leave in the final decades of the AD 1300s, with families and small groups moving short distances to build modest pueblos on patches of farmland. After a generation or two, Grasshopper was empty, although some people returned and briefly reoccupied the area around AD 1400 before the plateau was abandoned for good. What inspired this exodus? Archaeologists note that the plateau was not well suited for farming, and the number of people living there placed heavy demands on soils and other natural resources. Droughts after the mid-AD 1300s exacerbated the deteriorating conditions, and the tenuous strands of social integration could not withstand the stress and people left (Tuggle and Reid 2001:102–3; Whittlesey and Reid 2001:69).

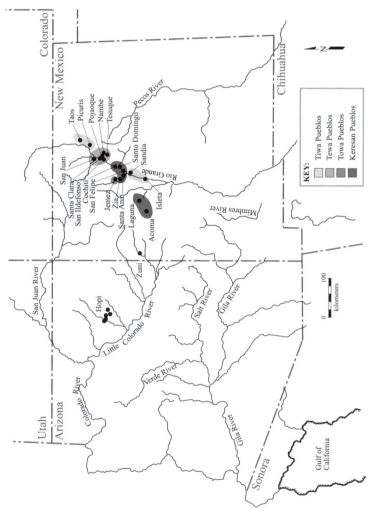

8.1 Many Pueblo people still live in the same locations as their ancestors did when the Spanish arrived in the American Southwest. A number of different languages are spoken in the Pueblos, including the three Tanoan languages – Tiwa, Tewa, and Towa – as well as Keresan, Zuni, and Hopi.

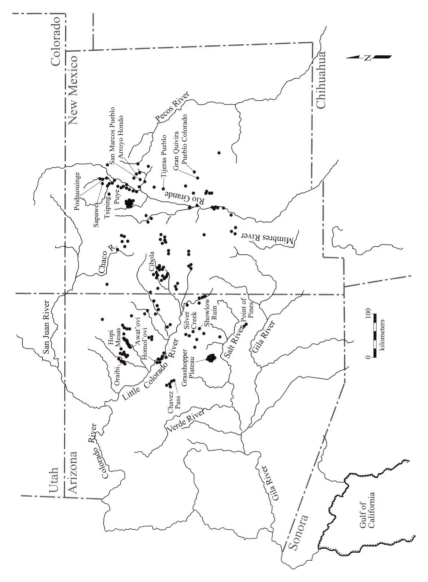

8.2 By AD 1300, most Puebloan towns were concentrated along the Little Colorado and Rio Grande drainages. Over the next few decades, populations rapidly decreased to the west and increased in the east.

Farther to the north, along the Little Colorado River, the same process was taking place (Figure 8.2). Pueblo towns here relied on the river
drainage, growing cotton that they traded with distant communities. The
Homol'ovi villages, for example, were economically allied with people
living along the Hopi Mesas. E. Charles Adams (2002:249–59) suggests
that Homol'ovi people traded cotton for yellow-ware pottery, perhaps
because the scarcity of wood made it difficult to produce pottery locally.
Extensive flooding in the late AD 1350s and 1380s, however, followed by
dry conditions in the AD 1390s, made it difficult to sustain a livelihood
along the Little Colorado, and by AD 1400 most people had left, with
many moving toward their allies – rapid growth of the Hopi Mesa villages
of Awat'ovi and Oraibi attest to this migration.

This process was repeated over and over again in the late AD 1300s
(Duff 2000:81). People left Chavez Pass south of the Little Colorado
by AD 1381, and the Silver Creek area was empty by AD 1384 with
the abandonment of Showlow Ruin (Figure 8.2). The 800-room Point
of Pines, even farther south, saw people disperse into small households
before leaving in the early AD 1400s (Stone 2002:395). And in the northern Rio Grande area, communities along the Chama River, the Pajarito
Plateau, and the Galisteo Basin began to be abandoned, inspired by severe
droughts at the turn of the century that contributed to a 50 percent
decline in population (Schroeder 1992; Wilcox 1991). Steven LeBlanc
(1999:248–9) points to the defensive postures of many new sites and
the widespread burning associated with abandonment to suggest that
warfare – or at least the *fear* of warfare – was one reaction to the resource
exhaustion, drought, and social disintegration that characterized the turn
of the century.

By the early AD 1400s, as a result of these abandonments, large areas
of the Puebloan Southwest were no longer permanently uninhabited,
resulting in sizeable "no-man's lands" between remaining concentrations
of people (compare Figure 8.2 with Figure 8.12). This is not to say that no
one ever ventured into these areas, for certainly they continued to provide
natural resources for Puebloans, abandoned villages served as important
features of the cultural landscape, and trails criss-crossed depopulated
regions as people engaged in long-distance interactions. But very little
habitation occurred until non-Puebloan people moved into these spaces
a few generations later.

Many groups, many plazas: Puebloan towns of the fifteenth century

As people vacated marginal regions, communities that persevered into the
middle decades of the AD 1400s experienced steady growth, resulting in
the largest Puebloan towns ever built. Poshuouinge, along the Chama

River, grew to as many as 2,000 adobe rooms in three stories around two large plazas, while the nearby town of Sapawe housed 3,000 people in adobe roomblocks around seven plazas (Lekson 1999b:16). Not far to the south, 85 percent of people on the Pajarito Plateau were concentrated in a dozen or so large towns (Walsh 2000:202), including Puye, a 1,000-room town built of volcanic tuff. And in the southern Rio Grande area, the Salinas Pueblos also grew, including a few exceeding 1,000 rooms (Graves and Spielmann 2000:49). The contraction of populations into fewer towns also occurred west of the Rio Grande. In the Cibola area, people who had been living in numerous villages, each with hundreds of rooms, aggregated into nine large towns by AD 1450 (Mills 1995:201). Hawikku is one of the largest, consisting of perhaps 800 masonry rooms among seven or more multistoried roomblocks (Figure 8.3).

These towns illustrate a trend seen over much of the Puebloan Southwest during the late pre-Contact period – a move away from communities oriented around one or two plazas and toward numerous large roomblocks clustered around many public spaces. "Street-oriented" layouts emerged in some Puebloan towns, in which linear roomblocks were arrayed parallel to one another, allowing room for narrow public spaces between them. These changes reflect the continuing trajectory of increasingly disparate groups living together. As vast expanses of the Southwest were depopulated and subsistence stress led to negative population growth, towns were inhabited by numerous small groups. Speaking different languages, practicing differing ceremonies, and perhaps even retaining ties with distant relatives, dense roomblocks like Grasshopper Pueblo and plaza-centered towns like Pueblo de los Muertos were susceptible to factionalism and fragmentation. Open layouts provided enough physical separation to allow for some group autonomy, while the expanding Kachina Cult helped to maintain communal identity (Adams 1991). Numerous open spaces also allowed disparate groups to practice their own ceremonies. Interestingly, however, at the Hopi town of Oraibi, the oldest section was still the location of the most important ceremonial spaces (Cameron 1992:180–1). Oraibi also exemplifies the perhaps unintentional integration provided by street-oriented town layouts – linear roomblocks made it difficult for clan members to build their homes next to one another, leading to substantial mixing of clan households as new families built on to the ends of each roomblock (Cameron 1992:178).

Feeding the masses

Densely populated towns, reduced mobility, and continuing droughts challenged every family to produce enough food. For northern Rio

8.3 Hawikku is one of several towns established in the Cibola region during the fourteenth century. By the time that the Spanish first visited the town, Hawikku had grown to around 800 rooms. Archaeologists in the early 1900s recovered nearly 1,000 burials from distinct cemeteries surrounding the town.

Grande farmers, the short growing season was exacerbated by the continuing cold of the Little Ice Age. Puebloan people responded by developing ingenious horticultural strategies. To conserve moisture, reduce erosion, and extend the growing season, Rio Grande groups used pebble-mulching, surrounding each plant with numerous small stones

(Lightfoot and Eddy 1995). Experimental plots show that this can produce 37 percent greater crop yields (see Maxwell 1995:7–8). Other horticultural strategies included "waffle gardens," earthen enclosures that controlled runoff in the same way that a waffle's surface holds syrup, and irrigation systems that became especially important along the Rio Grande in the AD 1400s (Greiser and Greiser 1995; Greiser and Moore 1995). Most towns were surrounded with fields using all possible strategies, ensuring that food was produced no matter what climatic conditions farmers faced in any given year (Anschuetz 1995).

While people successfully confronted many environmental challenges, large communities occupied for many generations substantially impacted the availability of natural resources. Decreasing quantities of game animals created the most severe problem, for these were a major source of protein and nutrients such as iron. Towns such as Arroyo Hondo in the Galisteo Basin ate fewer and fewer large animals, replacing them with rabbits and domesticated turkeys. In fact, turkey consumption, which had never been a major part of the diet except during times of crisis, doubled in Rio Grande towns between the fourteenth and sixteenth centuries (Spielmann and Angstadt-Leto 1996:85–93).

The relative ease of producing starchy crops, particularly maize, compared with the increasing difficulty in obtaining protein, resulted in poor nutrition. Dietary deficiencies lowered fertility, increased infant mortality, and made everyone susceptible to infectious disease. A comparison of late skeletal material with earlier collections reveals that people of the fourteenth and fifteenth centuries suffered the worst health in pre-Contact Puebloan history. Bioarchaeologist Debra Martin (1994:105) estimates that a third of the residents of Hawikku and the Galisteo Basin town of San Cristobal were impacted by disease. Previously unusual diseases also became more common, including non-venereal syphilis and a tuberculosis epidemic that hit San Cristobal. In some areas, the severity of poor health may explain decreasing population sizes and continuing abandonments.

Integration and inequity: the organization of fifteenth-century Puebloan towns

As fourteenth-century Puebloan communities dissolved and people reaggregated into fifteenth-century towns, their sociopolitical configuration reflected the diversity of resident groups. The Kachina Cult spread from the west toward the Rio Grande drainage, providing an important arena for integrating disparate elements of growing towns (Figure 8.4). Its importance is reflected in the frequency with which Kachina figures are

8.4 Located near the modern city of Albuquerque, Petroglyph National Monument features over 15,000 rock art elements, most of which date from AD 1300 into the Historic period. Included among the images are what appear to be Kachinas, such as the one illustrated here.

represented in rock art from this period (Schaafsma 1994). Older ceremonial sodalities also existed in some areas, providing yet another means for interaction. On the other hand, kin-focused organizations, particularly the clans that maintained their own ceremonial traditions, provided a more divisive component of community life.

What was going on inside Puebloan towns?

A series of studies at Hawikku provide insight into the complex sociopolitical landscape of protohistoric Puebloan towns (Figure 8.3). Built in the Cibola region around AD 1325, Hawikku grew to 800 rooms and played an important role in post-Contact history. Excavations in the late 1910s and early 1920s recovered almost 1,000 burials, most from cemetery clusters outside of the roomblocks. Interestingly, 67 percent of the burials were inhumations typical of the Anasazi mortuary pattern, while the remaining burials were cremations, a tradition commonly associated with the Hohokam.

Focusing on the 955 pre-Contact burials, Todd Howell (1996, 2001; Howell and Kintigh 1996) conducted a detailed mortuary analysis in an attempt to identify the structure of Hawikku leadership. His assumption was that the diversity of items interred with each burial reflected the number of roles the individual served during his or her life. Howell discovered that fourteen inhumations – only 1.5 percent of the population – stood out as having an inordinate diversity of burial goods. Of these, six were females. This included the richest of all Hawikku burials, which Native American excavators interpreted as a medicine sodality leader because of the presence of a shrine and medicinal plants. The remaining eight individuals were males, four with particularly high quantities of goods. Noting the presence of clubs, bows, arrows, knives, black pigments, and even a human scalp, Native American excavators believed that at least one of these males was a "bow priest," a highly ranked position in the Zuni political hierarchy responsible for protecting the town. Two other males were buried with fewer war-related items but more artifacts of ritual significance.

The rarity of these rich burials and the diversity of ceremonial and warfare-related roles they represented led Howell (1996:79) to conclude that authority roles at Hawikku were centralized in a few individuals. He also noted that females enjoyed access to important positions (Howell 1995). According to his interpretation, individuals who achieved concurrent leadership positions in a variety of sodalities and kin organizations – particularly the important ones such as those related to war and social control – were able to wield significant decision-making power. With so few burials representing this kind of authority, these leaders seem only to have appeared once or twice in every generation. This path to leadership probably characterized other Puebloan towns as well. Keith Kintigh (2000) used Howell's approach to investigate 255 burials at Kechiba: wa (Figure 8.5), another fifteenth-century Cibolan town, and he found a similar pattern. Kechiba: wa's most elaborate graves, however, were not as rich as those at Hawikku, nor did they include as many rare items of ritual importance. Apparently, leaders in only some Cibolan towns could achieve the centralized power seen at Hawikku.

How did Puebloan leaders attain the level of dominance exhibited at Hawikku? Howell and Kintigh (1996:552; Howell 2001:163) analyzed dental traits for the Hawikku cemetery populations and found not only that clusters of burials were linked by kinship, but that leaders came from the two largest cemeteries. This suggests that they belonged to the largest and perhaps oldest kin groups, which probably provided the legitimacy and support needed to attain such influential positions. Apparently a leader's kin benefited from this arrangement – while Hawikku's leaders

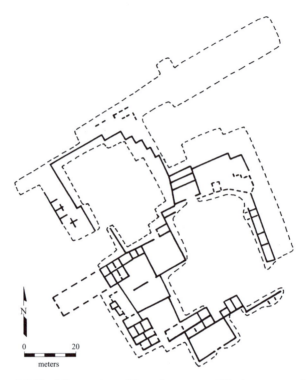

8.5 Kechiba:wa is a fifteenth-century Cibolan town of around 470 rooms surrounding two or three plazas. This town was a contemporary of Hawikku, and like that larger town, it was still occupied when the Spanish arrived in the sixteenth century.

did not enjoy improved health, their kin were slightly better off. Females particularly benefited from having a kin member as a town leader, a pattern further suggesting that kinship organization was matrilineal in these fifteenth-century towns.

Whether Cibolan towns are representative of sociopolitical organization in other protohistoric communities is unclear, as no comparable analyses have been conducted elsewhere. Some clues, however, indicate that other parts of the Puebloan world experienced the degree of centralization exhibited at Hawikku. In Homol'ovi and Hopi Mesa towns at the turn of the fifteenth century, for example, a variety of kivas were built both in plazas and in roomblocks, with a tendency for the largest, most communal kivas to occupy the plazas. Adams (2002:160–4) suggests that this variety of ceremonial spaces corresponded with a diversity of communal and exclusionary sodalities and kin groups, each with its own decision-making authorities. Adams proposes that individuals serving in leadership positions in a number of the most important groups were positioned to accrue a significant amount of power. In his scenario, kin groups controlling the most productive lands around Homol'ovi towns funded prestige-building ceremonies and monopolized the trade for cotton and other items needed for Kachina Cult activities, providing the material means for important roles to be concentrated in fewer authority figures.

Protohistoric towns were therefore dynamic places, composed of numerous kin, ethnic, and religious groups sharing the same social and political landscape and vying for decision-making authority. Older lineages and sodalities enjoyed greater status and enough economic advantage to contribute disproportionately to the town's ceremonial life, and in some places and times this apparently led to episodes of greater centralization. Counteracting this trend were the ease of fragmentation and continuing environmental instability that repressed economic inequity. As the fifteenth century progressed, however, and Puebloan people contracted into fewer areas – and as newly arrived nomadic societies such as the Athapaskans and Utes filled intervening spaces – economic differences between well-established families and newcomers probably became more marked, discouraging fissioning and further promoting centralized authority.

Was the world their oyster? Interaction beyond town boundaries

During the late thirteenth and the fourteenth centuries, the high degree of mobility and the resulting intensity of interaction had promoted networks of kinship and alliance across the Puebloan Southwest. The contraction of populations during the fifteenth century, in contrast, has led archaeologists to question whether this scale of interaction disappeared and more insular political unification occurred. Because protohistoric Puebloan towns were concentrating into clusters separated by growing "no-man's lands," it seems reasonable to expect that the most intensive interactions occurred among close neighbors. A detailed examination of regional clustering as the protohistoric era began, however, reveals a more complicated picture.

In many parts of the Puebloan world, population concentration brought together people who still interacted with their homelands. Andrew Duff (2000), for example, argues that late fourteenth-century town clusters mislead archaeologists into thinking that each was socially and ethnically unified and became more so as time passed. In his research on the Upper Little Colorado drainage, he found that communities located quite close to one another maintained separate connections. Duff examined the Table Rock and Rattlesnake Point communities, located only 16 km apart, and found that while Table Rock's ceramics revealed ties toward the north, including the Hopi Mesas, Rattlesnake Point was associated more closely with the Cibola region to the east (Duff 2000: 85–8). While plenty of pottery moved between the two villages, indicating friendly interaction, their ethnic ties were with different parts of the Southwest.

As clustering continued in the AD 1400s, changing ties between different towns impacted their regional status. Using trace-element analysis to determine where yellow-ware pottery was made and where it was moving, Wesley Bernardini (2002) found that during the fourteenth century, each Hopi village produced vessels that were traded with specific Homol'ovi towns, while the opposite was also true – each Homol'ovi town provided cotton to distinct Hopi villages. Adams (2002) argues that these relationships not only fueled inequities *within* Hopi and Homol'ovi towns, but that successful alliances such as those identified by Bernardini also promoted the *regional* power of particular towns. And as the Homol'ovi area was abandoned, the status of particular Hopi towns accordingly changed. Adams (2002:249–50) proposes that Awat'ovi became less prominent as allied Homol'ovi communities were abandoned and the cotton they supplied disappeared. In contrast, the Hopi town of Oraibi grew more powerful as it established ties with new cotton-producing lands to the west.

As disparate groups migrated and connections with their homelands were broken, the distinction between older towns dominated by local residents and those settled mostly by newcomers became important. For example, while Kintigh's (2000:107–11) comparison of mortuary patterns in the Cibolan towns of Kechiba: wa and Hawikku suggested that they were largely autonomous, each with a similar leadership structure, the towns did not enjoy equal regional status. Hawikku possessed greater political and ritual power, and items interred with its deceased were more unusual and numerous, leading Kintigh to suggest that this town was important in extra-community ceremonialism. Kechiba: wa, in contrast, had leadership roles largely distinguished by pottery rather than items of ritual importance. Pottery styles at Kechiba: wa suggest that it was established by immigrants from the Little Colorado who, while maintaining their independence, played secondary roles compared to older villages like Hawikku.

Particular communities also enjoyed higher status owing to relationships they were able to establish with non-Puebloan groups. In the southern Rio Grande drainage, many Salinas towns were facing the problem seen elsewhere at the turn of the fifteenth century: decreasing quantities of game because of habitat destruction and overhunting. James Potter (1995) examined animal remains from Gran Quivira and Pueblo Colorado, both established in the early AD 1300s and occupied into the post-Contact era, and found decreasing quantities of large game and increasing numbers of small animals. At Gran Quivira (Figure 8.6), however, Potter noticed that game was not as thoroughly processed as at Pueblo Colorado. He attributed this to Gran Quivira's relationships with Plains groups, from whom they acquired meat and other products from bison hunting. This not only resulted in improved health for the town's inhabitants, but also established Gran Quivira as the most influential town in the Salinas region. Compared to Pueblo Colorado, for example, trash deposits at Gran Quivira included substantial quantities of discarded glazeware serving vessels imported from the north (Graves and Spielmann 2000:55).

Ruling the world with glaze-painted pottery

Glazeware pottery played an important role in protohistoric Puebloan life, particularly along the Rio Grande (Figure 8.7). Originating in the polychrome traditions of the Cibola and Little Colorado regions as early as the late AD 1200s, glaze was produced from a mix of lead, copper, iron, and manganese to produce a black, opaque, and glassy paint (Peckham 1991:81–2; Shepard 1956:44–8). Evolving from older matte paints made of iron and manganese, glaze paint probably was discovered by accident, perhaps during attempts to achieve greater contrast between pigments on polychrome vessels. Glazewares did not differ much stylistically from their matte-painted contemporaries, replicating the same bold iconography associated with Salado Polychrome pottery and the Southwestern and Kachina Cults. What does differ is that the materials and skills needed to produce the glazes were not easy to find, and accordingly, the earliest glazewares, such as those made in the Cibola area in the AD 1300s, came from fewer sources than non-glaze pottery (Mills 1995). Although they do not exhibit a degree of standardization that would suggest centralized production, glazeware vessels did get larger over time, requiring even greater skill and adequate access to raw materials. As a result, glazeware vessels attained some value, particularly among people unable to produce them easily.

Glaze-painted pottery and perhaps even raw glaze material moved into the middle Rio Grande region by the fourteenth century, where local potters soon created the glazes themselves (Vint 1999:421). Its

8.6 Established in the AD 1300s, Gran Quivira became a dominant town in the Salinas region, probably owing to its trade with Plains people who provided products from bison hunting in exchange for farming surpluses.

8.7 This glazeware bowl was recovered from Pecos Pueblo and dates to the seventeenth century. This particular vessel displays the distinctive horned serpent motif. Pueblo people associate this icon with water in all its forms, suggesting further parallels with Mesoamerica, where the plumed serpent is associated with water and fertility.

appearance along the Rio Grande corresponds with a shift away from household production and consumption and toward a new pattern in which uniquely decorated ceramics were produced in fewer towns. Judith Habicht-Mauche (1995) refers to this as the result of "tribalization," through which distinct styles formed in specific parts of the Rio Grande, with some becoming commodities traded over longer distances. Glazeware fueled this trend – at the town of Arroyo Hondo through most of the AD 1300s, pottery exhibited uniform, matte-painted decorations, no matter whether they were produced locally or imported, but between the AD 1370s and AD 1420s up to 35 percent of pottery consisted of distinctive glaze-painted vessels imported from the Galisteo Basin (Habicht-Mauche 1995).

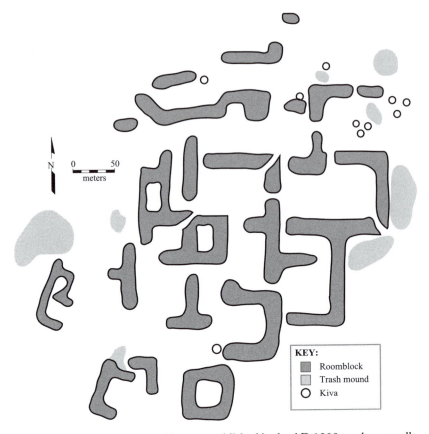

8.8 San Marcos Pueblo was established in the AD 1300s and eventually grew to as many as 5,000 adobe rooms, although not all rooms were occupied at the same time. In 1610–11, a Catholic church and convent were built in the town, and several hundred residents still lived at San Marcos until after the Pueblo Revolt of 1680.

By the early AD 1400s, a few towns in the central Rio Grande region dominated glazeware production, trading vessels as far south as the Salinas Pueblos, 120 km away. Thomas Motsinger (1997) proposes that most glaze pottery produced between AD 1430 and 1525 came from towns in the Galisteo Basin, perhaps because lead was available in the nearby Cerrillos Hills. He points to the increasing standardization of rim shapes as evidence of this village specialization and suggests that some rim designs were markers of their producers. One town in particular, San Marcos Pueblo, was probably a prominent production center (Figure 8.8). Established in the AD 1300s, this town grew to as many as 5,000 adobe rooms. Although not all rooms were occupied at the same time, San Marcos Pueblo was huge, and it remained important in the post-Contact period. Habicht-Mauche and her colleagues (2000) conducted trace-element analyses of glazewares and discovered that the paints produced at San Marcos Pueblo could be traced to sources in the nearby Cerrillos Hills. Glaze paints used in other towns relied on the same sources, but their glazes were chemically much less uniform, suggesting that they did not have regular access to raw materials. San Marcos Pueblo apparently controlled access to the lead mines, providing it with the kind of power that allowed it to grow rapidly. The town also may have maintained control over turquoise mines found in the Cerrillos Hills – the mineral occurs in very high frequencies at San Marcos Pueblo (Creamer 2000:108).

Why was glazeware pottery desirable, so much so that people living along the Rio Grande traded vessels over such long distances? A number of explanations have been proposed, and the possibility exists that it is was not the pottery that was important, but its contents (Habicht-Mauche 1993:47). A recent study by Matthew Chamberlin (2002), however, shows that glaze-painted jars were not well suited for transport, but they were effective for holding liquids and perhaps food for long periods of time. He argues that glaze jars were desired for their superior ability to store especially important liquids, food, seeds, and pollen used in ceremonial contexts. William Graves and Katherine Spielmann (2000:54) similarly suggest that because painted designs on glazewares reflected Southwestern Cult themes, glazeware bowls were the serving vessel of choice, particularly in ceremonial feasts during which bowls were prominently displayed. That the vessels were not easy to obtain further enhanced their value, fueling social inequities both among the producing towns that had access to the raw materials and within the towns that imported these vessels.

The demise of Casas Grandes

Skeletons of year-old macaws and shell ornaments have been found during excavations at Awat'ovi, Pecos Pueblo, and Gran Quivira, demonstrating that Puebloan trade far to the south persevered at least until AD 1400 (Bradley 1999, 2000; McKusick 2001:72). Most scholars agree that Casas Grandes continued to feed the Puebloan appetite for these goods. Interaction between the northern Southwest and the Chihuahuan Desert, however, steadily decreased – compared to the over 15,000 shell items and eight macaws found at Grasshopper Pueblo, only about 1,600 shell artifacts and two macaws were recovered at Pecos Pueblo. While Mesoamerican influences that had funneled through Casas Grandes continued to reverberate through Puebloan life, as illustrated in kiva murals,

8.9 The rock art panels at Petroglyph National Monument include imagery of macaws. Although petroglyphs are difficult to date, these are probably from the fourteenth or fifteenth century.

rock art (Figure 8.9), and pottery decoration (Smith 1952:149–51; Young 1989), the Chihuahuan center itself was fading.

The end for Casas Grandes occurred around AD 1450 (Phillips and Carpenter 1999). Charles Di Peso (1974) argued that the final blow came in a frenzy of warfare and destruction, perhaps by invaders coming from the west. LeBlanc (1999:252–3) agrees with Di Peso's interpretation, suggesting that many architectural features in the town were designed to repel such an onslaught. These measures apparently failed, and LeBlanc points to the 127 unburied skeletons recovered from excavated portions of the town. He believes they represent most of the residents living in Casas Grandes at that time. Alternative interpretations have been proposed. William Walker (2002), for example, builds a compelling argument suggesting that much of the burning and destruction was actually the result of ceremonial activity that perhaps included ritual abandonment.

Whether Casas Grandes was destroyed by an invading force or abandoned in an organized fashion, its final end was preceded by the cessation of major construction and the remodeling of public spaces to accommodate domestic use (Whalen and Minnis 2001b:200–2). What caused this decline? Overfarming and climate change are tempting candidates, but one possibility is that Casas Grandes became less prominent in long-distance exchange networks, as suggested by the declining quantities of Mesoamerican imports in towns to the north. The contraction of Puebloan people into isolated clusters of towns perhaps made trade over such long distances more difficult, particularly as nomadic societies filled the resulting vacant spaces. At the same time, competitors surrounding Casas Grandes probably challenged its preeminence in the region. Carroll Riley (1999) describes the emergence of "statelets" in the Sonoran Desert to the west of Casas Grandes that would have cut Casas Grandes off from sources of marine shell. Some scholars suggest that when Casas Grandes and its surrounding core area were finally abandoned, survivors moved to the west, both into the Sierra Madre, where cliff dwellings were constructed, and into the Sonoran Desert, where they joined the new Sonoran centers (Haas *et al.* 1994:224; Phillips and Carpenter 1999; Riley 1999:198–9).

The protohistoric sociopolitical landscape

Continuing climatic instability and the contraction of disparate groups provided opportunities for inequities to develop within fifteenth-century Puebloan towns. These were probably based on preferential access to the best resources, particularly arable lands, and it was most clearly manifested in the complex ceremonial life of these growing communities. Kin groups with the greatest antiquity were positioned to guide town activities, for they were the ones with the best lands, they were the ones maintaining the oldest and most important rituals, and they were the ones who could muster the resources needed to host ceremonies. Working against their dominance, however, was their inability to exert sustainable economic power – overt attempts to do so would have prompted people to "vote with their feet" and simply pack up and leave.

In this context, the Kachina Cult and other cross-cutting sodalities served two functions. They provided mechanisms to build unity across different factions. However, they also created opportunities for well-positioned groups and the individuals they promoted to expand their authority further. The evidence from Hawikku, for example, suggests that one route to power in these non-hierarchical and decentralized political systems was to fill leadership roles in a variety of sodalities – aspiring leaders did not seek a crown, but instead accumulated a number of hats that allowed them to guide community decision-making and benefit their supporters. And in some protohistoric towns, such as San Marcos Pueblo, the production and export of glazeware provided additional economic avenues to authority.

Despite the appearance of incipient centralized leadership in some fifteenth-century towns, and despite the greater influence that places like San Marcos Pueblo and Hawikku had over their neighbors, no evidence shows that regional political systems existed. Winifred Creamer (2000:107–10), for example, found that even though sixty-five protohistoric villages ranging from 300–3,000 rooms were established in the northern Rio Grande drainage, no region-wide hierarchy could be identified. Creamer does note that some of the areas she examined exhibited unusually regular spacing between towns, suggesting that competition among neighboring villages influenced settlement dynamics. LeBlanc (1999:246–50) agrees, arguing that many towns along the Rio Grande and its tributaries were built in inaccessible locations that allowed them to defend themselves. He further contends that in some cases, "confederacies" of autonomous towns maintained sizeable "no man's lands" between themselves and mutual enemies.

Puebloan towns clearly did engage in physical conflict during the protohistoric era. Martin (1994:106) summarizes research on trauma among Puebloan skeletal remains, finding that violence impacted a large proportion of protohistoric populations. While only about 2 percent of the individuals at the late fourteenth-century town of Tijeras Pueblo exhibited evidence of trauma, 17.5 percent of people at Hawikku had been injured. At San Cristobal, a 1,650-room town in the Galisteo Basin, one out of every five residents suffered traumatic injuries. Because the greatest frequencies are found in Puebloan communities occupied into the post-Contact era, some wounds are probably associated with warfare between Spanish and Pueblo people. However, the evidence also shows that the decades prior to European Contact were stressful for a number of reasons: a sharp decline in rainfall after the AD 1450s, pressure from surrounding nomadic groups by the early sixteenth century, and corresponding tension within closely packed Puebloan regions. With time-tested strategies of mobility and migration increasingly difficult to pursue – and perhaps less palatable to influential town leaders – conflict was resorted to more frequently.

By the early AD 1500s, regular interaction between Puebloan regions was decreasing. No longer did Galisteo Basin towns dominate glaze-ware production and exchange to the south, but instead local producers emerged to serve nearby consumers (Chamberlin 2002:273; Motsinger 1997:112–13). Warfare apparently structured Puebloan interaction to a degree not experienced earlier, and some towns reorganized their layouts with defense clearly in mind, such as occurred at the fortress-like Pecos Pueblo after the AD 1450s (Figure 8.10). By the time the Spanish began exploring the northern Southwest in the mid-sixteenth century, they remarked on the sophisticated battlefield tactics used by Puebloan people, including organized skirmish lines and trumpet signaling (Walker 2002:167). The Spanish noted the number of burned communities they encountered, and informants told them of epic battles between towns that caused many to be abandoned prior to their arrival. As seen throughout Puebloan history, the sociopolitical landscape was continually evolving, although nothing yet experienced would compare with changes that European Contact instigated.

Connecting the pre-Contact and post-Contact Puebloan worlds

A question that drives a considerable amount of anthropological and historical research is what the Puebloan world looked like immediately prior to European Contact. Many scholars are particularly interested in linking specific pre-Contact communities with the Pueblo towns known from the historical period. Some researchers are curious to draw the historical connections, while others want to know what pre-Contact towns looked like so they can understand how Europeans impacted Puebloan society and culture (see Boxes 8.1–8.4). In some cases, specific links between the past and the present have significant implications for contemporary issues such as land and water rights (e.g., Ellis 1974).

Unfortunately, the decades leading up to Spanish entry into the Southwest and the pre- to post-Contact connections are not well understood by archaeologists. Part of the reason is that much of the needed information is underneath towns still inhabited by Pueblo people – they are not "abandoned" sites and therefore are not readily available for investigation. Another problem is simply that the time frame is too

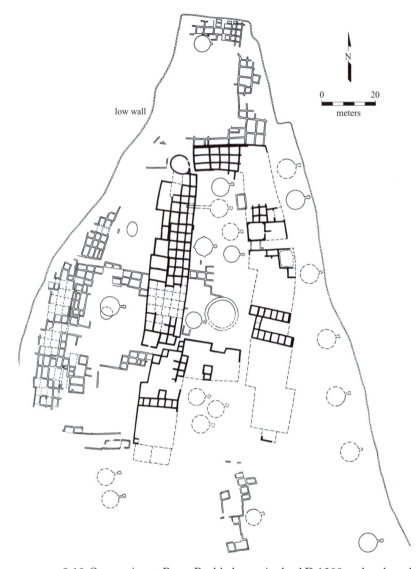

low wall

N

0   20
meters

8.10 Occupation at Pecos Pueblo began in the AD 1300s, when loosely
clustered roomblocks were established. By AD 1450, residents of the
town had built a much more defensive, multistoried structure of around
700 rooms and twenty kivas – shown here as the darker walls – enclosing
a large plaza area.

Box 8.2   Pueblo social organization in the ethnographic present

For Pueblo people of the ethnographic present, kinship relations serve as an important structure for all social, political, and religious activity. They therefore recognize important guidelines for organizing kin and determining who it is appropriate to marry. For the Hopi, the basic social unit is the matrifocal household, several of which are tied together through matrilineal descent. Two or more of these matrilineages are further united in twenty to thirty named and loosely ranked clans, which in turn are aligned into several unnamed phratries. The clans are arguably the most important social institutions, for they generally control property, ceremonies, and leadership positions. The Hopi are traditionally clan exogamous, meaning that one is supposed to marry outside of the clan. They also tend to be village endogamous – they marry within their villages (Levy 1992; Sekaquaptewa 1972; Titiev 1944). Similar social organization characterizes the other Western Pueblos, the Zuni and the Keresan Pueblos of Acoma and Laguna, although the traditions of the latter exhibit influence from the Rio Grande Pueblos.

Tanoan Pueblos along the Rio Grande also traditionally practice village endogamy, but unilineal descent groups are weak or absent. In fact, kinship relations are not especially important beyond the bilateral extended family, and property and other rights can pass to both sons and daughters. In place of unilineal descent is the dual moiety organization, for which one initially gains membership through one's father. In general, one marries within one's own moiety, but this is not a strict rule. Despite the overall flexibility of Tanoan organization, moieties are the most important social, political, and ceremonial social units, which has led scholars to suggest that this organization – and the lack of clans and lineages – must extend well back into the pre-Contact era (Hill 1982; Ortiz 1969).

The Rio Grande Keres reflect both their Western Pueblo roots and influence from the Tanoans. Villages again tend to be endogamous, but they feature both unilineal descent groups and a dual moiety organization. Unlike their Western counterparts, the family structure is less matrifocal and the matrilineal clans are not ranked and have little direct control over property or ceremonies; they primarily regulate exogamous marriage traditions. Several scholars believe that matrilineal clan organization was once more important, but faded when the Keres moved to the Rio Grande drainage (Dozier 1970; Ware and Blinman 2000). The patrilineal moieties are also not especially influential, and their primary role is in organizing the two principal dance-drama societies. Further adding to the complexity of Keresan organization are the medicine associations, influential sodalities with limited membership that control the political and ceremonial realms.

short – archaeological techniques are not easily applied to changes occurring over a few decades. And, finally, defining what "pre-Contact" and "post-Contact" mean is difficult, because very probably the *effects* of European Contact – Old World diseases, the disruption of long-distance exchange, even stories about the Spanish – entered the Southwest long before they physically arrived. The story of the pre-Contact decades is therefore not easy to reconstruct and linkages between past and contemporary Puebloan people are difficult to identify (Cordell 1995; Dongoske *et al.* 1997).

What can skeletal remains tell us?

Attempts to link the Puebloan past and present often consider information derived from skeletal analyses. These studies examine cranial measurements or discrete traits that have a strong genetic basis and that are resistant to environmental influence. The typical approach is to collect data from pre-Contact and historic skeletal populations and analyze them statistically to determine which groups were morphologically similar and therefore most likely to be related. The results, unfortunately, are ambiguous at best, particularly for attempts to link older Puebloan traditions with specific post-Contact Pueblo people.

One example of this approach is James Mackey's (1977) study of the origins of Jemez Pueblo. Although today Jemez is a single town, prior to Spanish Contact at least eight separate towns were occupied by Jemez ancestors. Mackey evaluated the hypothesis that these towns were established by immigrants moving from the San Juan River, through the Gallina area, and into the Jemez River valley. He recorded cranial measurements from fourteen pre-Contact and Contact-era skeletal populations, and found that, as predicted, remains from the hypothesized ancestral areas statistically linked with the Jemez population. Both groups were also morphologically similar to people from the protohistoric towns of Sapawe and Puye, located not far to the east along the Pajarito Plateau. However, Mackey's analysis suggested that Jemez people were also closely related to Hopi as well as to Hawikku in the Cibola region. Mackey's study reflects the intriguing yet often unclear results that these skeletal analyses produce.

Many skeletal studies yield contradictory results. Mahmoud El-Najjar (1978), for example, compared cranial measurements for several populations and found, among other results, that populations from twelfth-century Pueblo Bonito and the protohistoric town of Puye were quite different from one another; Puye, in fact, was most similar to Hawikku. Robert Corruccini (1972) found the opposite in his study of discrete cranial traits: Pueblo Bonito and Puye were most similar, while Puye and Hawikku were not. Differing conclusions may reflect different analytical techniques, but contradictions may also have a more interesting reason – analysts are looking at *different* skeletal assemblages from the *same* location. In the studies of El-Najjar and Corruccini, their data from Pueblo Bonito came from different samples.

Other studies confirm that different skeletal populations from the same area can show distinct relationships with other parts of the Southwest. El-Najjar found that skeletal remains from Hawikku, clearly ancestral to the Zuni, were associated with Little Colorado area populations, while burials from Zuni Pueblo itself were most similar to Sinagua and Kayenta populations. Craniometric analyses by Michael Schillaci and Christopher Stojanowski (2002) of several groups from Chaco Canyon found that their linkages were also quite varied. The West Cemetery in Pueblo Bonito, for example, was most similar to skeletal populations at Puye and Hawikku, while the North Cemetery was close to populations from the far northern Rio Grande. Remains from sites around Fajada Butte, on the other hand, were closest to those from the Pajarito Plateau protohistoric town of Tsankawi.

How can we interpret all of this? These skeletal analyses confirm that Puebloan communities consisted of many distinct groups – during cycles of abandonments, aggregations, and reabandonments, people left one area and moved elsewhere to join other similarly mobile people. This is why there are so many linkages from a place such as Chaco Canyon, and it is also why establishing ties between a twelfth-century site and a Contact-era town will never be possible – too much movement, resettlement, and intermarrying occurred in the intervening centuries. It is also why the West Cemetery at Pueblo Bonito links so closely with the protohistoric Zuni town of Hawikku, the protohistoric Pajarito Plateau town of Puye, and thirteenth-century sites near the modern town of Taos – all three are probably true, reflecting over 400 years of Puebloan history.

The most informative skeletal analyses focus only on populations from the protohistoric and Contact centuries. Schillaci (2001), for example, analyzed craniometric data from skeletal populations from eight protohistoric and historic cemeteries and found that towns physically located close to one another and culturally indistinguishable were often occupied by biologically diverse groups. His comparison of the towns of Hawikku and Heshotauthla, both ancestral to the modern Zuni, showed that they were occupied by people with quite distinct craniometric measurements. A contrasting pattern is revealed by Ethne Barnes's (1994) study of 354 individuals from protohistoric towns in the northern Rio Grande that are associated with modern Tewa Pueblos. She discovered that inhabitants of these towns exhibited very similar skeletal traits, suggesting a closely related population. She also found that females tended to be more similar to one another than did males, while the males also were fairly similar to one another, suggesting that people were organized into matrilineal groups into which local men married.

Schillaci's and Barnes's results suggest that the formation of the Zuni people and the Tewa people occurred through different processes – the aggregation of smaller groups of diverse people in the case of Zuni and the migration of larger groups in the case of the Tewa. Schillaci's work also found that remains from some ancestral Tewa towns were morphologically similar to non-Tewa populations in the northern Rio Grande, demonstrating that cultural features that allow us to label a town as "Tewa" do not necessarily indicate that all residents shared the same ancestral connections. And, most importantly, the reverse is true – biologically linked populations may have adopted or developed very different cultural characteristics as social groups fissioned and fused.

Say what? The linguistic evidence

Another approach employed to reconstruct protohistoric changes among Puebloan people is to analyze the languages spoken by their descendants. Two complementary approaches employed by anthropological linguists contribute to this effort. First, different languages and dialects can be compared to determine evolutionary relationships – usually, sets of fundamental words and basic grammatical features are compared to reconstruct historical links. Second, assuming that words and syntax change at a predictable rate, the difference between any two languages is used to estimate how long ago they diverged from a "proto" or "basal" language. While controversial, these techniques can be combined with the archaeological record to provide another source of information for understanding the protohistoric period.

According to linguistic reconstructions, the Hopi language traces back to 1,000 BC, perhaps having emerged among foragers living in what is now eastern California and southern Nevada (Sutton 2000:300). The origin of the Zuni language, however, is a mystery, for it shares little with other Southwest languages, making it less amenable to historical linguistic analysis (Hale and Harris 1979). Keresan also has no identifiable linguistic relatives. All Keresan speakers today understand one another, although dialects do distinguish the Western Keres – particularly the Acoma – from Keres living along the Rio Grande (Upham *et al.* 1994:187). This mutual intelligibility suggests a relatively recent origin for Keresan, with some estimates dating the emergence of current dialects to AD 1400–1500.

The Tanoan languages – which include Tewa, Towa, and Tiwa, all still spoken among northern Rio Grande people – first emerged around 2,000 to 3,000 years ago (Adler 1999; Hale and Harris 1979:171). The current languages, however, diverged much more recently from this basal Tanoan. Some estimates place the emergence of Towa at around AD 500–700, while Tewa, whose dialects are the most mutually intelligible, developed between AD 1050–1350. Tiwa, often considered closest to basal Tanoan, is further divided into those speakers living in the northernmost reaches of the Pueblo world and those living near the city of Albuquerque. This physical separation has made the two dialects nearly unintelligible.

While linguistic reconstructions can suggest when the *languages* emerged, their origins cannot easily be linked to geography or material culture. During the historic period, speakers of the same language often exhibited other characteristics that differed (Creamer 2000:111–12). For example, the towns of Pecos and Jemez, both speakers of Towa, produced distinctive ceramics – the former made glazewares while the latter produced whitewares. And the reverse also occurred – Towa-speaking Jemez adopted aspects of ceremonial organization from neighboring Keresan towns (Ware and Blinman 2000:395). Further complicating the picture is the mobility known from the historic period. During the Contact period, for example, most Tano speakers of the Galisteo Basin moved into Tewa towns to escape the Spanish, then moved to Hopi, where their descendants still speak Tewa. Linguistic reconstructions can tell us what happened to the languages themselves, but they do not directly tell us the histories of the people who speak them.

Building connections between past and present

Our understanding of how the protohistoric Southwest became the Contact-era Pueblo world is necessarily fuzzy, because culture, sociopolitical organization, and even language are not inextricably linked together. When the archaeological, linguistic, and skeletal data are considered together, however, a provisional picture does emerge of the late pre-Contact changes that led to the Pueblo world at the time of European Contact (see Boxes 8.1–8.4).

Box 8.3   Pueblo religious practice in the ethnographic present

Traditional religious practice among the different Pueblos universally focuses on weather control and community well-being, which includes the promotion of fertility, the purging of witchcraft and other misfortunes, and the general enhancement of communalism. How ceremonial activity is directed, however, is quite variable, and revolves around a combination of medicine societies, clan-based sodalities, and the Kachina Cult dance groups. Hunting and warfare sodalities also once enjoyed prominent roles in Pueblo ceremonial life, but the post-Contact era undermined their religious authority, with warfare sodalities disappearing entirely among some Pueblos (Ware and Blinman 2000: 390–1).

For the Hopi, religious practice is decentralized. Hopi sodalities serve a number of equivalent roles, including healing, and they are run by individual clans, which "own" the ceremonies, kivas, and ritual items used by each sodality. However, while sodalities are managed by specific clans, sodality *members* can come from any clan; participants in the highly public Kachina Cult can also come from any clan (Parsons 1939; Rushforth and Upham 1992; Underhill 1991). Zuni clans also regulate religious activity, but ceremonial sodalities are more independent than among the Hopi. The Zuni recognize about a dozen medicine sodalities, whose mandate is to protect the village from witchcraft, disease, and other misfortune. The Kachina Cult is also present among the Zuni, although it is restricted to men (Cushing 1979; Parsons 1939; Stevenson 1904).

Religious practice among the Keresan Pueblos differs between the Western and Rio Grande Keres. Acoma and Laguna ceremonial life is organized similarly to the Hopi and Zuni. The Keresan Pueblos along the Rio Grande, however, are somewhat different, for ceremonial activity is controlled by several non-kin-based sodalities, each with a specific function, including curing, clowning, and warfare. An association of sodality leaders also manages the Kachina Cult (Dozier 1970).

Ceremonial life also differs among the Tanoan Pueblos. Among the Tewa, for example, the dual moiety organization provides the structure for religious activity, with each moiety taking charge of ceremonies for only half the year. Each moiety has its own ranked sodalities involved in specific activities, as outlined in the oral historical account at the beginning of this chapter. Cross-cutting sodalities, however, are weak among the Tewa, with the two medicine associations involved primarily in individual curing. The Kachina Cult is also secondary to the ceremonial authority of the moieties. The Tewa pattern generally characterizes the other Tanoan Pueblos, with the northern Tiwa having the strongest moiety-based ceremonial life and no Kachina Cult activity at all, while the Towa are most like the Western Pueblos, with a more influential Kachina Cult (Dozier 1970; Hill 1982; Ortiz 1969).

Most data associate Hopi people with the Virgin and Kayenta Anasazi cultural traditions, while similarities with Great Basin and California languages suggest a western origin for their language. Some scholars also point to the Grand Canyon and Sinagua regions as places from which ancestral Hopi people emigrated to the Hopi Mesas (Ambler 1998:20; Euler 1999). Additional connections exist between Hopi and towns along the Little Colorado River to the south, and immigrants from the San Juan River region also moved into the Kayenta area, demonstrating that people came from all surrounding areas to form towns along the Hopi Mesas (Turner 1999; see also Turner 1993). Oral history is consistent with these archaeological reconstructions, and specific Hopi traditions can even be traced back hundreds of years to a diversity of specific sites. When the so-called Magician Burial at the twelfth-century Sinagua site of Ridge Ruin was discovered, for example, Hopi consultants accurately predicted the contents of the grave after being shown a small sample – many items were still tied to a specific Hopi clan, 800 years later (Ferguson et al. 2001:17). These diverse origins help to explain why the clan became the fundamental unit of Hopi sociopolitical organization, with different clans united through communal activities promoted by the Kachina Cult and the decision-making authority of the oldest clans.

The Zuni have a similar heritage, but one less well understood by archaeologists. Like the Hopi, Zuni people lived in several different towns prior to European Contact – perhaps nine Zuni towns were occupied in the early sixteenth century, one of which, Halona: wa, is today's Zuni Pueblo. Uncertainty regarding the origin of the Zuni language makes historical reconstructions more difficult, but oral histories tell of the migrations of many clans that finally united in the Cibola region. The archaeological evidence suggests that people from a variety of regions joined the local population, with groups immigrating from the Little Colorado drainage and the Mogollon Rim (Kintigh 2000:112). Some groups may have come from fairly far south. Spanish chroniclers, for example, describe the abandoned "fortress" of "Chichilticale," in what is now southeastern Arizona, as having been located on a trade route to Zuni, and native informants noted that Chichilticale's inhabitants moved to the Cibola region (Hartmann and Flint 2001). This aggregation of disparate groups in Zuni towns created sociopolitical organization similar to the Hopi, with ranked clans held together by the Kachina Cult and guided by leaders of the most powerful clans.

The heritage of the Keresan Pueblos is still debated. Some evidence shows that the Keres can trace their origins to people living just beyond the southeastern edge of the San Juan Basin (but see Ambler 1998). At Acoma, the oldest Keresan Pueblo that is still occupied, oral histories identify nearby sites as ancestral to specific clans, and research at these sites confirms a local connection back to the thirteenth century (Dittert and Brunson-Hadley 1999). Oral histories also refer to the immigration of other groups who joined the local population, including people who came from Mesa Verde through Chaco Canyon (Cordell 1995:205). J. Richard Ambler (1998) also argues that at least some Keres originated far to the west, where the San Juan River empties into the Colorado River, and that they gradually moved east. Perhaps all of these scenarios are correct, with Keresan ancestors coming to Acoma from a variety of places.

Archaeologists identify the turn of the fourteenth century as the point at which trade items from the east began to enter the Acoma region (Dittert and Brunson-Hadley 1999:67), providing a connection that allowed some Keres – as well as glazeware technology – to move toward the Rio Grande. By the mid-AD 1300s, Keres occupied communities on the southern edge of the Jemez Mountains, where they either displaced or joined local inhabitants – and perhaps sizeable groups of northern immigrants – along the lower Jemez drainage and the southern Pajarito Plateau. LeBlanc (1999:247) proposes that they moved into a "no-man's land" that had formed between local Puebloan groups. At European Contact, several Keresan towns were scattered along the Jemez Valley, several more were located along the Rio Grande south of the Pajarito Plateau, and Acoma Pueblo was occupied far to the west. Accordingly, the cultural traditions of the Keres include the clan organization seen at Hopi and Zuni, while moiety divisions reminiscent of the Tanoan Pueblos also exist. The most important sociopolitical authority, however, emanates from older religious sodalities, suggesting a stable and ancient organizational core.

The history of Tanoan groups is complicated by the many changes that took place along the Rio Grande both before and after Europeans arrived. Some scholars contend that "basal" Tanoan was spoken across much of the northern Colorado Plateau, including Mesa Verde and northern Rio

Grande areas. The Towa language, with linguistic origins as old as the AD 500s, may have been spoken around the San Juan River. Towa oral histories trace their roots to this area, and Mackey's (1977) skeletal analyses provide some support. Cheryl Ferguson (1980) also found similarities between skeletal remains from the Towa village of Pecos and those from the thirteenth-century occupation of Aztec. Archaeological evidence suggests that these northern residents migrated into the Jemez region in the AD 1300s, where they probably joined local Tanoan speakers. Eventually, some Towa moved beyond the eastern edge of the Galisteo Basin. By the AD 1500s, Towa speakers were concentrated in perhaps a dozen towns along the Jemez River and at Pecos Pueblo to the east. Towa contact with Keresan people may explain their sociopolitical similarities, including a focus on both clans and moieties and the locus of authority among the sodalities.

By the time of European Contact, Tewa-speaking people were living in a dozen towns north of the modern city of Santa Fe, as well as in a handful of communities in the Galisteo Basin. Oral histories recount the journey of Tewa people from the northwest – often Mesa Verde is indicated – down the Chama and Rio Grande valleys (Cordell 1995:205). These accounts tell of the movement of moieties that built villages along the way, with some settling along the Pajarito Plateau and in the Galisteo Basin before moving to their current locations. Archaeological evidence is consistent with these scenarios, for Mesa Verde-style pottery, masonry, and kiva styles are found among thirteenth-century towns of the northern Rio Grande (Buge 1980; Hawley 1950). On the other hand, although some evidence from northern San Juan sites suggests the presence of moiety organization there, their presence has not been confirmed at suspected ancestral Tewa sites along the Chama and Rio Grande drainages.

Historical linguistics suggests that the Tewa language diverged from basal Tanoan around AD 1050–1350, perhaps through contact with Keres people who moved into the Rio Grande drainage at this time. Archaeologists have tried to identify the resulting "Tewa–Keres" boundary on the Pajarito Plateau. Architectural, ceramic, and even lithic data confirm the cultural distinction, with ancestral Tewa sites characterized by plaza-oriented adobe architecture, D-shaped ceremonial rooms, and pottery painted with organic pigments, while ancestral Keresan sites exhibit detached kivas and glazeware pottery. This pattern – and the boundary north of Frijoles Canyon on the Pajarito Plateau – becomes most prominent at the turn of the fifteenth century, at which point little cultural material moved between the two areas (Creamer 2000:105; Van Zandt 1999:378–9; Vint 1999:461–2; Walsh 2000:208). Prior to this century, the boundary was more blurry, and Tewa–Keres interaction was probably more common. Evidence of this earlier interaction can still be seen today – the Kachina Cult is found among the Tewa and names of Tewa clown societies are Keresan cognates, although, in both cases, moieties and their leaders shape most town activity (Ware and Blinman 2000:386).

When the Spanish arrived, Tiwa speakers lived in perhaps fifteen towns located along the Rio Grande south of Albuquerque, with at least two Tiwa towns located far to the north near Taos. Separated by Keresan and Tewa speakers, the two Tiwa dialects diverged substantially. Oral histories suggest that this happened around AD 1100–1200, which roughly correlates with the first flood of immigrants moving from northwestern Puebloan areas into the middle Rio Grande. The Tiwa language may therefore have originated among the oldest inhabitants of the Rio Grande drainage as new groups moved in (Ware and Blinman 2000:402). Oral histories, however, also indicate that others contributed to Tiwa culture. The southern Tiwa describe how people came from the south as well as the north to form the Tiwa towns, while the famous Tiwa town of Taos Pueblo includes kiva sodalities that trace their heritage to the north (e.g., Eddy 1975:63). Nevertheless, the antiquity of Tiwa in the region may explain why their moiety organization is so strong and clans and the unifying Kachina Cult are absent.

Although the exact details will perhaps never be known, archaeologists do agree on the continuity between protohistoric Puebloan people and the Hopi, Zuni, Keres, and Tanoan speakers who occupy the Southwest today (see Boxes 8.1–8.4). The histories of other Puebloan groups

Box 8.4   Traditional Puebloan leadership in the ethnographic present

Despite the Spanish attempt to establish a hierarchical governing structure in most towns, the Pueblos retained their traditional forms of decision-making. While most Pueblos include councils of priests or similar groups of decision-makers, positions of authority tend to be ranked in importance. In general, this ranking is determined by sodality and/or clan membership and the corresponding access to and control over important ceremonial knowledge and ritual items. Kinship, religion, and politics are virtually inseparable among the Pueblo, which has led some scholars to suggest that the organization is decentralized and non-hierarchical. In fact, priestly leaders enjoy considerable behind-the-scenes power over Pueblo towns – they control the ritual calendar, they adjudicate disputes and have punitive authority, and they often manage property ownership (Brandt 1994; Reyman 1987).

Priestly leaders of the clan sodalities are the highest authorities among the Hopi, but they are not all considered equal. Instead, the Hopi sodalities are ranked according to when each clan is believed to have arrived in the village – the *kikmongwi*, or village chief, therefore typically comes from the Bear Clan, which "owns" the ancient and important Soyal Society and controls the most valuable farmlands (Levy 1992). Clan leadership – and thus village leadership for the Bear Clan – is passed from brother to brother or from maternal uncle to nephew in this matrilineal society (Sekaquaptewa 1972:241). A similar leadership structure is seen at Zuni, where the Dogwood Clan traditionally controls the two major offices (Reyman 1987:125). The Western Keres also mirror this political organization. At Acoma, for example, the Antelope Clan is the most highly ranked, and one of its lineages controls the office of *ha'actitcani*, the town chief. This position, however, is supposed to be approved by the medicine sodality priests, which can lead to conflicts between the clan and sodalities over leadership positions, a consequence seen in most Pueblos with multiple and overlapping forms of organization (Ware and Blinman 2000).

Among the Rio Grande Keres, leadership is based in the powerful and more restricted medicine sodalities rather than the weaker unilineal descent groups. Positions of authority are usually filled by the Flint medicine sodality – the sodality's head priest is also the village chief, and he appoints other political offices, forming a fairly hierarchical and centralized political structure (Ware and Blinman 2000:384–5). The Tanoan Pueblos, in contrast, organize leadership around the moieties, with the two moiety chiefs each in charge for half the year. These chiefs must come from one of the eight ranked sodalities found in each moiety (Ortiz 1969). Among some Tanoan Pueblos, however, one moiety chief enjoys greater decision-making authority, or yet a third chief is superordinate to the moiety chiefs.

encountered when Europeans arrived, however, are not well understood because their populations did not survive the Contact period intact. This includes the Piro and Tompiro, who lived along the southern Rio Grande and bore the brunt of Spanish Conquest (Schroeder 1979). The Piro occupied as many as forty towns where the Rio Puerco drains into the Rio Grande, and Spanish accounts describe their architecture and dress as similar to Tanoans to the north; some linguists believe Piro was a Tanoan language. To the east, in the Salinas area, the Spanish described perhaps ten towns occupied by Tompiro people, whose ancestry can be traced to protohistoric Salinas towns such as Gran Quivira and Pueblo Colorado, some of which were still occupied during the Contact period. The Tompiro were probably related to Piro speakers of the Rio Grande, but their interactions with Plains Indians, especially Apache, led to the development of a separate dialect. Although it seems likely that Piro and Tompiro ancestry can be partially traced to Mogollon groups, particularly those in the Jornada area, little is known of these people owing to the radical changes that impacted the Puebloan world beginning in the sixteenth century.

Disease, subjugation, and continuing change in the Pueblo world

In AD 1539, Fray Marcos de Niza, a Franciscan friar, left the heartland of New Spain to search for wealthy cities rumored to exist to the north (Figure 8.11). Traveling into what is now Arizona and then crossing into New Mexico, de Niza and his party entered the Cibola region, but when one of his companions was killed at Hawikku (Figure 8.3), the expedition returned to Mexico City. Although de Niza only viewed the Pueblo towns from a distance, he reported his discovery of the fabled "Seven Cities of Cibola," leading to stories that great riches could be found in the Pueblo world. The next year, an expedition led by Francisco Vásquez de Coronado set out with 300 Spanish soldiers, over 1,000 Mexican Indians, 1,000 horses and 600 pack animals, and six Franciscan friars. Reaching Hawikku on July 7, 1540, Coronado quickly defeated the town but was disappointed not to find gold. Spanish parties sent to Hopi failed to discover riches there either, and so Coronado turned east, taking the expedition to the Rio Grande, where again no wealth was found. After spending the winter among the Southern Tiwa Pueblos, and ruthlessly putting down a Pueblo rebellion by killing several hundred people, Coronado attempted to find treasure on the Plains before returning to New Spain. The Southern Tiwa never recovered from that winter of AD 1540–41, and their entire region was virtually abandoned (Dozier 1970; Simmons 1979).

Although a few more expeditions entered the Pueblo world during the late AD 1500s, interest waned as the expected wealth failed to materialize and Pueblo people became increasingly confrontational. Spanish attitudes toward the Southwest changed, however, at the end of the AD 1600s. At the prodding of the Catholic church, violent conquest

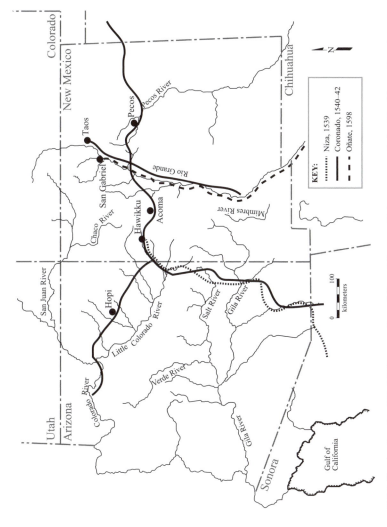

8.11 Beginning in AD 1539, a series of Spanish expeditions entered the Puebloan Southwest. The first *entradas* were led by Fray Marcos de Niza and Francisco Vásquez de Coronado; several more expeditions followed. Colonization began when Juan de Oñate led 400 people to the Pueblo of Yunqueyunque, where the Spanish established the colony of San Gabriel.

ostensibly was outlawed in favor of benevolent colonization and the conversion of indigenous peoples. In AD 1598, Juan de Oñate assembled a
force of 400 soldiers, colonists, friars, and Mexican Indians, marched up
the Rio Grande to the Keresan Pueblo of Santo Domingo, and demanded
the capitulation of all surrounding villages (Figure 8.11). Perhaps because
of the sacking of powerful Pecos Pueblo (Figure 8.10) by an expedition
several years earlier – despite its force of 500 warriors – Oñate faced
little resistance. His party established their colonial capital at the Tewa
Pueblo of Yunqueyunque, near present-day San Juan Pueblo, although
it was moved in AD 1610 to Santa Fe, which still serves as the capital
of New Mexico. Franciscans soon established missions at Pueblo towns
all over the northern Southwest. Although a few generations later, in AD
1680, Pueblo people rebelled and drove the Spanish south to El Paso,
they returned in force twelve years later, at which point European conquest and colonization of the Pueblo world was complete (Dozier 1970;
Simmons 1979).

The depopulation of the Pueblo world

Beginning with the first Spanish expeditions, Pueblo populations were
decimated through disease, battles, and punitive executions. Resistance
was brutally punished – when the Keresan Pueblo of Acoma killed his
nephew and fourteen other Spaniards in AD 1598, Oñate had the town
sacked, many people were executed, one foot was severed from each surviving man, and all men and women were sentenced to twenty years
of servitude. Such violence had a tremendous impact on Pueblo populations, but even more devastating were the diseases the Spanish introduced
and the demands that they placed on Pueblo towns.

Disease was not alien to Pueblo people, and they suffered from a variety of chronic and acute ailments, including tuberculosis and treponemal
disease (Stodder and Martin 1992:63–4). Just like humans everywhere,
they possessed a degree of resistance to indigenous pathogens. The Spanish, however, introduced foreign diseases that were much more virulent
owing to their long association with dense populations in the Old World,
including smallpox, measles, malaria, typhus, typhoid, dysentery, scar-
let fever, and chicken pox (Roberts and Ahlstrom 1997; Stodder and
Martin 1992). Because waves of disease probably preceded waves of
Europeans, perhaps following traditional trade routes from Mesoamerica, the full impact of Old World diseases on the Pueblo people may
never be understood. The number of deaths from Old World diseases –
most with mortality rates far in excess of 50 percent – must have been
extremely high. After Spanish colonization, priests and bureaucrats duly

recorded epidemics among native populations, such as the "pestilence" that reportedly killed 3,000 in AD 1640 (Stodder and Martin 1992:66). Documentary references, however, often make no reference to numbers of deceased, and they do not account for the impact of disease on Pueblo towns distant from the Spanish capital or where no missions existed.

Adding to the devastation of epidemic diseases were demands for supplies and labor that the Spanish placed on Pueblo towns, particularly those along the Rio Grande (Dozier 1970; Simmons 1979). Large Catholic missions were built by native populations and the friars demanded agricultural surpluses to support their activities. Many of the approximately 2,000 Spanish colonists during the seventeenth century were beneficiaries of the *encomienda* system, in which a colonist was granted the right to extract tribute and labor from a Pueblo town. Both missionaries and *encomenderos* routinely abused the limits imposed by the very distant Spanish Crown, and the indigenous population had to give up supplies they normally kept in reserve for the winter months or for droughts that hit the Southwest with increasing frequency in the mid-1600s (Rose *et al.* 1981). Meanwhile, nomadic groups surrounding the Rio Grande, particularly the Apache to the east, regarded the Pueblos as allies of the Spanish, and their raids of Pueblo towns accordingly grew in frequency and potency. A powerful attack in AD 1640, for example, led to the burning of 20,000 *fanegas* (about 1.6 bushels each) of maize (Simmons 1979:184).

The effect of all of these impacts was a rate of depopulation so severe that the majority of Pueblo towns were abandoned, with survivors seeking refuge with remaining communities. Exact numbers are hard to determine because of the difficulty in estimating how many people existed prior to Contact (Schroeder 1979). Based on accounts by the earliest Spanish explorers, as many as 135 named towns existed in the sixteenth century, with at least sixty-six of them larger than 300 rooms (Figure 8.12). By AD 1650, about half of these towns had been abandoned. Steadman Upham (1992:232) estimates that almost 132,000 people lived along the Rio Grande, with another 67,000 found in Pueblo towns west of the river. After reprisals exacted for the Pueblo Revolt of AD 1680, a census taken in AD 1706 of all but the Hopi towns recorded only eighteen towns with 6,440 Pueblo people (Simmons 1979:185).

The Cibola region provides a specific example of this depopulation. Early in the AD 1500s, thousands of ancestral Zuni occupied nine large Cibolan towns, and by AD 1598, after nearly three generations of sporadic Spanish contact, at least 12,000 people still lived in the surviving six towns. After seventeenth-century missionization and the reprisals of the Pueblo Revolt, however, only 1,500 people remained, all living in

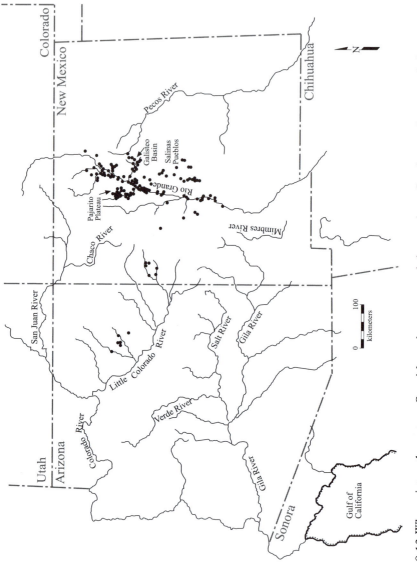

8.12 When sixteenth-century Spanish explorers entered the northern Southwest, they recorded over 130 Puebloan towns. Their population estimates ranged from 20,000 men up to 248,000 people. By 1706, a Spanish census of all but the Hopi Pueblos identified eighteen towns with fewer than 7,000 people.

8.13 Kivas at Acoma Pueblo are incorporated into the roomblocks, making them appear to the casual observer as if they are domestic quarters. This may have developed as a way to hide traditional ceremonial spaces from the Spanish, particularly from the missionaries intent on converting Pueblo people.

Halona: wa, where Zuni Pueblo is found today. Not all of the depopulation was due to death by disease or punitive attacks by the Spanish – some Zuni probably fled to live with other Pueblo groups or with the Athapaskans – but the effect on surviving town residents was profound (Simmons 1979:185).

Impact on the Pueblo way of life

The perseverance of the Pueblo way of life through the Contact era is a testament to the human spirit in the face of so many physical and socio-cultural challenges. It is impossible to appreciate how the experiences of this period tore at the threads of Pueblo culture, a topic that cannot be done justice in the remaining pages of this book. Both the archaeological and the historical record do, however, preserve clues to suggest some of the changes to Pueblo sociopolitical organization in response to Contact-era pressures.

Depopulation had the most substantial impact on Pueblo towns. Many kin groups – including clans, the fundamental organizing unit of many towns – ceased to exist when their numbers fell too low to make them viable. Sodality organization was also jeopardized as individual leaders succumbed to disease or were targeted by the Spanish, and as kin groups that often served as a sodality's foundation dissolved. Pueblo people confronted these challenges by frequently reorganizing, and ethnically related communities worked together to retrain religious authorities needed for critical ceremonies. Some towns tried to attract refugees to augment their numbers, in order to deter Spanish and Athapaskan attacks as well as to fill vacant ceremonial positions. Most towns ultimately were abandoned, with survivors splitting up and moving in with related clans in other communities. Some took refuge with the Spanish, going so far as to join the retreat to El Paso after the Pueblo Revolt of AD 1680, where Pueblo people established villages that still survive today (Schroeder 1979; Simmons 1979).

Laguna Pueblo provides a good example of post-Contact changes (Ellis 1979). It formed when a number of Keres and Towa fled several Rio Grande towns during the Spanish Reconquest. After first taking refuge at Acoma Pueblo, these survivors moved east with some Acoma people and established Laguna in AD 1697. Seven clans are said to have resulted from this original migration, but later additions included clans from Hopi, Zuni, Jemez, and Acoma. This resulted in Laguna Pueblo exhibiting features of Rio Grande Keres culture mixed with Hopi and Zuni characteristics. Similar ethnic blending occurred when Tewa-speaking people of the Galisteo Basin fled to Hopi after the Pueblo Revolt, where the Hopi allowed them to establish their own village, Hano, in a vulnerable location between the Hopi towns and potential Ute attackers (Stanislawski 1979). While Hano still exists today, other people who fled to Hopi to escape the Spanish eventually returned to the Rio Grande. Sandia Pueblo was abandoned when its Tiwa residents fled to Hopi during the Pueblo Revolt, but the town was resettled in the AD 1740s when some Tiwa returned, accompanied by a number of Hopi people (Brandt 1979).

Alongside the population movements and ethnic blending that occurred after Spanish arrival were other sociopolitical changes. Some scholars argue that the flexible social rules seen among Rio Grande Pueblos were necessary adjustments to the Contact period. Some Pueblos, for example, practice "bilocal postmarital residence," meaning that once a couple is married, they are free to live with either the husband's or the wife's kin. Rare among other horticultural people, it is particularly unusual to find it in societies that trace their descent along the maternal line, as do the Pueblo. Archaeological evidence confirms that matrilocal residence – in which the new couple moves in with the wife's family – was common prior to Spanish Contact. The implication is therefore that the bilocal pattern emerged in the challenging times of the sixteenth and seventeenth centuries, allowing for greater social flexibility at a time when entire kin groups were disappearing (Peregrine and Ember 2002:358).

Another change argued to date to the Contact period is the degree of political centralization found in many Pueblo towns. When the Spanish established control over the Pueblo world, particularly after the Reconquest, they created new political offices in each town, including a governor, lieutenant governor, *alcaldes* (councilmen), and an *alguacil* (constable). This new government allowed the Spanish to interact more easily with Pueblo towns, while also facilitating acculturation of the indigenous population by divorcing their political structure from the influential religious sodalities. While some scholars believe that this marks the beginning of centralized authority among the Pueblo, the archaeological record indicates that powerful individuals and sodalities certainly existed prior to Contact, and they continued to guide Pueblo life (see also Brandt 1994). In practice, the Spanish-imposed system was only employed for interactions with the Spanish – the traditional theocratic authority continued intact, often with native leaders secretly appointing and controlling the secular government (Dozier 1970:68).

Missionary efforts among Pueblo people also had unintended consequences. Franciscan friars, supported by the Spanish Crown, established sizeable missions in many Pueblo towns, rebuilding many – and replacing the martyred friars – after the Pueblo Revolt (Simmons 1979). The indigenous population contributed surpluses and labor, and many unwillingly went through the motions of conversion. Some people perhaps were prepared to try Catholicism, but few wanted to abandon their traditional belief system, as the new religion required. Attempts by the Franciscans forcibly to stamp out Pueblo religion, including burning and filling kivas, destroying Kachina iconography, and punishing "idolaters," drove people to hide their ceremonial lives. In some Pueblo towns, square rooms hidden away in domestic roomblocks replaced traditional subterranean plaza kivas, while sodality activities became even more secretive, further bolstering the control and thus value of the ceremonial knowledge that sustained theocratic authority (Brandt 1977, 1980) (see Fig. 8.13).

These are just a few changes to the sociopolitical structure of the Pueblo world after European Contact. Despite the abandonment of so many towns and the accompanying splintering and reaggregation of Pueblo communities, much of the pre-Contact culture persevered, including the different languages, religious traditions, and sociopolitical institutions. On the other hand, significant changes obviously occurred, just as they had in pre-Contact times when Puebloan people faced severe stresses. Areas that bore the brunt of Spanish conquest and colonization, exacerbated by attacks and raids by nomadic groups, were the most severely impacted, so much so that places like Sandia Pueblo in the eighteenth century were quite unlike what they looked like in the sixteenth century. Pueblo people situated on the fringe of the Spanish colony were less severely impacted, with the Hopi and northern Tiwa towns resisting change more successfully.

Social and political histories in the American Southwest

Although this book's story stops in the AD 1700s, the history of the Pueblo people does not. Many continue to occupy twenty Pueblo Reservations, while others live in cities and communities across the world. Pueblo languages are still spoken, and the ancestral traditions are still practiced, often well out of sight of non-Pueblo people. And, as they did throughout their long history, they continue to experience changes as the world in which we all exist influences our lives.

What anthropological lessons can be learned from the sociopolitical histories of the Puebloan people? First, the history is a story of continual change. Pueblo people today are not the same as Pueblo people of AD 1539, over twenty generations ago. And their pre-Contact ancestors of AD 1400 were quite different from Puebloan people living in AD 900 – some sixty generations before today! Certainly, biological and cultural threads tie all of these places and times together, and in many ways the Pueblo people of today are remarkably similar to their distant ancestors. Innumerable influences over many centuries, however, created the unique traditions that emerged and occasionally disappeared at particular moments in Puebloan history. The lesson is that we should not stop at Contact when relating the development of historic Pueblo culture, a point already appreciated by many scholars (e.g., Ware and Blinman 2000). Similarly, we cannot expect that the present – even the "ethnographic present" of the late nineteenth and early twentieth centuries – is a mirror of the Puebloan past, a point that perhaps is not as widely appreciated.

Another lesson from the pages of this book is that Puebloan people never "mysteriously disappeared," an idea that the popular literature on the American Southwest enjoys promoting. A characteristic that permeates the Puebloan experience is mobility, and at various times and places people packed up and left their communities to find greener pastures elsewhere. On occasion, this led to the depopulation of entire regions, but to archaeologists, as well as to Pueblo descendants, there are no mysteries as to where they went. Depopulation of one region led to increasing aggregation in other parts of the Puebloan world, part of the pattern of mobility that continued well into the post-Contact era. In some cases, places that were abandoned were later reoccupied, leading to recent challenges suggesting that the term "abandonment" is inappropriate because of the impression of finality that it evokes. Many Puebloan communities that we consider "abandoned" were in fact carefully closed down rather than haphazardly vacated, as if the inhabitants planned to return. And many "abandoned" sites continue to serve as important, even sacred, points on the Pueblo landscape.

The final lesson, and a guiding theme in this book, is that the history of change in the Puebloan world is not simply a record of responses to physical environmental stimuli. No one doubts that the unforgiving climate and landscape of the northern Southwest created remarkable challenges that Puebloan people had to overcome, particularly once farming became the primary means of subsistence. The Puebloan way of life has been shaped by these challenges and the particular adaptations that emerged. The paleoenvironmental record, however, is one of nearly constant change, and yet there are comparatively few "hinge points" – the episodes of substantial shifts in Puebloan history described in the first chapter and related throughout the book. The perspective advocated here is that changes were precipitated by a convergence of circumstances, particularly internal sociopolitical factors that often made Puebloan communities ripe for change. Characteristics of the physical environment operated much like catalysts, accelerating cultural changes, but not "causing" them in a direct way. Instead, the timing and nature of new cultural trajectories were – and still are – most directly shaped by competing and cooperating forces within Puebloan society.

A complex episode in the history of Keresan-speaking Laguna Pueblo, introduced earlier, encapsulates the perspective on cultural change advocated in this book (Brandt 1979; Ellis 1979). By the nineteenth century, Laguna was occupied by at least two factions. One group, the Conservatives, represented the traditional theocratic leadership that controlled both internal and external political offices, including the Puebloan and Catholic ceremonial life of the town. The Progressives, on the other hand, were guided by ambitious personalities that believed the future of Laguna lay in greater openness to non-Indian people and Protestant religions. After decades of brewing tensions, the traditional Conservative leadership packed up the ritual paraphernalia in AD 1879 and moved out. Led by the Kachina Chief, the refugees were eventually persuaded by religious leaders at Tiwa-speaking Isleta Pueblo, located almost 70 km away on the Rio Grande, to join their town, whose own ceremonial program was suffering – they had none of their own Kachina masks, and some of the old sodalities had faded away. Isleta's and Laguna's ceremonial and social traditions, however, differed to such a degree that this attempt to meld the two groups together failed. Ultimately, the Laguna refugees returned to a village near Laguna Pueblo, leaving only the Kachina masks they had promised to the Isleta leaders – and the Kachina Chief to tend them.

This Laguna story could have been anyone's – although the details of Puebloan society and culture are unique, the social and political forces that shape their histories can be seen in any people's history. Indeed, these same tensions between individual and group, between competition and cooperation, and between environment and culture impact us today and continue to structure our future. The story of the Puebloan people is, at its core, the story of humanity.

References

Adams, E. Charles. 1991. *The origin and development of the Pueblo Katsina Cult.* Tucson: University of Arizona Press.

1996. The Pueblo III–Pueblo IV transition in the Hopi area, Arizona. In *The prehistoric Pueblo world, A.D.1150–1350*, ed. Michael A. Adler, pp. 48–58. Tucson: University of Arizona Press.

2002. *Homol'ovi: an ancient Hopi settlement cluster.* Tucson: University of Arizona Press.

Adams, J. M., and H. Faure. 1997. Preliminary vegetation maps of the world since the last glacial maximum: an aid to archaeological understanding. *Journal of Archaeological Science* 24:623–47.

Adams, Karen R., and Vandy E. Bowyer. 2002. Sustainable landscape: thirteenth-century food and fuel use in the Sand Canyon locality. In *Seeking the center place: archaeology and ancient communities in the Mesa Verde region*, ed. Mark D. Varien and Richard H. Wilshusen, pp. 123–42. Salt Lake City: University of Utah Press.

Adler, Michael A. 1994. Population aggregation and the Anasazi social landscape: a view from the Four Corners. In *The ancient Southwestern community: models and methods for the study of prehistoric social organization*, ed. W. H. Wills and Robert D. Leonard, pp. 85–102. Albuquerque: University of New Mexico Press.

1996. Land tenure, archaeology, and the Ancestral Pueblo social landscape. *Journal of Anthropological Archaeology* 15:337–71.

1999. Picuris' place in the Pueblo world. In *Picuris Pueblo through time: eight centuries of change at a northern Rio Grande Pueblo*, ed. Michael A. Adler and Herbert W. Dick, pp. 189–207. Dallas, Texas: William P. Clements Center for Southwest Studies, Southern Methodist University.

Adler, Michael A., Todd L. VanPool, and Robert D. Leonard. 1996. Ancestral Pueblo population aggregation and abandonment in the North American Southwest. *Journal of World Prehistory* 10:375–438.

Adler, Michael A., and Mark D. Varien. 1994. The changing face of the community in the Mesa Verde region A.D. 1000–1300. In *Proceedings of the Anasazi Symposium 1991*, ed. Art Hutchinson and Jack E. Smith, pp. 83–98. Mesa Verde, Colorado: Mesa Verde Museum Association.

Agenbroad, Larry D. 1990. Before the Anasazi: Early Man on the Colorado Plateau. *Plateau* 61.

Akins, Nancy J. 1985. Prehistoric faunal utilization in Chaco Canyon: Basket-maker III through Pueblo III. In *Environment and subsistence of Chaco Canyon, New Mexico*, ed. Frances Joan Mathien, pp. 305–445. Chaco Canyon Studies Publications in Archeology 18E. Albuquerque: US Department of the Interior, National Park Service.

1986. *A biocultural approach to human burials from Chaco Canyon, New Mexico.* Reports of the Chaco Center 9. Santa Fe, New Mexico: US Department of the Interior, National Park Service, Branch of Cultural Research.

2001. Chaco Canyon mortuary practices: archaeological correlates of complexity. In *Ancient burial practices in the American Southwest: archaeology, physical anthropology, and Native American perspectives*, ed. Douglas R. Mitchell and Judy L. Brunson-Hadley, pp. 167–90. Albuquerque: University of New Mexico Press.

Akins, Nancy J., Pamela J. McBride, and Mollie S. Toll. 1999. Early Pit House Period household organization and subsistence in the Mogollon Highlands. In *Sixty years of Mogollon archaeology: papers from the Ninth Mogollon Conference, Silver City, New Mexico, 1996*, ed. Stephanie M. Whittlesey, pp. 153–6. Tucson, Arizona: SRI Press.

Allen, Wilma H., Charles F. Merbs, and Walter H. Birkby. 1985. Evidence for prehistoric scalping at Nuvakwewtaqa (Chavez Pass) and Grasshopper Ruin, Arizona. In *Health and disease in the prehistoric Southwest*, ed. Charles F. Merbs and Robert J. Miller, pp. 23–41. Anthropological Research Papers 34. Tempe: Arizona State University.

Ambler, J. Richard. 1998. An ethnohistoric, linguistic, and archaeological reconstruction of Hopi and Keres origins. Paper presented at the Transition from Prehistory to History in the Southwest, Albuquerque, New Mexico.

Anschuetz, Kurt F. 1995. Saving a rainy day: the integration of diverse agricultural technologies to harvest and conserve water in the lower Rio Chama Valley, New Mexico. In *Soil, water, biology, and belief in prehistoric and traditional Southwestern agriculture*, ed. H. Wolcott Toll, pp. 25–39. Special Publication 2. Albuquerque: New Mexico Archaeological Council.

Anyon, Roger, and Steven A. LeBlanc. 1984. *The Galaz Ruin: a prehistoric Mimbres village in southwestern New Mexico.* Albuquerque: Maxwell Museum of Anthropology.

Barnes, Ethne. 1994. Patterns of developmental defects in northern and central Pajarito Plateau skeletal collections. In *Proceedings of the Anasazi Symposium 1991*, ed. Art Hutchinson and Jack E. Smith, pp. 285–94. Mesa Verde, Colorado: Mesa Verde Museum Association.

Bernardini, Wesley. 1996. Transitions in social organization: a predictive model from Southwestern archaeology. *Journal of Anthropological Archaeology* 15:372–402.

1999. Reassessing the scale of social action at Pueblo Bonito, Chaco Canyon, New Mexico. *Kiva* 64:447–70.

2002. The gathering of the clans: understanding migration into the Hopi area, AD 1275–1400. Paper presented at the 67th Annual Meeting of the Society for American Archaeology, Denver, Colorado, 2002.

Berry, David Richard. 1983. Disease and climatological relationship among Pueblo III–Pueblo IV Anasazi of the Colorado Plateau. Unpublished PhD dissertation, University of California.

Betancourt, Julio L., Jeffrey S. Dean, and Herbert M. Hull. 1986. Prehistoric long-distance transport of construction beams, Chaco Canyon, New Mexico. *American Antiquity* 51:370–5.

Billman, Brian R., Patricia M. Lambert, and Banks L. Leonard. 2000. Cannibalism, warfare, and drought in the Mesa Verde region during the twelfth century A.D. *American Antiquity* 65:145–78.

Blake, Michael, Steven A. LeBlanc, and Paul E. Minnis. 1986. Changing settlement and population in the Mimbres Valley, SW New Mexico. *Journal of Field Archaeology* 13:439–64.

Blinman, Eric. 1989. Potluck in the protokiva: ceramics and ceremonialism in Pueblo I villages. In *The architecture of social integration in prehistoric Pueblos*, ed. William D. Lipe and Michelle Hegmon, pp. 113–24. Occasional Paper 1. Cortez, Colorado: Crow Canyon Archaeological Center.

Blinman, Eric, and C. Dean Wilson. 1993. Ceramic perspectives on northern Anasazi exchange. In *The American Southwest and Mesoamerica: systems of prehistoric exchange*, ed. Jonathon E. Ericson and Timothy G. Baugh, pp. 65–94. New York: Plenum Press.

Bradfield, Maitland. 1971. *The changing pattern of Hopi agriculture*. Royal Anthropological Institute Occasional Paper 30. London: Royal Anthropological Institute of Great Britain and Ireland.

Bradley, Bruce A. 1993. Planning, growth, and functional differentiation at a prehistoric Pueblo: a case study from SW Colorado. *Journal of Field Archaeology* 20:23–42.

1996. Pitchers to mugs: Chacoan revival at Sand Canyon Pueblo. *Kiva* 61:241–55.

Bradley, Ronna J. 1999. Shell exchange within the Southwest: the Casas Grandes interaction sphere. In *The Casas Grandes world*, ed. Curtis F. Schaafsma and Carroll L. Riley, pp. 213–28. Salt Lake City: University of Utah Press.

2000. Networks of shell ornament exchange: a critical assessment of prestige economies in the North American Southwest. In *The archaeology of regional interaction: religion, warfare, and exchange across the American Southwest and beyond*, ed. Michelle Hegmon, pp. 167–88. Boulder: University Press of Colorado.

Brandt, Elizabeth A. 1977. The role of secrecy in a Pueblo society. In *Flowers of the wind: papers on ritual, myth and symbolism in California and the Southwest*, ed. Thomas C. Blackburn, pp. 11–28. Socorro, New Mexico: Ballena Press.

1979. Sandia Pueblo. In *Southwest*, ed. Alfonso Ortiz, pp. 343–50. Handbook of North American Indians 9. Washington, DC: Smithsonian Institution Press.

1980. On secrecy and the control of knowledge: Taos Pueblo. In *Secrecy: a cross-cultural perspective*, ed. Stanton K. Tefft, pp. 123–46. New York: Human Sciences Press.

1994. Egalitarianism, hierarchy, and centralization in the Pueblos. In *The ancient Southwestern community*, ed. W. H. Wills and Robert D. Leonard, pp. 9–24. Albuquerque: University of New Mexico Press.

Breternitz, Cory Dale, David E. Doyel, and Michael P. Marshall. Editors. 1982. *Bis sa'ani: a Late Bonito Phase community on Escavada Wash, Northwest New Mexico*. Papers in Anthropology 14. Window Rock, Arizona: Navajo Nation Cultural Resource Management Program.

Brody, J. J. 1977. *Mimbres painted pottery*. Santa Fe: School of American Research Press.

Brown, David E. Editor. 1994. *Biotic communities: southwestern United States and northwestern Mexico*. Salt Lake City: University of Utah Press.

Brugge, David M. 1996. Navajo archaeology: a promising past. In *The archaeology of Navajo origins*, ed. Ronald H. Towner, pp. 255–72. Salt Lake City: University of Utah Press.

Buge, David. 1980. Big kivas and Tewa prehistory. *The Masterkey* 54:24–9.

Bustard, Wendy. 1996. Space as place: small and great house spatial organization in Chaco Canyon, New Mexico. PhD dissertation, University of New Mexico.

Buzon, Michele R., and Anne L. Grauer. 2002. A bioarchaeological analysis of subsistence strategies at the SU Site, New Mexico. *Kiva* 68:103–22.

Cameron, Catherine M. 1984. A regional view of chipped stone raw material use in Chaco Canyon. In *Recent research on Chaco prehistory*, ed. W. James Judge and John D. Schelberg, pp. 137–52. Reports of the Chaco Center 8. Albuquerque: National Park Service, Division of Cultural Research.

1992. An analysis of residential patterns and the Oraibi split. *Journal of Anthropological Archaeology* 11:173–86.

2001. Pink chert, projectile points, and the Chacoan regional system. *American Antiquity* 66:79–102.

Cannon, Michael D. 2000. Large mammal relative abundance in Pithouse and Pueblo period archaeofaunas from southwestern New Mexico: resource depression among the Mimbres–Mogollon? *Journal of Anthropological Archaeology* 19:317–47.

Carlson, John B. 1987. Romancing the stone, or moonshine on the sun dagger. In *Astronomy and ceremony in the prehistoric Southwest*, ed. John B. Carlson and W. James Judge, pp. 71–88. Papers of the Maxwell Museum of Anthropology 2. Albuquerque, New Mexico: Maxwell Museum of Anthropology.

Carlson, John B., and W. James Judge. Editors. 1987. *Astronomy and ceremony in the prehistoric Southwest*. Papers of the Maxwell Museum of Anthropology 2. Albuquerque, New Mexico: Maxwell Museum of Anthropology.

Chamberlin, Matthew A. 2002. Technology, performance, and intended use: glaze ware jars in the Pueblo IV Rio Grande. *Kiva* 67:269–96.

Chenault, Mark L., and Thomas N. Motsinger. 2000. Colonization, warfare, and regional competition: recent research into the Basketmaker III period in the Mesa Verde region. In *Foundations of Anasazi culture: the Basketmaker–Pueblo transition*, ed. Paul F. Reed, pp. 45–68. Salt Lake City: University of Utah Press.

Chrisman, Donald, Richard S. MacNeish, Jamshed Mavalwala, and Howard Savage. 1996. Late Pleistocene human friction skin prints from Pendejo Cave, New Mexico. *American Antiquity* 61:357–76.

Cook, E. R. 2000. Southwestern USA drought index reconstruction. In *Data Contribution Series No. 2000–0953*. Boulder, Colorado: International Tree-Ring Data Bank, NOAA/NGDC Paleoclimatology Program.

Cordell, Linda S. 1995. Tracing migration pathways from the receiving end. *Journal of Anthropological Archaeology* 14:203–11.

——— 1997. *Archaeology of the Southwest*. San Diego, California: Academic Press.

Cordell, Linda S., David E. Doyel, and Keith W. Kintigh. 1994. Processes of aggregation in the prehistoric Southwest. In *Themes in Southwest prehistory*, ed. George J. Gumerman, pp. 109–34. Santa Fe, New Mexico: School of American Research.

Cordell, Linda S., and George J. Gumerman. 1989. Cultural interaction in the prehistoric Southwest. In *Dynamics of Southwest prehistory*, ed. Linda S. Cordell and George J. Gumerman, pp. 1–18. Washington, DC: Smithsonian Institution Press.

Corruccini, Robert S. 1972. The biological relationships of some prehistoric and historic Pueblo populations. *American Journal of Physical Anthropology* 37:373–88.

Courlander, Harold. 1971. *The fourth world of the Hopis*. Albuquerque: University of New Mexico Press.

Crary, Joseph S., Stephen Germick, and David E. Doyel. 2001. Exploring the Gila Horizon. *Kiva* 66:407–45.

Creamer, Winifred. 2000. Regional interactions and regional systems in the protohistoric Rio Grande. In *The archaeology of regional interaction: religion, warfare, and exchange across the American Southwest*, ed. Michelle Hegmon, pp. 99–118. Boulder: University Press of Colorado.

Creel, Darrell G. 1989. A primary cremation at the NAN Ranch Ruin, with comparative data on other cremations in the Mimbres area, New Mexico. *Journal of Field Archaeology* 16:309–29.

——— 1999. The Black Mountain Phase in the Mimbres area. In *The Casas Grandes world*, ed. Curtis F. Schaafsma and Carroll L. Riley, pp. 107–20. Salt Lake City: University of Utah Press.

Creel, Darrell G., and Roger Anyon. 2003. New interpretations of Mimbres public architecture and space: implications for cultural change. *American Antiquity* 68:67–92.

Creel, Darrell G., and Charmion McKusick. 1994. Prehistoric macaws and parrots in the Mimbres area, New Mexico. *American Antiquity* 59:510–24.

Creel, Darrell G., Matthew Williams, Hector Neff, and Michael D. Glascock. 2002. Black Mountain Phase ceramics and implications for manufacture and exchange patterns. In *Ceramic production and circulation in the Greater Southwest: source determination by INAA and complementary mineralogical investigations*, ed. Donna M. Glowacki and Hector Neff, pp. 37–46. Los Angeles: The Cotsen Institute of Archaeology, University of California.

Crown, Patricia L. 1994. *Ceramics and ideology: Salado Polychrome pottery*. Albuquerque: University of New Mexico Press.

1995. The production of the Salado Polychromes in the American Southwest. In *Ceramic production in the American Southwest*, ed. Barbara J. Mills and Patricia L. Crown, pp. 142–66. Tucson: University of Arizona Press.

2000a. Gendered tasks, power, and prestige in the prehispanic American Southwest. In *Women and men in the prehispanic Southwest: labor, power, and prestige*, ed. Patricia L. Crown, pp. 3–42. Santa Fe, New Mexico: School of American Research Press.

2000b. Editor. *Women and men in the prehispanic Southwest: labor, power, and prestige*. Santa Fe, New Mexico: School of American Research Press.

Crown, Patricia L., and Timothy A. Kohler. 1994. Community dynamics, site structure, and aggregation in the northern Rio Grande. In *The ancient Southwestern community*, ed. W. H. Wills and Robert D. Leonard, pp. 103–18. Albuquerque: University of New Mexico Press.

Crown, Patricia L., Janet D. Orcutt, and Timothy A. Kohler. 1996. Pueblo cultures in transition: the northern Rio Grande. In *The prehistoric Pueblo world, A.D. 1150–1350*, ed. Michael A. Adler, pp. 188–204. Tucson: University of Arizona Press.

Crown, Patricia L., and W. H. Wills. 1995. Economic intensification and the origins of ceramic containers in the American Southwest. In *The emergence of pottery: technology and innovation in ancient societies*, ed. William K. Barnett and John W. Hoopes, pp. 241–54. Washington, DC: Smithsonian Institution Press.

Cruz Antillón, Rafael, and Timothy D. Maxwell. 1999. The Villa Ahumada Site: archaeological investigations east of Paquimé. In *The Casas Grandes world*, ed. Curtis F. Schaafsma and Carroll L. Riley, pp. 43–53. Salt Lake City: University of Utah Press.

Cummings, Linda Scott. 1994. Anasazi diet: variety and nutritional analysis. In *Proceedings of the Anasazi Symposium 1991*, ed. Art Hutchinson and Jack E. Smith, pp. 303–18. Mesa Verde, Colorado: Mesa Verde Museum Association.

Cushing, Frank Hamilton. 1890. Preliminary notes on the origin, working hypothesis, and primary researches on the Hemenway Southwestern Archaeological Expedition. In *Comptes-Rendus de la Septième Session, Congrès International des Américanistes, Berline, 1888*, pp. 152–94. Paris.

1896. *Outlines of Zuñi creation myths*. Annual Report of the Bureau of Ethnology 13. Washington, DC: Government Publishing Office.

1979. *Zuñi: selected writings of Frank Hamilton Cushing*. Lincoln: University of Nebraska Press.

Damp, Jonathan E., and Edward M. Kotyk. 2000. Socioeconomic organization of a late Basketmaker III community in the Mexican Springs area, southern Chuska Mountains, New Mexico. In *Foundations of Anasazi culture: the Basketmaker–Pueblo transition*, ed. Paul F. Reed, pp. 95–114. Salt Lake City: University of Utah Press.

Darling, J. Andrew. 1998. Mass inhumation and the execution of witches in the American Southwest. *American Anthropologist* 100:732–52.

Dean, Jeffrey S. 1970. Aspects of Tsegi Phase social organization: a trial reconstruction. In *Reconstructing prehistoric Pueblo societies*, ed. William A. Longacre, pp. 140–74. Albuquerque: University of New Mexico Press.

1992. Environmental factors in the evolution of the Chacoan sociopolitical system. In *Anasazi regional organization and the Chaco system*, ed. David E. Doyel, pp. 35–43. Anthropological Papers 5. Albuquerque, New Mexico: Maxwell Museum of Anthropology.

1996a. Demography, environment, and subsistence stress. In *Evolving complexity and environmental risk in the prehistoric Southwest*, ed. Joseph A. Tainter and Bonnie Bagley Tainter, pp. 25–56. Santa Fe Institute Studies in the Sciences of Complexity Proceedings 24. Reading: Addison Wesley Publishing Company.

1996b. Kayenta Anasazi settlement transformations in northeastern Arizona: A.D. 1150 to 1350. In *The prehistoric Pueblo world A.D.1150–1350*, ed. Michael A. Adler, pp. 29–47. Tucson: University of Arizona Press.

Dean, Jeffrey S., William H. Doelle, and Janet Orcutt. 1994. Adaptive stress, environment, and demography. In *Themes in Southwest prehistory*, ed. George J. Gumerman, pp. 53–86. Santa Fe, New Mexico: School of American Research Press.

Dean, Jeffrey S., and John C. Ravesloot. 1993. The chronology of cultural interaction in the Gran Chichimeca. In *Culture and contact: Charles C. DiPeso's Gran Chichimeca*, ed. Anne I. Woosley and John C. Ravesloot, pp. 83–103. Amerind Foundation New World Studies Series 2. Albuquerque: University of New Mexico Press.

Di Peso, Charles C. Editor. 1974. *Casas Grandes: a fallen trading center of the Gran Chichimeca*. Flagstaff, Arizona: Amerind Foundation, Dragoon, and Northland Press.

Dick, Herbert W., Daniel Wolfman, Curtis F. Schaafsma, and Michael A. Adler. 1999. Prehistoric and early historic architecture and ceramics at Picuris. In *Picuris Pueblo through time: eight centuries of change at a northern Rio Grande Pueblo*, ed. Michael A. Adler and Herbert W. Dick, pp. 43–100. Dallas, Texas: William P. Clement Center for Southwest Studies, Southern Methodist University.

Diehl, Michael W. 1996. The intensity of maize processing and production in upland Mogollon pithouse villages, A.D. 200–1000. *American Antiquity* 61:102–15.

1998. The interpretation of archaeological floor assemblages: a case study from the American Southwest. *American Antiquity* 63:617–34.

Diehl, Michael W., and Steven A. LeBlanc. 2001. *Early pithouse villages of the Mimbres Valley and beyond: the McAnally and Thompson sites in their cultural and ecological contexts*. Peabody Museum of Archaeology and Ethnology 83. Cambridge, Massachusetts: Harvard University Press.

Dittert, Alfred E. Jr., and Judy L. Brunson-Hadley. 1999. Identifying Acoma's past: a multidisciplinary approach. In *La Frontera: papers in honor of Patrick H. Beckett*, ed. Meliha S. Duran and David T. Kirkpatrick, vol. 25, pp. 59–69. Albuquerque: The Archaeological Society of New Mexico.

Dixon, E. James. 1999. *Bones, boats, and bison: archeology and the first colonization of western North America*. Albuquerque: University of New Mexico Press.

Dohm, Karen M. 1994. The search for Anasazi village origins: Basketmaker II dwelling aggregation on Cedar Mesa, southeast Utah. *Kiva* 60:257–76.

Dominguez, Steve, Karl J. Reinhard, and Kari Sandness. 1994. Termination of a life at the edge: the Dan Canyon burial. In *Proceedings of the Anasazi Symposium 1991*, ed. Art Hutchinson and Jack E. Smith, pp. 275–84. Mesa Verde, Colorado: Mesa Verde Museum Association.

Dongoske, Kurt E., Michael Yeatts, Roger Anyon, and T. J. Ferguson. 1997. Archaeological cultures and cultural affiliation: Hopi and Zuni perspectives in the American Southwest. *American Antiquity* 62:600–8.

Douglas, John E. 1995. Autonomy and regional systems in the late prehistoric southern Southwest. *American Antiquity* 60:240–57.

2000. Exchanges, assumptions, and mortuary goods in pre-Paquimé Chihuahua, Mexico. In *The archaeology of regional interaction: religion, warfare, and exchange across the American Southwest and beyond*, ed. Michelle Hegmon, pp. 189–208. Boulder: University Press of Colorado.

Doxtater, Dennis. 1991. Reflections of the Anasazi cosmos. In *Social space: human spatial behavior in dwellings and settlements*, ed. O. Gron, E. Engelstad, and I. Lindblom, pp. 155–84. Odense: Odense University Press.

2002. A hypothetical layout of Chaco Canyon structures via large-scale alignments between significant natural features. *Kiva* 68:23–47.

Dozier, Edward P. 1970. *The Pueblo Indians of North America*. New York: Holt, Rinehart and Winston.

Driver, Jonathan C. 2002. Faunal variation and change in the northern San Juan region. In *Seeking the center place: archaeology and ancient communities in the Mesa Verde region*, ed. Mark D. Varien and Richard H. Wilshusen, pp. 143–60. Salt Lake City: University of Utah Press.

Duff, Andrew I. 2000. Scale, interaction, and regional analysis in late Pueblo prehistory. In *The archaeology of regional interaction: religion, warfare, and exchange across the American Southwest*, ed. Michelle Hegmon, pp. 71–98. Boulder: University Press of Colorado.

Duff, Andrew I., and Richard H. Wilshusen. 2000. Prehistoric population dynamics in the northern San Juan region, A.D. 950–1300. *Kiva* 66:167–90.

Durand, Kathy Roler. 2003. Function of Chaco-era great houses. *Kiva* 69(2):141–70.

Durand, Stephen R. 1992. Architectural change and Chaco prehistory. Unpublished PhD dissertation, University of Washington.

Durand, Stephen R., and Kathy Roler Durand. 2000. Notes from the edge: settlement pattern changes at the Guadalupe community. In *Great house communities across the Chacoan landscape*, ed. John Kantner and Nancy M. Mahoney, pp. 101–10. Anthropological Papers 64. Tucson: University of Arizona Press.

Durand, Stephen R., Phillip H. Shelley, Ronald C. Antweiler, and Howard E. Taylor. 1999. Trees, chemistry, and prehistory in the American Southwest. *Journal of Archaeological Science* 26:185–203.

Eddy, Frank W. 1975. A settlement model for reconstructing prehistoric social organization at Chimney Rock Mesa, southern Colorado. In *Collected papers in honor of Florence Hawley Ellis*, ed. Theodore R. Frisbie, pp. 60–79. Papers of the Archaeological Society of New Mexico 2. Norman, Oklahoma: Hooper Publishing Company.

Eddy, Frank W., Dale R. Lightfoot, Eden A. Welker, Layne L. Wright, and Dolores C. Torres. 1996. Air photographic mapping of San Marcos Pueblo. *Journal of Field Archaeology* 23:1–13.

El-Najjar, Mahmoud Y. 1978. Southwestern physical anthropology: do the cultural and biological parameters correspond? *American Journal of Physical Anthropology* 48:151–8.

Elias, Scott A. 1997. *The Ice-Age history of Southwestern national parks.* Washington, DC: Smithsonian Institution Press.

Ellis, Florence Hawley. 1974. Archaeologic and ethnologic data: Acoma-Laguna land claims. In *American Indian ethnohistory, Indians of the Southwest: Pueblo Indians,* vol. 2, pp. 9–99. New York: Garland Publishers.

1979. Laguna Pueblo. In *Southwest,* ed. Alfonso Ortiz, pp. 438–49. Handbook of North American Indians 9. Washington, DC: Smithsonian Institution Press.

English, Nathan B., Julio L. Betancourt, Jeffrey S. Dean, and Jay Quade. 2001. Strontium isotopes reveal distant sources of architectural timber in Chaco Canyon, New Mexico. *Proceedings of the National Association of Science* 98:11891–6.

Ennes, Mark J. 1999. Evidence for migration in the eastern Mimbres region, southwestern New Mexico. In *Sixty years of Mogollon archaeology: papers from the Ninth Mogollon Conference, Silver City, New Mexico, 1996,* ed. Stephanie M. Whittlesey, pp. 127–34. Tucson, Arizona: SRI Press.

Euler, Robert C. 1999. The Grand Canyon Anasazi, their descendents, and other claimants. In *La Frontera: papers in honor of Patrick H. Beckett,* ed. Meliha S. Duran and David T. Kirkpatrick, vol. 25, pp. 71–8. Albuquerque: Archaeological Society of New Mexico.

Ezzo, Joseph A. 1993. *Human adaptation at Grasshopper Pueblo, Arizona: social and ecological perspectives.* Archaeological Series 4. Ann Arbor, Michigan: International Monographs in Prehistory.

Ezzo, Joseph A., and T. Douglas Price. 2002. Migration, regional reorganization, and spatial group composition at Grasshopper Pueblo, Arizona. *Journal of Archaeological Science* 29:499–520.

Feidel, Stuart J. 1999. Older than we thought: implications of corrected dates for Paleoindians. *American Antiquity* 64:95–116.

2000. The peopling of the New World: present evidence, new theories, and future directions. *Journal of Archaeological Research* 8:39–103.

Feinman, Gary M., Kent G. Lightfoot, and Steadman Upham. 2000. Political hierarchies and organizational strategies in the Puebloan Southwest. *American Antiquity* 65:449–70.

Ferguson, Cheryl. 1980. Analysis of skeletal remains. In *Tijeras Canyon: analyses of the past,* ed. Linda S. Cordell, pp. 121–48. Albuquerque: Maxwell Museum of Anthropology and University of New Mexico Press.

Ferguson, T. J., Kurt E. Dongoske, and Leigh J. Kuwanwisiwma. 2001. Hopi perspectives on Southwestern mortuary studies. In *Ancient burial practices in the American Southwest: archaeology, physical anthropology, and Native American perspectives,* ed. Douglas R. Mitchell and Judy L. Brunson-Hadley, pp. 9–26. Albuquerque: University of New Mexico Press.

Ferguson, T. J., and E. Richard Hart. 1985. *A Zuni atlas*. Norman: University of Oklahoma Press.

Fewkes, Jesse W. 1893. A-wa'-tobi: an archaeological verification of a Tusayan legend. *American Anthropologist* 6:363–75.

1896. The prehistoric culture of Tusayan. *American Anthropologist* 9:151–74.

Fish, Paul R., and Suzanne K. Fish. 1999. Reflections on the Casas Grandes regional system from the northwestern periphery. In *The Casas Grandes world*, ed. Curtis F. Schaafsma and Carroll L. Riley, pp. 27–42. Salt Lake City: University of Utah Press.

Fish, Paul R., Suzanne K. Fish, George J. Gumerman, and J. Jefferson Reid. 1994. Toward an explanation for Southwestern "abandonments". In *Themes in Southwest prehistory*, ed. George J. Gumerman, pp. 135–64. Santa Fe, New Mexico: School of American Research.

Force, Eric R., R. Gwinn Vivian, Thomas C. Windes, and Jeffrey S. Dean. 2002. *Relation of "Bonito" paleo-channels and base-level variations to Anasazi occupation, Chaco Canyon, New Mexico*. Archaeological Series 194. Tucson: Arizona State Museum, University of Arizona.

Fowler, Andrew P., and John R. Stein. 1992. The Anasazi great house in space, time, and paradigm. In *Anasazi regional organization and the Chaco system*, ed. David E. Doyel, pp. 101–22. Anthropological Papers 5. Albuquerque, New Mexico: Maxwell Museum of Anthropology.

Fowler, Andrew P., John R. Stein, and Roger Anyon. 1987. *An archaeological reconnaissance of west-central New Mexico: the Anasazi Monuments Project*. Santa Fe: State of New Mexico Office of Cultural Affairs, Historic Preservation Division.

Fritz, John M. 1987. Chaco Canyon and Vijayanagara: proposing spatial meaning in two societies. In *Mirror and metaphor: material and social constructions of reality*, ed. Daniel W. Ingersoll Jr. and Gordon Bronitsky, pp. 313–49. Lanham, Maryland: University Press of America.

Geib, Phil R. 2000. Sandal types and Archaic prehistory on the Colorado Plateau. *American Antiquity* 65:509–24.

Geib, Phil R., Kimberly Spurr, and Jim H. Collette. 2003. *Prehistory of the northern Kayenta Anasazi region: archaeological excavations along the Navajo Mountain Road (N16)*: vol. 3, *Basketmaker site descriptions*. Navajo Nation Archaeology Department Report 02–48. Gallup, New Mexico: Navajo Nation Historic Preservation Department, Branch of Roads.

Gilman, Patricia A. 1987. Architecture as artifact: pit structures and pueblos in the American Southwest. *American Antiquity* 52:538–64.

1989. Households, communities, and painted pottery in the Mimbres region of southwestern New Mexico. In *Households and communities: proceedings of the 21st Annual Chacmool Conference*, ed. Scott MacEachern, David J. W. Archer, and Richard D. Garvin, pp. 218–26. Calgary: Archaeological Association, University of Calgary.

1990. Social organization and Classic Mimbres Period burials in the SW United States. *Journal of Field Archaeology* 17:457–69.

1995. Multiple dimensions of the Archaic-to-Pit Structure Period transition in southeastern Arizona. *Kiva* 60:619–32.

Gilman, Patricia A., Veletta Canouts, and Ronald L. Bishop. 1994. The production and distribution of Classic Mimbres Black-on-White pottery. *American Antiquity* 59:695–709.

Gilpin, Dennis. 1994. Lukachukai and Salina Springs: Late Archaic/Early Basketmaker habitation sites in the Chinle Valley, northeastern Arizona. *Kiva* 60:203–18.

———. 1995. Anasazi community architecture on the lower Puerco River. Paper presented at the 60th Annual Meeting of the Society for American Archaeology, 1995.

Gladwin, Harold S. 1957. *A history of the Ancient Southwest.* Portland, Oregon: Bond Wheelwright.

Glowacki, Donna M., Hector Neff, and Michael D. Glascock. 1998. An initial assessment of the production and movement of thirteenth century ceramic vessels in the Mesa Verde region. *Kiva* 63:217–40.

Glowacki, Donna M., Hector Neff, Michelle M. Hegmon, James W. Kendrick, and W. James Judge. 2002. Resource use, red-ware production, and vessel distribution in the northern San Juan Region. In *Ceramic production and circulation in the Greater Southwest*, ed. Donna M. Glowacki and Hector Neff, pp. 67–73. Monograph 44. Los Angeles: The Cotsen Institute of Archaeology, University of California-Los Angeles.

Graves, William M., and Katherine A. Spielmann. 2000. Leadership, long-distance exchange, and feasting in the protohistoric Rio Grande. In *Alternative leadership strategies in the prehispanic Southwest*, ed. Barbara J. Mills, pp. 45–59. Tucson: University of Arizona Press.

Greiser, Sally T., and T. Weber Greiser. 1995. Prehistoric irrigation in the Taos Valley. In *Soil, water, biology, and belief in prehistoric and traditional Southwestern agriculture*, ed. H. Wolcott Toll, pp. 221–37. Special Publication 2. Albuquerque: New Mexico Archaeological Council.

Greiser, Sally T., and James A. Moore. 1995. The case for prehistoric irrigation in the northern Southwest. In *Soil, water, biology, and belief in prehistoric and traditional Southwestern agriculture*, ed. H. Wolcott Toll, pp. 189–95. Special Publication 2. Albuquerque: New Mexico Archaeological Council.

Grissino-Mayer, Henri D. 1996. A 2129-year reconstruction of precipitation for northwestern New Mexico, USA. In *Tree rings, environment, and humanity: radiocarbon 1996*, ed. J. S. Dean, D. M. Meko, and T. W. Swetnam, pp. 191–204. Tucson: Department of Geosciences, University of Arizona.

Grissino-Mayer, Henri D., Thomas W. Swetnam, and Rex K. Adams. 1997. The rare, old-aged conifers of El Malpais–their role in understanding climatic change in the American Southwest. *New Mexico Bureau of Mines and Mineral Resources Bulletin* 156:155–61.

Gumerman, George J. Editor. 1988. *The Anasazi in a changing environment.* Cambridge: Cambridge University Press.

Gumerman, George J., and Murray Gell-Mann. 1994. Cultural evolution in the prehistoric Southwest. In *Themes in Southwest prehistory*, ed. George J. Gumerman, pp. 11–32. Santa Fe, New Mexico: School of American Archaeology Press.

Haas, Jonathan, and Winifred Creamer. 1993. *Stress and warfare among the Kayenta Anasazi of the thirteenth century A.D.* Fieldiana: Anthropology N.S. 21. Chicago: Field Museum of Natural History.

———. 1996. The role of warfare in the Pueblo III period. In *The prehistoric Pueblo world, A.D.1150–1350*, ed. Michael A. Adler, pp. 205–13. Tucson: University of Arizona Press.

Haas, Jonathan, Edmund J. Ladd, Jerrold E. Levy, Randall H. McGuire, and Norman Yoffee. 1994. Historical processes in the prehistoric Southwest. In *Understanding complexity in the prehistoric Southwest*, ed. George Gumerman and Murray Gell-Mann, pp. 203–32. Santa Fe Institute Studies in the Sciences of Complexity Proceedings 26. Reading, Massachusetts: Addison Wesley Publishing.

Habicht-Mauche, Judith A. 1993. *The pottery from Arroyo Hondo Pueblo, New Mexico.* Arroyo Hondo Archaeological Series 8. Santa Fe, New Mexico: School of American Research Press.

———. 1995. Changing patterns of pottery manufacture and trade in the northern Rio Grande region. In *Ceramic production in the American Southwest*, ed. Barbara J. Mills and Patricia L. Crown, pp. 167–99. Tucson: University of Arizona Press.

Habicht-Mauche, Judith A., Stephen T. Glenn, Homer Milford, and A. Russell Flegal. 2000. Isotopic tracing of prehistoric Rio Grande glaze-paint production and trade. *Journal of Archaeological Science* 27:709–13.

Hack, John T. 1942. *The changing physical environment of the Hopi Indians of Arizona.* Papers of the Museum 35(1). Cambridge, Massachusetts: Peabody Museum of American Archaeology and Ethnology.

Hale, Kenneth, and David Harris. 1979. Historical linguistics and archeology. In *Southwest*, ed. Alfonso Ortiz, pp. 170–7. Handbook of North American Indians 9. Washington, DC: Smithsonian Institution Press.

Hartmann, William K., and Richard Flint. 2001. Migrations in late Anasazi prehistory: "eyewitness" testimony. *Kiva* 66:375–85.

Haury, Emil W. 1958. Evidence at Point of Pines for a prehistoric migration from northern Arizona. In *Migrations in New World culture history*, ed. Raymond H. Thompson, pp. 1–8. University of Arizona Bulletin 29(2). Tucson: University of Arizona Press.

———. 1985. Tla Kii ruin, Forestdale's oldest pueblo. In *Mogollon culture in the Forestdale Valley, East-Central Arizona*, ed. Emil W. Haury, pp. 1–133. Tucson: University of Arizona Press.

Hawley, Florence. 1950. Big kivas, little kivas, and moiety: houses in historical reconstruction. *Southwestern Journal of Anthropology* 6:286–302.

Hayes, Alden C. 1964. *The archeological survey of Wetherill Mesa, Mesa Verde National Park-Colorado.* Archeological Research Series 7A. Washington, DC: National Park Service, US Department of the Interior.

Haynes, C. Vance Jr. 1980. The Clovis culture. *Canadian Journal of Anthropology* 1:115–22.

———. 1991. Geoarchaeological and paleohydrological evidence for a Clovis-age drought in North America and its bearing on extinction. *Quaternary Research* 35:438–50.

Hays-Gilpin, Kelley A. 2000. Gender ideology and ritual activities. In *Women and men in the prehispanic Southwest: labor, power, and prestige*, ed. Patricia L. Crown, pp. 91–136. Santa Fe, New Mexico: School of American Research Press.

Hays-Gilpin, Kelley A., and Jane H. Hill. 1999. The flower world in material culture: an iconographic complex in the Southwest and Mesoamerica. *Journal of Anthropological Research* 55:1–37.

Hegmon, Michelle M. 1996. Variability in food production, strategies of storage and sharing, and the pithouse-to-pueblo transition in the northern Southwest. In *Evolving complexity and environmental risk in the prehistoric Southwest*, ed. Joseph A. Tainter and Bonnie Bagley Tainter, vol. 34, pp. 223–50. Reading: Addison Wesley Publishing Company.

——— 2002. Recent issues in the archaeology of the Mimbres region of the North American Southwest. *Journal of Archaeological Research* 10:307–57.

Hegmon, Michelle M., James R. Allison, Hector Neff, and Michael D. Glascock. 1997. Production of San Juan Red Ware in the northern Southwest: insights into regional interaction in early Puebloan prehistory. *American Antiquity* 62:449–63.

Hegmon, Michelle M., Margaret C. Nelson, Roger Anyon, Darrell G. Creel, Steven A. LeBlanc, and Harry J. Shafer. 1999. Scale and time–space systematics in the post-A.D. 1100 Mimbres region of the North American Southwest. *Kiva* 65:143–66.

Hegmon, Michelle M., Margaret C. Nelson, and Mark J. Ennes. 2000. Corrugated pottery, technological style, and population movement in the Mimbres region of the American Southwest. *Journal of Anthropological Research* 56:217–40.

Hegmon, Michelle M., Margaret C. Nelson, and Susan M. Ruth. 1998. Abandonment and reorganization in the Mimbres region of the American Southwest. *American Anthropologist* 100:148–62.

Hegmon, Michelle M., Scott G. Ortman, and Jeannette L. Mobley-Tanaka. 2000. Women, men, and the organization of space. In *Women and men in the prehispanic Southwest: labor, power, and prestige*, ed. Patricia L. Crown, pp. 43–90. Santa Fe, New Mexico: School of American Research Press.

Hegmon, Michelle M., and Wenda R. Trevathan. 1996. Gender, anatomical knowledge, and pottery production: implications of an anatomically unusual birth depicted on Mimbres pottery from southwestern New Mexico. *American Antiquity* 61:747–54.

Heidke, James M. 1999. Cienega phase incipient plain ware from southeastern Arizona. *Kiva* 64:311–38.

Hensler, Kathy Niles. 1999. Anasazi ceramic traditions: a view from the Cove. In *Anasazi community development in Cove and Redrock Valley: archaeological excavations along the N33 Road in Apache County, Arizona*, ed. Paul F. Reed and Kathy Niles Hensler, pp. 551–686. Navajo Nation Papers in Anthropology 33. Window Rock, Arizona: Navajo Nation Archaeology Department.

Herr, Sarah A. 2001. *Beyond Chaco: great kiva communities on the Mogollon Rim frontier*. Anthropological Papers 66. Tucson: University of Arizona Press.

Hill, W. W. 1982. *An ethnography of Santa Clara Pueblo, New Mexico*. Albuquerque: University of New Mexico Press.

Hogan, Patrick. 1994. Foragers to farmers II: a second look at the adoption of agriculture in northwestern New Mexico. In *Archaic hunter-gatherer archaeology in the American Southwest*, ed. Bradley J. Vierra, pp. 155–84. Contributions in Anthropology 13(1). Portales: Eastern New Mexico University.

Howell, Todd L. 1995. Tracking Zuni gender and leadership roles across the contact period. *Journal of Anthropological Research* 51:125–47.

1996. Identifying leaders at Hawikku. *Kiva* 62:61–82.

2001. Foundations of political power in ancestral Zuni society. In *Ancient burial practices in the American Southwest*, ed. Douglas R. Mitchell and Judy L. Brunson-Hadley, pp. 149–66. Albuquerque: University of New Mexico Press.

Howell, Todd L., and Keith W. Kintigh. 1996. Archaeological identification of kin groups using mortuary and biological data: an example from the American Southwest. *American Antiquity* 61:537–54.

Huckell, Bruce B. 1995. *Of marshes and maize: preceramic agricultural settlements in the Cienega Valley, Southeastern Arizona*. Anthropological Papers 59. Tucson: University of Arizona Press.

1996. The Archaic prehistory of the North American Southwest. *Journal of World Prehistory* 10:305–73.

Huckleberry, Gary A., and Brian R. Billman. 1998. Floodwater farming, discontinuous ephemeral streams, and Puebloan abandonment in southwestern Colorado. *American Antiquity* 63:595–616.

Hunter, Andrea A. 1997. Seeds, cucurbits, and corn from Lizard Man Village. *Kiva* 62:221–44.

Hunter-Anderson, Rosalind L. 1986. *Prehistoric adaptation in the American Southwest*. Cambridge: Cambridge University Press.

Hurst, Winston B. 2000. Chaco outlier or "wannabe"? Comments and observations on a provincial, Chacoesque great house at Edge of the Cedars Ruin, Utah. In *Great house communities across the Chacoan landscape*, ed. John Kantner and Nancy M. Mahoney, pp. 63–78. Anthropological Papers 64. Tucson: University of Arizona Press.

Irwin-Williams, Cynthia. 1967. Picosa: the elementary Southwestern culture. *American Antiquity* 32:441–57.

1973. *The Oshara tradition: origins of Anasazi culture*. Contributions in Anthropology 5(1). Portales: Eastern New Mexico University.

Irwin-Williams, Cynthia, and Phillip H. Shelley. 1980. *Investigations at the Salmon Site: the structure of Chacoan society in the northern Southwest*. Portales: Eastern New Mexico University Printing Services.

Judd, Neil M. 1954. *The material culture of Pueblo Bonito*. Smithsonian Miscellaneous Collections 124. Washington, DC: Smithsonian Institution.

Judge, W. James. 1973. *Paleoindian occupation of the central Rio Grande valley in New Mexico*. Albuquerque: University of New Mexico Press.

1979. The development of a complex cultural ecosystem in the Chaco Basin, New Mexico. In *Proceedings of the First Conference on Scientific Research in the National Parks*, vol. 2, ed. R. M. Linn, pp. 901–6. Transactions and

Proceedings Series 5. Washington, DC: US Department of the Interior, National Park Service.

1989. Chaco Canyon–San Juan Basin. In *Dynamics of Southwest prehistory*, ed. Linda S. Cordell and George J. Gumerman, pp. 209–62. Washington, DC: Smithsonian Institution Press.

1991. Chaco: current views of prehistory and the regional system. In *Chaco and Hohokam: prehistoric regional systems in the American Southwest*, ed. Patricia L. Crown and W. James Judge, pp. 11–30. Santa Fe, New Mexico: School of American Research Press.

1993. Resource distribution and the Chaco phenomenon. In *The Chimney Rock Archaeological Symposium*, ed. J. McKim Malville and Gary Matlock, pp. 35–6. General Technical Report RM-227. Fort Collins, Colorado: US Department of Agriculture, Forest Service, Rocky Mountain Forest and Range Experiment Station.

Kane, Allen E. 1993. Settlement analogues for Chimney Rock: models of 11th and 12th century northern Anasazi society. In *The Chimney Rock Archaeological Symposium*, ed. J. McKim Malville and Gary Matlock, pp. 43–60. General Technical Report RM-227. Fort Collins, Colorado: US Department of Agriculture, Forest Service, Rocky Mountain Forest and Range Experiment Station.

Kantner, John. 1996. Political competition among the Chaco Anasazi of the American Southwest. *Journal of Anthropological Archaeology* 15:41–105.

1997. Ancient roads, modern mapping: evaluating prehistoric Chaco Anasazi roadways using GIS technology. *Expedition Magazine* 39:49–62.

1999a. The influence of self-interested behavior on sociopolitical change: the evolution of the Chaco Anasazi in the prehistoric American Southwest. PhD dissertation, University of California at Santa Barbara.

1999b. Survival cannibalism or sociopolitical intimidation? Explaining perimortem mutilation in the American Southwest. *Human Nature* 10: 1–50.

2003a. Biological evolutionary theory and individual decision-making. In *Essential tensions in archaeological theory*, ed. Todd L. VanPool and Christine S. VanPool, pp. 67–87. Salt Lake City: University of Utah Press.

2003b. The Chaco World Database. http://sipapu.gsu.edu/chacoworld.html. 02/22/03.

2003c. Rethinking Chaco as a system. *Kiva* 69:207–28.

Kantner, John, Nate Bower, Jeffrey Ladwig, Jacob Perlitz, Steve Hata, and Darren Greve. 2000. Interaction between great house communities: an elemental analysis of Cibolan ceramics. In *Great house communities across the Chacoan landscape*, ed. John Kantner and Nancy M. Mahoney, pp. 130–46. Anthropological Papers 64. Tucson: University of Arizona Press.

Kantner, John, and Ronald Hobgood. 2003. Digital technologies and prehistoric landscapes in the American Southwest. In *The reconstruction of archaeological landscapes through digital technologies*, ed. Maurizio Forte, P. Ryan Williams, and James Wiseman, pp. 117–23. Oxford: Archaeopress.

Kantner, John, and Nancy M. Mahoney. Editors. 2000. *Great house communities across the Chacoan landscape*. Anthropological Papers 64. Tucson: University of Arizona Press.

Kearns, Timothy M., Janet L. McVickar, and Lori Stephens Reed. 2000. The early to late Basketmaker III transition in Tohatchi Flats, New Mexico. In *Foundations of Anasazi culture: the Basketmaker–Pueblo transition*, ed. Paul F. Reed, pp. 115–44. Salt Lake City: University of Utah Press.

Kelley, J. Charles. 1993. Zenith passage: the view from Chalchihuites. In *Culture and contact: Charles C. Di Peso's Gran Chichimeca*, ed. Anne I. Woosley and John C. Ravesloot, pp. 83–104. Dragoon, Arizona, and Albuquerque: Amerind Foundation and University of New Mexico Press.

Kenzle, Susan C. 1997. Enclosing walls in the northern San Juan: sociophysical boundaries and defensive fortifications in the American Southwest. *Journal of Field Archaeology* 24:195–210.

Kidder, Alfred V. 1958. *Pecos, New Mexico: archaeological notes*. Papers of the Robert S. Peabody Foundation for Archaeology 5. Andover, Massachusetts: Phillips Academy Foundation.

Kintigh, Keith W. 1985. *Settlement, subsistence, and society in late Zuni prehistory*. Anthropological Papers 44. University of Arizona Press, Tucson.

1994. Chaco, communal architecture, and Cibolan aggregation. In *The ancient Southwestern community*, ed. W. H. Wills and Robert D. Leonard, pp. 131–40. Albuquerque: University of New Mexico Press.

1996. The Cibola region in the Post-Chacoan era. In *The prehistoric Pueblo world, A.D. 1150–1350*, ed. Michael A. Adler, pp. 131–44. Tucson: University of Arizona Press.

2000. Leadership strategies in protohistoric Zuni towns. In *Alternative leadership strategies in the prehispanic Southwest*, ed. Barbara J. Mills, pp. 95–116. Tucson: University of Arizona Press.

Kintigh, Keith W., and Todd L. Howell. 1996. Archaeological identification of kin groups using mortuary and biological data: an example from the American Southwest. *American Antiquity* 61:537–54.

Kintigh, Keith W., Todd L. Howell, and Andrew I. Duff. 1996. Post-Chacoan social integration at the Hinkson Site, New Mexico. *Kiva* 61:257–74.

Kluckhohn, Clyde, and Paul Reiter. 1939. *Preliminary report on the 1937 Excavations, Bc 50–51, Chaco Canyon, New Mexico*. Anthropological Series 3(2). Albuquerque: University of New Mexico Press.

Kohler, Timothy A. 1992a. Field houses, villages, and the tragedy of the commons in the early northern Anasazi Southwest. *American Antiquity* 57:617–34.

1992b. Prehistoric human impact on the environment in the upland North American Southwest. *Population and Environment: A Journal of Interdisciplinary Studies* 13:255.

Kohler, Timothy A., and M. H. Matthews. 1988. Long-term Anasazi land use and forest reduction: a case study from southwest Colorado. *American Antiquity* 53:537–64.

Kohler, Timothy A., and Carla R. Van West. 1996. The calculus of self-interest in the development of cooperation: sociopolitical development and risk in the prehistoric Southwest. In *Evolving complexity and environmental risk in the prehistoric Southwest*, ed. Joseph A. Tainter and Bonnie Bagley Tainter, pp. 169–96. Santa Fe Institute Studies in the Sciences of Complexity Proceedings 24. Reading: Addison Wesley.

Kuckelman, Kristin A. 2000. The archaeology of Castle Rock Pueblo: a thirteenth-century village in southwestern Colorado. http://www.crowcanyon.org/castlerock. 09/16/2002.

Kuckelman, Kristin A., Ricky R. Lightfoot, and Debra L. Martin. 2002. The bioarchaeology and taphonomy of violence at Castle Rock and Sand Canyon Pueblos, southwestern Colorado. *American Antiquity* 67:486–513.

Lang, Richard W., and Arthur H. Harris. 1984. *The faunal remains from Arroyo Hondo Pueblo, New Mexico.* Arroyo Hondo Archaeological Series 5. Santa Fe, New Mexico: School of American Research Press.

LeBlanc, Steven A. 1983. *The Mimbres people, ancient Pueblo painters of the American Southwest.* New York: Thames and Hudson.

1989. Cultural dynamics in the southern Mogollon area. In *Dynamics of Southwest prehistory*, ed. Linda S. Cordell and George J. Gumerman, pp. 179–208. Washington, DC: Smithsonian Institution Press.

1999. *Prehistoric warfare in the American Southwest.* Salt Lake City: University of Utah Press.

2000. Regional interaction and warfare in the late prehistoric Southwest. In *The archaeology of regional interaction: religion, warfare, and exchange across the American Southwest and beyond*, ed. Michelle Hegmon, pp. 41–70. Boulder: University Press of Colorado.

2001. Warfare and aggregation in the El Morro Valley, New Mexico. In *Deadly landscapes: case studies in prehistoric Southwestern warfare*, ed. Glen E. Rice and Steven A. LeBlanc, pp. 19–49. Salt Lake City: University of Utah Press.

Lekson, Stephen H. 1982. Architecture and settlement plan in the Redrock Valley of the Gila River, southwestern New Mexico. In *Mogollon archaeology: proceedings of the 1980 Mogollon Conference*, ed. Patrick H. Beckett and Kira Silverbird, pp. 61–73. Ramona, California: Acoma Press.

1983. Dating the Hubbard tri-wall and other tri-wall structures. *Southwestern Lore* 49:15–23.

1984. *Great pueblo architecture of Chaco Canyon.* Publications in Archaeology 18b. Albuquerque, New Mexico: National Park Service.

1988. The idea of the kiva in Anasazi archaeology. *The Kiva* 53:213–34.

1991. Settlement patterns and the Chaco region. In *Chaco and Hohokam: prehistoric regional systems in the American Southwest*, ed. Patricia L. Crown and W. James Judge, pp. 31–56. Santa Fe, New Mexico: School of American Research Press.

1992. The surface archaeology of southwestern New Mexico. *The Artifact* 30.

1996. Southwestern New Mexico and southeastern Arizona, A.D. 900 to 1300. In *The prehistoric Pueblo world, A.D. 1150–1350*, ed. Michael A. Adler, pp. 170–6. Tucson: University of Arizona Press.

1999a. *The Chaco Meridian: centers of political power in the ancient Southwest.* Walnut Creek, California: AltaMira Press.

1999b. Great towns in the Southwest. In *Great towns and regional polities*, ed. Jill E. Neitzel, pp. 3–21. Albuquerque: University of New Mexico Press.

2002. War in the Southwest, war in the world. *American Antiquity* 67:607–24.

Lekson, Stephen H., Curtis P. Nepstad-Thornberry, Brian E. Yunker, Toni S. Laumbach, David P. Cain, and Karl W. Laumbach. 2002. Migrations in the Southwest: Pinnacle Ruin, southwestern New Mexico. *Kiva* 68:73–101.

Lekson, Stephen H., Thomas C. Windes, John R. Stein, and W. James Judge. 1988. The Chaco Canyon community. *Scientific American* 256:100–9.

Levy, Jerrold E. 1992. *Orayvi revisited: social stratification in an "egalitarian" society.* Santa Fe, New Mexico: School of American Research Press.

Lightfoot, Dale R., and Frank W. Eddy. 1995. The construction and configuration of Anasazi pebble-mulch gardens in the northern Rio Grande. *American Antiquity* 60:459–70.

Lightfoot, Kent G. 1983. Resource uncertainty and buffering strategies in an arid, marginal environment. In *Ecological models in economic prehistory*, ed. Gordon Bronitsky, pp. 189–218. Anthropological Research Papers 29. Phoenix: Arizona State University.

Lightfoot, Kent G., and Gary M. Feinman. 1982. Social differentiation and leadership development in early pithouse villages in the Mogollon Region of the American Southwest. *American Antiquity* 47:64–86.

Lightfoot, Ricky R., and M. C. Etzkorn. Editors. 1993. *The Duckfoot Site*: vol. 1, *Descriptive archaeology*. Occasional Paper 3. Cortez, Colorado: Crow Canyon Archaeological Center.

Lightfoot, Ricky R., and Kristin A. Kuckelman. 2001. A case of warfare in the Mesa Verde region. In *Deadly landscapes: case studies in prehistoric Southwestern warfare*, ed. Glen E. Rice and Steven A. LeBlanc, pp. 51–64. Salt Lake City: University of Utah Press.

Lipe, William D. 1995. The depopulation of the northern San Juan: conditions in the turbulent 1200s. *Journal of Anthropological Archaeology* 14:143–69.

2002. Social power in the central Mesa Verde region, A.D. 1150–1290. In *Seeking the center place: archaeology and ancient communities in the Mesa Verde region*, ed. Mark D. Varien and Richard H. Wilshusen, pp. 203–32. Salt Lake City: University of Utah Press.

Lipe, William D., and Mark D. Varien. 1999. Pueblo III (A.D. 1150–1300). In *Colorado prehistory: a context for the southern Colorado River basin*, ed. William D. Lipe, Mark D. Varien, and Richard H. Wilshusen, pp. 290–352. Denver: Colorado Council of Professional Archaeologists.

Lyneis, Margaret M. 1996. Pueblo II–Pueblo III change in southwestern Utah, the Arizona strip, and southern Nevada. In *The prehistoric Pueblo world A.D.1150–1350*, ed. Michael A. Adler, pp. 11–28. Tucson: University of Arizona Press.

McGregor, John C. 1943. Burial of an early American magician. *Proceedings of the American Philosophical Society* 86:270–98.

1965. *Southwestern archaeology.* Urbana: University of Illinois Press.

Mackey, James. 1977. A multivariate, osteological approach to Towa culture history. *American Journal of Physical Anthropology* 46:477–82.

McKusick, Charmion. 1986. *Southwest Indian turkeys: prehistory and comparative osteology.* Globe, Arizona: Southwest Bird Laboratory.

2001. *Southwest birds of sacrifice.* The Arizona Archaeologist 31. Phoenix: Arizona Archaeological Society.

Mahoney, Nancy M., Michael A. Adler, and James W. Kendrick. 2000. The changing scale and configuration of Mesa Verde communities. *Kiva* 66:67–90.

Malville, J. McKim. 1994. Astronomy and social integration among the Anasazi. In *Proceedings of the Anasazi Symposium 1991*, ed. Art Hutchinson and Jack E. Smith, pp. 149–64. Mesa Verde, Colorado: Mesa Verde Museum Association.

Malville, J. McKim, and Nancy J. Malville. 2001. Pilgrimage and periodical festivals as processes of social integration in Chaco Canyon. *Kiva* 66:327–44.

Malville, J. McKim, and Claudia Putnam. 1993. *Prehistoric astronomy in the Southwest*, 2nd edition. Boulder, Colorado: Johnson Printing Company.

Marlar, Richard A., Banks L. Leonard, Brian R. Billman, Patricia M. Lambert, and Jennifer E. Marlar. 2000. Biochemical evidence of cannibalism at a prehistoric Puebloan site in southwestern Colorado. *Nature* 407:74–8.

Marshall, Michael P., John R. Stein, Richard W. Loose, and Judith E. Novotny. 1979. *Anasazi communities of the San Juan Basin*. Santa Fe: Public Service Company of New Mexico and New Mexico Historic Preservation Division.

Martin, Debra L. 1994. Patterns of health and disease stress profiles for the prehistoric Southwest. In *Themes in Southwest prehistory*, ed. George J. Gumerman, pp. 87–108. Santa Fe, New Mexico: School of American Research Press.

1997. Violence against women in the La Plata River valley (A.D. 1000–1300). In *Troubled times: violence and warfare in the past*, ed. Debra L. Martin and David W. Frayer, pp. 45–76. Amsterdam, Netherlands: Gordon and Breach Publishers.

Martin, Debra L., and Nancy J. Akins. 2001. Unequal treatment in life as in death: trauma and mortuary behavior at La Plata (A.D. 1000–1300). In *Ancient burial practices in the American Southwest: archaeology, physical anthropology, and Native American perspectives*, ed. Douglas R. Mitchell and Judy L. Brunson-Hadley, pp. 223–48. Albuquerque: University of New Mexico Press.

Martin, Paul S. 1973. The discovery of America. *Science* 179:969–74.

Martin, Paul S., R. S. Thompson, and A. Long. 1985. Shasta ground sloth extinction: a test of the blitzkrieg model. In *Environments and extinctions: man in late glacial North America*, ed. J. I. Mead and David J. Meltzer, pp. 5–14. Orono: Center for the Study of Early Man, University of Maine.

Mathien, Frances Joan. 1984. Social and economic implications of jewelry items of the Chaco Anasazi. In *Recent research on Chaco prehistory*, ed. W. James Judge and John D. Schelberg, pp. 173–86. Reports of the Chaco Center 8. Albuquerque, New Mexico: Division of Cultural Research, National Park Service, US Department of the Interior.

1991. *Excavations at 29SJ 644: The Eleventh House Site, Chaco Canyon, New Mexico*. Reports of the Chaco Center 10. Santa Fe, New Mexico: Branch of Cultural Research, US Department of the Interior, National Park Service.

1993. Exchange systems and social stratification among the Chaco Anasazi. In *The American Southwest and Mesoamerica: systems of prehistoric exchange*, ed. J. E. Ericson and T. G. Baugh, pp. 27–64. New York: Plenum Press.

1997. Ornaments of the Chaco Anasazi. In *Ceramics, lithics, and ornaments of Chaco Canyon, analyses of artifacts from the Chaco Project, 1971–1978*, ed. Frances Joan Mathien, pp. 1119–1220. Publications in Archeology 18G. Santa Fe, New Mexico: US Department of the Interior, National Park Service.

2001. The organization of turquoise production and consumption by the prehistoric Chacoans. *American Antiquity* 66:103–18.

Mathien, Frances Joan, and Thomas C. Windes. 1988. *Historic structure report: Kin Nahasbas Ruin, Chaco Culture National Historical Park, New Mexico*. Santa Fe, New Mexico: US Department of the Interior, National Park Service.

Matson, R. G. 1991. *The origins of Southwestern agriculture*. Tucson: University of Arizona Press.

Maxwell, Timothy D. 1995. A comparative study of prehistoric farming strategies. In *Soil, water, biology, and belief in prehistoric and traditional Southwestern agriculture*, ed. H. Wolcott Toll, pp. 3–12. Special Publication 2. Albuquerque: New Mexico Archaeological Council.

Meyer, Daniel A. 1999. Masonry and social variability in the Chaco system. PhD dissertation, University of Calgary.

Mills, Barbara J. 1995. The organization of protohistoric Zuni ceramic production. In *Ceramic production in the American Southwest*, ed. Barbara J. Mills and Patricia L. Crown, pp. 200–30. Tucson: University of Arizona Press.

1999. The reorganization of Silver Creek communities from the 11th to 14th centuries. In *Living on the edge of the Rim: excavations and analysis of the Silver Creek Archaeological Research Project 1993–1998*, ed. Barbara J. Mills, Sarah A. Herr, and Scott Van Keuren, pp. 505–11. Archaeological Series 192. Tucson: Arizona State Museum, University of Arizona.

2002. Recent research on Chaco: changing views on economy, ritual, and society. *Journal of Archaeological Research* 10:65–117.

Mills, Barbara J., Andrea J. Carpenter, and William Grimm. 1997. Sourcing Chuska ceramic production: petrographic and experimental analysis. *Kiva* 62:261–82.

Mills, Barbara J., Sarah A. Herr, and Scott Van Keuren. Editors. 1999. *Living on the edge of the Rim: excavations and analysis of the Silver Creek Archaeological Research Project 1993–1998*. Archaeological Series 192. Tucson: Arizona State Museum, University of Arizona.

Milo, Richard G. 1994. Corn production on Chapin Mesa: growing season variability, field rotation, and settlement shifts. In *Proceedings of the Anasazi Symposium 1991*, ed. Art Hutchinson and Jack E. Smith, pp. 35–46. Mesa Verde, Colorado: Mesa Verde Museum Association.

Minnis, Paul E. 1985. *Social adaptation to food stress: a prehistoric Southwestern example*. Prehistoric Archeology and Ecology Series. Chicago: University of Chicago Press.

1989. Prehistoric diet in the northern Southwest: macroplant remains from Four Corners feces. *American Antiquity* 54:543–63.

Minnis, Paul E., Michael E. Whalen, Jane H. Kelley, and Joe D. Stewart. 1993. Prehistoric macaw breeding in the North American Southwest. *American Antiquity* 58:270–6.

Mobley-Tanaka, Jeannette L. 1997. Gender and ritual space during the pithouse to pueblo transition: subterranean mealing rooms in the North American Southwest. *American Antiquity* 62:437–48.

Motsinger, Thomas N. 1997. Tracking protohistoric glazeware specialization in the upper Rio Grande Valley, New Mexico. *Kiva* 63:101–16.

Muenchrath, Deborah A., and Ricardo J. Salvador. 1995. Maize productivity and agroecology: effects of environment and agricultural practices on the biology of maize. In *Soil, water, biology, and belief in prehistoric and traditional Southwestern agriculture*, ed. H. Wolcott Toll, pp. 303–33. Special Publication 2. Albuquerque: New Mexico Archaeological Council.

Muir, Robert J., and Jonathan C. Driver. 2002. Scale of analysis and zooarchaeological interpretation: Pueblo III faunal variation in the northern San Juan region. *Journal of Anthropological Archaeology* 21:165–99.

Munson, Marit K. 2000. Sex, gender, and status: human images from the Classic Mimbres. *American Antiquity* 65:127–43.

Neitzel, Jill E. 1989. Regional exchange networks in the American Southwest: a comparative analysis of long-distance trade. In *The sociopolitical structure of prehistoric Southwestern societies*, ed. S. Upham, K. G. Lightfoot, and R. A. Jewett, pp. 149–95. Boulder, Colorado: Westview Press.

1999. Examining societal organization in the Southwest: an application of multiscalar analysis. In *Great towns and regional polities*, ed. Jill E. Neitzel, pp. 183–213. Albuquerque: University of New Mexico Press.

2000. Gender hierarchies: a comparative analysis of mortuary data. In *Women and men in the prehispanic Southwest: labor, power, and prestige*, ed. Patricia L. Crown, pp. 137–68. Santa Fe, New Mexico: School of American Research Press.

Nelson, Ben A. 2000. Aggregation, warfare, and the spread of the Mesoamerican tradition. In *The archaeology of regional interaction: religion, warfare, and exchange across the American Southwest and beyond*, ed. Michelle Hegmon, pp. 317–37. Boulder: University Press of Colorado.

Nelson, Ben A., and Roger Anyon. 1996. Fallow valleys: asynchronous occupations in the Mimbres valley. *The Kiva* 61:275–94.

Nelson, Ben A., Timothy A. Kohler, and Keith W. Kintigh. 1994. Demographic alternatives: consequences for current models of Southwestern prehistory. In *Understanding complexity in the prehistoric Southwest*, ed. George J. Gumerman and Murray Gell-Mann, pp. 113–46. Santa Fe Institute Studies in the Sciences of Complexity Proceedings 16. Reading, Massachusetts: Addison Wesley.

Nelson, Ben A., Debra L. Martin, Alan C. Swedlund, Paul R. Fish, and George J. Armelagos. 1994. Studies in disruption: demography and health in the prehistoric Southwest. In *Understanding complexity in the prehistoric Southwest*, ed. George J. Gumerman and Murray Gell-Mann, pp. 59–112. Santa Fe Institute Studies in the Sciences of Complexity Proceedings 16. Reading, Massachusetts: Addison Wesley.

Nelson, Margaret C. 1996. Technological strategies responsive to subsistence stress. In *Evolving complexity and environmental risk in the prehistoric Southwest*, ed. Joseph A. Tainter and Bonnie Bagley Tainter, pp. 107–44. Santa Fe

Institute Studies in the Sciences of Complexity Proceedings 24. Reading, Massachusetts: Addison Wesley.

1999. *Mimbres during the twelfth century: abandonment, continuity, and reorganization.* Tucson: University of Arizona Press.

Nelson, Margaret C., and Michelle Hegmon. 2001. Abandonment is not as it seems: an approach to the relationship between site and regional abandonment. *American Antiquity* 66:213–35.

Nials, Fred, John Stein, and John Roney. 1987. *Chacoan roads in the southern periphery: results of Phase II of the BLM Chaco Roads Project.* Cultural Resources Series 1. Santa Fe: Bureau of Land Management, New Mexico State Office.

Olsen, John W. 1990. *Vertebrate faunal remains from Grasshopper Pueblo, Arizona.* Anthropological Papers 83. Ann Arbor: Museum of Anthropology, University of Michigan.

Ortiz, Alfonso. 1969. *The Tewa world: space, time, being, and becoming in a Pueblo society.* Chicago: University of Chicago Press.

Ortman, Scott G., and Bruce A. Bradley. 2002. Sand Canyon Pueblo: the container in the center. In *Seeking the center place: archaeology and ancient communities in the Mesa Verde region,* ed. Mark D. Varien and Richard H. Wilshusen, pp. 41–78. Salt Lake City: University of Utah Press.

Palkovich, Ann M. 1984. Disease and mortality patterns in the burial rooms of Pueblo Bonito: preliminary considerations. In *Recent research on Chaco prehistory,* ed. W. James Judge and John D. Schelberg, pp. 103–13. Reports of the Chaco Center 8. Albuquerque, New Mexico: National Park Service, Division of Cultural Research.

Parsons, Elsie Clews. 1926. *Tewa tales.* Memoirs of the American Folklore Society 19. New York: G. E. Stechert.

1939. *Pueblo Indian religion.* Chicago: University of Chicago Press.

Peckham, Stewart. 1991. *From this earth: the ancient art of Pueblo pottery.* Santa Fe: Museum of New Mexico Press.

Pepper, George H. 1920. *Pueblo Bonito.* Anthropological Papers 27. New York: American Museum of Natural History.

Peregrine, Peter N. 2001. Matrilocality, corporate strategy, and the organization of production in the Chacoan world. *American Antiquity* 66:36–46.

Peregrine, Peter N., and Melvin Ember. 2002. Response to Schillaci and Stojanowski. *American Antiquity* 67:357–60.

Petersen, Kenneth Lee. 1987a. Concluding remarks on prehistoric agricultural potential in the Dolores Project area. In *Dolores Archaeological Program: supporting studies: settlement and environment,* ed. Kenneth Lee Petersen and Janet D. Orcutt, pp. 235–48. Denver, Colorado: United States Department of the Interior Bureau of Reclamation Engineering and Research Center.

1987b. Summer warmth: a critical factor for the Dolores Anasazi. In *Dolores Archaeological Program: supporting studies: settlement and environment,* ed. Kenneth Lee Petersen and Janet D. Orcutt, pp. 61–71. Denver, Colorado: United States Department of the Interior Bureau of Reclamation Engineering and Research Center.

1987c. Reconstruction of droughts for the Dolores project area using tree-ring studies. In *Dolores Archaeological Program: supporting studies: settlement and environment*, ed. Kenneth Lee Petersen and Janet D. Orcutt, pp. 91–104. Denver, Colorado: United States Department of the Interior Bureau of Reclamation Engineering and Research Center.

1994. A warm and wet Little Climatic Optimum and a cold and dry Little Ice Age in the southern Rocky Mountains, U.S.A. *Climatic Change* 26:243–69.

1996. Environmental factors in the Mesa Verde–northern Rio Grande migration in the 13th and 14th centuries. Paper presented to AMQUA 1996: Global Warming: Interglacials, Interstadials, Climatic Optima, and Other Events, Flagstaff, Arizona, 1996.

Phillips, David A. Jr. 2000. The Chaco Meridian: a skeptical analysis. Paper presented to the 65th Annual Meeting of the Society for American Archaeology, Philadelphia, 2000.

Phillips, David A. Jr., and John P. Carpenter. 1999. The Robles Phase of the Casas Grandes culture. In *The Casas Grandes world*, ed. Curtis F. Schaafsma and Carroll L. Riley, pp. 78–83. Salt Lake City: University of Utah Press.

Pilles, Peter J. Jr. 1996. The Pueblo III period along the Mogollon Rim: the Honanki, Elden, and Turkey Hill Phases of the Sinagua. In *The prehistoric Pueblo world A.D.1150–1350*, ed. Michael A. Adler, pp. 59–72. Tucson: University of Arizona Press.

Pippin, Lonnie C. 1987. *Prehistory and paleoecology of Guadalupe Ruin, New Mexico*. University of Utah Anthropological Papers 112. Salt Lake City: University of Utah Press.

Plog, Fred T. 1974. *The study of prehistoric change*. New York: Academic Press.

Potter, James M. 1995. The effects of sedentism on the processing of hunted carcasses in the Southwest: a comparison of two Pueblo IV sites in central New Mexico. *Kiva* 60:411–28.

1997. Communal ritual and faunal remains: an example from the Dolores Anasazi. *Journal of Field Archaeology* 24:353–64.

2000. Pots, parties, and politics: communal feasting in the American Southwest. *American Antiquity* 65:471–92.

Potter, James M., and Elizabeth M. Perry. 2000. Ritual as a power resource in the American Southwest. In *Alternative leadership strategies in the prehispanic Southwest*, ed. Barbara J. Mills, pp. 60–78. Tucson: University of Arizona Press.

Powell, Valli S. 1996. Regional diversity in Mogollon Red-on-Brown pottery. *Kiva* 62:185–204.

Powers, Robert P., William B. Gillespie, and Stephen H. Lekson. 1983. *The Outlier Survey: a regional view of settlement in the San Juan Basin*. Reports of the Chaco Center 3. Albuquerque, New Mexico: Division of Cultural Research, National Park Service, US Department of the Interior.

Rautman, Alison E. 1996. Risk, reciprocity, and the operation of social networks. In *Evolving complexity and environmental risk in the prehistoric Southwest*, ed. J. A. Tainter and B. Bagley Tainter, pp. 197–222. Santa Fe Institute Studies in the Sciences of Complexity Proceedings 24. Reading, Massachusetts: Addison Wesley.

Ravesloot, John C. 1988. *Mortuary practices and social differentiation at Casas Grandes, Chihuahua, Mexico.* Anthropological Papers 49. Tucson: University of Arizona Press.

Reed, Lori Stephens, C. Dean Wilson, and Kelley A. Hays-Gilpin. 2000. From brown to gray: the origins of ceramic technology in the northern Southwest. In *Foundations of Anasazi culture: the Basketmaker–Pueblo transition*, ed. Paul F. Reed, pp. 203–20. Salt Lake City: University of Utah Press.

Reed, Paul F. Editor. 2000. *Foundations of Anasazi culture: the Basketmaker–Pueblo transition.* Salt Lake City: University of Utah Press.

Reed, Paul F., and Scott Wilcox. 2000. Distinctive and intensive: the Basketmaker III to early Pueblo I occupation of Cove-Redrock Valley, northeastern Arizona. In *Foundations of Anasazi culture: the Basketmaker–Pueblo transition*, ed. Paul F. Reed, pp. 69–94. Salt Lake City: University of Utah Press.

Reid, J. Jefferson, and Stephanie M. Whittlesey. 1997. *The archaeology of ancient Arizona.* Tucson: University of Arizona Press.

   1999. *Grasshopper Pueblo: a story of archaeology and ancient life.* Tucson: University of Arizona Press.

Renfrew, Colin. 2001. Production and consumption in a sacred economy: the material correlates of high devotional expression at Chaco Canyon. *American Antiquity* 66:14–25.

Reyman, Jonathan E. 1987. Priests, power, and politics: some implications of socioceremonial control. In *Astronomy and ceremony in the prehistoric Southwest*, ed. John B. Carlson and W. James Judge, pp. 121–48. Papers of the Maxwell Museum of Anthropology 2. Albuquerque, New Mexico: Maxwell Museum of Anthropology.

Riggs, Charles R. 2001. *The architecture of Grasshopper Pueblo.* Salt Lake City: University of Utah Press.

Riley, Carroll L. 1999. The Sonoran statelets and Casas Grandes. In *The Casas Grandes world*, ed. Curtis F. Schaafsma and Carroll L. Riley, pp. 193–200. Salt Lake City: University of Utah Press.

Roberts, Frank H. H. Jr. 1929. *Shabik'eshchee Village: a late Basket Maker site in the Chaco Canyon, New Mexico.* Bureau of American Ethnology Bulletin 92. Washington, DC: Smithsonian Institution.

Roberts, Heidi, and Richard V. N. Ahlstrom. 1997. Malaria, microbes, and mechanisms of change. *Kiva* 63:117–35.

Robins, Michael R., and Kelley A. Hays-Gilpin. 2000. The bird in the basket: gender and social change in Basketmaker iconography. In *Foundations of Anasazi culture: the Basketmaker–Pueblo transition*, ed. Paul F. Reed, pp. 231–47. Salt Lake City: University of Utah Press.

Rocek, Thomas R. 1995. Sedentarization and agricultural dependence: perspectives from the pithouse-to-pueblo transitions in the American Southwest. *American Antiquity* 60:218–39.

Rohn, Arthur H. 1971. *Mug House, Mesa Verde National Park – Colorado (Wetherill Mesa Excavations).* Archeological Research Series 7D. Washington, DC: National Park Service, US Department of the Interior.

Roney, John R. 1992. Prehistoric roads and regional integration in the Chacoan system. In *Anasazi regional organization and the Chaco system*, ed. David E. Doyel, pp. 123–31. Anthropological Papers 5. Albuquerque, New Mexico: Maxwell Museum of Anthropology.

1996. The Pueblo III period in the eastern San Juan Basin and Acoma-Laguna areas. In *The prehistoric Pueblo world, A.D. 1150–1350*, ed. Michael A. Adler, pp. 145–69. Tucson: University of Arizona Press.

Root, Matthew J. 1992. Casa del Rito, LA 3852. In *Bandelier Archaeological Excavation Project: summer 1990 excavations at Burnt Mesa Pueblo and Casa del Rito*, ed. Timothy A. Kohler and Matthew J. Root, pp. 5–36. Reports of Investigations 64. Pullman: Department of Anthropology, Washington State University.

Rose, Martin R., Jeffrey S. Dean, and William J. Robinson. 1981. *The past climate of Arroyo Hondo, New Mexico, reconstructed from tree rings*. Arroyo Hondo Archaeological Series 4. Santa Fe: School of American Research.

Rushforth, Scott, and Steadman Upham. 1992. *A Hopi social history*. Austin: University of Texas Press.

Saitta, Dean J. 1997. Power, labor, and the dynamics of change in Chacoan political economy. *American Antiquity* 62:7–26.

2000. Theorizing the political economy of Southwestern exchange. In *The Archaeology of regional interaction: religion, warfare, and exchange across the American Southwest and beyond*, ed. Michelle Hegmon, pp. 151–66. Boulder: University Press of Colorado.

Salzer, Matthew W. 2000. Temperature variability and the northern Anasazi: possible implications for regional abandonment. *Kiva* 65:295–318.

Sanchez, M. Guadalupe. 2001. A synopsis of Paleo-Indian archaeology in Mexico. *Kiva* 67:119–36.

Sayles, E. B. 1983. *The Cochise cultural sequence in southeastern Arizona*. Anthropological Papers 42. Tucson: University of Arizona Press.

Sayles, E. B., and Ernst Antevs. 1941. *The Cochise culture*. Medallion Papers 29. Globe, Arizona: Gila Pueblo.

Schaafsma, Curtis F., and Carroll L. Riley. 1999. The Casas Grandes world: analysis and conclusion. In *The Casas Grandes world*, ed. Curtis F. Schaafsma and Carroll L. Riley, pp. 237–49. Salt Lake City: University of Utah Press.

Schaafsma, Polly. 1994. The prehistoric Kachina cult and its origins as suggested by Southwestern rock art. In *Kachinas in the Pueblo world*, ed. Polly Schaafsma, pp. 63–79. Albuquerque: University of New Mexico Press.

Schachner, Gregson. 2001. Ritual control and transformation in middle-range societies: an example from the American Southwest. *Journal of Anthropological Archaeology* 20:168–94.

Schelberg, John D. 1992. Hierarchical organization as a short-term buffering strategy in Chaco Canyon. In *Anasazi regional organization and the Chaco system*, ed. D. E. Doyel, pp. 59–74. Anthropology Papers 5. Albuquerque: Maxwell Museum of Anthropology.

Schillaci, Michael A. 2001. Investigating gene flow and migration in the prehistoric American Southwest: Pueblo IV/Classic period sites from New Mexico. *NewsMAC: Newsletter of the New Mexico Archeological Council* 2001:7–9.

Schillaci, Michael A., Erik G. Ozolins, and Thomas C. Windes. 2001. A multivariate assessment of biological relationships among prehistoric Southwest Amerindian populations. In *Collected papers in honor of Phyllis S. Davis*, ed. Regge N. Wiseman, Cornelia T. Snow, and Thomas O. Laughlin. Papers 27. Albuquerque: Archaeological Society of New Mexico.

Schillaci, Michael A., and Christopher M. Stojanowski. 2002. Investigating social organization at Aztec Ruins using determinant ratio analysis. In *Forward into the past: papers in honor of Teddy Lou and Francis Stickney*, ed. Regge N. Wiseman, Thomas C. O'Laughlin, and Cordelia T. Snow, pp. 93–104. Papers 28. Albuquerque: Archaeological Society of New Mexico.

Schroeder, Albert H. 1979. Pueblos abandoned in historic times. In *Southwest*, ed. Alfonso Ortiz, pp. 236–54. Handbook of North American Indians 9. Washington, DC: Smithsonian Institution Press.

1992. Protohistoric Pueblo demographic changes. In *Recent research on the late prehistory and early history of New Mexico*, ed. Bradley J. Vierra, pp. 29–36. Special Publication 1. Albuquerque: New Mexico Archeological Council.

Sebastian, Lynne. 1992. *The Chaco Anasazi: sociopolitical evolution in the prehistoric Southwest*. Cambridge: Cambridge University Press.

Sekaquaptewa, Emory. 1972. Preserving the good things of Hopi life. In *Plural society in the Southwest*, ed. Edward H. Spicer and Raymond H. Thompson, pp. 239–60. New York: Interbook.

Shafer, Harry J. 1982. Classic Mimbres phase households and room use patterns. *The Kiva* 48:17–48.

1999a. The Classic Mimbres phenomenon and some new interpretations. In *Sixty years of Mogollon archaeology: papers from the Ninth Mogollon Conference, Silver City, New Mexico, 1996*, ed. Stephanie M. Whittlesey, pp. 95–105. Tucson, Arizona: SRI Press.

1999b. The Mimbres Classic and Postclassic: a case for discontinuity. In *The Casas Grandes world*, ed. Curtis F. Schaafsma and Carroll L. Riley, pp. 121–33. Salt Lake City: University of Utah Press.

Shafer, Harry J., and Harold Drollinger. 1998. Classic Mimbres adobe-lined pits, plazas, and courtyards at the NAN Ruin, Grant County, New Mexico. *Kiva* 63:379–99.

Shaffer, Brian S., Karen M. Gardner, and Joseph F. Powell. 1999. Sexual division of labor in the prehistoric Puebloan Southwest as portrayed by Mimbres potters. In *Sixty years of Mogollon archaeology: papers from the Ninth Mogollon Conference, Silver City, New Mexico, 1996*, ed. Stephanie M. Whittlesey, pp. 113–17. Tucson, Arizona: SRI Press.

Shaffer, Brian S., Karen M. Gardner, and Harry J. Shafer. 1997. An unusual birth depicted in Mimbres pottery: not cracked up to what it is supposed to be. *American Antiquity* 62:727–32.

Shepard, Anna O. 1956. *Ceramics for the archaeologist*. Publication 609. Washington, DC: Carnegie Institution of Washington.

Simmons, Marc. 1979. History of Pueblo–Spanish relations to 1821. In *Southwest*, ed. Alfonso Ortiz, pp. 178–93. Handbook of North American Indians 9. Washington, DC: Smithsonian Institution Press.

Skibo, James M., and Eric Blinman. 1999. Exploring the origins of pottery on the Colorado Plateau. In *Pottery and people: a dynamic interaction*, ed. James M. Skibo and Gary M. Feinman, pp. 171–83. Salt Lake City: University of Utah Press.

Skibo, James M., Eugene B. McCluney, and William H. Walker. Editors. 2002. *The Joyce Well Site: on the frontier of the Casas Grandes world*. Salt Lake City: University of Utah Press.

Smiley, Francis E. 1994. The agricultural transition in the northern Southwest: patterns in the current chronometric data. *Kiva* 60:165–90.

Smith, Watson. 1952. *Excavations in Big Hawk Valley, Wupatki National Monument, Arizona*. Museum of Northern Arizona Bulletin 24. Flagstaff: Northern Arizona Society of Science and Art.

Snow, David H. 1973. Prehistoric Southwestern turquoise industry. *El Palacio* 79:33–51.

Snygg, John, and Tom Windes. 1998. Long, wide roads and great kiva roofs. *Kiva* 64:7–25.

Sofaer, Anna. 1997. The primary architecture of the Chacoan culture: a cosmological expression. In *Anasazi architecture and American design*, ed. Baker H. Morrow and V. B. Price, pp. 88–132. Albuquerque: University of New Mexico Press.

Sofaer, Anna, and Rolf M. Sinclair. 1987. Astronomical markings at three sites on Fajada Butte. In *Astronomy and ceremony in the prehistoric Southwest*, ed. John B. Carlson and W. James Judge, pp. 43–70. Papers of the Maxwell Museum of Anthropology 2. Albuquerque, New Mexico: Maxwell Museum of Anthropology.

Spielmann, Katherine A. 1996. Impressions of Pueblo III settlement trends among the Rio Abajo and eastern border Pueblos. In *The prehistoric Pueblo world A.D.1150–1350*, ed. Michael A. Adler, pp. 177–87. Tucson: University of Arizona Press.

Spielmann, Katherine A., and Eric A. Angstadt-Leto. 1996. Hunting, gathering, and health in the prehistoric Southwest. In *Evolving complexity and environmental risk in the prehistoric Southwest*, ed. J. Tainter and B. B. Tainter, pp. 79–106. Santa Fe Institute Studies in the Sciences of Complexity Proceedings 24. Reading, Massachusetts: Addison Wesley.

Stanislawski, Michael B. 1979. Hopi-Tewa. In *Southwest*, ed. Alfonso Ortiz, pp. 587–602. Handbook of North American Indians 9. Washington, DC: Smithsonian Institution Press.

Stein, John R., and Andrew P. Fowler. 1996. Looking beyond Chaco in the San Juan Basin and its peripheries. In *The prehistoric Pueblo world, A.D.1150–1350*, ed. Michael A. Adler, pp. 114–31. Tucson: University of Arizona Press.

Stein, John R., and Peter J. McKenna. 1988. *An archaeological reconnaissance of a Late Bonito Phase occupation near Aztec Ruins National Monument, New Mexico*. Santa Fe, New Mexico: National Park Service, Southwest Cultural Resource Center, Branch of Cultural Resources Management, Division of Anthropology.

Stevenson, Matilda Coxe. 1904. *The Zuñi Indians: their mythology, esoteric fraternities, and ceremonies*. Annual Report 23. Washington, DC: Bureau of American Ethnology.

Steward, Julian H. 1937. Ecological aspects of Southwestern society. *Anthropos* 32:87–104.

Stodder, Ann L. W. 1987. The physical anthropology and mortuary practice of the Dolores Anasazi: an early Pueblo population in local and regional context. In *Dolores Archaeological Program: supporting studies: settlement and environment*, ed. Kenneth Lee Petersen and Janet D. Orcutt, pp. 339–504. Denver, Colorado: United States Department of the Interior Bureau of Reclamation Engineering and Research Center.

Stodder, Ann L. W., and Debra L. Martin. 1992. Health and disease in the Southwest before and after Spanish contact. In *Disease and demography in the Americas*, ed. John W. Verano and Douglas H. Ubelaker, pp. 55–73. Washington, DC: Smithsonian Institution Press.

Stoltman, James B. 1999. The Chaco-Chuska connection: in defense of Anna Shepard. In *Pottery and people: a dynamic interaction*, ed. James M. Skibo and Gary M. Feinman, pp. 9–24. Salt Lake City: University of Utah Press.

Stone, Tammy. 2002. Kiva diversity in the Point of Pines region of Arizona. *Kiva* 67:385–411.

Stubbs, Stanley A. 1954. Summary report on an early Pueblo site in the Tesuque Valley, New Mexico. *El Palacio* 61:43–5.

Sullivan, Alan P. III. 1994. Frontiers, barriers, and crises today: Colton's methods and the Wupatki survey data. In *The ancient Southwestern community: models and methods for the study of prehistoric social organization*, ed. W. H. Wills and Robert D. Leonard, pp. 191–207. Albuquerque: University of New Mexico.

Sutton, Mark Q. 2000. Prehistoric movements of northern Uto-Aztecan peoples along the northwestern edge of the Southwest: impact on Southwestern populations. In *The archaeology of regional interaction: religion, warfare, and exchange across the American Southwest and beyond*, ed. Michelle Hegmon, pp. 295–316. Boulder: University Press of Colorado.

Tainter, Joseph A., and Fred Plog. 1994. Strong and weak patterning in Southwestern prehistory: the formation of Puebloan archaeology. In *Themes in Southwestern prehistory*, ed. G. J. Gumerman, pp. 109–34. Santa Fe, New Mexico: School of American Research Press.

Teague, Lynn S. 2000. Outward and visible signs: textiles in ceremonial contexts. In *The archaeology of regional interaction: religion, warfare, and exchange across the American Southwest and beyond*, ed. Michelle Hegmon, pp. 429–50. Boulder: University Press of Colorado.

Thompson, Marc. 2000. The evolution and dissemination of Mimbres iconography. In *Kachinas in the Pueblo world*, ed. Polly Schaafsma, pp. 93–106. Salt Lake City: University of Utah Press.

Till, Jonathan D., and Winston B. Hurst. 2002. Trail of the ancients: a network of ancient roads and great houses in southeastern Utah. Paper presented to the 67th Annual Meeting of the Society for American Archaeology, Denver, Colorado, 2002.

Titiev, Mischa. 1944. *Old Oraibi: a study of the Hopi Indians of Third Mesa*. Papers of the Peabody Museum of American Archaeology and Ethnology 22(1). Cambridge, Massachusetts: Harvard University Press.

Toll, H. Wolcott. 1991. Material distributions and exchange in Chaco Canyon. In *Chaco and Hohokam: prehistoric regional systems in the American Southwest*, ed. Patricia L. Crown and W. James Judge, pp. 77–108. Santa Fe, New Mexico: School of American Research Press.

2001. Making and breaking pots in the Chaco world. *American Antiquity* 66:56–78.

Toll, H. Wolcott, and Peter J. McKenna. 1997. Chaco ceramics. In *Ceramics, lithics, and ornaments of Chaco Canyon*, ed. Frances Joan Mathien, pp. 17–530. Publications in Archeology 18G. Santa Fe, New Mexico: National Park Service, US Department of the Interior.

Towner, Ronald H., and Jeffrey S. Dean. 1996. Questions and problems in pre–Fort Sumner Navajo archaeology. In *The archaeology of Navajo origins*, ed. Ronald H. Towner, pp. 3–18. Salt Lake City: University of Utah Press.

Triadan, Daniela. 1997. *Ceramic commodities and common containers: production and distribution of White Mountain Red Ware in the Grasshopper Region, Arizona*. Anthropological Papers 61. Tucson: University of Arizona Press.

Triadan, Daniela, Barbara J. Mills, and Andrew I. Duff. 2002. From compositional to anthropological: fourteenth-century red-ware circulation and its implications for Pueblo reorganization. In *Ceramic production and circulation in the greater Southwest: source determination by INAA and complementary mineralogical investigations*, ed. Donna M. Glowacki and Hector Neff, pp. 85–97. Monograph 44. Los Angeles: The Cotsen Institute of Archaeology, University of California.

Truell, Marcia L. 1992. *Excavations at 29SJ 627, Chaco Canyon, New Mexico*. Reports of the Chaco Center 11. Santa Fe, New Mexico: US Department of the Interior, National Park Service, Branch of Cultural Research.

Tuggle, H. David, and J. Jefferson Reid. 2001. Conflict and defense in the Grasshopper region of east-central Arizona. In *Deadly landscapes: case studies in prehistoric Southwestern warfare*, ed. Glen E. Rice and Steven A. LeBlanc, pp. 85–105. Salt Lake City: University of Utah Press.

Turner, Christy G. II. 1993. Southwest Indian teeth. *National Geographic Research and Exploration* 9:32–53.

1999. The dentition of Casas Grandes with suggestions on epigenetic relationships among Mexican and Southwestern U.S. populations. In *The Casas Grandes world*, ed. Curtis F. Schaafsma and Carroll L. Riley, pp. 229–36. Salt Lake City: University of Utah Press.

Turner, Christy G. II, and Jacqueline A. Turner. 1999. *Man corn: cannibalism and violence in the prehistoric American Southwest*. Salt Lake City: University of Utah Press.

Umberger, Melissa, Nicholas Beale, Amy Vest, and Cynthia Hotujec. 2002. Status differences in a prehistoric Chaco Anasazi community. Paper presented to the 67th Society for American Archaeology Annual Meeting, Denver, Colorado, 2002.

Underhill, Ruth. 1991. *Life in the Pueblos*. Santa Fe, New Mexico: Ancient City Press.

Upham, Steadman. 1987. The tyranny of ethnographic analogy in Southwestern archaeology. In *Coasts, plains, and deserts: essays in honor of Reynold J. Ruppe*, ed. S. W. Gaines, pp. 265–81. Anthropological Research Papers 38. Tempe: Arizona State University.

1992. Population and Spanish contact in the Southwest. In *Disease and demography in the Americas*, ed. John W. Verano and Douglas H. Ubelaker, pp. 223–36. Washington, DC: Smithsonian Institution Press.

Upham, Steadman, Patricia L. Crown, and Stephen Plog. 1994. Alliance formation and cultural identity in the American Southwest. In *Themes in Southwest prehistory*, ed. George J. Gumerman, pp. 183–210. Santa Fe, New Mexico: School of American Research Press.

Upham, Steadman, Richard S. MacNeish, Walton C. Galinat, and Christopher M. Stevenson. 1987. Evidence concerning the origin of Maiz de Ocho. *American Anthropologist* 89:410–19.

Van Dyke, Ruth M. 1997. Tracking the trachyte boundary: a southern perspective on exchange and interaction among Chacoan communities. Paper presented to the 62nd Annual Meeting of the Society for American Archaeology, Nashville, Tennessee, 1997.

1999. The Chaco connection: evaluating Bonito-style architecture in outlier communities. *Journal of Anthropological Archaeology* 18:471–506.

2000. A Chacoan landscape: the view from the Red Mesa Valley. In *Great house communities across the Chacoan landscape*, ed. John Kantner and Nancy Mahoney, pp. 91–100. Tucson: University of Arizona Press.

2003. Bounding Chaco: great house architectural variability across time and space. *Kiva* 69:117–40.

Van Keuren, Scott. 1999. *Ceramic design structure and the organization of Cibola White Ware production in the Grasshopper region, Arizona*. Archaeological Series 191. Tucson: Arizona State Museum, University of Arizona.

2000. Ceramic decoration as power: late prehistoric design change in east-central Arizona. In *Alternative leadership strategies in the prehispanic Southwest*, ed. Barbara J. Mills, pp. 79–94. Tucson: University of Arizona Press.

Van West, Carla R. 1994a. *Modeling prehistoric agricultural productivity in southwestern Colorado: a GIS approach*. Reports of Investigations 67. Pullman: Washington State University Department of Anthropology.

1994b. Reconstructing prehistoric climatic variability and agricultural production in southwestern Colorado, A.D. 901–1300: a GIS approach. In *Proceedings of the Anasazi Symposium 1991*, ed. Art Hutchinson and Jack E. Smith, pp. 25–33. Mesa Verde, Colorado: Mesa Verde Museum Association.

1996. Agricultural potential and carrying capacity in southwestern Colorado, A.D. 901 to 1300. In *The prehistoric Pueblo world, A.D.1150–1350*, ed. Michael A. Adler, pp. 214–27. Tucson: University of Arizona Press.

Van Zandt, Tineke. 1999. Architecture and site structure. In *The Bandelier Archeological Survey*, ed. Robert P. Powers and Janet D. Orcutt, pp. 309–88. Intermountain Cultural Resources Management Professional Paper 57. Santa Fe, New Mexico: Intermountain Region, National Park Service, Department of the Interior.

VanPool, Christine S., and Todd L. VanPool. 1999. The scientific nature of post-processualism. *American Antiquity* 64:33–53.

Vargas, Victoria D. 1995. *Copper bell trade patterns in the prehistoric U.S. Southwest and northwest Mexico.* Archaeological Series 187. Tucson: Arizona State Museum.

Varien, Mark D. 1999. *Sedentism and mobility in a social landscape: Mesa Verde and beyond.* Tucson: University of Arizona Press.

Varien, Mark D., and Ricky R. Lightfoot. 1989. Ritual and nonritual activities in Mesa Verde region pit structures. In *The architecture of social integration in prehistoric Pueblos,* ed. William D. Lipe and Michelle Hegmon, pp. 73–88. Occasional Paper 1. Cortez, Colorado: Crow Canyon Archaeological Center.

Varien, Mark D., William D. Lipe, Michael A. Adler, Ian M. Thompson, and Bruce A. Bradley. 1996. Southwestern Colorado and southeastern Utah settlement patterns: A.D. 1100 to 1300. In *The prehistoric Pueblo world, A.D. 1150–1350,* ed. Michael A. Adler, pp. 86–113. Tucson: University of Arizona Press.

Varien, Mark D., Carla R. Van West, and G. Stuart Patterson. 2000. Competition, cooperation, and conflict: agricultural production and community catchments in the central Mesa Verde region. *Kiva* 66:45–66.

Vint, James M. 1999. Ceramic artifacts. In *The Bandelier Archeological Survey,* ed. Robert P. Powers and Janet D. Orcutt, pp. 389–468. Intermountain Cultural Resources Management Professional Paper 57. Santa Fe: Intermountain Region, National Park Service, Department of the Interior.

Vivian, Gordon, and Tom W. Mathews. 1965. *Kin Kletso: a Pueblo III community in Chaco Canyon, New Mexico.* Technical Series 6. Globe, Arizona: Southwestern Monuments Association.

Vivian, Gordon, and Paul Reiter. 1960. *The great kivas of Chaco Canyon and their relationships.* Monograph 22. Santa Fe, New Mexico: School of American Research.

Vivian, R. Gwinn. 1990. *The Chacoan prehistory of the San Juan Basin.* San Diego, California: Academic Press.

1997a. Chacoan roads: function. *Kiva* 63:35–68.

1997b. Chacoan roads: morphology. *Kiva* 63:7–34.

2000. Basketmaker archaeology at the millennium: new answers to old questions. In *Foundations of Anasazi culture: the Basketmaker–Pueblo transition,* ed. Paul F. Reed, pp. 251–8. Salt Lake City: University of Utah Press.

Vivian, R. Gwinn, Dulce N. Dudgen, and Gayle H. Hartmann. 1978. *Artifacts from Chaco Canyon, New Mexico: the Chetro Ketl collection.* Anthropological Papers 32. Tucson: University of Arizona Press.

Walker, William H. 2002. Stratigraphy and practical reason. *American Anthropologist* 104:159–77.

Walker, William H., and James M. Skibo. 2002. Joyce Well and the Casas Grande religious interaction sphere. In *The Joyce Well Site: on the frontier of the Casas Grandes world,* ed. James M. Skibo, Eugene B. McCluney, and William H. Walker, pp. 167–75. Salt Lake City: University of Utah Press.

Walsh, Michael R. 1998. Lines in the sand: competition and stone selection on the Pajarito Plateau, New Mexico. *American Antiquity* 63:573–94.

2000. Material evidence for social boundaries on the Pajarito Plateau, New Mexico. *Kiva* 65:197–213.

Walters, Harry, and Hugh C. Rogers. 2001. Anasazi and *'Anaasází:* two words, two cultures. *Kiva* 66:317–26.

Ware, John A. 2001. Chaco social organization: a peripheral view. In *Chaco society and polity: papers from the 1999 Conference,* ed. Linda S. Cordell, W. James Judge, and June-el Piper, pp. 79–93. Special Publication 4. Albuquerque: New Mexico Archeological Council.

Ware, John A., and Eric Blinman. 2000. Cultural collapse and reorganization: the origin and spread of Pueblo ritual sodalities. In *The archaeology of regional interaction: religion, warfare, and exchange across the American Southwest,* ed. Michelle Hegmon, pp. 381–409. Boulder: University Press of Colorado.

Warren, A. Helene. 1980. Production and distribution of pottery in Chaco Canyon and northwestern New Mexico. Unpublished manuscript available at National Park Service Southwest Regional Office Library.

Webster, Laurie D., and Kelley A. Hays-Gilpin. 1994. New trails for old shoes: sandals, textiles, and baskets in Basketmaker culture. *Kiva* 60:313–28.

Whalen, Michael E. 1994. Moving out of the Archaic on the edge of the Southwest. *American Antiquity* 59:622–38.

Whalen, Michael E., and Paul E. Minnis. 1996. Ball courts and political centralization in the Casas Grandes region. *American Antiquity* 61:732–46.

1999. Investigating the Paquimé regional system. In *The Casas Grandes world,* ed. Curtis F. Schaafsma and Carroll L. Riley, pp. 54–62. Salt Lake City: University of Utah Press.

2000. Leadership at Casas Grandes, Chihuahua, Mexico. In *Alternative leadership strategies in the prehispanic Southwest,* ed. Barbara J. Mills, pp. 168–79. Tucson: University of Arizona Press.

2001a. Architecture and authority in the Casas Grandes area, Chihuahua, Mexico. *American Antiquity* 66:651–68.

2001b. *Casas Grandes and its hinterland: prehistoric regional organization in northwest Mexico.* Tucson: University of Arizona Press.

2003. The local and the distant in the origin of Casas Grandes, Chihuahua, Mexico. *American Antiquity* 68:314–32.

White, Tim D. 1992. *Prehistoric cannibalism at Mancos 5MTUMR-2346.* Princeton: Princeton University Press.

Whiteley, Peter M. 1988. *Deliberate acts: changing Hopi culture through the Oraibi split.* Tucson: University of Arizona Press.

Whittlesey, Stephanie M., and J. Jefferson Reid. 2001. Mortuary ritual and organizational inferences at Grasshopper Pueblo, Arizona. In *Ancient burial practices in the American Southwest: archaeology, physical anthropology, and Native American perspectives,* ed. Douglas R. Mitchell and Judy L. Brunson-Hadley, pp. 68–96. Albuquerque: University of New Mexico Press.

Wilcox, David R. 1991. Changing contexts of Pueblo adaptations, A.D. 1250–1600. In *Farmers, hunters, and colonists: interaction between the Southwest and the Southern Plains,* ed. Katherine A. Spielmann, pp. 128–54. Tucson: University of Arizona Press.

1993. The evolution of the Chacoan polity. In *The Chimney Rock Archaeological Symposium*, ed. J. McKim Malville and Gary Matlock, pp. 76–90. General Technical Report RM-227. Fort Collins, Colorado: US Department of Agriculture, Forest Service.

1996. Pueblo III people and polity in relational context. In *The prehistoric Pueblo world, A.D. 1150–1350*, ed. Michael A. Adler, pp. 241–54. Tucson: University of Arizona Press.

1999a. A peregrine view of macroregional systems in the North American Southwest, A.D. 750–1250. In *Great towns and regional polities*, ed. Jill E. Neitzel, pp. 115–41. Albuquerque: University of New Mexico Press.

1999b. A preliminary graph-theoretic analysis of access relationships at Casas Grandes. In *The Casas Grandes world*, ed. Curtis F. Schaafsma and Carroll L. Riley, pp. 93–104. Salt Lake City: University of Utah Press.

Wilcox, David R., and Jonathan Haas. 1994. The scream of the butterfly: competition and conflict in the prehistoric Southwest. In *Themes in Southwest prehistory*, ed. George J. Gumerman, pp. 211–38. Santa Fe: School of American Research.

Williams, Jerry L. Editor. 1986. *New Mexico in maps*, 2nd edition. Albuquerque: University of New Mexico Press.

Wills, W. H. 1988. Early agriculture and sedentism in the American Southwest: evidence and interpretations. *Journal of World Prehistory* 2:445–88.

1989. Patterns of prehistoric food production in west-central New Mexico. *Journal of Anthropological Research* 45:139–57.

1995. Archaic foraging and the beginning of food production in the American Southwest. In *Last hunters, first farmers: new perspectives on the prehistoric transition to agriculture*, ed. T. Douglas Price and Anne Birgitte Gebauer, pp. 215–42. Santa Fe, New Mexico: School of American Research Press.

2000. Political leadership and the construction of Chacoan great houses, A.D. 1020–1140. In *Alternative leadership strategies in the prehispanic Southwest*, ed. Barbara J. Mills, pp. 19–44. Tucson: University of Arizona Press.

2001. Ritual and mound formation during the Bonito Phase in Chaco Canyon. *American Antiquity* 66:433–51.

Wills, W. H., and Thomas C. Windes. 1989. Evidence for population aggregation and dispersal during the Basketmaker III period in Chaco Canyon, New Mexico. *American Antiquity* 54:347–69.

Wilshusen, Richard H. 2002. Estimating population in the central Mesa Verde region. In *Seeking the center place: archaeology and ancient communities in the Mesa Verde region*, ed. Mark D. Varien and Richard H. Wilshusen, pp. 101–20. Salt Lake City: University of Utah Press.

Wilshusen, Richard H., and Scott G. Ortman. 1999. Rethinking the Pueblo I period in the San Juan drainage: aggregation, migration, and cultural diversity. *Kiva* 64:369–99.

Wilson, C. Dean, and Eric Blinman. 1995. Changing specialization of white ware manufacture in the northern San Juan region. In *Ceramic production in the American Southwest*, ed. Barbara J. Mills and Patricia L. Crown, pp. 63–87. Tucson: University of Arizona Press.

Windes, Thomas C. 1984. A new look at population in Chaco Canyon. In *Recent research on Chaco prehistory*, ed. W. James Judge and John D. Schelberg, pp. 75–87. Reports of the Chaco Center 8. Albuquerque, New Mexico: National Park Service, Division of Cultural Affairs.

1987. *Investigations at the Pueblo Alto Complex, Chaco Canyon, New Mexico, 1975–1979*. Chaco Canyon Studies Publications in Archeology 18F. Santa Fe, New Mexico: US Department of the Interior, National Park Service.

1991. The prehistoric road network at Pueblo Alto, Chaco Canyon, New Mexico. In *Ancient road networks and settlement hierarchies in the New World*, ed. Charles D. Trombold, pp. 111–31. Cambridge: Cambridge University Press.

1992. Blue notes: the Chacoan turquoise industry in the San Juan region. In *Anasazi regional organization and the Chaco system*, ed. David E. Doyel, pp. 159–68. Anthropological Papers 5. Albuquerque, New Mexico: Maxwell Museum of Anthropology.

1993. *The Spadefoot Toad Site: investigation at 29SJ 629 in Marcia's Rincon and the Fajada Gap Pueblo II Community*, vol. 1. Reports of the Chaco Center 12. Santa Fe, New Mexico: Branch of Cultural Research, Division of Anthropology, National Park Service.

2001. House location patterns in the Chaco Canyon area: a short description. In *Chaco society and polity: papers from the 1999 Conference*, ed. Linda S. Cordell, W. James Judge, and June-el Piper, pp. 31–46. Special Publication 4. Albuquerque: New Mexico Archeological Council.

Windes, Thomas C., Rachel Anderson, Brian K. Johnson, and Cheryl A. Ford. 2000. Sunrise, sunset: sedentism and mobility in the Chaco East community. In *Great house communities across the Chacoan landscape*, ed. John Kantner and Nancy Mahoney, pp. 39–59. Tucson: University of Arizona Press.

Windes, Thomas C., and Dabney Ford. 1996. The Chaco Wood Project: the chronometric reappraisal of Pueblo Bonito. *American Antiquity* 61:295–310.

Windes, Thomas C., and Peter J. McKenna. 2001. Going against the grain: wood production in Chacoan society. *American Antiquity* 66:119–40.

Woodson, M. Kyle. 1999. Migrations in late Anasazi prehistory: the evidence from the Goat Hill site. *Kiva* 65:63–84.

Woodson, M. Kyle, Thomas E. Jones, and Joseph S. Crary. 1999. Exploring late-prehistoric mortuary patterns of southeastern Arizona and southwestern New Mexico. In *Sixty years of Mogollon archaeology: papers from the Ninth Mogollon Conference, Silver City, New Mexico, 1996*, ed. Stephanie M. Whittlesey, pp. 67–79. Tucson, Arizona: SRI Press.

Woosley, Anne I., and Bart Olinger. 1993. The Casas Grandes ceramic tradition: production and interregional exchange of Ramos Polychrome. In *Culture and contact: Charles C. DiPeso's Gran Chichimeca*, ed. Anne. I Woosley and John C. Ravesloot, pp. 105–32. Dragoon, Arizona: Amerind Foundation.

Wright, Barton. Editor. 1988. *The mythic world of the Zuni, as written by Frank Hamilton Cushing*. Albuquerque: University of New Mexico Press.

Young, M. Jane. 1989. The Southwest connection: similarities between Western Puebloan and Mesoamerican cosmology. In *World archaeoastronomy: selected papers from the 2nd Oxford International Conference on Archaeoastronomy*, ed. A. F. Aveni, pp. 167–79. Cambridge: Cambridge University Press.

Zedeño, Maria Nieves. 1994. *Sourcing prehistoric ceramics at Chodistaas Pueblo, Arizona*. Anthropological Papers 58. Tucson: University of Arizona Press.

2002. Artifact design, composition, and context: updating the analysis of ceramic circulation at Point of Pines, Arizona. In *Ceramic production and circulation in the greater Southwest: source determination by INAA and complementary mineralogical investigations*, ed. Donna M. Glowacki and Hector Neff, pp. 74–84. Monograph 44. Los Angeles: The Cotsen Institute of Archaeology, University of California.

Zedeño, M. Nieves, and Daniela Triadan. 2000. Ceramic evidence for community reorganization and change in east-central Arizona. *Kiva* 65:215–33.

Zeilik, Michael. 1987. Anticipation in ceremony: the readiness is all. In *Astronomy and ceremony in the prehistoric Southwest*, ed. John B. Carlson and W. James Judge, pp. 25–42. Papers of the Maxwell Museum of Anthropology 2. Albuquerque, New Mexico: Maxwell Museum of Anthropology.

Zubrow, Ezra B. W. 1975. *Prehistoric carrying capacity: a model*. Menlo Park, California: Cummings Publishing.

Index

Figures and boxes appear in italics.

314